THE CONCE
OF HUMAN DIGNITY
IN HUMAN RIGHTS
DISCOURSE

Edited by

David Kretzmer

and

Eckart Klein

The Minerva Center for Human Rights
The Hebrew University of Jerusalem
Tel Aviv University

KLUWER LAW INTERNATIONAL
THE HAGUE / LONDON / NEW YORK

A C.I.P. Catalogue record for this book is available from the Library of Congress

ISBN 90-411-1783-0

Published by Kluwer Law International,
P.O. Box 85889, 2508 CN The Hague, The Netherlands.

Sold and distributed in North, Central and South America
by Kluwer Law International,
101 Philip Drive, Norwell, MA 02061, U.S.A.
kluwerlaw@wkap.com

In all other countries, sold and distributed
by Kluwer Law International, Distribution Centre,
P.O. Box 322, 3300 AH Dordrecht, The Netherlands.

Printed on acid-free paper

All Rights Reserved
© 2002 Kluwer Law International
Kluwer Law International incorporates the publishing programmes of
Graham & Trotman Ltd, Kluwer Law and Taxation Publishers,
and Martinus Nijhoff Publishers.

No part of the material protected by this copyright notice may be reproduced or
utilized in any form or by any means, electronic or mechanical,
including photocopying, recording or by any information storage and
retrieval system, without written permission from the copyright owner.

Printed in the Netherlands.

FOREWORD
Eckart Klein and David Kretzmer

The Universal Declaration of Human Rights opens with the statement that recognition of the inherent dignity and of the equal and inalienable rights of all members of the human family is the foundation of freedom, justice and peace in the world. The International Covenant on Economic, Social and Cultural Rights and the International Covenant on Civil and Political Rights, which were adopted in the wake of the Universal Declaration and together with it comprise the International Bill of Rights, go one step further and declare that the inalienable rights of all persons derive from the inherent dignity of the human person. The concept of human dignity also plays a major role in the debate over the 'universalism' or 'relativism' of human rights.

'Human dignity' has become a central concept not only in international instruments that deal with human rights, but in many modern constitutions as well. Thus article 1 of the German Basic Law states:

> The dignity of man is inviolable. To respect and protect it shall be the duty of all public authority.

Israel's Basic Law: Human Dignity and Liberty declares that its object is to protect human dignity and liberty, so as to entrench in a basic law the values of the State of Israel as a Jewish and democratic state.

South Africa's new constitution also grants a central place to the concept of human dignity. Article 1 declares that the Republic of South Africa is founded on certain values, the first-mentioned of which are "human dignity, the achievement of equality and the advancement of human rights and freedoms." The Bill of Rights included in the Constitution affirms democratic values of human dignity, equality and freedom, and permits restrictions on protected rights only if, inter alia, they are reasonable and justifiable in an open and democratic society based on human dignity, equality and freedom. Furthermore, when interpreting the Bill of Rights, the Courts are obligated to promote the values of an open and democratic society based on human dignity, equality and freedom. Finally, according to the South African approach, human dignity is not only an underlying value. Article 10 of the Constitution states:

> Everyone has the inherent right to have their dignity respected and protected.

While the concept of human dignity now plays a central role in the law of human rights, there is surprisingly little agreement on what the concept actually means. In the international instruments mentioned above, the reference is to a concept from which other values, peace, justice and human rights, are derived. However, even in these documents the term 'human dignity' is not confined to the preamble which sets out the underlying values of human rights. Article 10 of the International Covenant on Civil and Political Rights refers to the right of all persons deprived of their liberty to be treated with humanity and with respect for the inherent dignity of the human person. Article 13 of the International Covenant on Economic, Social and Cultural Rights provides that education shall be directed to the full development of the human personality and the sense of its dignity, and shall strengthen the respect for human rights and fundamental freedoms.

The provision in the German Basic Law has been interpreted as referring to the most fundamental of the rights of man, a right that must not be violated in any circumstances. In the developing Israeli jurisprudence the concept of human dignity has become a kind of 'super-right,' which contains within it the kernel of all the other rights recognized in international instruments and modern constitutions. The Israeli courts have not accepted the German approach that human dignity must never be violated. Like most other rights, it may be limited in certain circumstances in order to cater to other clashing values. As can be seen from the provisions cited above from the South African constitution, the notion of human dignity plays a dual role: as a general underlying value and as a right that must be respected and protected.

The concept of 'human dignity' is obviously not confined to legal discourse. It has deep roots in the theology of many religions, moral and political philosophy and anthropology. The articles in this book are part of an attempt to examine different approaches to the concept of human dignity, the role it played in the historical development of religious and legal approaches to human rights, and the extent to which the approaches of other disciplines can contribute to a better understanding of the term in human rights discourse.

The articles grew out of a joint project of the Minerva Center for Human Rights of the Hebrew University of Jerusalem and Tel Aviv University and the Menschenrechtszentrum der Universität Potsdam. They were originally presented at a conference that took place at the Hebrew University to celebrate the fiftieth anniversary of the Universal Declaration of Human Rights. The questions regarding the meaning of human dignity have obviously not been solved in the articles. But it is our hope that they do shed light on the concept and pave the way for further research and discussion.

Foreword vii

The editors wish to express deep appreciation to Francine Kershman Hazan who organized the original conference and was responsible for preparing the articles for publication and to Krista Beverage who assisted Ms. Hazan in copy-editing.

TABLE OF CONTENTS

Foreword
Eckart Klein and David Kretzmer   v

Historical Roots

On the Necessary and Sufficient Conditions for the
Emergence of the Doctrine
of the Dignity of Man and His Rights
Yehoshua Arieli   1

'Dignity of Man' and '*Persona*' in Stoic Anthropology:
Some Remarks on Cicero, *De Officiis* I, 105-107
Hubert Cancik   19

Legal Roots of Human Dignity in German Law
Joern Eckert   41

Human Dignity in Religious Thought

Blood and the Image of God: On the Sanctity of Life
in Biblical and Early Rabbinic Law, Myth, and Ritual
Yair Lorberbaum   55

Can Ethical Maxims be Derived from Theological
Concepts of Human Dignity?
Dietrich Ritschl   87

Human Dignity in a Rabbinical Perspective
Chana Safrai   99

Human Dignity in International Law

The Founding Function of Human Dignity in the
Universal Declaration of Human Rights
Klaus Dicke   111

Human Dignity in International Law
Jochen Abr. Frowein   121

Comparative Constitutional Perspectives

Human Dignity as a Constitutional Value
Arthur Chaskalson   133

Human Dignity in German Law
Eckart Klein   145

Human Dignity in Israeli Jurisprudence
David Kretzmer   161

The Religious and Philosophical Background of Human Dignity and its Place in Modern Constitutions
Christian Starck   179

Human Dignity: Philosophical Aspects

Dignity as a Modern Virtue
Michael Meyer   195

Humiliation, Dignity and Self-Respect
Daniel Statman   209

Concepts of Dignity and Honor

Honor and Dignity Cultures: The Case of *Kavod* and *Kvod Ha-Adam* in Israeli Society and Law
Orit Kamir   231

Honor, Dignity and the Framing of Multiculturalist Values
David Weisstub   263

Index   297

ON THE NECESSARY AND SUFFICIENT CONDITIONS FOR THE EMERGENCE OF THE DOCTRINE OF THE DIGNITY OF MAN AND HIS RIGHTS

Yehoshua Arieli

Let me start with two methodological remarks: One cannot understand the meanings of the concepts and terms used in the Universal Declaration of Human Rights of December 1948, and its subsequent formulations, if we deal with the expressions 'the dignity of man' or the 'inherent dignity of man' without reference to their textual context, namely, 'and of the equal and inalienable rights of all members of the human family.'[1] Nor can we adequately understand their meanings unless we see them in their historical context, in the perspective of the colossal events of the 20th century, and beyond that in the wider perspective of the last two centuries going back to the age of the Enlightenment.

In such a context, one should see them as the essence of the lesson which the initiators of the Universal Declaration drew from their past experience, and in particular from the terrifying events of this century, making the Universal Declaration of Human Rights and the concept of the Dignity of Man the cornerstone and the foundation on which the United Nations sought to reconstruct the future international order of mankind and of public life in general.

Only the catastrophe of two World Wars and the Holocaust, only the threat of a world dominated and enslaved by a ruthless power which rejected the fundamental principles and norms of the spiritual and moral heritage of the West, could have called into being a document of the newly created world organizations such as the Universal Declaration of Human Rights. By its intent, the Universal Declaration proclaimed the belief in the inherent dignity of man, in his equality and his inalienable rights, as the principles on which a

---

[1] 'The Universal Declaration of Human Rights,' *Basic Documents on Human Rights*, Jan Brownlie, ed., (Oxford 1994) p. 21.

new world order should be established. This aspect reveals the fundamental difference between the nature and the aim of the League of Nations and that of the United Nations. Both aimed at the establishment of an international order for the prevention of war, which had proved destructive beyond all measure not only for the nations involved but also for the very survival of the social and political order of the West and of the world. The Covenant of the League of Nations sought to establish instruments which would transcend the principles of national sovereignty and the systems of alliances which had been an immediate cause for World War I and create a quasi-parliamentary, supranational world confederation which aimed, as the Preamble of the Covenant of the League of Nations stated, 'To promote international co-operation and achieve international peace and security; by the acceptance of obligations not to resort to war; by the prescription of open, just and honourable relations between the Nations; by the firm establishment of the understandings of international law as the actual rule of conduct among the Governments.'[2]

Yet the Covenant refrained from defining its purposes in terms of ideals and norms even in the vague terms of the Wilsonian principles as expressed in his 14 points.[3] The difference between these two conceptions, of the League of Nations and the United Nations, derived obviously from the difference of the threat revealed by the nature of the aggressors and their war aims. The destruction brought about by World War I, which the League of Nations faced, was caused by the struggle for mastery of the world by the Great Powers, and derived in the last respect from the inherited conception developed with the rise of the modern state that the relations between the sovereign states were solely determined by the limits set by their capacity to mobilize power. Yet the victory of either side did not present a total challenge to the survival of the defeated nations, as they possessed similar political and social regimes and common normative traditions and values.[4] The UN, on the other hand, faced the historically unprecedented attempt to subject the whole world to the

---

[2] See the text of 'The Covenant of the League of Nations,' *Introduction to Contemporary Civilization in the West*, (Columbia University Press, New York 1954) vol. II, p. 1220 *ff.*

[3] See Wilson defining the War aims before the Congress (the 14 Points) on January 8, 1918, to establish an international order 'a world fit and safe to live in' based on 'the principle of justice to all peoples and nationalities, and their right to live on equal terms of liberty and safety with one another whether they be strong or weak,' in *Documentary History of American Life* (New York 1966) vol. VI, pp. 247, 249. While Article 22 of the Covenant which deals with mandatories, control of colonies and Territories, still reveals a tutelary 'white man's burden' attitude toward the well-being and development of the people ruled as 'sacred trust of Civilization,' Article 23 (social activities) envisions the securing of fair conditions of labor and other social obligations by the establishment of international organizations which point toward the developments realized by the UN.

[4] See among others A.J.P. Taylor, *The Struggle For Mastery in Europe 1848-1918*, (Oxford 1954).

permanent rule of a Master Race by conquest, enslavement and genocide. Against this the Preamble of the Charter of the United Nations made the normative intent of a new world order the cornerstone of the Charter. Imitating the opening words of the founding charter of the United States of America, the Federal Constitution, the Charter of the United Nations declared:

> WE THE PEOPLES OF THE UNITED NATIONS, DETERMINED to save succeeding generations from the scourge of war which twice in our lifetime has brought untold sorrow to mankind, and to reaffirm faith in fundamental human rights, in the dignity and worth of the human person, in the equal rights of men and women and of nations large and small ... and to promote social progress and better standards of life in larger freedom, AND FOR THESE ENDS to practice tolerance and live together in peace with one another as good neighbours and to unite our strength to maintain international peace and security ... and to employ international machinery for the promotion of the economic and social advancement of all peoples, have resolved to combine our effort to accomplish these aims.[5]

Against this background, the invocation of the dignity and rights of man has to be seen as counter-thesis and counter-ideology of the Free World to the ideologies of the Axis Powers and in particular to National Socialism. This is plainly expressed in the preamble of the Universal Declaration:

> *Whereas* recognition of the inherent dignity and of the equal and inalienable rights of all members of the human family is the foundation for freedom, justice and peace in the world, *Whereas* disregard and contempt for human rights have resulted in barbarous acts which have outraged the conscience of mankind [...] *Whereas* it is essential, if man is not to be compelled to have recourse, as a last resort, to rebellion against tyranny and oppression, that human rights should be protected by the rule of law.[6]

It was the Universal Declaration of Human Rights adopted by the United Nations General Assembly on December 10, 1948, that turned the United Nations from an instrument of ordering the international relations between the nations and powers into an instrument for the reconstruction of the international community upon the highest ideals and ethical norms of a humanistic conception of man and mankind.

---

[5] 'The Preamble in the Charter of the United Nations' in *Introduction to Contemporary Civilization in the West*, (Columbia University Press, New York 1994) pp. 1233-34.

[6] Preamble to the Universal Declaration, *op. cit.*

Surveying the different versions of the Universal Declaration of Human Rights adopted since 1948, the question of whether they were not utopian in their character both in their common sense meaning as aiming at the realization of an ideal social and political international order and in the sense of the impracticality of their proposed reforms and changes, becomes inevitable. The Universal Declaration of Human Rights actually related to this question by defining itself as regulative ideal in the Kantian sense, or in its own words, 'as a common standard for achievement for all peoples and all nations, to the end that every individual and every organ of society, keeping this declaration constantly in mind, shall strive by teaching and education to promote respects for these rights and freedoms and by progressive measures, national and international, to secure their universal and effective recognition and observance, both among the peoples of the Member States themselves and among the peoples of the territories under their jurisdiction.'[7]

The history of half a century, which has passed since its inception, has unquestionably proven the growing impact of the Universal Declaration of Human Rights on the peoples and the nations of the world, and on world opinion in general. Whether as lip-service or as genuine acceptance of its principles and their integration into the political, legal and conceptual structure of the members-states of the United Nations, the Universal Declaration of Human Rights served as standard of achievement, as a regulative ideal and guideline for both the founding members and the growing number of new members of the UN.[8]

Standing on the threshold of twenty-first century, one is permitted to say that the conception of humanity as expressed by the Universal Declaration of Human Rights has become the only valid framework of values, norms and principles capable of structuring a meaningful and yet feasible scheme of national and international civilized life. Such a development demands explanation. Was it the self-evident truth and power of persuasion, the inherent justice and equity of the human message of the Declaration that explained this progress? Did the fact that this ideological conception was from the beginning

---

[7] The Preamble, *op. cit. Ibid.* p. 22.

[8] The process of the acceptance of the enumerated rights of the Universal Declaration of Rights by the member states of the UN and their incorporation in the legal and political framework of the same occurred in the main in three forms: by the acceptance and confirmation of specific Conventions of the United Nations setting specific standards (such as the prohibition of slavery); by the acceptance and confirmation of general standard setting declarations or conventions such as the Universal Declaration of December 1948, or the International Covenant on Civil and Political Rights of 1966, or by joining convention based on geopolitical divisions such as the European Convention of Human Rights and its five protocols. See the survey of the conventions, and standard setting declarations given in *Basic Documents on Human Rights*, Jan Brownlie, ed., 3rd Edition, (Oxford 1994); also Y. Arieli, 'The Proclamation of Independence: A Forty-Year Perspective,' *The Jerusalem Quarterly*, No. 51, (Summer 1989), for Israel's way to conform to the human rights standards set by the UN.

intimately connected with the United Nations indicate that it was the only possible common framework for the community of nations? Without a doubt, the pre-eminent role of the United States and the West in the defeat of the Axis Powers and in the shaping of the UN was an important, and perhaps decisive, factor in the growing acceptance of its principles. Still, I believe that no other ideological framework could have become the basis for the reconstruction of the world community because of the inherent equity of its human message as well as its seemingly self-evident truth defined in the meta-language of rational categories of universal generalizations bestowed upon it a particular force of persuasion.

The concepts, values and ideas which make up the different versions of the Universal Declaration of Human Rights, were in their essence the direct offspring of the great ideas of the 18th century Enlightenment, of the American and French revolutions, of the movement toward democracy and of liberalism which shaped modern history. On the surface they reflect the democratization and universalization of values and norms which have always been held as of supreme, existential importance by men, tribes, nations the world over and by the ruling classes, at least in the West. Liberty, dignity and the right of self-determination were claimed by the Greek citizen in the *politea* and the *civis romanus*, as well as by the nobility and the *Buerger* in the European medieval societies. The terms *homo liber* and *libertas*, the privileges, the liberties and freedoms, the suffrages and franchises as well as the codes of honor of the aristocracies were all indications of their supreme importance and were the motivating force for all rebellions, upheavals and violence throughout the ages.[9] In a deeper sense, the theory of the 'Rights of Man' was the lesson that, since the Enlightenment, the intellectual leaders of the West proclaimed to have drawn from past beliefs, traditions and experiences. Such was the explicit contention underlying the proclamation of man's inalienable rights in the Declaration of Independence of the United States of America, which became the cornerstone of the American polity and, to a great degree, the substance of American national identity.[10]

As credo of the French Revolution, the '*Declaration des droits de l'homme et du citoyen*' became the exemplary model and guiding star for all revolutionary movements, be they democratic, liberal, national or social, that aimed at refashioning the framework of political and social life in modern history.[11]

---

[9] As for the differences of the concepts of liberty in the classical heritage as against that of medieval and modern history, see C. Wirszubski, *Libertas as Political Ideal: Rome During the Late Republic and the Early Principate*, (Cambridge 1950).

[10] See Y. Arieli, *Individualism and Nationalism in American Ideology*, (Cambridge, MA 1964), and Peter Gay, *The Enlightenment, The Science of Freedom*, (London 1973) vol. II.

[11] See Toqueville, who compared the French Proclamation of the Rights of Man as the fundament on which mankind would establish a new order of man with the

The revolutionary force of all these movements lay in their conviction that the instauration of the rights of man as foundation of the political, social and legal order was only the reestablishment of principles which, had it not been for 'the abandoned confederacy [of kings, nobles and priests] against the happiness of the people,'[12] had always been valid as they were founded on the law of nature and reason. They all shared the basic conviction of the Enlightenment that the law of nature and reason which inheres in the nature of man and humanity[13] enabled man to shape his own fate and future; that reason and experience, rightly understood, and inborn moral sense enabled man to create a social and political order in which freedom, social cooperation and justice would be harmonized But this common ideological outlook stemmed from a deeper layer of conceptions. It stemmed from the fundamental awareness of the Western elites since the dawn of modern history—since the Renaissance, the Humanist movement and the Age of discoveries, since the rise of science and philosophy in the 16th and 17th century—that mankind was standing on the verge of an unprecedented new era. That its essential significance lay in the potentiality of mastering the forces of nature, increasing thereby the powers of man to create a new world befitting the original promise given to man to be the appointed master and trustee of the created world under God.[14] Immanuel Kant expressed this awareness in his programmatic essay: 'What Is the Enlightenment.' 'Enlightenment is man's exodus from his self-incurred tutelage. Tutelage is the inability to use one's understanding without the guidance of another. Dare to know (*Sapere aude*)! Have the courage to use your own understanding: This is the motto of the Enlightenment.'[15]

The growing inclination of the 'New Era,' the modern era, is the renunciation of man's desire to know the transcendental for the sake of gaining true knowledge of the created world. It is the ideal of human autonomy; the promise of the self-emancipation of man as individual and as species; the future-directedness of man and the Promethean new awareness of man's power

---

persuasive power of the great religions. Alexis de Toqueville, *L'Ancien Regime*. Edit. G.W. Headlam, livre I, (Oxford 1969) Ch. 3.

[12] See letter of Thomas Jefferson to George Wythe, Aug. 13, 1776, in *Jefferson Writings*, P. L. Ford, ed., (New York 1892-1899) iv, p. 296.

[13] On the Higher Law background of the concept of the rights of man see E.S. Corwin, *The Higher Law Background of American Constitutional Law*, (Ithaca 1967); L. Strauss, *Natur und Geschichte*, (Stuttgart 1956); H. Medick, *Naturzustand und Naturgeschichte der Bürgerlichen Gesellschaft*, (Göttingen 1973).

[14] See Hans Blumenberg, *Die Legitimität der Neuzeit*, (Frankfurt a.M. 1966); Y. Arieli, 'Modern History as Reinstatement of the Saeculum: A Study in the Semantics of History,' *Jewish History*, (Haifa University Press, Haifa 1994) vol. VIII, nos. 1-2, pp. 205-228; also Richard Koebner, 'Die Idee der Zeitwende,' *Geschichte, Geschichtsbewusstsein, und Zeitwende*, (Bleicher Verlag, Gerlingen, Germany 1990).

[15] Immanuel Kant, 'What Is the Enlightenment?' in *Introduction to Contemporary Civilization in the West*, vol. I, p. 1071.

to shape his future. Human history is thus the successive realization of man's freedom and of the potentialities inherent in Mankind.

If one looks for a philosophical underpinning for the principles contained in the Universal Declaration of Human Rights, Kant may serve as guide, as his philosophy presents a feasible link between a possible metaphysic and secularism which is the existential dimensions of modernity and of modern history. This was basically the core contention of Immanuel Kant. Whether dealing with the nature and limits of pure reason or the nature of ethics, morality, human freedom and history, or the true aims of a cosmopolitan order, his basic assumption is man's capacity to shape his individual and collective existence according to the highest ideals implied in the concept of the dignity of man and his existential autonomy and freedom. His admirable short essay on a possible philosophy of history called '*Idee zu einer allgemeinen Geschichte in welbürgerlicher Absicht*' (Ideas of a Universal History on a Cosmopolitical Plan) together with his pragmatic treatise 'Zum Ewigen Frieden' (Perpetual Peace) are probably the closest approximations to the conceptions of a new world order as developed by the founding documents of the United Nations on human rights. As history is conceived as the movement toward human autonomy, the concept of the city of man—the saeculum—has been reinstated and has inherited the city of God.[16]

The Enlightenment's philosophy of man, its belief in the basic unity of man and humanity, of the nature and power of reason and morality, were clearly based on a deistic or theistic worldview, and derived ultimately from a humanistic and secularizing reinterpretation of the fundamental beliefs of Jewish-Christian monotheism. Their conceptions harmonized with those which were derived from classical, scholastic and humanistic views of man and the great rationalistic philosophical systems of the 17th and 18th centuries. Man's position in the universe was unique, both of and beyond nature and endowed with attributes that connected him to the source of the divine. Only in the light of these fundamental beliefs did the basic assumptions of the human rights theory of the Enlightenment make sense and could its postulates of the unity of mankind, of the inherent dignity and the existential equality of all man, their inalienable right to freedom and self-determination claim validity. It was therefore sufficient for Jefferson's Declaration of Independence to state: 'We hold these truths to be self-evident, that all men are created equal, that they are endowed by their Creator with certain inalienable rights, that among these are Life, Liberty and the pursuit of Happiness. That to secure these rights,

---

[16] Kant, 'Ideen zu einer allgemeinen Geschichte in weltbürgerlicher Absicht,' *Schriften zu Geschichts philosophie* (Stuttgart 1974) and *Zum Ewigen Frieden,* vol. VIII in the collected works of Kant as edited by the Prussian Academy of Sciences. See also Yirmiahu Yovel, *Kant and the Philosophy of History* (Princeton 1980), and by the same, 'Kant and the History of Reason,' *Philosophy of History and Action,* first Jerusalem Philosophical Encounter, 1974, (The Magnes Press, The Hebrew University of Jerusalem 1978); also B. Bury, 'German Speculation on Progress,' *The Idea of Progress,* (Dover Publication, New York 1952) Ch. 13.

Governments are instituted among Men, deriving their just powers from the consent of the governed.' Just as it was sufficient for him to justify the right for the American people to assume independence as entitlement given by the laws of Nature and Nature's God.[17]

Such justification could not be used in the Universal Declaration of Human Rights, embracing all people and cultures. It is therefore defined in the meta-language of a universal secular order, which is capable of addressing the community of nations and cultures in the neutral terms of secularity. They are formulated in part as self-evident truth and in part postulated as necessary condition for the achievement of the highest good, namely freedom, justice and peace in the world. 'Whereas recognition of the inherent dignity and of the equal and inalienable rights of all members of the human family is the foundation for freedom, justice and peace in the world.' The truth of the same principles is confirmed by historical experience, namely, 'That the disregard and contempt for human rights have resulted in barbarous acts which have outraged the conscience of mankind.'[18] In this way the truth of the principles of the Universal Declaration and the necessity to adopt them as such have been proven without taking recourse to the sources and foundations on which these principles were reared.

But there is one term in the Universal Declaration that cannot be tucked away nor separated from its sources, namely, 'the Inherent Dignity of all human beings.'

It is the concept and term of 'the inherent Dignity' that carries the whole burden of being the fountainhead from which the equal rights of man follow which leads us back to the deistic or theistic worldview. Though article 1 of the Declaration attempts to define this concept also as a right, stating: 'All human beings are born free and equal in dignity and rights. They are endowed with reason and conscience and should act to one another in the spirit of brotherhood.'[19] It is clear that this right to respect the dignity of each person, does not exhaust the significance of the term stated in the preamble, 'the

---

[17] See the religious overtones in 'The Unanimous Declaration of Independence of the Thirteen United States of America' which are immediately introduced in the preamble, 'When in the course of events, it becomes necessary ... to assume among the powers of the earth, the separate and equal station to which the laws of nature and of Nature's God entitle them' and again toward the concluding end of the Declaration: 'We ... the Representatives of the United States of America ... appealing to the Supreme Judge of the world,' quoted from Julian P. Boyd, et al., eds., *The Papers of Thomas Jefferson I*, (Princeton 1950) pp. 429-433. See Carl L. Becker, *The Declaration of Independence*, (New York 1922), and by the same *The Heavenly City of the Eighteenth Century Philosophers*, (New Haven 1932). As for the general attitudes toward the church at the eve of the French Revolution, see Daniel Mornet, 'Conclusion,' in *Les Origines Intellectuelles De La Revolution Francaise, 1715-1787*, (Librarie Armand Colin, Paris 1954) p. 469 *ff*.

[18] Preamble to the Universal Declaration of Human Rights, *Basic Documents on Human Rights*, Jan Brownlie, ed., 3rd Edition, (Oxford 1994).

[19] *Ibid.*, article 1, p. 22.

Inherent dignity of all human beings.' We find the difficulty in legitimating the concept of 'dignity' in purely secular terms in the Basic Law: Human Dignity and Liberty, adopted by Israel, which stands for a bill of rights enumerating 'Respect for Life, Body and Dignity,' 'the Protection of Property,' of 'Personal Liberty,' 'Freedom of Movement' and the 'Right to Privacy and Personal Confidentiality.'

There are actually two versions of this law. The first law enacted by the Israeli Legislature in 1992, defines the purpose of this law as follows: 'The purpose of this Basic Law is to protect human dignity and liberty, in order to entrench in a basic law the values of the state of Israel as a Jewish and democratic state.' Obviously, this does not provide a substantive explication of the meaning and significance of the concept of dignity. This version was therefore emended in 1994 by prefacing the law with a declaration of the 'fundamental principles,' stating: Fundamental human rights in Israel are founded on the recognition of the value of the human being, the sanctity of human life, and the principle that all persons are free; these rights shall be respected in the spirit of the principles set forth in the Declaration on the Establishment of the State of Israel. The reference to the text of the Declaration of Independence is directed to the enumeration of rights as well as to the introductory statement that the norms of the state of Israel will be based 'on freedom, justice and peace as envisaged by the prophets of Israel.' This reference to the Prophetic vision of the ontological status of man is exceptional, as the clear separation from all metaphysical and religious assumptions is the fundamental requirement for the universal acceptance of the principles of the Universal Declaration. For the same reason, the supreme place that the assertion of human dignity holds in the German Basic Law as the legitimizing basis of the state[20] is not explained, but appears as a normative command addressed to the State, which makes the dignity of man the constitutive principle in the system of basic rights.[21]

The expression 'the inherent dignity of man' refers not to another right but defines the ontological status of man which derives ultimately from the fundamental conceptions of the West created by the fusion of Jewish-Christian monotheism with those derived from classical and humanistic conceptions of man. In all these, man's position in the universe is unique, both of and beyond nature, and endowed with attributes that connected him to the source of the divine. Though the classical sources point to the same direction and could be therefore absorbed by Christianity, the main inspiration lies undoubtedly in the Jewish-Christian monotheistic view according to which the Creation of the world itself, and the course and purpose of history are bound up with the destiny of man and his I-Thou relationship with God.[22]

---

[20] See Eckart Klein's article inthis volume 'Human Dignity in German Law.'

[21] See Art. 1 para. 1. cl. 1. and E. Klein, *op. cit.*

[22] I believe it to be superfluous to elaborate this point, suffice it to mention some basic concepts: The Jewish conception of the sanctification of the world, the chiliastic and apocalyptic concepts of history in post-biblical Judaism and the Christian conception

This feeling of awe, of pride and humility in the relationship between man and God which lies at the basis of the concept of the inherent dignity of man is given exemplary expression, maybe for the first time, in Psalm 8:

> When I consider thy heavens, the work of thy fingers, the moon and the stars, which thou hast ordained: What is man that thou art mindful of him? And the son of man, that thou visitest him? For Thou has made him a little lower than the Angels and hast crowned him with glory and honour. Thou hast made him to have dominion over the works of thy Hands; thou hast put all things under his feet.[23]

This conception of the unique status of man in the Universe is also the vital center of the classical view of man from Plato to Boetius' 'De consolatione philosophiae.' It is reaffirmed in the Neoplatonic and Stoic conceptions of man, in *De Legibus* and *De Natura Deorum* of Cicero.

Reformulated in the scholastic theology and the humanistic interpretation of the Renaissance, this view became the central message of Humanism.[24] For Lorenco Valla, Marsilio Ficino, Pico della Mirandola, and Ludovico Vives the existential freedom, the potential powers of man to raise himself to the highest levels of excellence in understanding, virtue, holiness and creativity, his capacity of change and progress, raise man to the central position in the created world. This was the message of Maneti's *De excellencia et dignitate hominis* and of the famous oration of Pico della Mirandola, *De Dignitate Hominis* which became the watchword and central expression of Humanism. Seen in this light, freedom and the possibility for self-determination are the necessary attributes for man and the rights follow logically from man's status of worth, dignity and creativity.[25]

---

of 'Geschichte als Heils-Geschichte.' See Karl Löwith, *Meaning in History*, (University of Chicago, Chicago 1958).

[23] But in Hebrew it says 'little lower than the Gods [*Elohim*],' and the Hebrew term for honor [*kavod*] stands both for honor and for dignity.

[24] See Cassierer, Kristeller Randall, eds., *The Renaissance Philosophy of Man*, (University of Chicago, Chicago 1945); J. H. Randall, Jr. *The Making of the Modern Mind* (New York 1940); Giuseppe Tofanin, 'The Classical Heritage from The Fathers to Saint Thomas,' *History of Humanism*, trans. Elio Gianturco (Las Americas Publishing Co., New York 1954); Richard C. Dales, 'A Medieval View of Human Dignity' *Journal of the History of Ideas, Oct.-Dec. 1977*, as quoted by Nathan Rotenstreich, *Man And His Dignity*, (Magnes Press, Jerusalem 1983) p. 15. See also K. Brandi, *Die Mittelalterliche Welianschauung, Humanismus, und nationale Bildung*, (Berlin 1925).

[25] Burkhardt, *Die Kultur der Renaissance in Italien*, (München 1960); K. Brandi, 'Die Renaissance,' *Die Gotik und Renaissance, 1250-1500*, Propylaen Weltgeschichte. Herschel Baker, 'The Renaissance View of Man,' *The Image of Man*, (Harper Torch Books, New York 1961); John Huizinga, *The Waning of the Middle Ages*, (Penguin 1955).

Western Civilization evolved out of the Fusion of two Universal-historical heritages, the Jewish-Christian monotheism and the heritage of the classical culture and thought, each of which held in its own way the idea of the unique status which man holds in the universe as central message of its spiritual and existential experience. On the basis of this assumption we tried to explain two traits which are specific to the West: its tendency to conceive its basic assumptions and norms as possessing universal validity and the fact that only in the West a culture and society developed which aimed to base its first principles and basic values on secular norms and principles. Yet we did not analyze the underlying assumption, which would explain why Western Culture contented that its basic values and intellectual assumptions do possess universal validity. Questions like these relate to the type of analysis for which Max Weber remains exemplary.[26] In order to understand phenomena which achieved universal historical significance and were as such evaluated, one should examine, according to Max Weber, the configuration of circumstances, and conditions which would explain why in the West, and only there, cultural, intellectual, moral and technical trends did develop which would claim and achieved universal significance and validity. Max Weber claimed this characteristic for almost all expressions and productions of Western culture and civilization: in science, architecture, the Arts and literature; in its institutions, its character of general and professional education; its professional bureaucracy without which modern society and the state could no function. Such characteristics are even more pronounced in the conception of the state as institution [Anstalt] as framework for the public sphere, based on constitutional rules and principles, on a body of legal procedures and institutions and a trained professional bureaucracy.[27]

The common ground, according to Weber, was to be found in the classical rationalistic inheritance developing into the modern modes of rationalistic thought and action which penetrate not only all forms of Western activity but also its ethos and purposes. Its rationalistic character is basic to the pattern of its social relations and is the condition for the development of modern capitalism called by Weber '*die schicksalstvolle Macht des modernen Leben.*'[28]

Max Weber emphasized the uniqueness of Western law and jurisprudence, and this despite similar beginnings in India, (the Mimamsa School) and in the systematic codifications of laws in the ancient Near East. They all lacked the strict juridical schemata and forms of reasoning which characterized the Roman Law and its offspring, the western jurisprudence.[29]

---

[26] See Max Weber, 'Vorbemerkung zu den gesammelten Aufsatzen zur Religionssoziologie,' *Soziologie Weltgeschichtliche Analysen, Politik*, (Alfred Kröner, Stuttgart 1956) p. 341*ff.*

[27] *Ibid.*, p. 343.

[28] *Ibid.*, p. 341. See 'Die Protestantische Ethik und der Geist des Kapitalismus,' *Gesammelte Aufsatze zur Religionssoziologie*, 1 Bd.

[29] *Ibid.*

The principle and theory of the inherent dignity of man and human rights is undoubtedly an outstanding example of a great idea embodying a system of values, which claim universal validity. It embodies the central belief which shaped the civilization of the West: its universalistic conception of man's unique position in the universe, which pertains to the Jewish-Christian monotheism and the conception of man in the classical heritage of thought and culture. These elements are the necessary condition for the development of legal-political thought of universal significance. Yet they same achieved their characteristic definition only after they absorbed the cultural and legal conceptions created in the Middle Ages and the intellectual and normative revolution contained in the development of modern history.

Such development cannot be explained only in terms of a systematic rationalization, as Max Weber maintained. It must be seen as a conscious endeavor to dissolve the ties that bound the conception of man to their religious transcendental source and translate them to the central existential claim of modernity—man's autonomy, his capacity to be lord of his fate and the shaper of his future.

The fusion of these two ultimate conceptions of human life into one civilization, which took place with the Christianization of the Roman Empire, seems to be a prescription for instability. Yet it was indeed this permanent tension between the secular authority of the Empire and the religious authority of the Church, the co-existence of church and state, which was decisive for the shaping of the mentality of the West and the emergence of a secular culture and civilization which characterize Modern History.

On Roman Law

This is particularly evident in the role Roman Law played in Western History. Two archetypes of legal systems may be distinguished: systems whose laws are based on a method and body of rational categorization and principles which relate to the needs of society and are defined and empowered by the authority of its collective will, the res-publica. The other archetype bases the principles of law and their authority on the transcendent source of divinity, revealed in sacred teaching, and by those authorized to interpret its revealed will.

The Roman Law is the outstanding example of the first type, as a rational system of a secular law, which has been unique in its capacity to stand the test of time and the immense revolutions occurring in the history of the West. Remaining an intrinsic factor in shaping its legal and political mind and order during almost two millennia, it has been at the same time a vehicle as well as a witness to the enduring influence that the Greco Roman Mind and civilization had on the shaping of the West in general and that of its modern period in particular. The crystallization of the Roman law reflects the growth of Rome from the its republican origins to that of a world embracing Empire, a development during which it absorbed the attitudes, the theories and the legal procedures of the Hellenistic world. Its true achievement lies in the fusion of these elements into a coherent system of legal assumption, thought and practice, and the systematic definition and categorization of all matters subject to the realm of jurisprudence as well as of the techniques of inquiry and adjudication. In tracing the sources of the rise of a secular system of law and judicature, claiming universal validity, it is relevant to observe that, the *Codex Justinianus*, was the first complete systematic representation of the whole field of the jurisprudence; that it was undertaken in order to put the Roman empire which was to be the universal empire of the whole Christendom under an uniform rule of law and order and that, by subjecting the legal practice of the World-Empire to general principles, it realized the Greek ideal of a turning the jurisprudence into a rational discipline.[30] In achieving this aim the influence of the Stoic philosophy, first that of Panaitos and Poseidoniaos and of later Stoicism was of great importance. Standing on the verge of becoming an Empire dominating the known world (*imperium orbis terrarum*), Rome adopted the vision of the Stoic philosophers which would justify its rule: to unify the *Oikumene,* the whole civilized World under one law to establish the rule of justice and order. In other words, to become a Cosmopolis exemplifying and realizing the unity of mankind. The Empire and the Stoic philosophy became partners in a covenant, which became fortified through the adoption of Christianity as religion of the Empire, and as such it shaped the legal and political conceptions of the Middle Ages and the intellectual outlook of Early Modern History

Upon closer examination one realizes that the stoic conception of man and mankind became the basis upon which all universalistic conceptions of the political philosophy since the Renaissance were raised and it prepared the ground for the revolutionary change of the social and political thought in the Age of the Enlightenment.[31]

---

[30] George H. Sabine, 'The Theory of the Universal Community,' *A History of Political Theory*, (New York 1937) p. 141*ff*; 'Cicero and the Roman Lawyers,' *Ibid*, Ch. IX. E. Meynial 'Roman Law,' *The Legacy of the Middle Ages*, (Oxford 1951) p. 363*ff*; See also Elmer Bund, 'Recht,' *Der kleine Pauli*, (München 1979) vol. IV.

[31] This refers to the rebirth of the secularized version of the theory of the Law of Nature, starting with Suarez and Althusius, who introduced the theory of the contract as basis of social and political relations; to Hugo Grotius who, trying to discover and formulate the law and the rules which should regulate the relations between sovereign states, reformulated the principles which rule the *ius gentium* , namely the *ius naturale* as law of reason without which neither a society nor the community of states and nations can exist. The immense importance of Grotius lies in the complete secularization, well beyond that formulated by the Stoa and Cicero, of the law of nature. He based its validity on the most basic needs of human existence, namely its need to live in society and to preserve a peaceful social order. Being an intrinsic good, the conditions of its maintenance, discovered by reason, have by necessity to be observed, constituting the law of nature and of reason. See his definition of the law of nature in *De iure belli ac pacis*. Bk. I, Ch. I, sec. X, as quoted by George Sabine, *A History of Political Theory*, p. 424. See Ch. XXI to Ch. XXVI. On the impact of Stoicism and the 'Law of Nature' on the development of

According to the Stoa, man's soul and reason participate in the cosmic reason, the *Logos*, and as he is destined to live in society, he aims and endeavors to live in a rational society that embraces all men. [32] Consequent to these assumptions, the ontological equality of man followed. This principle determines the status of man in society, in the polity, in law and ethics. To this aspect of Stoic thought referred Lord Acton in his *History of Freedom*, stating, 'Owing to Stoic teaching mankind was freed from its subjection to despotic Government and their enlightened and sublime views on life served as bridge between the Ancients and the Christian polity and led the way to liberty.'[33]

Though the later Stoa endeavored to adjust the political ideals of classical Greece to the pluralistic society of the Roman Empire, it preserved the norms and spirit of the Polis, by emphasizing the supreme importance of responsible citizenship. Its conception of the inherent equality of man created an universal republican ideal according to which the state, beyond being a community of interests, presents a moral partnership for achieving the common good, the *res-publica* of Cicero, and not a framework of power to rule its subjects according to its absolute will.

It was foremost the concept of the 'law of nature,' *jus naturale*, which became the link between the political-philosophic thought of the Stoa and the conceptions of the Roman Law. By identifying the Law of nature with that of reason, which rules the universe and nature, the Stoa also based man's social existence on the rule of reason without which society cannot exist. Such conception also inspired the views of Cicero whose views and writings on the nature of law, of citizenship and of the res-publica, influenced the political and legal philosophy of future generations down to the 18th century. He based the equality of man on the identity between the rules of justice and law and that of reason. This was the meaning of his famous pronouncement in his book on the Republic.[34]

'There is in fact a true law-namely, right reason-which is in accordance with nature, applies to all men and is unchangeable and eternal. By its command this law summons all men to the performance of their duties; by its

---

Western thought in general, see Ernst Troeltsch, *Aufssatze zur Geistesgeschichte und Religionssoziologie*, herausg. Hans Baron, (Tübingen 1925) pp. 122-190, 374-429. See also Gilbert Murray, *The Stoic Philosophy*, (Oxford 1915); Paul Barth, *Die Stoa*, 4th edition, (Stuttgart 1922).

[32] W. Klaus, 'Logos,' *Der Kleine Pauli*, vol. III.

[33] Lord Acton, 'The History of Freedom in Antiquity,' *Essays on Freedom and Power*, selected by G. Himmelfarb, (Meridian Books, New York 1955), pp. 75-76.

[34] Cicero, Republic, III, 22. On the enduring influence of the writings and the image of Cicero on the European mind see: Giuseppe Toffanin, History of Humanism, *op. cit.* pp. 78-92, 279 *ff*; also Wilhelm Windelband, *History of Philiosophy*, (Harper Row, New York 1958) vol. I, p. 175; H. McIlwain, *The Growth of Political Thought in the West*, (New York 1932) Ch. IV, and Jacques Denis, *Histoire des théories et des idées morales dans l'antiquit* as quoted by Sabine, p. 154 *ff*. See also Hayim Wirschubski, 'Cicero Today,' *Eschkolot*, (Jerusalem 1964) vol. 4.

prohibitions it restrains them from wrong.' On the basis of these assumptions Cicero and the jurists and lawyers, who came after him, defined the fundamental structure of the Roman Law. Though the lawyers of the Principate and the Empire, Gaius, Papinian, Celsus, Paulus and Ulpian, refrained from basing their legal conceptions on philosophical grounds, they were undoubtedly based on similar considerations. The stoic conception of the law of nature, as identical with true reason, underlies their conception of justice.[35] Though this concept undoubtedly reflects the Stoic idea of the congruence of reason and nature, it is gained as a legal term by a process of generalization and systematic abstraction, a process which characterizes the categorization of the *Codex Justinianus* in general. This is evident in the categorization of its subject matter. In consequence of this proceeding the distinction between the law dealing with the relations of men as social beings (*ius*), and *fas*, the law dealing with the rules covering man's relation to the divine (*sacrum*), is gained.[36] Further substantive division of the saecular sphere establishes the distinction between civil law (*ius privatum*) and constitutional law, (*ius publicum*) and between positive law (*ius civile*) and (*jus gentium*) the law of nations. It is from the latter that the *ius naturale*, the law of nature, is gained. Namely that which is common to all man and nations represents the law of nature and reason.

The Roman law was not only the first secular law that claimed universal validity but as such it continued to influence and shape the fundamental legal and political conception of the West. Though its distinction between the sphere of the *sacrum* and the *saeculum* secured the independence of either, its influence on the development of the Catholic Church, its doctrine and in particular on the Canon law was decisive.[37] With the renaissance of the Roman law, concurrent with the secularization of society, the law of nature would become the basis for the formulation of the rights of man till our time.[38]

This leads us to the basic problem of the autonomy of the secular sphere in Western History.

On the Autonomy of the Secular Realm in the History of the West

In dealing with the influence of the Roman Law in the history of the West, we assumed also the enduring division of Western society into a secular and a

---

[35] See Dig. I, 1, pr, as quoted by E. Bund, 'Recht,' in *Der kleine Pauli*, p. 1355. Both, '*jus*' and '*justitia*' are guided, according to Ulpian, by the law of nature. '*ius naturale est, quod natura omnia animalia docuit.*' Ulp. Dig. 1, 1, 1, 3 *ibid.* p. 1355.

[36] See E. Bund, 'Recht,' *ibid.*

[37] See Gabriel Le Bras, 'Canon Law,' in *Legacy of the Middle Ages*, C.G. Crump, ed., (Oxford 1951) p. 321 *ff*; also Ed. Meynial, 'Roman Law,' on the renaissance of Roman Law in the twelfth century in *Legacy*, p. 367 *ff.*

[38] See notes 30 and 33 on the role which the concept of the law of nature played in the development of the political philosophy and the theory of rights in the early modern period and my discussion on its role in the ideology of the Enlightenment above.

religious sphere and this despite having embraced Christianity as the obligate belief of its society down to recent times. It is the fusion of the secular realm and the spiritual, religious realm, without destroying the autonomy of either sphere, which endowed the West with its unique character. This kind of fusion was possible because of the character of Catholic Christianity as compared to the other Monotheistic religions, that of Judaism and the Islam.

Both, the Islam and Judaism negate the coexistence and the right to coexistence of the World, the *Saeculum*, as autonomous sphere in which society orders its existence according to its needs, exigencies, purposes and understanding. Both reject the Augustinian division between the city of God, the church, and the city of man, the 'world,' as well as its theory of the two swords, the spiritual and the temporal, the church and the empire. The Islam, decisively influenced by Jewish conception of the all-embracing law, the Tora-Halacha, does not acknowledge the distinction between a spiritual and a temporal realm, between religious and secular activities. Both realms form a unity under the all-embracing authority of the Shari'a. Both recognize only one authority and one law- the revealed will of God in the Torah given to Moshe on Sinai, and to Mohammed in the Koran. The law is not man-made; it was given as command of precepts to all Israel in Judaism and to the whole world in the Dar el Islam. One law and rule of beliefs order the behavior and relations of men in society and their beliefs and faith in the Islam through the Shari'a and in Judaism through the Halacha. Being derived by an unbroken chain of interpretation to the source of all truth, they are binding for all generations and all believers. It is of the essence of every law, obligation, Idea, concept and institution that they have their point of reference in the Shari'a, or in the Halacha, in the divinely revealed prophetic Law of the Torah and the Koran to sanctify the world and hasten the coming of the kingdom of God.

For these reasons there is no room for the development of independent philosophical, theoretical, political, legal, social thought or reasoning, or for the very idea of the *res-publica*, the commonweal as an independent frame work, responsible and expressing the ordered life of the community. In Judaism, enduring the Galut and cutting itself loose from the contingencies of History, the all-embracing validity of the Halacha has replaced all marks the World and its kingdoms. In Islam where society, is identical with the community of the believers, the Law of the Koran claims absolute authority in the direction, and relations of human life: in man's obligations toward God, toward society and toward himself. According to its teaching the Islam tends toward an absolute theocracy, though this turned out to become an absolute Monarchy which was limited solely by the decisions of the 'Ulamá.[39]

---

[39] Erwin Rosenthal, *Political Thought in Medieval Islam*, (Cambridge, England 1958); see also Bernard Lewis, *The Arabs in History*, (Harper and Row, New York 1966); Hava Lazarus Jaffe, *HaKoran u'Mitzwot HaYesod b'Islam, Perakim b'Toldot HaAravim w'HaIslam*, (Reschafim, Tel Aviv 1967). As for the Halacha, see E.E. Urbach, *Hasa'l—Pirkei Emunoth weDeoth*, (The Magnes Press, Jerusalem 1978); and L. Jacobs, 'Halakha,' *Encyclopedia Judaica*, (Jerusalem 1971).

Christianity, on the other hand defined itself as 'church' (*ecclesia*), as institution of *salvation and grace which rules itself by its appointed ministry, (ecclesia* saccerdotium), inside the world and yet outside it. Such self-definition enabled Christianity to coexist within the world, and yet independent of it. Since the church as the community of all believers and saints (*ecclesia omnium fidelium et sanctorum*) represented the kingdom of God, it possessed a monopoly on grace and salvation. (Heilsanstalt). The uniqueness of this development lies in the fact that the apparent contradiction between the claims to universal validity of the powers and authority of the church as against the common wealth, the Empire, were resolved by the institutional separation between the realm of the sacred and that of the saeculum, each side recognizing the defined authority of the two kingdoms. As the world-embracing Empire, Rome was in need of a universal religion whose Kingdom is not of this world. So was Catholic Christianity, claiming the mission of universal salvation, in need of a universal Empire. In this process, both sides were influenced by the teaching of the Hellenistic philosophies and in particular by Platonism and the teaching of the Stoa. While the former was instrumental in the formulation of the Dogma, the later Stoa strongly influenced Christian ethics and its theology.[40]

This recognition of two legitimate spheres of authority is new in the history of the civilization. The reception of the stoic philosophy by the church influenced its attitude toward the 'World,' society and government. The existence of the Church as realm of the sacred deepened the secular character of the 'World,' and strengthened the process of secularization of the society and the state, which started the Era of the Renaissance and became the main characteristic of the Modern Period. In other words, the necessary historical condition for the rise of the Modern Period as the age of the Saeculum lay in the initial recognition of the coexistence of the spheres of the sacred and the secular. With this, I believe that the demand of Max Weber has been fulfilled, to examine the configuration of circumstances and conditions that would explain why in the West, and only there, did develop secular cultural, intellectual, moral and technical trends, attitudes and capacities which would claim universal significance and validity.

---

[40] 'Church,' *The Oxford Dictionary of the Christian Church*, F.L. Cross, ed., (New York 1958); Troeltsch, *The Social Teaching*, p.143; Karl Lowith, *Meaning in History*, (Chicago 1958) Ch. IX; Johannes Weiss, *Earliest Christianity*, F.C. Grant, trans., (Harper and Row, New York 1959) vol. II, Ch. XXI; Hans Lietzman, *A A History of the Early Church*, trans. B.L. Woolf (World Publishing Co., Cleveland 1961) vol. I, Ch. 5, 7, 8.

'DIGNITY OF MAN' AND *'PERSONA'* IN STOIC ANTHROPOLOGY: SOME REMARKS ON CICERO, *DE OFFICIIS I* 105-107[1]

Hubert Cancik

I. The First 'Persona'

1. The Core Text: Cicero, 'On Appropriate Actions' (I 105-107)

i. Topic and Aim

The expression 'dignity of man' was coined in Stoic anthropology. Formulated in the second/first century BCE by Panaetius of Rhodes and Marcus Tullius Cicero in Rome, it did not become a common term for the ancient Stoic authors. The original Latin term *dignitas hominis* denotes worthiness, the outer aspect of a person's social role which evokes respect, and embodies the charisma and the esteem presiding in office, rank or personality. It is concrete dignity inherent in the rational persona, given by Nature and to all human beings.

Stoic anthropology was transmitted, with or without the term 'dignity of man,' by Renaissance philosophers in the humanist tradition, by Ciceronian philology, and by the jurists and politicians who developed natural law in the 16th and 17th centuries. Through the mediation of these authors, natural law and Stoic anthropology permeated to the American and French declarations of human rights.

In this paper, I focus on the first appearance and the original meaning of the expression 'dignity of man.' Therefore, I would like to translate and explain a core text, Cicero's 'On Appropriate Actions;' to analyze some words, metaphors and the context of the expression 'dignity of man' in Stoic philosophy; and, finally, to offer a perspective on the reception of this text.

---

[1] I am indebted to Ms. Mareile Haase and M. Matthias Peppel (both of Tübingen) for their cooperation in bibliographical matters and for helpful discussions.

ii. Date, Addressee, Genre of Cicero's Treatise

Cicero uses the word *dignitas*, meaning rank or worth, quite often in his speeches and his rhetorical and philosophical treatises. Only once, however, does he apply it to mankind: in the treatise 'On Appropriate Actions' ('On Duties'). This text was written in the fall of 44 BCE, the year that Caesar was murdered. It was dedicated to Cicero's son, who studied philosophy in faraway Athens and was in need of money and, so the father supposed, of moral admonition. The genre of the three books on appropriate actions is exoteric, popular and personal.[2]

The author, Marcus Tullius Cicero, born 106 BCE, was an elder statesman who, at that time, had risked his life to maintain the aristocratic form of the Roman republic. He had been consul (in 63) in a colonial empire that embraced the Mediterranean from Spain to Syria—clearly a situation in which universal concepts in law, religion and philosophy were needed.[3] He had been a successful lawyer. As a governor of Cilicia, he had worked hard, but in vain, to obtain a blood-stained triumph in Rome. He was killed by his political enemies on the 7th of December 43, one year after the publication of his treatise *De Officiis* ('On Duties').

iii. The Text

The text (1.30.105-107) reads as follows:

> *Sed pertinet ad omnem officii quaestionem semper in promptu habere, quantum natura hominis pecudibus reliquisque bestiis antecedat; illae nihil sentiunt nisi voluptatem ... (106) Ex quo intellegitur corporis voluptatem non satis esse dignam hominis praestantia ... Itaque victus corporis ad valetudinem referatur et ad vires, non ad voluptatem. Atque etiam si considerare volumus, quae sit in natura hominis excellentia et dignitas, intellegemus quam sit turpe diffluere luxuria et delicate ac molliter vivere, quamque honestum, parce continenter severe sobrie.*

> But it is important for any disquisition on appropriate action to bear in mind how much the nature of man has precedence over cattle and other beasts; those feel but pleasure ... (106) Thereof it can be seen that the pleasure of the body is not worthy enough of

---

[2] On exoteric and esoteric philosophy cf. Cicero, *De Finibus* 5.5.12: Gr. *exoterikón* (ἐξωτερικόν) *populariter; limatius in commentariis.* Aristotle wrote *De Moribus* to his son Nikomachos: Cicero, *Fin.* 5.5.12.

[3] Cf. Hubert Cancik/Hildegard Cancik-Lindemaier, 'Patria peregrina universa. Versuch eine Typologie der universalistischen Tendenzen in der Geschichte der römischen Religion,' in Ch. Elsas et.al., eds., *Tradition und Translation. Zum Problem der Übersetzbarkeit religiöser Phänomene. FS für Carsten Colpe zum 65. Geburtstag* (Berlin, New York 1994) pp. 64-74.

the preeminence of man ... The nourishment of the body, therefore, should be measured with regard to health and strength, not to pleasure. But also, if we consider what excellence and dignity is in the nature of man, we'll recognize how shameful it is to be dissolved in luxury and to live in a spoilt and weak way, and how virtuous in a moderate, continent, severe, and sober way.

2. Context and Source

i. *Decorum* (splendid, decent) and *personae* (roles)

The text sets forth Stoic anthropology and morals as follows: The human mind (*ratio* reason) constitutes the fundamental difference between man and animal; it is the foundation of moral decision (*honestum*) and behaviour (*decorum*). Nature herself has imposed this *persona* (mask, role); it is common to all human beings.[4] This is the 'first *persona*;' it bestows excellence and distinction on man over all other living beings (*excellentia, praestantia*). From it, the dignity of man is derived.

The second role is individuality; the third is formed by the historical situation by which we are shaped; and the fourth is made by our own free will.

From this anthropological statement some moral demands are derived: You have to keep up your role; you must preserve the dignity of your *persona*;[5] your mind should control your drives, emotions, boundless desire (*voluptas*) and you should rule over them as over wild beasts.[6]

This, then, is the context for the first emergence of the formula 'dignity of man:' stoic anthropology and morals in Late Republican Rome. To the best of my knowledge, this is the first instance for the use of this term. Some scholars claim that the term is found in the Bible; I could not, however, find a single piece of evidence there.[7]

---

[4] Cic., *Off.* 1.97: *Nobis autem personam imposuit ipsa Natura magna cum excellentia praestantiaque animantium reliquorum.*

[5] Cicero, *De Inventione* 21.29: *personarum dignitates servare* (context: rules on narrative).

[6] Cf. Cic., *Off.* 1.101: *appetitus, impetus*: Greek *hormé* (ὁρμή); 1.14.—The opposition 'pleasure' (Epicureanism) versus '*dignitas*:' Cic., *De Finibus*, 3.1.1.

[7] August Buck, *Giovanni Pico della Mirandola, Über die Würde des Menschen* (1990) Introduction p. VII: '*Indem man bei der Beantwortung dieser Frage* (sc. '*Wesen des Menschen*') *auf den sowohl in der Bibel als auch in der Antike verwendeten Begriff der Wesenswürde des Menschen zurückgriff, erhielt dieser eine neue Bedeutung.*' (without references). Even in *Psalm* 8.5 ff. (*ma enosch*) the Vulgate translates with *gloria*: *minues eum paulo minus a Deo/gloria vel decore coronabis eum.*—Cf. Hiob 19.9: 'my *kavod*' the Vulgate translates as 'glory:' *spoliavit me gloriâ meâ.*—Cf. 1. Mose 45.13 (the glory of Joseph in Egypt). Nowhere are the different Hebrew passages translated with *dignitas hominis*; there is no immediate evidence of the conjunction *kvod ha-adam.*

ii. Panaetius of Rhodes

The source of Cicero's doctrine of the four *personae*, moral goodness and its visible beauty, is well known: Panaetius of Rhodes, *peri kathekónton* (περὶ καθηκόντων) 'On Appropriate Actions.' Cicero himself quotes him several times.[8] What he added to the Greek text can readily be discerned, e.g., Roman examples and allusions to contemporary politics (the death of Caesar, the rise of Octavianus, the future Augustus). Scholars agree, therefore, that our passage is taken over from Panaetius, and with it, probably, the term 'dignity of man.' This would bring us, for the first occurrence of the term, up to ca. 128 BCE, the year in which Panaetius probably composed his treatise.

Unfortunately, however, the Greek text is lost. In addition, the discourse on *persona* and *dignitas* cannot easily be translated into Greek.[9] In any case a term like *timé (*τιμή) or *axíoma anthrópou (*ἀξίωμα ἀνθρώπου) is not found in our fragments of Greek Stoicism.[10] At present, therefore, Cicero remains our first instance for the formula 'dignity of man.'

II. Dignity and Rule of Reason

1. Dignitas

i. Visible and Social Quality

'Dignity' is one of the most characteristic concepts of Cicero and was very frequently used by him.[11] He defines it as follows:[12]

---

[8] Cic. *Off.* 1.90; 2.76; cf. Cic. *Epistulae ad Atticum* 16.11.4, see A. Dyck, *A Commentary on Cicero, De Officiis*, p. 18 *ff.*

[9] For Gr. *prósopon* (πρόσωπου) cf. Annekathrin Puhle, *Persona. Zur Ethik des Panaitios*, Diss. (Berlin 1986). For Gr. *timé* (τιμή) cf. M. Forschner, *Stoische Ethik*, pp. 165, 168.

[10] For Gr. like or *axíoma* (ἀξίωμα) cf. Auct. ad Herennium 4.17 f.: *dignitas—* ornament, beauty = *axíoma* (ἀξίωμα); Athanasius, contra Apollinarem (ad Psalm. 109.1): *ouk anthrópou axíoma alla theoú* (οὐκ ἀνθρώπου ἀξίωμα ἀλλὰ θεοῦ)—the Latin translation in Migne has *dignitas*. For Gr. *axía* (ἀξία) cf. Seneca, *Epist.* 71.33: His (i.e., Gr. *agathá* (ἀγαθά) *pretium erit aliquod, ceterum dignitas non erit.*)

[11] E. Remy, 'Le concept cicéronien de la dignitas,' in: *Nova et Vetera* 5 (1922) p. 129; there is no adnotation to *Off.* 1.106.

[12] Cicero, *De Inventione* 2.55.166; context: the four cardinal virtues; the discourse is popular philosophy in the frame of rhetoric. Cf. H. Lausberg, *Handbuch der literarischen Rhetorik*, (1960) (index s.v.) Cf. Cic. *Invent.* 1.21.29: *si personarum dignitates servabuntur* (in the narrative); 2.53.161: *Iustitia est habitus animi, communi utilitate conservata, suam cuique tribuens dignitatem. Eius initium a natura profectum ... naturae ius est, quod non opinio genuit sed quaedam in natura vis insevit, ut religionem, pietatem.* There is a strict connection from this early rhetoric treatise to the late philosophical treatise 'On Appropriate Actions.'

Dignitas est alicuius honesta et cultu et honore et verecundia digna auctoritas.

Dignity is someone's virtuous authority which makes him worthy to be honored with regard and respect.

This definition (a) points to the concrete, visible quality of a person and (b) brings social aspects, like rank and prestige, into the foreground, not anthropological values. Both parts of the definition fit the etymology and the common use of this word in Latin.

Dignitas, Decus, Decorum

Roman dignity can be seen, it has splendor; it shines; it is an ornament (*decus, decorum*).[13] It is a quality of the body as is health, strength or swiftness.[14] What charm (*venustas*) is in the female, dignity is in the male.[15] The opposite is 'obscure, dirty, ugly, contemptible.'[16]

Dignitas and *Maiestas*

Roman dignity is marked by social and political connotations. The Roman people itself, its government and state have *dignitas*.[17] Qualities like 'majesty' (*maiestas*) and 'greatness' (*amplitudo*) can be added.[18] The magistrate bears the role (*persona*) of the state and he should, therefore, by lawful administration, preserve its 'dignity and splendor.'[19] All parts and members of the Roman State, the citizenship, the empire have a share in this collective dignity:[20] the province of Sicilia;[21] the senate;[22] the praetor; the consul;[23] the

---

[13] Cicero, *In Verrem* II.2.45.111; *Inv.* 2.177 (*corporis virtus*); *Vatin.* 25 (*dignitas et splendor*); *Sull.* 1; *Marcell.* 24.

[14] *Rhet. Herenn.* 3.6.10: *corporis sunt ...: velocitas, vires, dignitas, valetudo* etc.; cf. Cic. *Inv.* 2.2; *De Orat.* 3.155; Livy 45.40.4: *cum dignitate alia corporis tum senecta ipsa maiestatem prae se ferens*; Cic. *Fin.* 5.17.47: Tacitus, *Ann.* 11.16.8; 11.28.27; 12.51.22.

[15] Cic. *Off.* 1.130; cf. Gellius 14.4.2 (from Chrysippos): *reverendae cuiusdam tristitiae dignitate*; Cic. *Off.* 1.94: *id dignum viro et decorum videtur*. Digesta 26.22 (Ulpianus): *dignitas maior est in sexu virili*.

[16] Cic. *Fin.* 5.17.47; cf. *turpitudo, humilis, obscurus; sordida plebs*.

[17] Cic. *Phil.* 3.19; *Imp. Pomp.* 11; *Cat.* 4.20; *Mur.* 1.

[18] Cic. *De Orat.* 2.164.

[19] Cic. *Off.* 1.124: *debere eius* (sc. *civitatis*) *dignitatem et decus sustinere, servare leges* ... For *persona* combined with magistrate cf. Pliny, *Epist.* 1.23.5: *sed tu ... plurimum interest quid esse tribunatum putes, quam personam tibi imponas; quae sapienti viro ita aptanda est ut perferatur ..*, see H.P. Bütler, *Die geistige Welt des jüngeren Plinius* (1970) p. 21.

[20] Cic. *Dom.* 1.4; *Epist. Fam.* 4.6.1: *ut eorum luctum ipsorum dignitas consolaretur ea quam ex re publica consequebantur*. Cf. Cic. *Imp. Pomp.* 14; *Phil.* 10.7; *Mur.* 1.1: *Quodsi illa sollemnis comitiorum precatio ... tantam habet in se vim et religionem, quantam rei publicae dignitas postulat*. Livy 37.54.14 ff.

augures.[24] To diminish this collective dignity (*maiestatem minuere*) is a grave crime.[25] The *crimen laesae maiestatis* of the state or, in later epochs, of the emperors (*lese-majesty*) was high treason and was punished by exile or death.[26]

To conclude this short history of Roman *dignitas*: there are many texts, in Cicero and in Roman literature in general, that concern themselves with the dignity of the state, the citizen and the male; there is but one on the dignity of human nature.

2. Ratio and Natura

i. Natura and Ius Naturale

Human dignity, Cicero claims, resides 'in human nature,' and it is Nature herself who has imposed the first and the second mask upon all and everyone: she gave reason and freedom of moral decision to all human beings and a specific individuality to everybody. Man is born free and rational 'by N/nature.'[27]

The use of 'Nature' and 'Reason' in this summary of Cicero's teaching on the dignity of man requires a short comment.

Nature, *kosmos*, *physis* (κόσμος, φύσις), and Reason, *logos* (λόγος), are key concepts of Stoic physics and ethics.[28] Nature herself is rational; reason, thought of as an energetic, fiery substance, is dispersed in all things, inorganic and organic, in different form and concentration. *Natura* is creative, she acts according to rational rules ('laws of nature'). Nature is a positive, normative force,[29] which may even give certain 'prescriptions:'[30]

---

[21] Cic. *Verr.* II.2.45.111.

[22] Cic. *Pis.* 64.

[23] *Consularis dignitas*: Cic. *Agr.* 2.2.3; *Pis.* 24: *Magnum nomen est, magna species, magna dignitas, magna maiestas consulis*; *Verr.* II.3.38.87 *praetoris dignitas*. For 'Amt und Würde' cf. Cic. *Epist. Fam.* 11.17; *Mur.* 13; *Scaur.* 27; *Rosc.* 12.33. Livy 22.40.4: *cum dignitates ('dignitaries') abessent*.

[24] Cic. *Brutus* 1.1; cf. Livy 10.7.12: *reddere honorem sacerdotiis dignatione sua*.

[25] Cic. *De Or.* 2.64: *si maiestas est amplitudo ac dignitas civitatis is eam minuit, qui exercitum hostibus populi Romani tradidit*. *Part. Orat.* 105: *maiestas est in imperii atque nominis* (!) *populi Romani dignitate, quam minuit is, qui ... ad seditionem vocavit*; *Inv.* 2.53: *maiestatem minuere est de dignitate aut amplitudine aut potestate populi ... aliquid derogare*; cf. *ibid.* 2.55.

[26] Cf. G. Rotondi, *Leges publicae populi Romani*, 1912 (= 1962) p. 339 f.: lex Varia de maiestate (90 BCE; *bellum sociale*); p. 360: Lex Cornelia de maiestate (81 BCE); cf. Cic. *Epist. Fam.* 3.11.2 (Asconius ad locum); Tac. *Ann.* 1.72.

[27] Ulpianus, in *Digesta* 1.1.4 = *Institut.* 1.5 pr.; cf. Ulpianus (?), in *Institut.* 1.2.2: *iure enim naturali ab initio omnes homines liberi nascebantur*.

[28] Sources: Cicero, *De Legibus*, book I; *De Natura Deorum*, book II.

[29] For the opposite evaluation of 'Natura' cf. J. Taubes, *Vom Kult zur Kultur*, (1996) pp. 34, 70.

Nature prescribes that man should help man for the only reason that he is human.

All of us are bound by one and the same law of nature (*una continemur omnes et eadem lege naturae*).

By natural law, there is unity and equality amongst mankind. Stoic universalism declares the whole world to be one common state for everybody. In this *kosmo-polis* Cicero even imagines 'a kind of *ius civile* (civil right)' for all men (*quasi ius civile*).[31] In this way, natural law, rule of reason, and natural rights, equal for all men, are linked together.

ii. *Ratio*

It is *ratio* (mind, reason) through which man excels beasts. Reason is, according to Stoic anthropology, the distinctive quality of man.[32] What is morally good (*honestum*) and beautiful (*decorum*) is derived from this faculty to foresee, to plan, to select and to decide according to the rules of nature and reason. The mind functions as the steering center, *hegemonikón* (ἡγεμονικόν), of human actions. It controls the drives (*hormé* (ὁρμή), *impetus*) and represses the irrational affects (*páthos* (πάθος), *affectus*). In this way reason governs; it rules our actions.[33] The Stoics developed this topic in great detail in books dealing with 'actions' *peri práxeon* (περὶ πράξεων), *de actionibus*. Cicero does not postulate the extinction of urges or desire, nor the mortification of man, but instead moderation and respect (*verecundia*). It is from this rule of reason over the irrational forces that Cicero derived the 'dignity of our nature.' The dignity of man resides in his first *persona*, reason and free moral decision.

---

[30] Cic. *Off.* 3.5.7; 3.5.23 (no enrichment to the disadvantage of others): *neque vero hoc solum naturâ, id est iure gentium, sed etiam legibus populorum constitutum est*. This text is quoted in Lactantius, *Inst. Div.* 6.6. Ambrosius, *Off.* 3.24. Hieronymus, *Epist* 133.1. Cf. Corpus Iuris Civilis *Institut*:1.2 (*ius naturale est, quod natura omnia animantia docuit*).

[31] Cic. *Fin.* 3.19.64: (*mundum esse*) *quasi communem urbem et civitatem hominum et deorum, et unumquemque nostrum eius mundi esse partem*. 67: *quasi ius civile*, but there is no legal society between man and animal. Cf. *Fin.* 4.3.7. Cf. M. Schofield, *The Stoic Idea of the City*, (Cambridge 1991).

[32] M. Forschner, *Stoische Ethik*, p. 59 f. In comparison to other Stoics, Panaetius intensifies the difference between rational/irrational and, by analogy, between man and beasts. See Dyck, p. 260: 'Panaetius differed from the the older Stoa in recognizing the *hormé* (ὁρμή) as an irrational element, independent of the *logos* (λόγος);' cf. *ibid.*, pp. 263, 267.

[33] Cic. *Off.* 1.36.132 and 2.5.18: *ratio* rules over *appetitus, impetus, voluptas*. Cf. Cic. *Fin.* 5.9.

Drives and emotions, then, are subject to reason according to the law of nature: *subiecti lege naturae*.[34] This hierarchy is repeated in the relationship of man and animal. Since animals, according to Stoic assumptions, have only senses and sensuality, they are fixed in the present and have only a limited foresight and memory.[35] Man should rule over beasts as over his own sensuality, emotions, drives. There is no legal relationship between man and animal; the bounds of law are valid only among humans.[36] Therefore man can make use of animals without doing wrong (*sine iniuria*); he can eat beasts, birds, fish. He has subdued animals to pull wagons, he has tamed elephants and trained dogs. With considerable self-assurance, Cicero praises the success of human rule over the world: engineering, building, heating and shipping. Man alone has the rule, he has the rule over everything:[37] *moderationem nos soli habemus-omnis est in homine dominatus*.

In Augustan time, Ovid, in his poem on the beginning of the world, has put into perfect verses this will to power:[38]

> *sanctius his animal mentisque capacius altae*
> *deerat adhuc et quod dominari in cetera posset*

> There was still need, in the beginning, of a more sublime animal
> and one with a higher mental capacity and which could be the
> master of the others.

Enters homo sapiens.

Samuel Pufendorf, when reviewing the Stoic anthropology, is perfectly right in quoting these verses in order to characterize this philosophical system. But before moving on to the history of the reception of Cicero's formula, it might be useful to formulate an interim result.

3. Interim results

'Dignity of man' is a unique coinage of Cicero's in his book on appropriate actions. It is a philosophical expression, a part of an anthropological and ethical argument.

---

[34] Cic. *Off.* 1.102, 105 (*nihil sentiunt nisi voluptatem*); cf. Dyck ad loc. Cic. *Inv.* 2.54.165: *temperantia est rationis in libidinem atque in alios non rectos impetus animi firma et moderata dominatio*.

[35] Cic. *Off.* 1.4.11; cf. 1.28.101 (*animals impetus appetitus*); 1.30.105. Cicero has a more positive picture of animals in *Fin.* 2.109: They show *indicia pietatis, cognitionem, memoriam in multis etiam desideria videmus*; they exhibit images of human virtues.

[36] Chrysippos in Cicero *Fin.* 3.20.66: *ut bestiis homines uti possint sine iniuria*. On the connection between repression of desire and power see N. Elias, *Über den Prozeß der Zivilisation*, Bern 1969 (=Frankfurt 1976). Cf. H. Cancik, 'Römische Rationalität,' in idem, *Antik Modern*, (1998) pp. 55-97.

[37] Cic. *Nat deor.* 2.57.151.

[38] Ovid, *Metamorphoses* 1.76 f.; cf. 1.89 *ff*.

The 'dignity of man' is based on his reason, his self-control, and his rule over beasts and the world. Reason and the capacity for free moral decision form the first *persona*; it is decidedly universal, common (*communis*). The word *dignitas* has a specifically Roman ring. It calls to mind the majesty of the Republic and the magistrate or Caesar. *Dignitas* denotes rank, authority, splendor.

The first occurrence of the expression 'dignity of man' is neither derived from religious concepts nor molded from theological language. It is a philosophical expression, tinged with Rome's political tradition, invented by a Greek aristocrat, Panaetius of Rhodes, and translated into Latin by a Roman nobleman. The eventual connection of the concept of the dignity of man with Stoic theology required a further step: the logic of its relationship to the transcendent or divine qualities of Nature, Cosmos, Reason had to be clarified. Cicero, however, in his treatise on appropriate actions, avoided expanding the argument into theology. It was solely his stress upon anthropology, rationality, and the simple but strong everyday experience that man rules over all other animals that guaranteed the astonishing success of his discourse on the excellence, the pre-eminence and the dignity of man. The expression could be understood as pure ethics and thus could be combined with Judaeo-Christian beliefs.

III. The Ciceronian Formula *dignitas hominis* in Manetti, Pico, Pufendorf

1. Text, Commentaries and Translations of Cicero's De Officiis

Cicero's treatise on appropriate actions was used by Lactantius, Ambrosius and Jerome. It became part of the bloodstream of Western culture, as Andrew Dyck, in his monumental commentary, stated with unusual emphasis.[39] There are about 700 manuscripts from the 14th-15th centuries. The text was printed for the first time in Mainz on the Rhine (by Fust and Schoeffer, 1465).[40] Desiderius Erasmus published an edition with notes and a famous recommendation of Cicero's moral teaching.[41] Philipp Melanchthon (1497-1560) wrote a commentary;[42] Johannes Sturmius[43] and Joachim Camerarius,[44] and some others printed notes and famous prefaces. The result of my provisional survey is that nowhere is the formula *dignitas hominis* commented

---

[39] Dyck, *supra* n. 8, p. 43.
[40] *Ibid.*, p. 44.
[41] P.S. Allen, *Opus epistolarum Des. Erasmi Roterodami* 2nd edition (1906) esp. epist. 151 (to James Batt, April 5th, 1501), epist. 152 (to James Voecht, April 28th, 1501). Editions 1501; 1520 (with Frobenius in Bale). Cf. G. Vallese, 'Erasmo e Cicerone: le lettere-prefazioni erasmiane al De officiis e alle Tuscolane,' in: *Le parole e le idee* 11, (1969) pp. 265-272.
[42] P. Melanchthon, *Argumenta et Scholia in officia Ciceronis*, 1525; *ibid.*, *Eruditae Annotationes in officia Ciceronis recens editae*, (Wittenberg 1562); cf. G. Binder, *Philipp Melanchthon*, (1998) pp. 21-31.
[43] J. Sturmius, *M. T. Ciceronis, de officiis lib. III*, (1553).
[44] J. Camerarius, *M. T. Ciceronis, libri de officiis*, (Lipsiae 1548).

upon in great detail. Cicero's anthropology and morals are approved of, the doctrine of the persons is explained, but even after Pico's famous *Oratio* was published, the commentators did not recognize the momentum of this expression.

The first translation into German was printed in Augsburg (Bavaria) 1488 (by Hans Schobser).[45] Here, for the first time, 'Wyrde des Menschen' appears in German literature.

2. Dignitas hominis in Quattrocento Italy

i. Gianozzo Manetti (1396-1459)

In Quattrocento Italy, there emerged a series of treatises on the nature and condition of man. The titles used Cicero's anthropological terminology: on the excellence, the privilege, the nobility and, finally, the dignity of man.[46]

Gianozzo Manetti, an erudite jurist from Florence, had the title written in golden letters in the dedication copy from 1452: *De Dignitate et Excellentia Hominis*.[47] Since 1583, his book has been on the Index of forbidden books; Manetti refutes Pope Innocent III, who wrote centuries ago on the misery of mankind.[48] He proves the preeminence of man by quoting Aristotle, the Bible, Cicero and Hermetism.[49] To offer only one example of this specific synthesis:[50]

---

[45] Peter Kesting, in: *Deutsche Literatur des Mittelalters. Verfasserlexikon* 1, (1978) pp. 1274-1282, esp. p. 1277 f. Johann Neuber, *Cicero der Römer zu seynem Sune Marco. Von den tugentsamen ämptern und zugehörungen eynes wol und rechtlebenden Menschen*, (Augsburg 1531) (bey Heynrichen Steyner), I c. XXV: 'So wir auch die ubertreflicheyt und wyrde menschlicher natur betrachten, wird leycht gemerckt, ...' The prologue refers polemically to former translations which are to be improved. The translation is dedicated to Johann von Schwarzenberg (1463/65-1528) who organized the work, embellished the book with pictures of Hans Weidlitz and gave a more agreeable form to Neuber's literal translation. Cf. Gustav Radbruch, 'Zu Johann von Schwarzenbergs Officien-Übersetzung,' in *Archiv für Rechts- und Sozialphilosophie* 35 (1942) pp. 143-154.

[46] Cf. E. Garin, 'La "Dignitas Hominis" e la letteratura patristica,' in: *Renascita* 1 (1938) 102-146; A. Buck, l.c., p. XVII; P.O. Kristeller, 'Frater Antonius Bargensis and His Treatise on the Dignity of Man,' in: *idem, Studies in Renaissance Thought and Letters* II, (Roma 1985) pp. 531-560.

[47] Edition by Elizabeth R. Leonhard, (Padova 1975) esp. p. XIV (title). German translation by Hartmut Leppin, (Hamburg 1990), with introduction by August Buck and bibliography.

[48] Lotario dei Segni (Pope Innocent III, 1160-1216), *De Miseria Condicionis Humanae*. Lotario writes in the prologue on '*dignitas humanae naturae*' as antithesis to '*vilitas humanae condicionis.*'

[49] Manetti, *De Dignitate* 2.19. Manetti 3.3 quotes Cic. *Off.* 1.2.7.; Manetti 3.7 quotes Cic. *Leg.* 1.7.

[50] Manetti 3.49.

> *itaque omnipotens Dominus ei in tanta ac tam sublimi dignitate constituto suâpte naturâ indidit, ut se ipsum conservandi sui causa diligeret [...] ut rerum omnium dominaretur.*

> Therefore the almighty Lord imposed on him, whom he has established in so great and distinguished a dignity, by his own nature that he loves himself for the sake of maintaining himself [...] that he rules over all things.

Self-consciousness, self-love and conservation of the self are key terms of Stoic anthropology; nature is still a protagonist, but the director of the world's theatre has become the almighty Lord. The Christianization of Stoicism, however, did not change the result: the dignity of man resides in the wonderful fabric of his body (*dignitas corporis*), the incredible gifts of his mind,[51] and his position over all animals and things. They are his subjects (*subiecta*).[52] It is man's honor (*honos*) to have the domination over the world.[53] Biblical and Stoic quotations converge smoothly into a high-spirited encomion on mankind, especially its male component, and, at the peak of this hierarchy, the king, Alfonsus of Aragon in Naples.[54] The king is a living example of a perfect man: *deo quasi similis*.[55] This appears to be a somewhat disappointing political narrowing of a philosophical discourse on the common nature of man.

ii. Giovanni Pico della Mirandola (1463-1494), *Oratio* (1486)

In 1486, Giovanni Pico della Mirandola composed an introductory speech which he was unable to deliver because he was tried and banned by the Inquisition. After his premature death in 1494, what Giovanni Pico had called *Oratio* was printed under the title *Oratio de hominis dignitate*. The *autographon* is lost, the first printing was overseen by Pico's nephew Gian Francesco Pico, and it is to him that the speech owes its title.[56] This title continues the series of Quattrocento treatises on the nature of man.[57] It sounds definitely Ciceronian and has some support in Pico's works.[58] A new edition

---

[51] Manetti 4.71: *animi celsitudo ac sublimitas*; the attribution of these gifts by the creator and by Nature is corroborated by quotations from Cicero, *De Natura Deorum* 2.134-146 in: *Dign.* 1.7; 1.9; 1.11; 1.12.

[52] Manetti 3.37, quoting *Psalm 8* (*ma enosch*).

[53] Manetti 1.50: *illi tantum honoris attribuit ut rerum omnium dominaretur.*

[54] Manetti 4.73.

[55] Manetti, *Dign.*, *praefatio*.

[56] First edition by Gian Francesco Pico (Bologna 1496) (Benedictus Hectoris; Hain 12 992); cf. Tognon's edition, p. IX. At the end of the Oratio the title reads *de homine*.

[57] Pico himself points to the genre by his praeteritio in *Oratio* §1: *multa de humanae naturae praestantia afferuntur a multis.*

[58] Pico, *Heptaplus* 5.6: *in animo trinitatis imago ... unde et dignitas ei propria ... quo etiam factum, ut servire illi (homini) nulla creata substantia dedignetur*; 5.7: *in tanta dignitate constituti*. *Regulae XII*, no.8: *hominis dignitas et natura.*

was published in Strasbourg (1504, Joh. Prüss der Ältere) with a preface by Jacob Wimpfeling (1450-1528), who in several letters recommended Pico's work.[59] At this point, one may assume, a second track emerged beside Cicero's own works through which the term 'dignity of man' spread in Western Europe.[60]

Pico extols man as the center of the world, the knot that binds together the mortal elements and unites the mortal with the eternal; he praises the penetrating force and swiftness of the human mind and its rule over the world. In general, this is in harmony with Manetti, or even Cicero's less speculative anthropology and sober moral teaching. Pico's sources, however, are Greek rather than Roman: Florentine Platonists, Hermetic, Jewish and Christian traditions on the first man, his fall and salvation. The tone is elevated and highly speculative; he dwells on the doctrine of *Imago Dei* and the mysteries of the Trinity;[61] there is no argument on natural law, on free and equal birth, on *kosmopolis*. I do not know whether there is any connection to the tradition from which the ideas of the 'rights of men and citizens' were to arise.[62]

3. Stoic Concepts in the Anthropology of Samuel Pufendorf (1632-1694)

The first author to bring the concept of dignity of man into a central position in anthropology was Samuel Pufendorf.[63] Hans Welzel, who put forward this

---

[59] Wimpfeling, Introductory letter, March 21st, 1504 (ed. Herding-Mertens, nr.156); cf. Wimpfeling to Peter of Eberbach, January 21st, 1506 (*ibid.* nr.205), to Hans of Schoenau, June 1st, 1509 (*ibid.* nr.252). The edition is made from the Bolognese print of 1496 by Hieronymus Emser. Cf. J. Benzing, *Die Buchdrucker des 16. und 17. Jahrhunderts im deutschen Sprachgebiet* 2nd Edition (1982).

[60] Cf. A. Buck, *Introduction* (1990) p. XXII ff.: Italy, France, England, Hungary; no information on the dissemination of the title and its use as a term in early modern anthropology.

[61] Pico, *Heptaplus* I.IV: *De mundo humano, id est de hominis natura; IV 6: ... factum a Deo hominem ad suam imaginem ut praeesset piscibus, avibus et bestiis ... unde illi in bruta ditio et imperium. Sic etenim a natura institutus homo ut ratio sensibus dominaretur ...* [Because of the original sin, however we started] *servire bestiis nostris [i.e., ira, libidinis furor et appetentia] ... cupidi terrenorum, obliti patriae, obliti patris, obliti regni, et datae in nobis [in] privilegium pristinae dignitatis.*

[62] Manetti and Ficino are not in the index of authors quoted in Pufendorf's *De Iure Naturae et Gentium*.

[63] Hans Welzel, *Die Naturrechtslehre Samuel Pufendorfs* (Diss. Jena 1928). Revised edition (1958) p. 47: '*Bei Pufendorf erscheint zum ersten Male der für die Folgezeit (bis einschließlich Kant) so wichtige Begriff der "Menschenwürde" an zentraler Stelle des naturrechtlichen Begründungszusammenhanges, während z. B. noch Grotius von dignitas humana nur innerhalb des Bestattungsrechts im Hinblick auf den entseelten menschlichen Körper spricht. Da nun Pufendorf diese in der Menschenwürde begründete oberste Norm des Handelns im Gebot der "Sozialität" ausgesprochen fand, mußte sich für ihn eine eminente soziale Struktur des Naturrechts ergeben.*' Cf. *ibid.*, *Naturrecht und materiale Gerechtigkeit* (1951) 4th Edition 1962=1980, pp. 140-142; p. 141: '*Die auf der sittlichen Freiheit gegründete Idee der Menschenwürde steht im Mittelpunkt des naturrechtlichen Systems*

thesis in his dissertation (Jena 1928) analyzes Pufendorf's anthropology and quotes a striking proof from *De iure naturae et gentium* (1672):[64]

> *Requirebat humanae naturae dignitas, et praestantia, qua caeteras animantes eminet, ut certam ad normam ipsius actiones exigerentur, quippe citra quam ordo, decor, aut pulcritudo intelligi nequit. Maxima inde homini dignatio, quod animam obtinet immortalem, lumine intellectus, facultate res diiudicandi et eligendi praeditam ... Ob quam ille audit sanctius reliquis animal mentisque capacius altae et quod dominare in caetera posset (Ovid, Metamorphoses 1.76 f.).*

> The dignity and pre-eminence of human nature by which it excels over other living beings required that human acts were judged according to a fixed norm, because there cannot be conceived of any order, splendor or beauty beyond this dignity. The greatest dignity for man derives from this, that he has an immortal soul which is distinguished by the light of intelligence, the capacity of deciding and choosing ... Because of his soul man is called an animal more holy than the other, capable of a deep mind, and able to rule over the other animals.

The text reproduces Stoic anthropology, modified by the Platonic (or Christian) doctrine of the immortality of the soul. Moreover, the text assimilates Ciceronian phrases from *De Officiis* and the specific terminology of the Good and Beautiful (*decorum*).[65] There is more evidence that Pufendorf uses Cicero directly, and not as mediated by authors of Neo-Stoicism.[66] He does not name Cicero for every quotation, nor does he do so in the cases of other classics, like Virgil and Ovid, whose verses he inserts without giving any details on authors or works. He indicates his sources only when referring to scarcely known texts from Solinus, Manilius, Libanius or the Greek author Oppian (in which case he adds a Latin version).[67] Pufendorf studied classics at

---

Pufendorfs. Sie erfüllt den Sozialitätsgedanken mit seinem eigentlichen Inhalt ...' Welzel's philosophical and historical analysis seems convincing to me; less so, however, his emphasis on *diginitas hominis*. This phrase is very rare in Pufendorf and cannot be taken as a central term of the author. But *socialitas*, the emphatic use of *homo* (normative and social), *intellectus* etc. prove that Stoic anthropology and morals are the core of Pufendorf's argument.

[64] Pufendorf, *De Iure* 2.1.5.
[65] Cicero, *Off.* 1.30.105-107, see above §1.1.3.
[66] Cf. e.g. Pufendorf, *De Iure* 1.3.1: Ex hoc igitur dignitas hominis prae brutis maxime elucet. 1.3.4: Animantia bruta, quae infra nostram condicionem posita sunt ... etc.
[67] Pufendorf, *De Iure* 2.1 §5 (Ovid, Metamorphoses 1.76 f.); §7 (Virgil, Aeneid); §6 (Oppian, Kynegetica 3).

Leiden; he could expect readers who knew the books of the Stoics, Seneca, Epictetus, Marcus Antonius (Aurelius).[68]

In Pufendorf, the formula 'dignity of man'—the history of which I have endeavored to outline in this paper—appears integrated in a modernized, but still genuine, Stoic context. In the fabric of Pufendorf's natural law, Stoic concepts are the structural framework: Nature;[69] unity of mankind;[70] equality of men;[71] the human as a deficient animal depending on society;[72] *homo* (man) as a normative and social term;[73] self-consciousness, self-love, self-conservation as principles of human life; the doctrine of *persona*;[74] the comparison man/animal as a method of anthropological thought; the doctrine of *intellectus* and moral action;[75] even the doctrine of *oikeíosis* (o⇒κε⇔ωσις, *conciliatio*; 'reconciliation of man and nature'). Thus, in the 17th century, the phrase 'dignity of man' emerges in a decidedly Stoic context. This is important enough, even if this phrase does not denote the center of Pufendorf's system.[76]

The works of Samuel Pufendorf, the humanist and jurist from Saxony, became known in Europe and, through the writings of John Wise (1652-1725) who used an English translation from 1710, in the colonial states of America. It was Hans Welzel, again, who pointed out that John Wise propagated the teaching of Pufendorf, his Chief Guide and Spokes-man.[77] In the debate on the

---

[68] Pufendorf, *De Iure*, Preface of the edition of 1688 (Oldfather vol. I, p. 2 verso = vol. II p. iv; cf. vol. I p. 3).

[69] Pufendorf, *De Officio* 1.3.11; *De Iure* 1.3.1-3; §3: *naturalis rectitudo; intellectus hominis naturaliter rectus.*

[70] Pufendorf, *De Iure* 2.3.6: *cognatum et aequalem*; 2.3.18: *a natura cognatum animal.*

[71] Pufendorf, *De Iure* 2.3.6; cf. Cicero, *Off.* 3.26.

[72] Cf. Welzel, *Pufendorf*, pp.43 f.

[73] Pufendorf, *De Iure* 2.3.18; cf. Cicero, *Off.* 3.27; cf. Welzel, *Pufendorf*, p. 47. Do *imago-Dei*-metaphors occur in Pufendorf's works?

[74] Pufendorf, *De Iure* 1.1.7 with quotation of Cicero, *Off.* 1.28 (= 30.105-109): *Nobis primam imposuit ipsa Natura magna cum excellentia praestantiaque animantium reliquorum.*

[75] Pufendorf, *De Iure* 1.3: *De intellectu hominis prout concurrit ad actiones morales*; Pufendorf uses the following terms: *res adpetendae/reiiciendae; intellectus rectus; assensus* Gr. *synkatáthesis* (συγκατάθεσις).

[76] This modification of Welzel's thesis seems necessary because of Pufendorf's scant use of the phrase.

[77] John Wise, *A Vindication of the Government of New-England Churches* (1717; 2nd Edition, 1772). A Facsimile Reproduction with an Introduction by Perry Miller, Gainsville (Florida): Scholars' Facsimiles and Reprints (1958) p. 32; cf. P. Miller's Introduction, p. XV: 'For the content of his second demonstration Wise relied heavily upon an English translation (1710) of Baron Samuel Pufendorf's *De Iure Naturae et Gentium* (first published in 1672). A few of his paragraphs are substantial paraphrases. (Wise appears to have been entirely unaware of Locke.) But even when he borrowed, he inserted twists of his own, colloquialisms that come from the New England community. And his blanket assertion of the superiorities of democracy over both monarchy and aristocracy is not Pufendorf's; it is pure Wise.' Cf. Leonard

constitution of the Congregational Churches in New England, Wise quotes Pufendorf's text on equality, liberty and dignity of man. His golden Maxims read as follows:[78]

> Particular 1. That the People or Fraternity under the Gospel, are the first Subject of Power; or else Religion sinks the Dignity of Humane Nature into a baser Capacity with relation to Ecclesiastical, then it is in, in a Natural State of being with relation to Civil Government.
>
> Particular 2. That a Democracy in Church or State, is a very honourable and regular Government according to the Dictates of Right Reason. And therefore,
>
> Particular 3. That these Churches of New-England in their ancient Constitution of Church Order; it being a Democracy, are manifestly Justified and Defended by the Law & Light of Nature.

It was Pufendorf and Wise who handed down ancient traditions of natural law, Stoic anthropology, and with it, the formula of 'dignity of man' to the constitutional discourse of the 18th century in America and France.[79]

4. The Stoic impact on Kant's concept of dignity of man

In 1941, there appeared in Leipzig (Saxony) an attractive little volume entitled *Immanuel Kant, Von der Würde des Menschen*. The title may surprise, and even more the date and place. The volume, however—number 228 in the *Insel-Bücherei*—does not contain an essay by Kant, but rather excerpts from his writings pertaining to the topic 'dignity of man,' arranged on 77 pages by the editor Hans Thomae.[80] The *florilegium* is not authorized in a specific outline

---

Krieger, *The Politics of Discretion. Pufendorf and the Acceptance of Natural Law* (Chicago 1965).

[78] John Wise, *A Vindication*, p. 67 f.

[79] Neither in the Virginia Bill of Rights (1776), nor in the French Declaration of 1791 nor in the French Constitution of 1793 appears 'dignity of man.' The connection to the modern discourse that led to the UN Charter (1945) is unknown to me.

[80] I. Kant, *Von der Würde des Menschen*, ed. Hans Thomae (Leipzig 1941), reprints: 1944; 1948. H. Thomae (born in 1915) was an 'Assistant' of Philipp Lersch at the University of Leipzig (1939-1943), became Professor of psychology in Erlangen (1953) and Bonn (1960). The topic was used in basic statements, formulated at that time in German opposition and exile groups. The National Committee '*Freies Deutschland*' proclaimed (July 19, 1943), '*[...] Aufhebung aller gegen die Freiheit und Menschenwürde gerichteten Zwangsgesetze der Hitlerzeit,*' in: Wolfgang Benz, (ed.), *Bewegt von der Hoffnung aller Deutschen. Zur Geschichte des Grundgesetzes*, 1979, p.92 (Manifest an die Wehrmacht und das deutsche Volk). Compare the postulates which the '*Kreisauer Kreis*' formulated in August 1943 (*ibid.* p.95), '*3. Brechung des totalitären Gewissenszwangs und Anerkennung der unverletzlichen*

by Kant himself. Nevertheless, it offers a useful collection of some, not all, Kantian texts that exhibit the term 'dignity'—of person, man, mankind. *Menschenwürde* occurs five times in Kant's *oeuvre*. *Würde*, however, has 2450 instances; it is frequently combined with *Menschheit* (humankind), or *menschliche Natur* (human nature).[81] Kant himself explicitly acknowledges the Stoic tradition, which he modified and modernized:[82]

> *Diese Philosophen* [sc. the Stoics] *nahmen ihr allgemeines moralisches Prinzip von der Würde der menschlichen Natur, der Freyheit (als Unabhängigkeit von der Macht der Neigungen), her; ein besseres und edleres konnten sie auch nicht zu Grunde legen. Die moralischen Gesetze schöpften sie nun unmittelbar aus der, auf solche Art, allein gesetzgebenden und durch sie schlechthin gebietenden Vernunft, [...].*

This text sounds like a summary of Cicero, but represents rather the stoicizing tradition of moral philosophy in the 18th century. Another text strongly resembles Cicero's educational endeavors. Kant, in an essay on pedagogy, writes:[83]

> *Daß der Mensch in seinem Innern eine gewisse Würde habe, die ihn vor allen Geschöpfen adelt und seine Pflicht ist es, diese Würde der Menschheit in seiner eigenen Person nicht zu verleugnen. Die Würde der Menschheit aber verleugnen wir, wenn wir zum Exempel uns dem Trunke ergeben, unnatürliche Sünden begehen, alle Art von Unmäßigkeit ausüben usw., welches alles den Menschen weit unter die Tiere erniedrigt. Ferner wenn ein Mensch sich kriechend gegen andere betätigt, immer Komplimente macht, um sich durch ein so unwürdiges Benehmen, wie er wähnt, einzuschmeicheln, so ist auch dieses wider die Würde der Menschheit. Die Würde des Menschen würde sich auch dem Kinde schon an ihm selbst bemerkbar machen lassen [...].*

Würde der menschlichen Person als Grundlage der zu erstrebenden Rechts- und Friedensordnung.'

[81] Gottfried Martin, ed., *Allgemeiner Kantindex zu Kants gesammelten Schriften*, Berlin 1967, vol. 17, 'Wortindex zu Band 1-9' (bearbeitet von Dieter Krallmann und Hans A. Martin) vol. 2 (L-Z), s.v. Rudolf Eisler, *Kant-Lexikon* (Berlin 1930) pp. 612-13: 'Würde'.

[82] I. Kant, *Die Religion innerhalb der Grenzen der bloßen Vernunft*, Königsberg (1793), 2nd Edition 1794, Zweytes Stück, p. 709, note (edition by W. Weischedel, vol. 7, 1968).

[83] I. Kant, *Über Pädagogik* (1803), in: *Kant's Werke*, vol. IX, Friedrich Theodor Rink, ed., notes by Paul Natorp (Akademie-Ausgabe, Berlin Leipzig 1923) pp. 437-499; p. 489: '*Die Pflicht gegen sich selbst aber besteht, wie gesagt, darin, daß der Mensch die Würde der Menschheit in seiner eigenen Person bewahre.*'

This is the most extensive and coherent text in Kant's *oeuvre* in which the term 'dignity of man' is used several times and as a basic term.[84] It is rather perplexing that this occurs in a text on children's education, teaching good manners, modesty, cleanliness, no drinking, no unnatural sins, sharing bread and butter. This reminds us of Cicero's attempt to bring his son to self-control and restraint; his argument, too, was the excellence and dignity of man over beasts.[85]

The impact of Stoicism on Kant is generally agreed upon.[86] It was effective by virtue of the ancient authors themselves and their contemporary translators and, indirectly, through Kant's teachers and colleagues (Christian Wolff, Alexander G. Baumgarten, Christian Garve).[87] Max Wundt recognized[88] that Kant started his foundation of the metaphysics of morals as an *Anti-kritik* of the translation and the meditations on Cicero's treatise *On Appropriate Actions*, which Christan Garve (1742-1798) published in 1783.[89] His translation of our core text (Cic., *Off.* 1,30) reads as follows:[90]

> *Zur Beobachtung dieser Pflicht aber, so wie aller andern, ist es ein großes Hülfsmittel, sich die Vorstellung von der Würde des Menschen, und seinem über die Thiere erhabenen Range gegenwärtig zu erhalten [...] Ein inneres Gefühl sagt uns also,*

---

[84] More important for philosophical anthropology than for the history of ideas are fundamental statements in Kant's *Grundlegung zur Metaphysik der Sitten* (1785), pp. 393 ff.; 439 etc.; cf. G. Löhrer, *Menschliche Würde. Wissenschaftliche Geltung und metaphorische Grenze der praktischen Philosophie Kants* (Freiburg München 1995) passim.

[85] Cicero, *Off.* 1.30.105. In Kant's pedagogy the editor (p. 496) has rightly commented Kant's teaching on sex and shame by Cicero's passage on this topic from *Off.* 1.35.

[86] Katharina Franz, *Der Einfluß der stoischen Philosophie auf die Moralphilosophie der deutschen Aufklärung*, 1940; Willi Schink, 'Kant und die stoische Ethik,' in: *Kant-Studien* 18 (1913) pp. 419-475; Maximilian Forschner, *Über das Handeln im Einklang mit der Natur*, (Darmstadt 1998), pp. 60-68; 104-107; G. Löhrer, *Menschliche Würde*, p. 35 with notes 3 and 4.

[87] Klaus Reich, *Kant und die Ethik der Griechen* (Tübingen 1935) p. 27 ff.: Panaetius Cic., *Off.*; Carlos Melches Gibert, *Der Einfluß von Christian Garves Übersetzung Ciceros 'de officiis' auf Kants 'Grundlegung zur Metaphysik der Sitten'* (Regensburg 1994, Dissertation Trier 1991) 102 pp.

[88] Max Wundt, *Kant als Metaphysiker* (Stuttgart 1924) p. 306; Reich, *Kant*, p. 27 f. quotes a letter of Johann Georg Hamann to Johann Gottfried Herder, February 8, 1784, 'Kant soll an einer Antikritik über Garvens Cicero arbeiten.'

[89] Chr. Garve, *Abhandlung über die menschlichen Pflichten in drey Büchern aus dem Lateinischen des Marcus Tullius Cicero übersetzt von C.G.*, Breslau bey Wilhelm Gottlieb Korn (1783); the book is dedicated to Frederick II, King of Prussia. Together with the translation, Garve published his *Philosophische Anmerkungen und Abhandlungen zu Ciceros Büchern von den Pflichten* (Breslau 1783). The fourth edition of the translation and explanation printed in Breslau (Wroclaw) 1792 has a few changes.

[90] Garve, *Abhandlung*, pp. 79-80.

> *daß das körperliche Vergnügen der Würde unserer Natur nicht angemessen genug sey; und daß [...] In der That, wenn wir bedenken, was der Mensch sey, welche Kräfte in seiner Natur liegen, zu welcher Vortreflichkeit er gelangen könne: so werden wir seiner nichts unwürdiger finden, als in Weichlichkeit diese Kräfte zu verzehren [...]*

In the discourses where Garve deals with several topics from Cicero's treatise, Garve does not pay any attention to the passage on the dignity of man. The term 'dignity of man' has little systematic relevance in Kant; it is irrelevant for Garve. There are, on the other hand, some hints that, already in the last decades of the 18th century, the rhetoric of dignity became irksome.

In 1797, Friedrich Schiller published a couple of epigrams on political topics. One out of this series runs as follows:[91]

> *Würde des Menschen.*
> *Nichts mehr davon, ich bitt euch. Zu essen gebt ihm, zu wohnen.*
> *Habt ihr die Blösse bedeckt, giebt sich die Würde von selbst.*

IV. Results for a History of the Formula 'Dignity of Man'

In my short notes on the formula 'dignity of man,' seven stages may be discerned. It is but a sketch dealing exclusively with the formula, not the idea, the concept, nor opinions, images, vague notions which should have existed much earlier; my concern is the word, the formula, and its context and influence.[92]

1) Rome ca.128/44 BCE
   First emergence of the terms '*dignitas hominis*' and '*prima persona*' in Stoic anthropology.
2) Italy, Quattrocento (1452; 1496)
   The formula is used for the first time as a title (Manetti; Pico) out of Ciceronian tradition, but apparently without influence on the discourse on natural law and human rights.
3) Bavaria (Germany), 1488 (and 1531)
   First occurence in a German dialect translation of Cicero, *De Officiis*.

---

[91] F. Schiller, *Musenalmanach* (1797) pp. 32-33. English version: 'No more on this, I pray you. Give him food and shelter; When you have covered his nakedness, dignity will follow by itself.' The titles of the other epigrams: '*An die Gesetzgeber;*' '*Die beste Staatsverfassung;*' '*Politische Lehre;*' '*Würde des Menschen;*' '*Majestas Populi;*' '*Das Ehrwürdige.*'

[92] The formula is '*dignitas hominis (et excellentia, praestantia),*' not: *humana dignitas* (which is, e.g., in Thomas of Aquino, STh II II q. 64.2) nor *dignitas humanae substantiae* (which was in Christian liturgy, and is now abolished).

4) Sweden, 17th century[93]
   The formula appears, for the first time, in a more or less 'central position' (Hans Welzel) and in a juridical system - direct influence of Cicero - the context is neo-Stoic.
5) Massachusetts, 18th century
   First appearance in an English[94] draft constitution; direct influence of Pufendorf.
6) Prussia (Germany), 1787-1803
   The term *Menschenwürde* gains a certain subordinate place in Kant's anthropology; direct and indirect influence of Stoic tradition and Cicero.
7) Leipzig (Germany), 1941
   First appearance of an anthology in German with the title *Von der Würde des Menschen*; Kantian anthropology and morals.

Historical sentences, which claim the first occurence of something are liable to be disproved soon. Nevertheless they give, I hope, a certain orientation in a broken ground of intellectual history. The various stages of this history are not strongly interconnected. There is no 'evolution' from Pico to Pufendorf, nor from Pufendorf to Kant. Up until the middle of this century, it is mainly the text of Cicero and a general Ciceronian tradition which bestows a certain coherence on the history of the formula 'dignity of man.'

---

[93] Pufendorf, *De Iure Naturae et Gentium* was published in Lund (1672) and Frankfurt (1684).

[94] Earlier probably in an English translation of Cicero, *De Officiis*. The earliest instances in the British Museum Catalogue of Printed Books are: (a) *The thre bookes of Tullyes offyces, bothe in latyne tonge & in englysshe*, lately translated by Roberte Whytinton poete laureate. (Wynkyn de Worde, London 1534); (b) *Marcus Tullius Ciceroes thre bokes of duties, to Marcus his sonne, turned out of latine into english*, by Nicolas Grimalde. (Richard Tottle, Lindon 1556). The translation of Cicero's, *On Old Age*, by T. Tiptoft, Earl of Worcester, was printed in 1481 by Caxton. (Researched and kindly communicated by Ms. Christine Baatz, Tübingen).

Bibliography

1. Ancient works and authors

Arnim, Hans von. *Stoicorum Veterum Fragmenta*. Stuttgart 1905, reprint 1965 (SVF).

Cancik, Hubert. 'Persona and Self in Stoic Philosophy.' *Self, Soul & Body in Religious Experience*. A.I. Baumgarten with J. Assmann & G.G. Stroumsa, eds. Leiden 1998.

Colish, Marcia L. *The Stoic Tradition from Antiquity to the Early Middle Ages*. vol. I: 'Stoicism in Classical Latin Literature.' Leiden etc. ^{2}1990 (chap.2: Cicero; chap.6: Stoicism in Roman Law; rich bibliography).

Dyck, Andrew. *A Commentary on Cicero, De Officiis*. Ann Arbor 1996.

Forschner, Maximilian. *Die stoische Ethik. Über den Zusammenhang von Natur-, Sprach- und Moralphilosophie im altstoischen System*. Darmstadt 1981.

Gill, C. 'Personhood and Personality. The Four-personae Theory in Cicero, De Officiis 1.' *Oxford Studies in Ancient Philosophy* 6 (1988).

Gundel, H. 'Der Begriff maiestas im politischen Denken der römischen Republik.' *Historia* 12 (1963).

Pöschl, Viktor. *Der Begriff der Würde im antiken Rom und später*. Sitzungsberichte der Heidelberger Akademie der Wissenschaften, Philosophisch-Historische Klasse, Heidelberg 1989.

Puhle, Annekathrin. *Persona. Zur Ethik des Panaitios*. Frankfurt etc. 1987.

Rémy, E. 'Dignitas cum otio,' *Le Musée Belge* 32 (1928) 113-127.

Rist, John. *Stoic Philosophy*. Cambridge 1969.

Wegehaupt, Helmut. *Die Bedeutung und Anwendung von dignitas in den Schriften der republikanischen Zeit*. Diss. Breslau 1932.

Wilkin, Robert N. 'Cicero and the Law of Nature.' *Origins of the Natural Law Tradition*. Arthur L. Harding, ed. Dallas 1954.

Wirszubski, C. 'Cicero's cum dignitate otium: A Reconsideration.' *Journal of Roman Studies* 44 (1954).

2. Reception of Stoic Philosophy

Buck, August. *Giovanni Pico della Mirandola, Über die Würde des Menschen*. Hamburg 1990.

Cancik, Hubert. 'Die Würde des Menschen ist unantastbar.' Religions- und philosophiegeschichtliche Bemerkungen zu Art.I, Satz 1 GG, (1987), id., *Antik—Modern. Beiträge zur römischen und deutschen Kulturgeschichte.* R. Faber, B. v. Reibnitz, J. Rüpke, Stuttgart, eds. Weimar 1998.

Forschner, Maximilian. *Über das Handeln im Einklang mit der Natur.* Darmstadt 1998.

Franz, Katharina. *Der Einfluß der stoischen Philosophie auf die Moralphilosophie der deutschen Aufklärung.* Halle 1940.

Garve, Christian. *Ciceros Abhandlung über die menschlichen Pflichten.* Breslau 1783.

Löhrer, Guido. *Menschliche Würde. Wissenschaftliche Geltung und metaphorische Grenze der praktischen Philosophie Kants.* Freiburg - München 1995.

Manetti, G. *De dignitate et excellentia hominis.* E. Leonhard, ed. Padova, 1975.

Melches Gibert, Carlos. *Der Einfluß von Christian Garves Übersetzung Ciceros de officiis auf Kants Grundlegung zur Metaphysik der Sitten.* Regensburg 1994.

Pico della Mirandola, Giovanni. *De dignitate hominis.* E. Garin, ed. Bad Homburg 1968.

Pico della Mirandola, Giovanni. *Discorso sulla dignitá dell'uomo.* a cura di G. Tognon, Brescia 1987.

Pufendorf, Samuel. 'De iure naturae et gentium.' *Samuel Pufendorf, Gesammelte Werke*, vol. 4. F. Böhling, ed. 1998.

Radbruch, Gustav. 'Verdeutschter Cicero. Zu Johann von Schwarzenbergs Officien-Übersetzung.' *Archiv für Rechts- und Sozialphilosophie* 35 (1942).

Reich, Klaus. *Kant und die Ethik der Griechen.* Tübingen 1935.

Welzel, Hans. *Die Naturrechtslehre Samuel Pufendorfs.* Berlin 1958.

Welzel, Hans. 'Ein Kapitel aus der Geschichte der amerikanischen Erklärung der Menschenrechte (John Wise und Samuel Pufendorf).' *Rechtsprobleme in Staat und Kirche. Festgabe für Rudolf Smend.* Göttingen 1952.

Wise, John. *A Vindication of the Government of New England Churches* (1717. ²1772). A Facsimile Reproduction with an Introduction by Perry Miller. Gainesville (Florida): Scholars' Facsimiles and Reprints, 1958.

Zielinski, Thaddaeus. *Cicero im Wandel der Jahrhunderte.* Leipzig ⁴1929.

LEGAL ROOTS OF HUMAN DIGNITY IN GERMAN LAW
Joern Eckert

In modern times, human dignity has become central to constitutions and international legal instruments. The preamble of the Charter of the United Nations of 26 June 1945 provides:

> We the Peoples of the United Nations determined ... to reaffirm faith in fundamental human rights, in the dignity and worth of the human person...

Similarly, the preamble of the programmatic Universal Declaration of Human Rights of 10 December 1948 provides:

> Whereas recognition of the inherent dignity and of the equal and inalienable rights of all members of the human family...

Article 1 of the Declaration reads as follows:

> All human beings are born free and equal in dignity and rights. They are endowed with reason and conscience and should act towards one another in a spirit of brotherhood.

The *Grundgesetz* of the Federal Republic of Germany (Basic Law) of 23 May 1949 stipulates in article 1:

> (1) The dignity of man is inviolable. To respect and protect it shall be the duty of all public authorities.

> (2) The German people therefore uphold human rights as inviolable and inalienable, and as the basis of every community of peace and justice in the world.

Clauses concerning human dignity are in the top position of many modern constitutions, e.g., art. 1 of the Portuguese Constitution of 1976/82; art. 14 para. 4 of the Turkish Constitution of 1961/73; art. 2 para. 1 of the Greek

Constitution of 1975; and preamble and art. 10 para. 1 of the Spanish Constitution of 1978.[1]

However, as most of the clauses are declarative and are influenced by a great variety of philosophical, theological, ideological and natural-law traditions, it is difficult to seize the judicial meaning of the concept of human dignity. Therefore, some might even characterize human dignity as an '*empty formula amongst others.*'[2] Even if one does not agree and tries to define the specific legal essence of the concept of human dignity, a very wide range of application still remains. That range includes, on the one hand, obligations for the state to take action, e.g., to guarantee a humane existence for everyone, to protect unborn life or to prevent its artificial creation. On the other hand, it also includes prohibitions to interfere, e.g., the abolition of the death penalty, prohibition of cruel and unusual punishment and restrictions on the enforcement of life imprisonment.[3] As the concept of human dignity is closely connected to humanity's earliest religious and cultural traditions, it is not a surprise that the question of its legal roots causes various problems.

Human dignity has a wide range of historical, political, theological and philosophical foundations.[4] Its development was influenced by ancient and Christian-biblical ideas as well as Humanism, Natural Law and the political philosophy of the modern era, especially the Enlightenment. The concept of human dignity, however, is fairly new in constitutional and international law. Therefore, a definition of its legal roots is rather difficult to find. The study of the concept of a person and the classification of human beings as persons laid the foundations of the acknowledgement of human dignity. However, the link between the concept of a person, human dignity and human rights was not recognized for a long time. Human dignity, therefore, did not have the quality of a legal norm binding the state.

The paper will start with a short overview of the foundations of human dignity within the history of ideas, followed by a presentation of the legal roots of the concept in German law.

---

[1] Peter Häberle, 'Die Menschenwürde als Grundlage der staatlichen Gemeinschaft,' in Josef Isensee and Paul Kirchhof, eds., *Handbuch des Staatsrechts der Bundesrepublik Deutschland* (Grundlagen von Staat und Verfassung, Heidelberg 1987), vol. I, p. 818; Stern, *Das Staatsrecht der Bundesrepublik Deutschland* III/1, (1988) p. 40.

[2] Kondylis, Würde, in *Geschichtliche Grundbegriffe. Historisches Lexikon zur politisch-sozialen Sprache in Deutschland*, Otto Brunner, ed., (Stuttgart 1992) vol. VII, p. 677.

[3] Christian Starck, 'Menschenwürde,' in *Staatslexikon*, Görres-Gesellschaft, ed., 7th edition, vol. III, p. 1120.

[4] Stern, 'Idee der Menschenrechte und Positivität der Grundrechte,' in *Handbuch des Staatsrechts der Bundesrepublik Deutschland*, Isensee and Kirchhof, eds., (Allgemeine Grundrechtslehren, Heidelberg 1992) vol. V, p. 11.

I. Historical Background

Although the idea of human dignity dates back to ancient times, its close link to human and fundamental rights remained unknown until the modern era. Traditionally, human dignity was regarded just as a religious or philosophical idea, not having legal relevance or providing inalienable rights.

In ancient history, the concept of human dignity had two different meanings. On the one hand, it referred to the social rank of a person, and on the other hand, to the distinction between human beings and other creatures. Plato (427-347 BC) reports that according to the sophist Protagoras (ca 485-415 BC) the essential equality of all men was based on 'decency and law,' the gifts of Zeus were bestowed upon all men. Due to this special relationship to divinity, all men were of the same kind and differed from the animals.[5] Similarly, the Stoic school proclaimed that all men shall hold man sacred because they all share the divine reason of the world.[6]

In Rome, too, human dignity had no legal relevance. Cicero, for instance, did not consider dignity as universal human dignity, but as a special dignity according to rank.[7] He explicitly used the concept of dignity to criticize democracy for not respecting the necessary differentiations of dignity according to rank. Even when the people control everything—no matter how much justice and moderation they may display—still equality itself is inequitable when it has no regard to degrees of rank (*aequabilitas est iniqua, cum habet nullos gradus dignitas*).[8]

In early Christianity and the Middle Ages, human dignity was completely based on the distinguishing feature given to all human beings by God. Since man was created by God in his own image, he had a special standing and dominion over all other creatures. In *Genesis*, it says that God made man in his own image and after his likeness.[9] For that reason, shedding man's blood is a primary offense punishable by death.[10] In *Psalms* 8, the psalmist marvels that God 'has put all things under the feet' of the son of man who, then, was so small and frail;[11] he has made him 'but a little lower than God,'[12] which is

---

[5] Plato, *Protagoras*, 322 c/d.
[6] Bielefeldt, *Zum Ethos der menschengeschichtlichen Demokratie: eine Einführung am Beispiel des Grundgesetzes*, (Würzburg 1991) p. 18; Coing, 'Der Begriff der menschlichen Person und die Theorien der Menschenrechte,' *Deutsche Landesreferate zum III. Internationalen Kongress für Rechtsvergleichung in London 1950*, Ernst Wolff, ed., (Berlin 1950) p. 194; Welzel, *Naturrecht und materiale Gerechtigkeit*, 4th edition, (Göttingen 1962) p. 37.
[7] Bielefeldt, *Ethos* (6), p. 19; Kondylis, *Würde* (2), pp. 638, 644.
[8] Cicero, *De Republica* I, 27, 43.
[9] *Genesis* 1:26; critical: Hubert Cancik, 'Die Würde des Menschen ist unantastbar' (Human dignity is inviolable). Religions-und philosophiegeschichtliche Bemerkungen zu Art. 1, Satz 1 Grundgesetz, in Funke, *Utopie und Tradition. Platons Lehre vom Staat in der Moderne*, (1987) p. 77.
[10] *Genesis* 9:6.
[11] *Psalm* 8:6.

impressive evidence of the special standing of the human being. Another major argument for human dignity was the incarnation. Human nature is entitled to boundless dignity because of its relation to Christ. As he is regarded as God's image, the human being differs from all other creatures. The likeness of man to God constituted human dignity or the dignity of human nature. St. Thomas Aquinas (1225-1274), in particular, used *dignitas humana* in that sense.[13] He, too, considered dignity differentiated according to rank as a principle of God, as even men in paradise and angels in heaven lived divided into ranks.[14]

Renaissance as well as Italian Humanists in the fifteenth century confirmed the likeness of man to God as the outstanding feature of all human beings. Giovanni Pico della Mirandola (1463-1494) based his '*Oratio de hominis dignitate*' of 1486 on the idea of this likeness. He regarded the human being as a microcosm containing the aptitude for all kinds of behaviour. The destiny of man was to find a rational decision on the basis of his *anima rationalis*. Thus, *hominis dignitas* was constituted by man's ability to make autonomous decisions.[15]

The modern era gave more priority to the elements of reason and ability to think. Incorporating the concept of human dignity into his doctrine of natural law, Samuel von Pufendorf (1632-1694) added the idea of natural equality of all human beings. According to Pufendorf, man had human dignity because of his 'immortal soul' and because he was 'indu'd with the Light of Understanding.'[16] Since everyone was endowed with it, all human beings were equal by nature. Pufendorf put special emphasis on the social nature of man, his *socialitas*. According to him, social nature was the very heart of human nature, which could only develop its peculiarity and reach its completion in the social context. Only human relations could give real dignity to human beings (*dignatio nominis humani*).[17] The works of Pufendorf were translated into all European national languages of the seventeenth and eightteenth century and, thus, became widespread all over Europe. In America, Pufendorf's ideas influenced the works of John Wise and the author's of the Virginia Bill of Rights of 1776.[18]

At the beginning of the modern era, a process of fundamental rethinking led to a loss of legitimacy for the traditional orders based on dignity according to hiearchical ranks. This process was followed by the recognition of the universal and equal human dignity as a major principle of law and politics. Due to the crisis of the traditional orders, it became possible and necessary to

---

[12] *Psalm* 8:5.
[13] Kondylis, *op. cit.*, p. 649.
[14] St. Thomas, Summa Theologica, I. 96. 3.; I. 50. 4.
[15] Stern, Staatsrecht III/1 (n. 1), p. 7; cf. Cancik, Würde (9), p. 78; Kondylis, *op. cit.*, p. 661.
[16] Pufendorf, *De iure naturae et gentium*, English Edition, (1703) II. 1. 5.
[17] Stern, *op. cit.*, p. 10.
[18] Cancik, *op. cit.*, p. 89.

give political and legal effect to the idea of human dignity in the meaning of universal human rights.[19]

The Reformation and the fracturing of the Catholic world not only challenged the religious authorities but undermined the traditional religious foundations of political power.[20] This development caused a crisis of authority and led to the religiously motivated civil wars in the seventeenth and eighteenth centuries. Religious and political crises and wars resulted in demands for tolerance and freedom of conscience, especially in Calvinism. The religious civil wars were replaced by a cease-fire maintained by the force of an absolutist police state. However, the absolutist state was not able to cope with the crisis. Excluding nobility and clergy from the political scene, the state itself began to question the corporate society. To the extent that nobility was deprived of its political function, its privileges were more and more doubted. At the beginning of the French Revolution, representatives of the nobility, too, renounced their privileges and questioned the legitimacy of the traditional order. Part of the nobility also supported the *Declaration of Human and Civil Rights* of 26 August 1789. The events of the French Revolution led to the realization that the idea of dignity could only be justified by separating dignity from rank and acknowledging dignity as an innate element of every human being. The universal and equal human dignity had to be inviolable and inalienable.[21]

English philosophers had a major influence on the development of human rights, as well. John Milton (1608-1674), the secretary of Cromwell, demanded the right of self-determination for each human being, of religious tolerance, of freedom of speech, freedom of the press and the abolition of censorship.[22] According to Thomas Hobbes (1588-1679), human beings had natural rights, but only in the primeval condition. If the sovereign did not guarantee protection and security for everyone, these rights would lead to *bellum omnium contra omnes*. The social contract placed the rights at the disposal of the sovereign. In the discussion about the *Petition of Rights*, Edward Coke (1552-1634), who had been Chief Justice for many years and member of Parliament, emphasized the importance of the existence and the legal effect of fundamental rights of the English people.[23] In his mind, fundamental rights meant protection against groundless arrest and protection of property. The disputes between King and Parliament resulted in legal stipulations based on these ideas (*Habeas Corpus Act of 1679*, Declaration of Rights of 1688, Bill of Rights of 1689). In the beginning, these rights simply confirmed traditional privileges and parliamentary freedoms. Due to the idea of equality in natural law, they were developed into rights of all free citizens

---

[19] Bielefeldt, *op. cit.*, p. 21.
[20] Kondylis, *op. cit.*, p. 662.
[21] Kondylis, *op. cit.*, p. 22.
[22] Stern, Handbuch V (n. 4), p. 9.
[23] *Ibid.*, p. 10.

and, eventually, all human beings. Coke developed the idea of the three core elements of the human rights conception: the rights to life, freedom and property. But it was only John Locke (1632-1704) who considered these natural rights a part of the social contract with immediate effect on the governing power, too.[24] There was nothing very original about these ideas, but the way that Locke worked out his system of ideas was original and, thus, it could convince especially the Americans one century later.

In Germany, the ideas of the French Revolution, in particular, had decisive influence on the change in thinking. For Immanuel Kant (1724-1804), as well as for Pufendorf, human dignity was based on the reason of the human being. But contrary to Pufendorf, Kant emphasized moral autonomy and individuality. He regarded human beings as unique creatures possessing not only material value—as relative to mankind—but also a deeper value in the sense of dignity. Kant chose a subjective starting point, when stating:

> Man does not exist as a mere means for any use or will, but as an end in himself. Thus, he always has to be regarded, in all his actions both towards himself and to other reasonable beings, as the end, too.[25]

The *categorical imperative* worked out by Kant was quite formal and appeared to have not much content.[26] But he developed it into the *practical imperative* and restated:

> Act in such a way as to treat humanity, whether in your own person or in that of another, always as the end, never merely as the means.[27]

But only a person endowed with morality, self-responsibility and the ability of rational self-determination could possess this dignity. According to Kant, dignity required the fulfilment of certain criteria of reason and morality. A human being did not have dignity just because of his existence. Seemingly, for Kant, dignity was not related to the single human being as individual, but to humanity as such, or even morality, as an objective principle.[28] It is morality—and humanity, as far as it has the ability for morality—that solely has dignity.[29]

The idea of individuality can also be traced in the works of *Wilhelm von Humboldt* (1767-1835). Humboldt demanded that the state abandon judging human beings by their race or religion, as he considered this way of thinking as

---

[24] Coing, *Rechtsbegriff* (6), p. 194; Hoffmann, 'Die Grundrechte 1749–1949–1989,' *NJW* (1989) p. 3177.
[25] Kant, *Grundlegung zur Metaphysik der Sitten*, 2nd edition, (1786 works), Cassirer, ed., (1922) vol. IV, p. 286.
[26] Stern, *Staatsrecht* III/1 (1), p. 8.
[27] Kant, *Metaphysik der Sitten* (25), p. 287.
[28] Stern, *Staatsrecht* III/1 (1), p. 8.
[29] Kant, *Metaphysik der Sitten* (25), p. 293.

inhumane, prejudiced and contrary to true human dignity, and rather judge them by their individual features.[30]

The concept of human dignity became a political catch-phrase in the middle of the last century. The demand for humane conditions of existence was one of the most prominent slogans of the socialist movement. *Ferdinand Lassalle* (1825-1864) declared that the working and lower middle classes had, like everyone else, the legitimate right for a humane existence. According to him, the state, therefore, had to endeavor to improve the situation of the lower classes, who had fallen into poverty and starvation, and thus provide a true humane existence for everyone.[31]

II. Legal Roots of Dignity in German Law

Christian, humanist and enlightened traditions of human dignity influenced law right from the very beginning. As early as in the 13th century, *Eike von Repgow*[32] postulated equality in the *Sachsenspiegel*, based on the fact that man was created in the image of God. The idea of equality entered positive German law in the sixteenth century when the legal capacity of the individual was acknowledged. Previously, the human being was regarded as able to have rights, as well as duties, only as a member of some form of superordinate society or association (e.g., family, tribe, cooperative). The legal capacity of the individual was discovered only at a higher stage of the development of law.[33] This process was mainly influenced by the increasing importance of the legal concept of a person, meaning a legal subject having rights and duties. The modern legal concept of a person also developed within a long legal tradition.

Foundations of the concept of a person can also be traced in the books of the *Prophets of Israel*. There, the single human being is taken out of the community and has to individually bear the iniquity. Ezekiel says, in that sense:

> The idea that man was made in the image of God became another aspect of the concept of a person. As God created man in his own image and God himself is regarded as a person, the individual human being, too, has to be regarded as a person.

In ancient Rome, the term 'person' did not refer to a legal concept with a specific content, but was used synonymously for human being. The jurisprudence of the Middle Ages retained this usage. The modern concept of a

---

[30] Humboldt, *Politische Denkschriften*, (1903), Gutachten zum Preussischen Emanzipationsedikt vom 17, Juli 1809, vol. I.
[31] Lassalle, 'Gesammelte Reden und Schriften,' *Das Arbeiterprogramm*, E. Bernstein, ed., (1919) vol. II, p. 173.
[32] Eike von Repgow, *Landrecht* III, 42.
[33] Stern, *Staatsrecht III/1* (n. 1), p. 13.

person was developed only by the systematic jurisprudence in the sixteenth and seventeenth century. *Hugo Donellus* (1527-1591), a Huguenot who taught at the university of Altdorf near Nuremberg, created the link between the concept of a person and the Roman law doctrine of the three statuses of man (*status libertatis, civitas* and *familiae*). Thus, the concept of a person became a legal concept. A human being was regarded as a person and could participate in legal relations only when he had a status. According to Donellus, the rights to life, freedom from bodily harm and public reputation belonged to the person.[34] Emphasizing the integration of all human beings into society, *Johannes Althusius* (1557-1638) had already used more general terms: *Persona est homo iuris communionem habens.*[35] He considered all human beings equal and the people sovereign. In his mind, human beings were not subject to anyone's power, unless they voluntarily submitted to the power by delegating their rights to it.[36]

This idea prevailed throughout the time of *usus modernus pandectarum*, although *status naturalis*, describing the important features for legal capacity (age, sex, mental health, etc.), was added to the Roman status-doctrine.[37] *Hugo Grotius* (1583-1645) considered the natural rights of human beings to be inalienable. According to him, any state sovereign had to respect these rights because of their relationship to the reasonable nature of the human being.[38]

During the Enligthenment, natural law doctrine took up this concept. Replacing Roman doctrine with a more general concept, it gave the concept the content that is still valid today.[39] Samuel Pufendorf regarded 'person' as '*homo consideratus cum statu suo.*'[40] He used status in his definition of all legal features influencing the rights and duties of man, e.g., being a member of nobility. Pufendorf acknowledged innate rights, but denied their effect on the state.[41] His main concern, though, was to subjugate the power of the state to the law of nature. The sovereign himself defined the public good, and only the rationale of the state limited the power of the sovereign. The state's aim, therefore, was not to preserve the rights of the individual, but security and public welfare.

The modern doctrine can first be found in the works of Christian Wolff (1679-1754). He stated:

---

[34] Coing, *Rechtsbegriff* (6), p. 196; Stern, *Handbuch V* (4), p. 8.
[35] Althusius, *Epitome Dicaeologicae Romanae, Jurisprudentiae Romanae Methodice Digestae Libri Duo*, 5th edition (1623) p. 6; Coing, *op. cit.*, p. 196.
[36] O. von Gierke, *Johannes Althusius und die Entwicklung der Naturrechtlichen Staatstheorien*, (1929) p. 47.
[37] Coing, *op. cit.*, p. 196.
[38] Stern, *Handbuch V* (4), p. 9.
[39] Coing, *op. cit.*, p. 197.
[40] Pufendorf, *De iure naturae et gentium*, English Edition, 1703, I. 1. 12.
[41] Stern, *Handbuch V* (4), p. 9.

> *Homo persona moralis est, quatenus spectatur tamquam subjectum certarum obligationum etque iurium certorum. Atque hinc status eius moralis dicitur qui per obligationes et iura determinatur.*[42]

Wolff regarded the unique status, as well as the general legal capacity of man, as the main criteria constituting a person. This general legal capacity characterized the human being as a legal subject able of having rights and duties.

Under the influences of Natural Law and Enlightenment, the idea of innate rights of all human beings gained acceptance in Germany. At that time, the traditional idea that man is a person because God is a person and man is created in his image became secularized. The conviction that the individual human being, as such, is a person and has dignity because he is a distinct individual has prevailed until today. Due to this influence, the *Codex Maximilianeus Bavanicus Civilis* (Bavarian Code) of 1756 stipulated the rights of the individual, stating that man was endowed with rights and duties by nature (I. 3. 1., 2.). The definition of the *Preußisches Allgemeines Landrecht* (*ALR*, Prussian Code) of 1794 used an even clearer wording:

> Man shall be called 'person' as far as he is endowed with certain rights in society.[43] (*translation by the author*)

The *ALR* thus made clear that a human being and a person did not have identical meaning in law. Neither the human being as such nor all human beings were necessarily regarded as persons. Since being regarded as a person depended on having certain rights, the two concepts were not even identical as far as legal considerations were concerned. Thus, the *ALR* did not yet grant rights to the human being as such.[44]

Three years later, the *Bürgerliches Gesetzbuch für West-Galizien* (Civil Code of Western Polish Galicia) of 1797 took this step by providing in its first part:

> sect. 26 Considering their rights, men shall be regarded as persons. Persons only, and not objects, shall have rights.
>
> sect. 29 Innate rights of men are the following ... (*translation by the author*)

These phrases contain both ideas that are important for understanding the modern concept of human dignity: the general legal capacity and the innate rights of every human being. The *Allgemeines Bürgerliches Gesetzbuch* (Austrian Civil Code) of 1811 stipulated more precisely in its sect. 16: 'Each

---

[42] Wolff, *Institutiones Juris Naturae et Gentium* (1750) sect. 96.
[43] ALR, § 1 I 1.
[44] Stern, *Staatsrecht III/1* (1), p. 14.

man has innate rights, which are obvious because of reason, and shall therefore be regarded as person.' (*translation by the author*)

Similarly, several other civil laws in the nineteenth century accepted all human beings, without exception, as persons. Although that did not include individual rights towards the state, it laid the foundations for the development of such rights in positive law. Thus, the civil law realized the major demand of Natural law and Enlightenment, the identity of person and human being.

Jurisprudence in the nineteenth century still fostered this way of thinking. However, the features of the concept of a person were reduced to the function of a person as an element in legal relations. According to *Anton Friedrich Justus Thibaut* (1772-1840), one could only be regarded as a person when one had claim to some rights, in particular civil rights.[45]

Following the philosophy of Immanuel Kant, the *Historische Rechtsschule* (historical German school) narrowed further the concept of the legal person. *Friedrich Carl von Savigny* (1779-1861) developed his doctrine of legal personality and subjective right on the basis of Kant's ideas. In his mind, the legal personality was based on moral freedom. He stated that all law existed for the sake of moral freedom being inherent to every human being. For that reason, the original concept of a person as a legal subject had to coincide with the concept of human being. He expressed the original identity of the two concepts with the following formula: 'Each individual has legal capacity.'[46] Thus, Savigny reduced the human being to a mere element of legal relations. As each legal relationship consisted of a relationship between two persons, the nature of persons needed closer investigation. Therefore, the questions had to be who could be the *subject of* a legal relationship and who was *able* to have rights and legal capacity.[47]

With this theory, Savigny denied the decisive role of human beings in law. In his opinion, the single individual could only serve its purpose by accepting the law revealed by history and by deliberately integrating into legal relations, which were believed to be predestined. In later years, the rising liberal middle class tried to create a synthesis of the conservative doctrine of Savigny and the heritage of the law of reason. The clearest expression of this attempt can be found in the *Sächsisches BGB* (Saxon Code) of 1863/65:

> sect. 30   Each man has legal capacity.
>
> sect. 31   Slavery, servitude and execution of all violence relating thereto are contrary to the law.
>
> sect. 32   The legal capacity of a person starts with his birth. The unborn are regarded as already born from the time of conception as far as their advantage is concerned. Still-born are regarded as if they had never been conceived.

---

[45] Thibaut, *System des Pandektenrechts*, 2nd edition (1805) 1 sect. 207.
[46] Savigny *System des heutigen römischen Rechts*, 1840–1849, II. 2.
[47] *Ibid.*, XI. 60.

sect. 36 The legal capacity ends with death. (*translation by the author*)

Whereas legal capacity remained the main feature characterizing the human being as a person, the prohibition of slavery and servitude provided the larger framework for this idea in everyday life.

Due to the influence to the school of *Positivismus*, the close connection between a person, legal capacity and human rights disappeared in the second half of the 19th century.[48] The opinion that the subjective right is just a reflex of the objective one prevailed. According to *Bernhard Windscheid* (1817-1892), in particular, subjective rights consisted of an order to a certain behavior which had been issued by the legal system on the basis of concrete facts, the order then being placed at the disposition of a beneficiary.[49]

This development did not remain without criticism. Stating that the right of being regarded as person is the fundamental subjective right that penetrates all particular subjective rights and which all other subjective rights are based upon,[50] *Otto von Gierke* (1841-1921) regarded the *Allgemeines Persönlichkeitsrecht*—the amalgamation of all individual rights and personal dignity—as the foundations for all private and public rights.[51]

Although the opinion that all human beings are persons simply by nature prevailed in the legal systems of the nineteenth century, this acknowledgement still remained limited to civil law. The idea of legal personality and legal capacity of human beings was not yet connected to the doctrine of human rights. The legal system only acknowledged the personality of a human being, its quality as legal subject.

III.

In Germany, the link between the concept of a person and human rights was established by the explicit acknowledgement of human dignity, which today is guaranteed in the first paragraph of the constitution and has utmost priority within the legal system. Whereas neither the *Virginia Bill of Rights* of 12 June 1776, nor the *French Declaration of Human and Civil Rights* of 26 August 1789 refer to human dignity, it was mentioned in the discussions of the Frankfurt Parliament. There, the delegate Mohr proposed:

> Society shall guarantee a humane existence for everyone corresponding to human dignity, providing
>
> a. security for the person;
>
> b. freedom;

---

[48] Coing *op. cit.*, p. 203.
[49] Windscheid, *Lehrbuch des Pandektenrechts*, , 6th edition, (1887) vol. I p. 97.
[50] Gierke, *Deutsches Privatrecht I*, (1895) p. 702.
[51] Coing *op. cit.*, p. 203.

> c. resistance against suppression;
>
> d. development of one's talents and abilities;
>
> e. means for easily making a living satisfying the need of life and insuring standing in society.[52]

Although this motion was not admitted, the idea of human dignity can be found in the constitution drafted by the Frankfurt Parliament, e.g., sect. 139 (prohibition of inhuman and degrading punishment) was based on the idea of human dignity:[53]

> Free people shall respect even the human dignity of a criminal.
> (*translation by the author*)

The Constitution of the Weimar Republic of 11 August 1919, adopted the wording of the socialist demand of the 19th century for a humane existence in art. 151 para. 1:

> The organization of economic life must respect fundamental justice and provide a humane existence for everyone.

Human dignity had already determined the character of one part of the constitution. Humane existence for everyone was guaranteed and human dignity was the limit to the economic freedom of the individual. The relation to fundamental justice, in particular, demonstrated the great importance this clause about human dignity was meant to have.[54]

The first legal provision of dignity and freedom of the individual is to be found in the preamble of the *Constitution of Ireland* of 1 July 1937:

> And seeking to promote the common good, with due observance of prudence, justice and charity, so that the dignity and freedom of the individual may be assured, true social order attained, the unity of our country restored, and concord established with other nations.[55]

The idea of human dignity was decisively strengthened by developments after the Second World War. After the terrible crimes and contempt towards mankind by the Nazis, there was a sudden surge for stronger protection of human dignity. The provisions of the Charter of the United Nations and the Universal Declaration of Human Rights, cited at the beginning, had their roots in this development. It also influenced the authors of the *Constitutions of the German Länder* after Second World War (e.g., art. 100 of the Bavarian Constitution of 2 December 1946) and the *Grundgesetz*. Article 100 of the *Bavarian Constitution* of 2 December 1946, with regard to the events during

---

[52] Eckhart, *Die Grundrechte vom Wiener Kongress bis zur Gegenwart*, (1913) p. 92.
[53] Stern, *Staatsrecht III/1* (1), p. 16.
[54] Häberle, *Menschenwürde* (1), p. 817.
[55] *Jahrbuch des öffentlichen Rechts der Gegenwart* (JöR) 25 (1938) p. 357.

the previous years, when the dignity of the human being was trodden down stipulated:[56]

> Legislative, executive and judicial powers shall respect the dignity of the human being. (*translation by the author*)

Similarly, article 5 para. 1 of the Constitution of Bremen of 21 October 1947 provides:

> The state shall recognize and respect the dignity of the human being. (*translation by the author*)

The constitutions of the German *Länder* Hesse (art. 1 of the Constitution of 1 December 1946), *Rhineland-Palatinate* (preamble of the Constitution of 18 May 1947) and *Saarland* (art. 1 of the Constitution of 15 December 1947) also contained similar stipulations.[57] In 1948, the draft of the so-called Assembly of Herrenchiemsee took up the ideas of these stipulations and proposed in art. 1:

> (1) The State shall exist for the sake of man and not man for the sake of the State.
>
> (2) The dignity of the human personality is inviolable. All public authority shall respect and protect human dignity. (*translation by the author*)

Although the exact wording and the theological and philosophical roots of human dignity were highly contested in the *Parlamentarischen Rat* (Parliamentary Council), all agreed that human dignity should be placed at the top position of the constitution.[58] From now on, human dignity and human rights should be the foundations of the Constitution. Thus art. 1 sect 1 contains one of the most important enactments of the entire *Grundgesetz*.

German law, eventually, harmonized the judicial concept of a person with that of human dignity and innate human rights. When the *Grundgesetz* came into effect, German law moved from the mere judicial concept of a person within the civil law to making the theological and philosophical meaning of human dignity a constitutionally binding force.

---

[56] *Decisions of the Bavarian Constitutional Court*, vol. I, p. 29 (32); Stern, *Staatsrecht III/1* (1), p. 17.
[57] *Ibid.*, p. 17.
[58] *Ibid.*, p. 18.

BLOOD AND THE IMAGE OF GOD: ON THE SANCTITY OF LIFE IN BIBLICAL AND EARLY RABBINIC LAW, MYTH, AND RITUAL[*]

Yair Lorberbaum

I. Introduction

The concept of human dignity and the sanctity of human life is historically bound up—at least in the Jewish tradition (and to a great extent in early Christianity, which draws upon the former)—with the biblical idea of humankind created in the divine image. This is insufficient, of course, to make the claim that *Imago Dei* constitutes the sole basis for the concept of human dignity in Western culture, but there is no doubt that the idea that man is in God's image is one of its primary sources. This theological perception is largely responsible for establishing the meaning we tend to assign to this central and heavily-laden idea, and the normative and legal understandings derived from it.

The origin of the idea of *Imago Dei* is to be found in Mesopotamia and perhaps in ancient Egypt as well. In the view of the royal theology prevalent in the ancient Near East, the Mesopotamian king (in Assyria and Babylonia) is the *salamu* [cognate to Biblical *tselem*] and the *mussulu* ['image'] of a god. Bible scholars offer the opinion that the *Genesis* brought about a democratization of this outlook, which had at first been applied solely to the king. The theological message underlying the first chapters of *Genesis* is that it is not the king alone who reflects the divine image, but that humanity—every human being—is created or born in His image. (See *Genesis* 1:26-27, 5:1, 9:6.)

---

[*] I would like to thank Ari Ackerman for translating the core of this article and Peretz Rodman for editing the manuscript and for additional translation. For the translations of the rabbinic sources we have consulted J. Neusner's translations of the Talmud and that published by Soncino Press; H. Danby's translation of the Mishna and J. Lauterbach's translation of the Mekhilta. Nevertheless, many changes have been introduced to these translations for substantive and stylistic reasons.

From here, in part, humanity derives its ability to impose its dominion upon the earth (*Genesis* 1:26).

Many interpretations of the concept of *Imago Dei* in *Genesis* have been offered. Some have taken it to refer to the human shape, others to the rational faculty, the conscience, the ability to discern between right and wrong, and other aspects of humanity. One of the ancient concepts of God's image in *Genesis*—one close to the original plain meaning of the term there, in my view—is offered by the Sages (the rabbis of the first centuries of the common era). According to this concept, the term 'image' [*tselem*] is to be taken quite literally, as a visual image. The relation between the divine and human person is iconic, and thus the prototype—God (who bears anthropomorphic features, including personality and shape)—is present in His image. Man, in all his physical and mental manifestations, is therefore a reflection of God. To use Platonic language, man takes part in God. According to this interpretation, *Genesis* describes God as creating for himself an image to serve as a sort of extension of Him on earth.

However we interpret the term 'image,' all those interpretations share the assumption that there is a divine 'spark,' as it were, in human beings. This element establishes man's humanity and grants him unique status among the creatures in God's creation, or in other words, his dignity.[1] In this view, the concept of the divine image is also the basis for the equality in principle among human beings, for all are in the image of the Creator. In this context it is interesting to note that the Hebrew term for 'dignity,' *kavod*, is ascribed in the Bible first and foremost to God, or, better, to the divine presence in the world (what rabbinic tradition later labels *shekhinah*). (See, e.g., *Exodus* 33:18-33, *Leviticus* 9:6,23.) The term itself is derived from the root *k-b-d* (literally, 'weight' or 'heaviness'), which signifies existence or substance. The phrase 'God's *kavod*' usually means God's substance descended to earth and present there.[2] The modern Hebrew phrase *kvod ha-adam* ('human dignity') and its common rabbinic counterpart, *kvod ha-beriot*, apparently derive from the Biblical phrase.[3] In the Bible, in the traditions preserved in rabbinic literature, and in many strands of Jewish (and Christian) literature in later

---

[1] It is important to note that the perception that all human beings are created in the divine image is not shared universally. Maimonides, for example, who understands the divine image as referring to the active intellect, thought that only one who actualized his intellect and reached the highest level of epistemological attainment is in the divine image. In his view, most, if not all, human beings are not in God's image. [See my article, 'Maimonides on *Imago Dei*: Philosophy and Law – The Felony of Murder, the Criminal Procedure and Capital Punishment' (Hebrew), *Tarbiz* 68 (1998-99) pp. 533-556.] Maimonides notwithstanding, the common interpretation of *Imago Dei* does indeed ascribe it equally to all humans.

[2] See Moshe Weinfeld, 'God the Creator in Gen. 1 and the Prophecy of Second Isaiah,' *Tarbiz* 37 (1967-68) pp. 103-132 [henceforth Weinfeld, 'God the Creator'].

[3] For *kvod ha-beri'ot*, see *Babylonian Talmud* Berakhot 19b.

periods, 'God's *kavod*' is radiated onto humanity, for the human being is made in God's image.[4]

The Bible does not simply make do with describing man as created in God's image. It derives normative meanings from that stand as well: 'Whoever sheds the blood of man by man shall his blood be shed, for in God's image did He make man' (*Genesis* 9:6). This verse stands at the focus of the covenant made with Noah after the Flood (*Genesis* 9:1-8), which establishes a new world order. Moshe Greenberg has pointed out that this verse expresses the basic principle of Biblical criminal law. In his words:

> The sense of the invaluableness of human life underlies the divergence of the biblical treatment of the homicide from that of the other law systems of the Near East. [...] A precise and adequate formulation of the jural postulate underlying the biblical law of homicide is found in *Genesis* 9:5f.: 'For your lifeblood I shall require a reckoning; of every beast shall I require it... Whoever sheds the blood of a man, by man shall his blood be shed; for in the image of God was man made.' [...] [T]hat man was made in the image of God... is expressive of the peculiar and supreme worth of man. [...] A beast that kills a man destroys the image of God and must give a reckoning for it. [...] This view of the uniqueness and supremacy of human life has yet another consequence. It places life beyond the reach of other values. The idea that life may be measured in terms of money or other property, and a fortiori the idea that persons may be evaluated as equivalences of other persons, is excluded. Compensation of any kind is ruled out. The guilt of the murderer is infinite because the murdered life is invaluable; the kinsmen of the slain man are not competent to say when he has been paid for. An absolute wrong has been committed, a sin against God which is not subject to human discussion. The effect of this view is, to be sure, paradoxical: because human life is invaluable, to take it entails the death penalty.[5]

Greenberg emphasizes that what characterizes the Biblical outlook in comparison with other views current in the ancient Near East is the realization that human life is immeasurable. Its practical legal expression is that murderers incur capital punishment. This 'legislation' is not grounded solely in considerations of prevention or deterrence. Such considerations are subject to being pushed aside by other considerations of a pragmatic, economic nature, as was in fact practiced in most ancient legal systems. Thus, for example, those

---

[4] This nexus of God's image and God's glorious 'presence' is common as far back as the Mesopotamian royal theology; see Weinfeld, 'God the Creator.'

[5] M. Greenberg, 'Some Postulates of Biblical Criminal Law' in *Yehezkel Kaufmann Jubilee Volume*, M. Haran, ed., (Magnes Press, Jerusalem 1960) pp. 5-28 [henceforth: Greenberg, 'Criminal Law']. Quote from pp. 15-16.

systems saw no impediment to granting the relatives of the murder victim the option of substituting monetary indemnification in place of the death penalty.[6] This verse, then, expresses in practice the concept of the inestimable value of human life. The legal application of the idea of creation in the divine image in *Genesis* embodies a revolution in theology and legal norms, for this is the first appearance, in western culture at least, of the idea of the sanctity of human life. Paradoxically, this idea is expressed in the opening chapters of the Bible in the statement that the only adequate punishment for bloodshed is death.

As we shall see below, early rabbinic exegesis of this biblical passage is sensitive to this paradox and turned this law on its head. On the basis of the Bible's own reasoning—'for in God's image did He make man'—the Rabbis concluded that the death penalty is not to be applied, for even damage inflicted upon the divine image (i.e., murder) cannot justify additional damage to that image (by capital punishment). To the best of my knowledge, this demurral is the first expression of a principled negative attitude toward the death penalty, and one specifically connected to the concept of human dignity. From a normative perspective, this too is a substantial revolution.

The relationship between the idea of the creation of the human being in the divine image in the Bible (along with its interpretation in ancient Jewish literature) and the idea of human dignity in the modern era is complex and multifaceted, and it is worthy of a full-scale study. The subject of the following inquiry is an examination of the meanings attributed to *Genesis* 9:6 in early rabbinic literature within a particular context: the mode of punishment for murder and the Rabbis' attitude toward capital punishment. It need not be stated that the literature in question attained a formative status in the formulation of the historic Jewish tradition. As will become clear, the Rabbis derived from this foundational verse theological perceptions, laws, and rituals that conflict and even stand in direct opposition to each other. They did not refrain from deciding between them. The following study is a sort of 'archaeological' reconstruction of the early meanings ascribed to this idea of

---

[6] Additional examples of the differences of approach on this point between laws of the ancient Near East and classical Greece on the one hand and biblical law on the other are: attitudes toward abortion—see M. Weinfeld, 'The Genuine Jewish Attitude toward Abortion' [Hebrew], *Zion* 42 (1976-77) pp. 129-142 [following V. Aptovitzer, 'The Status of the Fetus in Israel's Criminal Law' [Hebrew], *Sinai* 11 (1951-52) pp. 10-33]; attitudes toward the murder of slaves; and attitudes toward committing a debtor to servitude—see J. Guttmann, 'The Subjugation of the Person for Debt in Jewish Law' [Hebrew] in *Dinaburg Jubilee Volume*, Y. Baer et al., ed., (Jerusalem 1948-49) pp. 68-82. For a critique of Greenberg's view, see S. Loewenstamm, 'The Laws of Adultery and Murder in Biblical Law and Mesopotamian Law' [Hebrew], *Bet Miqra* 7:1 (no. 13) (1962) p. 55; B. Jackson, 'Reflections of Biblical Criminal Law,' *JJS* 24 (1973) pp. 8-38. (See the response by M. Weinfeld, 'On the Concept of Law in Israel and Elsewhere' [Hebrew], *Bet Miqra* 8:1-2 (1963) pp. 58-63); M. Greenberg, 'More Reflections of Biblical Criminal Law' in *Studies in the Bible* [=*Scripta Hierosolymitana* 31] S. Japhet, ed., (Jerusalem 1986) pp. 1-17.

creation in the divine image and thus of human dignity. This treatment uncovers surprising connections between myth, theology, ethics, law, and rituals of atonement.

The relevance of a presentation of ancient perceptions, myths, and rituals connected to the idea of creation in God's image to an analysis of the concept of human dignity in our time is to be found, in my view, in the words of Paul Ricoeur, according to which 'the symbol gives rise to thought.' 'It gives,' continues Ricoeur, an 'occasion for thought. Something to think about... a philosophy instructed by myths arises at a certain moment in reflection, and, beyond philosophical reflection, it wishes to answer a certain situation of modern culture.'[7] The hermeneutics of ancient symbols, Ricoeur thinks, is an appropriate (or better, necessary) starting point for philosophical conceptualization.

Connections of the sort that Ricoeur speaks of—between ancient myths and symbols of evil and modern philosophical speculations about evil—exist, in my estimation, between biblical and rabbinic myths and rituals that embody the idea of human creation in the divine image on one hand, and the modern idea of human dignity on the other. In this study, other than some reflections that appear at the end, I make no claim of uncovering these connections, but only of reconstructing part of the early foundations of the perception of blood in general and human blood in particular and the idea of creation in the divine image in rabbinic literature. The connections between these and the modern idea of human dignity according to the philosophical hermeneutics proposed by Ricoeur must be the subject of a separate study.

The point of departure of the following discussion is the law of beheading in tannaitic halakhah. As we shall see, this mode of execution—which applies in practice only to murderers—is extraordinary in comparison to other forms of judicial execution in rabbinic literature. This study will focus on the Rabbis' reasons for forming this mode of execution and the antinomy between these reasons and the Rabbis' attitude toward capital punishment.

II. Introducing the Issue

Beheading (*hereg*)—which entails the 'cutting off the head [of the convict] with a sword'—is exceptional among the judicial executions of the tannaim (the early rabbinic sages of the period of the Mishnah). Recent studies have showed that the tannaim shaped the means of judicial executions in a manner such that serious damage was not inflicted upon the victim's body.[8] They

---

[7] Paul Ricoeur, *Symbolism of Evil*, trans. from the French by E. Buchanan (Boston 1967) p. 348.

[8] See M. Halbertal, Interpretative Revolutions in the Making, [Hebrew] (Jerusalem 1997) [henceforth: Halbertal, Revolutions] Ch. 7; and following him Y. Lorberbaum, '*Imago Dei*: Early Rabbinic Literature, Maimonides and Nahmanides,' Ph. D. Thesis (Hebrew University, Jerusalem 1997) [henceforth, Lorberbaum, 'Image']. N. Brill and A. Buechler already alluded to this principle: Brill, 'Various Glosses' [Hebrew] *Beit Ha-Talmud* 4 (1985) pp. 7-11; Buechler, 'Die Todesstrafen

achieved this in two ways: they refashioned biblical forms of execution so that they would limit corporeal damage to the convict and they introduced a new means of execution that avoided disfigurement to an even greater degree.

The tannaim replaced the Biblical capital punishment of burning with internal burning whereby a flaming wick [or: melted lead bar—see Sanhedrin 52a] was thrown into the mouth of the convict and 'his entrails were burnt' (Sanhedrin 7:2). The principle that led them to refashion the punishment of burning was 'burning the soul with the body intact' (Sanhedrin 52a). Likewise, the biblical punishment of stoning that crushes the convict's body was changed to the convict being pushed from a limited height ('twice the height of a man'), thereby again limiting the corporeal damage inflicted (Sanhedrin 6:4, 45a).

The tannaim also fashioned a new type of execution that is not mentioned in pre-tannaitic sources, namely strangulation: 'Put a towel of coarse stuff within one of soft stuff and wrap it around his neck; one [witness] pulled one end towards him and the other pulled one end towards him until his life departed' (Sanhedrin 7:3). Death by strangulation is a means of execution that completely refrains from disfiguring the victim's corpse. The tannaim even prevent the rope from inflicting a minor bruise on the convict's neck by instructing the executioner to wrap it with a soft towel. The tannaim based the establishment of the punishment of strangulation on the following principle that they attribute to Judah ha-Nasi, the editor of the Mishnah: 'Just as death inflicted at the hand of heaven is such that there is no physical mark [on the body], so death inflicted at the hands of man should be death in which there is no physical mark [on the body].'[9] It is likely that this principle lies at the center of their shaping of the different means of the capital punishments. What is more, strangulation, was designated by the tannaim as the default judicial execution: 'In any passage in the Pentateuch in which there is a reference to the death penalty without further specification, it is to be inflicted only through strangulation.'[10] That is, in the absence of an explicit directive in the Pentateuch regarding the means of judicial execution, the transgressor should be punished with strangulation because strangulation brings about the least corporeal damage. In addition, it is likely that, on account of its general

---

der Bibel und der judisch-nachbiblischen Zeit,' *MGWJ* 50 (1906) [henceforth: Buechler, 'Todesstrafen'], pp. 542-562, 664-706.

Analyzes of the Talmudic sources and a comparison with the pre-tannaitic Jewish and contemporary non-Jewish sources testify that the laws in the Mishnah and parallel sources are not a result of a passive inheritance of earlier halakhic traditions. Instead, they reflect exegetical and halakhic innovation based on principles that I will detail below. See Halbertal, Revolutions; following him Lorberbaum, 'Image,' *idem*; cf. E.E. Urbach, 'The Courts of Twenty-Three and the Laws of Judicial Execution,' [Hebrew] *The World of the Sages*, (Jerusalem 1988) pp. 294-305 [henceforth: Urbach, 'Courts'].

[9] *Mekhilta de-Rabbi Ishmael*, Nezikin 5, Horovitz-Rabin, ed. pp. 265-266; Sanhedrin 52b. On the first part of this principle ('death inflicted at the hand of heaven is such that there is no physical mark') see Lorberbaum 'Image,' pp. 190-191.

[10] *Mekhilta de-Rabbi Ishmael, idem*; Sanhedrin, *idem*.

formulation, the principle that lies at the foundation of the creation of the judicial execution of strangulation also led to the refashioning of the other types of capital punishment.

The Biblical practice of *teliyah*—impaling the corpse of an executed criminal on a pole—which itself moderated the practice current in the ancient Near East, was subject to a significant additional reduction at the hands of the tannaim. Pentateuchal law apparently applies this treatment to all those convicted of a capital crime and executed, permitting the corpse to be exposed only for a single day and mandating its removal at nightfall (*Deuteronomy* 21:22-23). In contrast, the tannaim delimit this practice to convicted blasphemers (those who have cursed God) and idolatrous, whose corpses are to be exposed after being stoned to death, and they refashion the practice in such a manner that it becomes merely symbolic—'one person ties him on and [immediately] the other releases him, in order to uphold the commandment of *teliyah*' (Sanhedrin 46a).

The aforementioned studies have also suggested the claim that the fashioning of the methods of execution was based on the conception that the human being—including one condemned to capital punishment—was created in God's image.[11] According to this conception, the human body is part of God's image and therefore any corporeal damage in the course of the judicial execution should be avoided.[12]

Beheading, however, is exceptional. Its singularity immediately raises the following question: what led the tannaim to deviate from the principle that they themselves established: 'death inflicted at the hands of man is death in which there is no physical mark,' and to fashion a means of execution that brings about so much corporeal damage?

It is important to note that the question of the origin and rationale of beheading as a capital punishment in rabbinic law should also be posed without reference to its irregular nature. Even if we take no notice of the principle underlying the other forms of judicial execution—the integrity of the corpse, a principle that I am convinced is at work—we may still wonder why the tannaim fashioned a form of execution to which, as will be shown, there is

---

[11] This thesis has a basis in tannaitic sources that explain the symbolic *teliyah* in the following manner: the person who is hanged is an (identical) twin of God and in order to refrain from damaging His image, he is lowered immediately with the hanging. And as Rashi explains: 'No time seperates them.' See Sanhedrin, *idem*; *Tosefta* Sanhedrin 9:7, Zuckermandel, ed., p. 429. These sources should be read with the statement of R. Meir in Sanhedrin 6:5. This explanation, we shall argue, applies not only to *feliylah* but to all types of judicial execution (with the exception of beheading). See Halbertal, *Revolutions, idem*; Lorberbaum, 'Images' pp. 159-167, 188-193.

[12] See Halbertal, *Revolutions, idem*; Lorberbaum, 'Image,' Ch. 6, particularly pp. 186-191. It is important to underscore that the corporeal dimension—depite its centrality—does not exhaust the tannaitic conception of God's image. On this notion and its theological and anthropological import see Lorberbaum 'Image,' pp. 159-192.

no reference of any substance in the Bible, nor in any pre-tannaitic Jewish sources. While such a point of origin for an inquiry blunts the distinctiveness of beheading among the forms of judicial execution—for one can pose the same question, with the same reasoning, about each of them—it does nothing to diminish the force of either the problem raised or the solution proposed below.

III. Purging the Defiled Blood

1. Sword and Axe: Shaping the Capital Punishment of Beheading

The following is the Mishnah's depiction of beheading (*hereg*):[13]

> The procedure of beheading: they would cut off his head with a sword as the [Roman] government does. R. Judah says: This is damaging [nivul][14] for him; instead, they place his head on a block and chop it off with an axe [kofitz]. (Sanhedrin 7:3)

Executing the convict by beheading him with a sword (in the view of the anonymous sages) or an axe[15] (R. Judah) severely harms the convict's body. The disagreement between R. Judah and the sages is recorded several times in Talmudic literature.[16] The version of the disagreement in these sources seems incongruent with what is stated in the Mishnah.[17] In either case, this type of judicial execution is exceptional and requires an explanation. What are the sources and reasons for this execution? Can they explain its exceptional nature?

First, we should note that the dispute between R. Judah and the sages does not touch upon the source of beheading but only the matter of its implementation.[18] The sages prefer beheading with a sword, because they maintain that it produces less bodily harm, while R. Judah rejects this manner not because of any claim that it produces greater disfigurement, but because of

---

[13] The word *hereg* in the Bible and Talmudic literature is a general term for capital punishment (see for example *Deuteronomy* 13:10-11) and it is exchanged occasionally by the rabbis with death by sword. See P. Segal, 'Capital Punishment and Punishment at the Hands of Heaven' [Hebrew], Ph. D. Thesis (Hebrew University, Jerusalem 1980) [henceforth Segal, 'Punishment'] p. 147, note 9; S. Krauss, 'A Chapter in Corporeal Punishments' [Hebrew] *Devir* 1 (1923), pp. 88-112, particularly pp. 96, 104-105.

[14] Nivul in rabbinic literature refers to embarrassment that is engendered by disfiguring and damaging the body.

[15] On the term *kofitz* see Segal, 'Punishment,' p. 112 and the references that he cites. See also below.

[16] See Sanhedrin 52b; Tosefta Sanhedrin 9:11, Zuckermandel, ed., p. 430; and Palestinian Talmud Sanhedrin 7c.

[17] For an examination of these sources and their relationship to one another see the appendix to the article.

[18] Compare with Segal, 'Punishment,' *idem*.

its resemblance to the ordinance of the Gentiles.[19] His position emerges from the Tosefta and the baraita recorded in the Babylonian and Palestinian Talmuds.[20] According to these sources, which complement the Mishnah's statement, the sages reply to R. Judah: 'there is no death more damaging than this (axe);' and he responds: 'I also know that this death is damaging, but what can I do, for the Pentateuch states: "You shall not follow their ordinances."'[21] The Mishnah's phrase 'as the government does'—whose meaning is the Roman custom[22]—does not indicate the source of the law of beheading, as scholars maintain.[23] Rather, the sages only employ it as a description of the means of implementation.[24] This claim is based on a number of reasons: First,

---

[19] See Sifra, Ahare Mot 9:8 Finkelstein, ed., p. 370: '"You shall not copy the practices of the land of Egypt, ... or of the land of Canaan." One might conclude that one cannot build their buildings or plant their plants. Therefore, it states: "You shall not follow their ordinances." We include only those laws that were promulgated for them, their fathers and forefathers. "And what would they do? A man would marry a man and a woman would marry a woman; a man would marry a woman and her daughter; a woman would be married to two men." Therefore it states: "You shall not follow their ordinances."' In this category matters of style are not included but only laws that were unique to Gentiles. See also *idem* 13:9 (Finkelstein, ed., p. 372-373): '"Nor shall you follow their laws." Now what is the Scripture establishing that it has not already stated? For it has previously stated: "Let no one be found among you who... or one who inquires of the dead" (*Deuteronomy* 18:10-11). What does "nor shall you follow their ordinances" come to teach? It is that you should not follow their customs that have been established by law, like going to their theaters, circuses and playing fields. R. Meir states: these are prohibited, because of "the ways of the Amorites" which the sages have specified.' See M. Herr, 'External Influences on the Sages of the Land of Israel: Absorption and Rejection' [Hebrew], *Acculturation and Assimilation: Continuity and Change in the Cultures of Israel and the Nations*, eds. Y. Kaplan and M. Stern, (Jerusalem 1989) pp. 88-91; and E.E. Urbach, *The Sages: Their Concepts and Beliefs*, (Jerusalem 1979) pp. 379-380.

[20] See n. 12 above and the appendix.

[21] This is the version in the baraita in Sanhedrin 52b. See the appendix.

[22] The meaning of the term 'government' (*malkhut*) is generally Rome. See Segal, 'Punishment,' p. 115. On beheading in Rome, see below, n. 22.

[23] See Segal, 'Punishment,' pp. 112-116.

[24] This is also apparent from the *Babylonian Talmud* (Sanhedrin 52b), which explains the view of the sages in the following manner: 'Since death by sword is written in Scripture, we are not learning it [i.e., death by sword] from them [i.e. the Gentiles].' See also the Tosefta, which states: 'Four modes of execution were given to the court, but to the regime was given only death by sword' (Sanhedrin 9:10). One should not infer from here that the source for death by sword is the civil regime. It should be noted that the regime (*rashut*) in Tosefta Sanhedrin is the Jewish regime. See Urbach, 'Courts,' p. 45; Segal, 'Punishment,' *idem*. The sword is indeed the mode of execution usually attributed to the civil regime (see for example Berakhot 32b; *Leviticus Rabbah* 6:5, Margulies, ed., pp. 137-138; see also Josephus, *Jewish Antiquities* 15:4-8; *idem, The Jewish Wars* 14:480.) However, as we shall demonstrate below, it is not from here that the tannaim derive death by sword. On this issue see Ketubot 30b; the parallel discussions in the *Babylonian Talmud*; and

the Mishnah does not cite the source of the other forms of capital punishment but offers only a depiction thereof. It is difficult to assume that beheading is exceptional in this regard. Second, preventing bodily harm or avoiding a foreign type of execution cannot of itself serve as a source for the law of beheading, because other types of capital punishment are both far less damaging and far less similar to Roman forms of execution. As was noted above regarding burning, stoning and in particular strangulation, which does not bring about corporeal damage, these forms of execution are hardly mentioned in contemporary sources.[25] The main reason that led scholars to claim that the source of execution by sword is Roman law is that the Romans employed it as the means of judicial execution of murderers conducted by the civil regime. But the Romans did not in fact execute those convicted of murder by the sword.[26] Moreover, the Romans perceived death by sword as a 'good death' and designated it for the upper class (*honestiores*).[27] Thus the question remains: whence did the Tannaim learn the law of beheading?

2. Beheading and the Prohibition of Murder

The scriptural basis for beheading (*hereg*)—in contrast with other types of capital punishment—is derived in tannaitic sources from the transgressions for which this punishment applies, namely a city of enticers ('*ir ha-nidahat*) and homicide (*Sanhedrin* 9:1). Regarding the latter,[28] the Pentateuch mandates: 'Put the inhabitants of the town to the sword' (*Deuteronomy* 13:17). The city of enticers is unique among Biblical transgressions whose punishment is death, because its form resembles more closely a prescribed war than a process of judicial execution.[29] Thus, Biblical and Talmudic sources testify that the category of war is a more appropriate classification for the punishment— which was apparently implemented by the king and not the judge[30]—that applies to the city of enticers. The sole transgression, then, to which the judicial execution of beheading (*hereg*) truly applies is homicide.

V. Aptovitzer, 'Observations on the Criminal Law of the Jews,' *JQR* 15 (1924-1925) pp. 55-118, n. 88.

[25] Lorberbaum, 'Image,' p. 158.

[26] See Macmullen, 'Savagery' pp. 148, 154 and the references collected there in note 1. He cites burning (in the case of the murder of a master by his slave), throwing into a pit of wild animals (in the case of murder by poisoning) and poisoning (in the case of unintentional murder or death brought about by negligence) as the modes of capital punishment for murder.

[27] Mommsen, *Romisches*, p. 927; P. Garnsey, 'Legal Principles in the Roman Empire,' *Past and Present* 41 (1968) pp. 3-24; and K. Koleman, 'Fatal Charades: Roman Executions Staged as Mythological Enactments,' *The Journal for Roman Studies* 80 (1990) pp. 44-73.

[28] A 'city of enticers' is a city whose residents have been enticed into idol worship.

[29] See Halbertal, Revolutions, *idem*.

[30] See also *Joshua* 11:11.

3. Blood in Biblical Literature

Before we investigate the Talmudic sources that relate to the punishment of the murderer and the form that it takes, we shall first turn to the Bible. The punishment for murder is designated after the flood, and it is connected to a detailed law regarding animal blood.[31] As part of the covenant that God establishes with Noah, He permits him to eat animal flesh (*Genesis* 9:3) but warns him against consuming blood: 'You must not, however, eat flesh with its life-blood in it' (9:4). The transgression is more severe regarding consuming human blood: 'But for your own life-blood I will require a reckoning: I will require it of every beast, of man, too, will I require a reckoning of human life of every man for that of his fellow man' (*idem* v. 5). This requirement is elucidated in the subsequent verse: 'Whoever sheds the blood of man, by man shall his blood be shed.' A similar punishment is mentioned in *Leviticus* 17:14 regarding consuming blood: 'For the soul [*nefesh*] of all flesh—its blood is its life ... I say to the Israelite people: You shall not partake of the blood of any flesh for the soul of all flesh is its blood. Anyone who partakes of it shall be cut off.'[32] In *Numbers* 35, different matters relating to the transgression of murder are cited: intentional and unintentional murder, city of refuge, and blood-redeemer, *inter alia*. There, after establishing the obligation of the blood-redeemer to murder(!) the murderer (19:6-27) and the prohibition of taking a ransom for the life of a murderer or in lieu of a flight to a city of refuge (v. 31-32), a final proclamation is presented that acts as a summary of the entire chapter: 'And the land can have no expiation for blood that is shed on it' (v. 33).[33]

From these verses—which scholars have classified as part of the Priestly source in the Bible[34]—emerges a conception that identifies the animal's soul with its blood.[35] The Priestly source deduces obligations and prohibitions

---

[31] See T. Frymer-Kensky, 'The Atrahasis and Its Significance for Our Understanding of *Genesis* 1-9,' *Biblical Archeologist* 40 (1977) pp. 147-155. She notes that previously murderers did not receive capital punishments. On the contrary, Cain, the first murderer, was given special protection against blood-avengers (*Genesis* 4:15). See also the matter of Lemech (*idem*, v. 24).

[32] On the punishment of being 'cut off,' see S. Loewenstamm, 'Karet, Hakaret' Encyclopedia Mikrait [Hebrew] 4: 330. Compare A. Shemesh, 'The Punishment of Lashes in Tannaitic Sources,' Ph. D. Thesis, (Bar-Ilan University 1994) p. 222.

[33] See M. Greenberg, 'Criminal Law.'

[34] See Y. Knohl, *The Sanctuary of Silence*, (Minneapolis 1995) [henceforth: Knohl, *Sanctuary*], pp. 99, 104. He attributes the anthropomorphic verses of *Genesis* 9 to the Priestly school, but to a period that precedes the appearance of the sublime Tetragramaton. See *idem*, p. 178. Phenomenologically, there is a similarity between these verses and those in *Numbers* 35, which is part of the literary creation of the Holiness School.

[35] See also Psalms 72:14, 94:21. For a good overview of blood in the Bible and other sources in the ancient Near East see the entry 'Blood' in the *Theological Dictionary of the Old Testament*, G. J. Botterweck, ed., (1989) vol. III, pp. 234-250.

whose violation requires expiation from the substantive-animistic features of the blood. The expiation resembles an act of purification that utilizes the purifying characteristics of blood.[36] The most severe of these transgressions is called 'spilling of the blood' and in light of the conception that identifies blood with the soul, one should not take this phrase metaphorically but as a literal depiction of the act of killing. From the spilled blood emerges an 'outcry'[37] for revenge-redemption-expiation (all of these echo in the Biblical conception of blood) that can be 'quieted' only through shedding the blood of the murderer. The demand to expiate the blood of the victim through the blood of the murderer—and not with other blood—is a magic-ritual objectification of the feeling of revenge and the principle of reciprocal punishment that are latent in the phrase 'redeemer of blood.' According to this conception, the 'redeemer of the blood' causes the situation to revert to a balance that was disturbed through the act of the murder. The killing of the murderer by a family member of the victim—unlike the execution in other transgressions, which is performed by the witnesses and the congregation[38]—reflects the conception that the blood of the victim that runs through the veins of his relatives wreaks vengeance, as it were, for the damage inflicted upon him.[39]

In fact, it seems that the Priestly source attributes to blood a singular and sacred status that transcends that of any other earthly matter or substance. The identification of blood with the soul, that is with the sustaining principle of the world; its danger and promise; and the rituals surrounding it—all of these perhaps testify to its divine source. It may be that confirmation of this is to be found in *Genesis* 9:6. There the declaration 'Whoever sheds the blood of man

---

[36] On blood as possessing demonic (and miasmatic) characteristics, on the one hand, and as 'purifying matter' on the other hand, see Jacob Milgrom, 'The Function of the Hatta't Sacrifice,' *Tarbiz* 40 (1969-70) pp. 1-8 [henceforth: Milgrom, 'Function']; compare with H. C. Brichto, 'On Slaughter and Sacrifice, Blood and Atonement' *HUCA* 47 (1976) pp. 19-55. On sacrificing the blood of the animals as expiation for slaughtering them, see Cana Wermen, 'Consumption of the Blood and Its Covering in the Priestly and Rabbinic Traditions' *Tarbiz* 63 (1993-94) pp. 173-183 [henceforth: Wermen, 'Consumption of the Blood'] and the studies she refers to in n. 10.

[37] See *Genesis* 4:10: 'Hark! Your brother's blood cries out to me from the ground' and *idem* 37:22, 42:22; see also *Midrash ha-Gadol, Exodus*, M. Margulies, ed., (Jerusalem 1976) p. 127: '"You shall not murder" – One shall not permit [the shedding of] the blood, so that it cries out toward you,' and other similar sources that are found there.

[38] See, for example, *Leviticus* 24:14; *Numbers* 15:35; *Deuteronomy* 21:21.

[39] On the 'redeemer of blood' as reflecting the conception that the entire congregation (family or tribe) is one body, in contradistinction to later conceptions that see particular human beings as individuals, see S. Mowinckel, *The Psalms in Israel's Worship* (Oxford 1962) p. 42.

by man shall his blood be shed' is justified by the assertion 'For in God's image did He make man.'[40]

Deuteronomy also identifies blood with the soul. In chapter 12, which deals with laws of eating meat, it states: 'But make sure that you do not partake of the blood; for the blood is the life, and you must not consume the life along with the meat' (v. 23). In this Biblical document the transgression of homicide is also depicted with the phrase 'spilling of the blood' (19:10), and its punishment, which involves the 'redeemer of blood,' is also characterized as 'purging the blood of the innocent' (vv. 10, 13). The demand of purging the blood of the victim is particularly evident in the ritual of the broken-necked heifer (`egla `arufa) that comes for a corpse 'the identity of [its] slayer not being known' (21:4-9):

> 'The Elders of the town (...) shall break the heifer's neck. (...) [They] shall wash their hands over the heifer whose neck was broken in the wadi. And they shall make this declaration: 'Our hands did not shed this blood. (...) Absolve O Lord, Your people Israel whom You redeemed and do not let guilt for the blood of the innocent remain among Your people Israel.' And they will be expiated for the guilt of the blood. Thus you will purge from your midst guilt for the blood of the innocent.'

Scholars have tended to emphasize the difference between the conception of blood in the Priestly document and its meaning in *Deuteronomy*. According to their approach, *Deuteronomy*'s depiction of blood is a prime example of that blood's secular, rationalistic and anti-mythic tendency, which openly polemicizes with the Priestly tradition. In their reading, the Book of *Deuteronomy* removes from blood its polluting (miasmatic) character; removes its magical-ritualistic dimension and transforms it into a symbol that functions only in the moral-social realm.[41] However, another reading of the verses of *Deuteronomy* identifies the 'stain' of blood with intentions (in the phenomenological sense) in the moral-social realm. But it still retains its 'objective' core, so that the blood also functions on the ritualistic-magical plane.[42] Although according to *Deuteronomy* the blood does not defile the land[43] or the temple, the conception that 'the blood is the soul' appears often (Ch. 12) and its spilling—at least from the human being—requires expiation.

---

[40] On the divine source of blood in Babylonian and Egyptian myths, see Weinfeld, 'God the Creator,' p. 114 and the references in n. 51.

[41] This is Weinfeld's interpretation (*Deuteronomy*, pp. 210-211, 226) of the ritual of the broken-necked heifer. The effectiveness of the expiation is based, in his opinion, on the elders' words of confession and not on the spilling of the blood.

[42] This is the approach of J. Milgrom ('The Alleged "Demythologization and Secularization" in *Deuteronomy*,' *IEJ* 23 (1973) pp. 156-161). He claims that *Deuteronomy*, in fact, expands upon the magical dimension in the Priestly work.

[43] But Milgrom (*idem*) notes that the conception of the impurity of the land exists also in *Deuteronomy*. See *Deuteronomy* 24:4, 21, 23 and *Joshua* 8:29, 10:27.

Deuteronomy expresses the need for expiation through the phrase 'purge the blood of the innocent'—that seems to relate to the blood of the victim[44]—which also appears in relation to the ritual of the broken-necked heifer.[45] Whatever its proper reading, *Deuteronomy* is similar to the Priestly literature in regard to the issue that interests us: the normative requirement for expiation through the blood of the murderer. This point was not lost on the tannaim.

4. The Source of the Law of Beheading

The Talmud and the Midrash, in contrast to critical scholarship, read the Pentateuch as a complete and unitary work. This certainly has to be the starting point for an inquiry into them.[46] The rabbinic sources generally, and in this issue in particular, do not distinguish between the different Biblical documents. They read the Priestly source and *Deuteronomy* together and see in them a commandment for expiating the blood of the victim through the *blood of the murderer*. Although they also discover in blood social and moral intentions as well, they learn the laws of beheading from its objectified-ritualistic dimensions.

A passage from the *Mekhilta de-Rabbi Ishmael* (Nezikin 4, ed. Horovitz-Rabin pp. 261-262) examines the punishment of the murderer and emphasizes that the death of the murderer must be through spilling his blood:

'[He who fatally strikes a man] shall be put to death' (*Exodus* 21:12)—by the sword. [You say by the sword].[47] Perhaps it

---

[44] There were commentators who explained the term 'blood of the innocent' as 'the blood of the innocent murderer.' See, for example, R. Saadia's commentary on this verse and Weinfeld, *Deuteronomy*, p. 116, n. 2. But, according to the simple reading of the verse, the 'blood of the innocent' refers to the blood of the victim, which receives expiation or redemption through the blood of the murderer. See Sifri *Deuteronomy* 200 (p. 244) and Nahmanides' and Ovadiah Seforno's commentaries on the verse.

[45] Milgrom (*idem*) claims that implicit in the law of the broken-necked heifer is the conception that the blood of the murderer impurifies the land. A. Rofe notes the linguistic-literary relationship between the laws of inadvertent and intentional murder and that of a corpse 'the identity of [its] slayer not being known' and emphasizes the ancient roots of the section concerning a broken-necked heifer ('The History of Cities of Refuge in Biblical Law' [Hebrew] *Beit Mikra* 31 (1983) p. 115).

[46] Along with this, the conclusion of scholarship will at times determine the centrality of a particular Biblical tradition in the different streams within Talmudic literature that dominates over other Biblical traditions through interpretation. For a similar methodology with different conclusions see Knohl, *Sanctuary*, p. 223, and compare with G. Alon, *Studies in Jewish History in the Times of the Second Temple*, [Hebrew] (Israel 1967) vol. I, pp. 175-176.

[47] The additions and alternative versions that are contained within the brackets follow MS. Oxford 151. These alternative readings have been documented by A. Shemesh ('These Are the Ones to Be Killed: A Study of a Chapter in the Penal Teachings of

means by strangulation? And you must reason thus: here the expression 'shall be put to death' is used and there (*Leviticus* 20:10), in the case of the adulterer, the expression 'shall be put to death' is used; just as there it means strangulation [alternative version: death by sword] so too here it means by strangulation [alternative version: death by sword]. You compare the case of murderer to the case of adulterer. But I compare it to the case of blasphemer: Here the expression 'shall be put to death' is used,[48] and there (*Leviticus* 24:16), in the case of the blasphemer, the expression 'shall be put to death' is used. Just as there it means by stoning, so also here it means by stoning. If you would compare him to the adulterer, I could compare him to the blasphemer. And if you would compare him to the blasphemer,[49] I could compare him to the adulterer. But Scripture says: 'Whoever sheds the blood of man' etc. (*Genesis* 9:6).

Still I might say that he should be bled from other [alternative version: two][50] organs so that he dies thereby. But Scripture says: 'and shall break the heifer's neck in the wadi' (*Deuteronomy* 21:4); 'So shall you purge the innocent blood from your midst' (*idem*, v. 9). This declares shedders of blood to be like the heifer whose neck is to be broken. Just as the latter is killed by cutting off its head, so all shedders of blood are to be killed by decapitation.

The anonymous author of this midrash begins with the judgment that when the Pentateuch designates that one should be killed for murder without stating the form of capital punishment, it is with a sword. He then attempts to identify the scriptural basis of this ruling. In this regard, he opens with a dilemma regarding the appropriate transgression that can serve as a source for the punishment of the murderer. On the one hand, an analogy can be drawn between the laws of the murderer and the law of the adulterer who receives the

---

Hazal,' Shenaton Ha-Mishpat Ha-Ivri (forthcoming) [henceforth: Shemesh, 'Penal Teachings']). The subsequent textual-philological notes regarding this passage are based on this article. I would like to thank Dr. Shemesh for providing me a prepublication copy of his article.

[48] From 'and there in the case of the adulterer the expression "shall be put to death" is used' to 'there the expression "shall be put to death" is used' does not appear in MS Munich 117, seemingly because of a homoioteleuton. See Shemesh, 'Penal Teachings.'

[49] 'And if you would compare him to a blasphemer' is missing from MS Oxford but does appear in MS Munich. Here also its absence can be explained as a homoioteleuton. This reference is from Shemesh as well.

[50] Epstein explains that the reference here is to bleeding him from between his two arms (see *Leshonenu* 15 (1957) p. 103. Cited in Shemesh, 'Penal Teaching').

punishment of strangulation[51] (as is done in all places where the mode of capital punishment is not recorded explicitly in the Pentateuch).[52] On the other hand, one can compare the murderer to a blasphemer who receives the punishment of stoning. The oscillation between these two transgressions is not only a result of the Pentateuch's failure to enumerate the particular punishment they receive—there exist many other such transgressions. These two transgressions, as well as the transgression of murder, are designated in tannaitic halakhah as extremely severe. These are the three prohibitions in regard to which one must choose to die a martyr's death rather than committing any of them.[53] The Midrash, however, neutralizes both possibilities by playing one off the other. This serves as a rhetorical device to underscore the singularity of the manner of execution for murder, which is with a sword. According to this understanding, one should read the words 'And you must reason thus' in the same breath with the preceding words 'perhaps it means by strangulation?' Thus, the role of the first part of the Midrashic passage is to demonstrate that one cannot derive the laws of execution for murder from the manner of execution of other transgression, even those that possess a similar level of severity. Instead, the Midrash shows that one must turn to another source—the verses that relate directly to the transgression under investigation. In my mind, this functions as a declaration regarding the singularity of the transgression of murder and its punishment.

According to the version of MS Oxford 151, the first part of the Midrashic passage possesses a different meaning. The Midrashic author attempts to prove that the murderer receives judicial execution with a sword initially by analogy ('And you must reason thus, etc.') with the laws of adultery. This analogy—by means of which he also attempts to address the question: 'perhaps it means by strangulation'—is apparently based on a unique tradition regarding the punishment for adultery. In contrast with the view of the Mishnah and other tannaitic sources,[54] this version of the Midrashic passage maintains that adultery is punished by capital punishment by the sword.[55] This analogy is rejected because of the possibility of building a conflicting alternative analogy to blasphemy, which is punished by stoning. Consequently, the Midrashic author turns to a different sort of derivation—an interpretation that focuses on verses relating to the nature of the transgression

---

[51] This is according to the version found in the edition of Horovitz-Rabin, ed., which follows the position of the Mishnah regarding the punishment for an adulterer. See also *Mekhilta de-Rabbi Ishmael*, M. Ish-Shalom, ed. (Vienna 1870) p. 80, note 10; and Yalkut Shimoni 247, 322.

[52] See *Mekhilta de-Rabbi Ishmael*, Nezikin 5 (pp. 265-266) and many other places.

[53] See Sanhedrin 74b and the parallel sources. Adultery is a classic example of a case of illicit sexual relations (see *idem*), and blasphemy is a classic example of idolatry. See *Sifre Deuteronomy* 221, pp. 253-254; Sanhedrin 45b and compare with Ezekiel 16:39-40.

[54] See Sanhedrin 10:1 and *Sifre*, Mekhilta de-Arayot 9:11, Weiss, ed. (92a).

[55] A. Shemesh offers this interpretation.

of murder. Our reading of the end of the Midrashic passage also applies to this version.

The source that the Midrashic passage relies upon is the verse of *Genesis* 9:6, which is understood in a literal fashion. Thus 'by man shall his blood be shed' is understood as stating that one should spill the blood of the murderer; that is, he should receive the death penalty ('by man'). Moreover, his death should be precisely through bloodshed ('his blood shall be shed') and consequently his head is cut off with a sword.[56] This interpretation is underscored through the question: 'Still I might say that he should be bled from two organs so that he dies thereby,' and through the answer that is based on the ritual of the broken-necked heifer. The verse 'you will purge the blood of the innocent' is compared with the act of breaking the neck. In the Biblical context, the meaning of these words, which conclude the section concerning the broken-necked heifer is unclear: do they relate to the ritual, so that its purpose is (again) cited and subsequently the necessity of observing it is underscored? Or is a new law established here that dictates that if the murderer is apprehended after performing the ritual, an obligation exists to execute him?[57] The Midrash derives this law from a different verse,[58] and our Midrashic author is closer to the first alternative, for he learns from the verse the ritual dimension of the law of the judicial execution by sword: just as the breaking of the heifer's neck purges (=expiates) the blood of the innocent (=the victim),[59] so, too, the beheading of the murderer 'cleanses' the blood of his victim. The analogy, however, is incomplete, because the breaking of the heifer's neck in tannaitic halakhah is with an axe,[60] while the beheading of the

---

[56] Compare with Sanhedrin 57b. There a tanna of the school of Manasseh interprets the phrase 'by man shall his blood be shed' as 'within the man' and therefore concludes that a Gentile receives the punishment of strangulation for murder. In contrast, the sages—seemingly following the interpretation in the Midrash—conclude that the Gentile receives the same punishment as the Jew, namely death by sword. Compare also to the allegorical interpretation of Philo, *De Specialibus Legibus* 3:28, 130-152. See also the interpretation of this verse in *Genesis* Rabbah 34:6, Theodor-Albeck, ed. (Jerusalem 1956) pp. 325-326; Sanhedrin, *idem*; and *Palestinian Talmud* Kiddushin 1:1, 58c.

[57] Rashi and other exegetes accept the first option, but see R. Abraham Ibn Ezra's comments on *Deuteronomy* 21:9.

[58] The answer to this question will be investigated below. Cf. also the view of Rava in Kerithot 26a.

[59] The latter part of the Midrashic passage—with slight alterations—appears in the baraita in Sanhedrin 52b; Ketubot 37b; and see *Palestinian Talmud* Sanhedrin 7:3 (24d). It is interesting to compare this Midrashic passage to *Sifre Deuteronomy* 187 (Finkelstein, ed., p. 227) 210 (p. 244) and see the references of the editor on p. 151, note 7, where the Midrashic phrase 'purge the sinner of Israel' is connected to the phrase 'purge the evil from among you/ from Israel' that appears frequently in this Midrashic work.

[60] See Sotah 9:6; *Sifre Deuteronomy* 207 (p. 242).

murderer is with a sword. It is, as it were, a 'phenomenological analogy,'[61] because more than touching upon the technique of breaking the neck, it focuses on the essence of the ritual—spilling of the blood as a means of expiation. This Midrashic passage fits with the view of the sages[62] that exchanged the axe for the sword in order to minimize corporeal damage.

In this Midrash, there are two stages that both underscore a single point: one executes the murderer by spilling his blood. The first part of the Midrash derives from the verse in *Genesis* the very necessity of an execution that involves the spilling of the blood and the second part derives from the ritual of the broken-necked heifer that this is accomplished through beheading.

I noted that the Midrashic passage interprets *Genesis* 9:7 literally. The punishment of the murderer is cited in the Bible in four places. The motif of blood appears in two of them;[63] in the two other places, it states that he is executed but without specifying the mode of execution.[64] Thus, according to the Bible, the means of execution is not apparent. In addition, the motif of expiation with blood, which is seemingly cited in two of the sources, can easily be explained metaphorically as denoting the principle of reciprocal punishment ('Whoever sheds the blood of man, by man shall his blood be shed'). Indeed, the Book of Jubilees bases the laws of murder on this principle. The following is its depiction of the first murderer, Cain, and the appropriate punishment for all murderers: 'At the end of that jubilee Cain was killed one year after him. And his house fell upon him, and he died in the midst of his house. And he was killed by its stones, because he killed Abel with a stone,[65] and with a stone he was killed by righteous judgment. Therefore it is ordained in the heavenly tablets: With the weapon with which a man kills his fellow he shall be killed just as he wounded him thus shall they do to him.' (4:31-32).[66] Philo and

---

[61] See Y. Gilat, 'The Development of the Gezerah Shavah' [Hebrew] *Milet* 2 (1985) p. 85-92 and previously S. Lieberman, *Hellenism in Jewish Palestine* (New York 1950) p. 61.

[62] Compare with Segal, 'Punishment,' p. 115 and Buechler, 'Todesstrafen,' pp. 695-696.

[63] *Genesis* 9:6; *Numbers* 35.

[64] *Exodus* 21:12-14 (the verse with which our Midrashic passage begins); *Deuteronomy* 19:11-13.

[65] Compare with *Genesis Rabbah*, Theodor-Albeck, ed., p. 214.

[66] *The Old Testament Pseudepigrapha*, J.H. Charlesworth, ed. (Garden City, New York 1985) p. 64. Reciprocal punishment is the main principle of punishment in the Book of Jubilees. It is reasonable to assume that this is the manner in which the Book of Jubilees understood *Genesis* 9:6 ('Whoever sheds the blood of man, by man shall his blood be shed'). This verse is included in this work in 6:9. What is surprising about this passage is the appearance of the notion of God's creating man in the image of God. The Book of Jubilees bases its depiction of the creation of man (Ch. 2) on *Genesis* 2:7, while ignoring the additional notion in the verse that man is created in God's image (on this issue see Lorberbaum, 'Image,' Ch. 9, n. 19). This single place in the work that this notion is mentioned is in God's words to Noah after the flood, when He commands him among other things, regarding execution for

Josephus also fail to mention expiation through blood regarding the punishment of the murderer. Philo claims that the murderer is crucified: 'Since there are no bounds to the iniquities of evil natures and they are ever committing a superabundance of enormities and extending and exalting their vices beyond all means and all limits, the lawgiver would, if he could, have sentenced them to die times beyond number. But since this was impossible, he ordained another penalty as an addition, and ordered the manslayer to be crucified.'[67] Josephus seemingly maintains that the punishment for murder is stoning, which is for him the punishment that a convict receives when the mode of punishment is not cited explicitly in the Biblical verse:

> ...let him be led forth by their own hands without the city, followed by the multitude, and stoned to death; and, after remaining for the whole day exposed to general view, let him be buried at night. Thus shall it be too with all who howsoever are condemned by the laws to be put to death.[68]

From what is known about the law of murderer in pre-tannaitic sources (and seemingly in the Bible) one can conclude that the exegetical move of the *Mekhilta* is innovative, because the execution of beheading and the demand for expiation with blood does not appear in these sources.

5. Expiation and Blood

Let us return to the Mishnah. It is difficult to ignore the similarity between beheading with a sword and the law regarding sacrifices, according to which the expiatory element of sacrifices in general, and of the sin- and guilt-offerings in particular, is not the blood that remains in the animal after death but the 'blood of the soul'—that is, the blood that spills from the animal as its 'soul exits.' This blood is sprinkled by the priest 'before the LORD, in front of the curtain' and/or 'at the base of the altar'[69] while the remaining blood is 'poured out on the base of the altar.'[70] According to tannaitic halakhah, the

---

murder. In this context, the Book of Jubilees cites *Genesis* 9:6 and also the end of the verse ('for in God's image ...'). It seems to me that the Book of Jubilees uses this verse for the principle of reciprocal punishment that is emphasized therein. Shemesh ('Penal Teachings') cites a similar (perhaps early) tradition that emerges from tannaitic sources. See Mekhilta de-R. Shimon bar Yohai (Epstein-Melamed, ed., p. 169). If his claim is correct, one can see this Midrashic interpretation (and other Midrashic passages based on a similar conception) as an innovative approach in relation to this tradition.

[67] Philo, *The Special Laws* 3:150-152 trans. F. H. Colson (Cambridge, MA) p. 571 and the comments of the editor in note C.

[68] *Antiquities* 4:265. We should note that according to Josephus, the corpses of all those who receive the punishment of stoning (including murderers) are displayed after their death.

[69] See, for example, *Leviticus* 4:6, 7, 17, 30, 34.

[70] See for example *idem*, v. 30, 18:7.

'blood of the soul' is the mechanism for expiation, while the blood that remains in the body is not effective (and engenders the invalidation of the sacrifices).[71] Consequently, the killing of the animal for sacrifice can only be done through ritual slaughtering.[72] For this reason, the murderer's punishment is derived from the breaking of the heifer's neck and not any other means of killing. The demand for beheading of the convict, which is emphasized in the *Mekhilta* by the rejection of the option of being bled slowly from two organs (a means of death that does not involve the 'blood of the soul'),[73] is also grounded in the conception of judicial execution as a ritual of expiation.[74]

An additional detail in the laws concerning the broken-necked heifer that indicates that expiation is through the spilling of the blood is the tannaitic law that the heifer's neck is broken only for a corpse whose blood was spilt but not for one who died through strangulation or hanging.[75] For our concerns, the phenomenology of this law is important even if its purpose is merely to limit the circumstances when one is commanded to perform the ritual of breaking the heifer's neck. In addition, it is important to emphasize that the judicial execution of beheading is applied to all acts of murder, even if they do not involve the spilling of blood.

The demand for ritual expiation for bloodshed is related to the religious dimension of bloodshed, which is emphasized in the following midrash in *Sifre Numbers*:

> 'And you shall not defile the land'—[...] Scripture says that the spilling of blood defiles the land and causes the Shekhinah [Divine Presence] to depart.[76]

One should not understand this midrashic statement as expressing merely a moral value or social interest (such as punishment serving as deterrent or

---

[71] This conception is found in the Bible (see Milgrom, 'Function') and particularly in tannaitic law. See, for example, *Sifra*, Hovah 3:7; Keritut 5:1; Tosefta Zevahim 8:17; and N. Zohar, 'The Sin Offering in the Teachings of the Tannaim,' M. A. Thesis (Hebrew University, Jerusalem 1988) p. 21, *passim*.

[72] This is certainly true for the Priestly code in *Leviticus* 17 that obligates ritual slaughtering and sacrifice for all animals 'as an offering to the LORD, before the LORD's tabernacle' (v. 4) as a condition of permitting the consumption of their meat. Regarding the sinner, it states: 'Bloodguilt shall be imputed to that man: he has shed blood; that man shall be cut off from among his people.' See also *idem*, v. 10.

[73] On this phrase see above, note 47.

[74] On the conception of the sin offering as a substitute for the sacrifice of the person in tannaitic literature see A. Buechler, *Studies in Sin and Atonement in the Rabbinic Literature of the First Century* (London 1928) pp. 441-442.

[75] See *Sifre Deuteronomy* 205 (p. 240) and its parallels; see also the comment of the editor, Finkelstein, there in note 7; see also Sotah 9:2, Palestinian Talmud Sotah 9:1 (23c) and S. Lieberman, 'After Life in Early Rabbinic Literature,' *Harry Wolfson Jubilee Volume*, Eng. section, (Jerusalem 1965) vol. I, p 514.

[76] *Sifre Numbers* 161, H.S. Horovitz, ed., p. 222.

prevention). This language underscores unequivocally the religious dimension of the act of murder—the spilt blood 'defiles the land and causes the Shekhinah to depart.' The ritual expiation for the blood of a murder victim emerges from a passage in *Midrash Ha-Gadol* (*Exodus*, pp. 227-228) as well: 'Bloodshed is harsh, for it has no expiation other than through *retsihah* [literally, murder], as Scripture says, 'and the land can have no expiation for blood that is shed on it, except by the blood of him who shed it' (*Numbers* 25:33).' These passages from *Sifre Numbers* and *Midrash Ha-Gadol*, which read *Numbers* 25:33 quite unmetaphorically, are in line with the midrash in the *Mekhilta*, which bases the law of beheading on a literal reading of the *Genesis* verse that enjoins 'by man shall his blood be shed' (9:6). Taken together (along with other passages as well), these rabbinic sources form a cohesive and coherent legal-ideational approach.

In this context, it is worthwhile to underscore the singularity of the means of derivation of the law of beheading (*hereg*). Unlike all other forms of execution, derived in rabbinic midrash from sources unrelated to the particular transgressions for which they are the punishment,[77] the law of beheading is learned directly from the (sole) transgression punishable by that form of execution. It is as if to say that the means of executing the murderer is anchored in the nature of the prohibition that the murderer has transgressed.

The demand for blood in exchange for blood shed emerges also from a passage in Avot de-Rabbi Natan that touches upon the first appearance of death in the Bible:

> For three offenses women die when they are giving birth: for carelessness in regard to menstrual purity, the dough offering and lighting the Sabbath lamp;[78] Why were the commandments of menstrual purity given to woman and not to man? Because Adam was the blood of the Holy One, blessed be He; Eve came and spilt it. Consequently, the commandments of menstrual purity were given to her so that [the sin involved in] the blood that she spilled might be atoned for.[79]

For causing Adam's downfall with the tree of knowledge, the woman was punished with the onset of her menstrual cycle that creates a set of obligations and prohibitions whose transgression precipitates death. This Midrash provides a mythic etiology of the woman's menstrual blood that is grounded in the Biblical conception of the blood that expiates for the bloodshed. The uniqueness of this Midrashic passage is in the fact that it expresses the mythic-theosophical dimension of the sacred state of human blood: 'Adam was the blood of the Holy One, blessed be He.' It seems that the

---

[77] See Lorberbaum, 'Image,' Ch. 5, pp. 100-158.
[78] *Shabbat* 2:6.
[79] *The Fathers According to Rabbi Natan*, transl. and comm. A.J. Saldarini (Leiden 1975) Ch. 9, p. 83.

source of this connection is *Genesis* 9:6, where the prohibition of bloodshed and the obligation of expiation for the bloodshed with the murderer's blood are given the justification: 'for in God's image did He make man.'[80] This Midrashic passage presumably alludes to the fact that the meaning of man's being in God's image is, *inter alia*, that the divine blood is merged with his blood.[81] The spilling of 'the Divine matter,' as it were, demands expiation (with the very same matter). We shall return to this Midrashic passage below.

Beheading is unique in tannaitic laws of judicial executions, which strive to keep the body intact. As we have seen, death by sword, as a judicial execution, is applied to only one transgression—murder. Regarding this transgression, there are explicit verses that enjoin the spilling of the murderer's blood for the purpose of the expiation of the land (*Numbers* 35) and/or the victim's blood (*Deuteronomy* 19:6-21). The Bible, as it were, compels itself upon the tannaim and 'prevents' them from fashioning a mode of execution that is not harmful to the convict's body. This is not to say that the tannaitic authors attributed to blood, in its different contexts, a meaning similar to that of the Bible. If in the Bible the meaning of blood is not readily apparent (as the debate between the scholars attests), its meaning in the Talmud is even more uncertain and requires a systematic and comprehensive study.[82] Scholars have recently pointed out differences between the tannaitic and Biblical (especially Priestly) laws regarding blood in sacrifices,[83] the covering and consumption of blood and other issues.[84] In the laws regarding the punishment for murderers, we are witness to a different tendency, in which the tannaim uphold the Biblical law, particularly the version present in the Priestly source. It is obvious that these opposing tendencies present an obstacle to understanding the conception of blood in tannaitic literature.[85]

---

[80] Compare with M. Kister, *Studies in Avot de-Rabbi Natan*, [Hebrew] (Jerusalem 1998) p. 95; and see my article, 'Murder, Capital Punishment and *Imago Dei* (Man as the Image of God)' [Hebrew] *Plilim: Israel Journal of Criminal Justice* 7 (Dec. 1998) pp. 223-272 [henceforth: Lorberbaum, 'Murder'], no. 116.

[81] This Midrashic passage recalls Egyptian and Babylonian myths according to which man is created from God's blood. It is important to underscore that in these myths, this motif is also connected with the conception that man (and in the Babylonian texts, the king and/ or the priest) is in the image of God. See Weinfeld, 'God the Creator,' p. 114 and his references in note 51; and the entry 'Blood' in *Theological Dictionary of the Old Testament*, pp. 237-289; cf. also Kister, *Avot*, n. 76. Regarding the possible Biblical context, see M. Miller, 'Image and Likeness of God' *JBL* 91 (1972) [henceforth: Miller, 'Image'].

[82] On studies regarding the conception of blood in rabbinic literature see N. Zohar, 'Ancient Rituals Transmitted by R. Judah—Evidence of a Transformed Understanding of "Blood is Life"' *Tarbiz* 58 (1988-89) pp. 525-530 [henceforth: Zohar, 'Rituals'], n. 1.

[83] Zohar, 'Rituals.'

[84] Werman, 'Consumption of the Blood,' pp. 174-175.

[85] From the halakhic differences that the tannaim established, we need not infer that early rabbinic literature adopted a symbolic conception of blood (as Zohar claims,

IV. Death by Sword and the Prevention of Disfigurement

As noted above, the Bible's normative pronouncements regarding the mode of execution for the murderer, that being the shedding of the murderer's blood, play a decisive role in the shaping of the judicial executions of beheading. These verses, which have no parallel in any other verses that depict transgressions whose punishment is execution, explain the deviation of the tannaitic law from the central principle that guided the formation of the other modes of judicial execution, namely, the prevention of harm to the convict's body. The demand for expiation through the convict's blood, which is unique to the transgression of murder, caused the tannaitic sages to deviate from the principle that accompanied them in the shaping of the other forms of execution and thereby legislate the law of beheading (*hereg*).

In addition, the tannaim also attempted with the formation of the punishment of beheading (*hereg*) to prevent corporeal damage. It is not entirely evident why, according to the sages, beheading with a sword is less damaging than beheading with an axe. It is possible that the axe, unlike the sword, 'damages the flesh on both sides of the area where the cutting takes place' as R. Meir Abulafi, the twelfth century talmudic commentator, claims.[86] Or, it inflicts greater insult, because it compares man with animal. In any event, it is clear that prevention of disfigurement is the consideration that causes the sages to deviate from precisely replicating the mode of killing in the broken-necked heifer, which is the Biblical source for this mode of execution. R. Judah's view is grounded in his desire not to follow the ordinances of the Gentiles, but it is clear that his position is also influenced somewhat by the (relatively) limited consideration of preventing damage and shame to the victim's body. His approach is reflected also in the laws of execution by burning where he opposed the use of a rope that prevents corporeal damage (for it is surrounded by a soft towel) to compel the convict to open his mouth, preferring instead the more damaging tongs.[87] R. Judah's attitude is also evident in his view that a woman is to be stoned while naked (but one 'covers her up in front and behind'), while the sages maintain that she is stoned clothed (*Sanhedrin* 6:4).[88] It is possible that underlying this dispute is an essential

---

['Rituals,' p. 530]) or that the laws regarding it are 'a collection of ordinances' (Werman, 'Consumption of the Blood,' p. 183, regarding the approach of R. Akiva). The latter suggestion is particularly perplexing, because it is logical that this would not allow any deviation from the Biblical law and it certainly cannot explain the changes that the sages brought about in the details of the laws regarding blood in the various halakhic spheres. In addition, from the rejection of the Biblical identification of blood and the soul, there is no necessity of inferring that the early rabbinic sages accepted a dualistic anthropology, whereby the soul has an independent existence.

[86] Commentary of Ramah on Sanhedrin 52b s.v. '*mitzvat ha-neheragin.*'
[87] See Sanhedrin 7:1.
[88] In the discussion of the *Babylonian Talmud* (Sanhedrin 45a) his position is explained as preferring the principle of preventing suffering (her death is hastened by falling naked rather than clothed). But it is more reasonable that his position

disagreement regarding the innovation that the sages brought to the laws of judicial execution, namely prevention of corporeal damage.[89]

This principle is also raised by the *Babylonian Talmud*, which emphasizes in its discussion of beheading that besides decapitation, it is prohibited to damage the body ('pierce it') or to slice it ('cut it in half').[90] This halakhah is also mentioned in tannaitic sources regarding the city of inciters: '[Put the inhabitants of the town] to (*lefi*) the sword' (*Deuteronomy* 13:16)— 'with the cutting edge (*lefiha*) of the sword, so that one does not damage them.'[91]

V. Judicial Execution and Diminishing the Divine Image

1. Abolishing Capital Punishment

The conception that stands at the foundation of beheading in the tannaitic sources requires, at least in the case of murderers, the actualization of the execution. Consequently, it is surprising to find the following famous Mishnah:

> A Sanhedrin that executes once in seven years is called murderous. R. Eleazar b. Azariah states: once in seventy years. R. Tarfon and R. Akiva states: if we were members of the Sanhedrin there would never be executions. R. Simon b. Gamliel states: they would multiply the shedders of blood in Israel (*Makot* 1:10).

After it lays out the penal procedure, the modes of execution and numerous transgressions that receive the death penalty, the *Mishnah* concludes the body of law concerning capital cases (the section that discusses judicial execution) by presenting views according to which the conviction and execution of a person is infrequent, and more accurately, unwanted.[92] The anonymous tanna, R. Eleazar b. Azariah, R. Akiva and R. Tarfon are not actually disagreeing.

---

follows from the traditional position that shaming the convict is part of the execution by stoning. See *Palestinian Talmud* Sanhedrin 6:4 and the following note.

[89] See also the dispute in Sanhedrin 6:3 and particularly Tosefta Sanhedrin 9:6, Zuckermandel, ed., p. 429 and cf. Urbach, 'Courts,' p. 45.

[90] Halbertal, *Revolutions* Ch. 7, n. 24) makes this point.

[91] *Sifre Deuteronomy* 94 Finkelstein, ed., p. 155) and see Tosefta Sanhedrin 14:6 (p. 374): 'One does not execute them with arrows and spears or the head of the sword, but only with the cutting edge, as it states "to the sword."' In the *Mekhilta de-Rabbi Ishmael*, Amalek 1 (p. 181) regarding the war against Amalek, it states: '"By sword" – not to engender shame but to judge them mercifully.'

[92] The tractate of *Makot* was originally part of tractate *Sanhedrin*. See J.N. Epstein, *Introduction to Tannaitic Literature* [Hebrew], (Jerusalem 1957) p. 417; and H. Albeck, *Commentary on the Mishnah: Nezikin* [Hebrew], (Jerusalem 1959) p. 165, 216. The issue of capital crimes begins with chapter 4 of tractate Sanhedrin and continues until the end of tractate *Makkot*.

Organizing their views in ascending order ('once in seven years;' 'once in seventy years;' 'never') is a rhetorical device whose purpose is expressing a fundamental opposition to capital punishment. But one who is conversant with tannaitic law will not be surprised by this *Mishnah*, because the procedural obstacles are such that they prevent conviction for a capital crime.[93] The procedure—which includes *inter alia* the warning of the suspect at the time of the crime and extreme demands in the realm of testimony[94]—is not a product of the concern for killing the innocent; nor is it based on considerations of procedural justice. Rather, it is grounded in the conception that capital punishment is a form of murder and therefore it is prohibited, irrespective of the guilt of the suspect.[95] For our concern, the fact that the view of the tannaim in our Mishnah applies also to the transgression of murder is significant. This is evident from the response of R. Simon b. Gamliel: 'They [i.e., the anonymous tanna and the three previously cited sages] increase the shedding of blood in Israel.' R. Simon b. Gamliel is not the only tanna who expresses this view. In *Midrash Tannaim* (ed. Hoffmann, p. 115) similar views are cited, one in the name of Eliezer:

> 'You must show him no pity' (*Deuteronomy* 19:13). This is a warning that one should not show pity to a murderer, so that one does not declare: 'This one was already killed and what purpose will be served by killing another person.' You will then be negligent in killing him [i.e., the murderer]. Instead, you must kill him [i.e., the murderer]. Aba Hanun in the name of R. Eliezer states: whenever the verse states an unworthy punishment, it declares: 'You must show him no pity. Thus you will purge the blood of the innocent' (*idem*). When you purge the world of murderers you bring goodness to the world.

These views are directed at murderers where there is no doubt regarding their guilt and they seemingly polemicize with the approach of R. Akiva and his colleagues. R. Eliezer and, following him, R. Simon b. Gamliel are not

---

[93] Many scholars have noted this. See, for example, G. F. Moore, *Judaism in the First Centuries of the Christian Era*, (Cambridge, MA 1927-1930) vol. III, p. 187; G. S. Blidstein, 'Capital Puishment in Classical Jewish Discussion,' *Judaism* 14 (1965) [henceforth: Blidstein, 'Capital Punishment'], p. 163; Greenberg, 'Criminal Law,' p. 29; E. P. Sanders, *Judaism, Practice and Belief 63 BCE- 66CE*, (London and Philadelphia 1992) p. 420, 469; A. Kirshenbaum, 'The Place of Punishment in the Jewish Penal Code' [Hebrew], *Iyyunei Mishpat* 13 (1988) pp. 253-273 [henceforth: Kirshenbaum, 'Place'] paragraph 1; and A. Enker, 'Fundamentals in Jewish Penal Law,' [Hebrew] *Mishpatim* 24 (1994) pp. 177-206 [henceforth: Enker, 'Fundamentals'], p. 180.

[94] For a complete list of the obstacles that prevent convicting the suspect and consequently executing him or her, see Lorberbaum, 'Murder,' paragraph 2 and the references cited therein.

[95] See Blidstein, 'Capital Punishment;' compare with Kirshenbaum, 'Place' and Enker, 'Fundamentals.'

prepared to relinquish the social benefit—deterrence and prevention ('purge the world of murderers')—that capital punishment engenders.[96]

2. Murder and Capital Punishment—Diminishing the Image

The conception that lies at the heart of R. Akiva's and R. Tarfon's demurral from capital punishment is implicit, in my estimation, in a number of tannaitic sources (some of them integrated into tractate *Sanhedrin* of the *Mishnah*). For our concerns, the most important of them appears in the *Tosefta* (*Yebamot*, Ch. 8). The following midrash is attributed there to R. Akiva:

> R. Akiva states: whoever spills blood destroys the image; as it states, 'whoever sheds the blood of man, by man shall his blood be shed, for in God's image did He make man.'[97]

From the double meaning of the term 'image' [*demut*]—the figurative God and man—R. Akiva derives that harm to man, who is in God's image, is like harming God or a certain dimension of Him. An act of murder does not just 'destroy' a human being; it also 'destroys' or 'diminishes the image.'[98] The bloodshed has actual consequences in the divine realm, which is not completely divorced from the human realm.[99]

A passage resembling R. Akiva's homily and seemingly inspired by it appears in *Mekhilta de-Rabbi Ishmael*: 'How was the decalogue given? Five on one tablet and five on another. It is written: 'I am the LORD your God''

---

[96] We should note that R. Eliezer and R. Simon b. Gamliel do not base their views regarding the need to kill murderers on the requirement for ritual expiation of the blood. It should also be noted that these tannaim seemingly possessed another law that allowed for the conviction of suspects. See Lorberbaum, 'Murder.'

[97] In order to clarify the interpretation of the verse here I quoted the entire verse. See S. Leiberman, *Tosefta Ki-Feshutah*, Yebamot, New York, p. 74, and the parallel discussions in *Genesis Rabbah* 34:9, Theodor-Albeck, ed., pp. 326-327 and Yebamot 63b; see also *Deuteronomy Rabbah*, S. Lieberman, ed., p. 10.

[98] This is the version in *Genesis Rabbah, idem*.

[99] The interpretation of R. Akiva makes use of the etymological and similarity between the Hebrew words *dam* (blood), *adam* (human being) and *demut* (image) and plays one off another. S. Lieberman notes that *adam* in Galilean Aramaic means blood. [See S. Lieberman, *Ha-Yerushalmi Ki-Feshuto*, (Jerusalem 1983) p. 72.] The appearance of the term *demut* in the interpretation is perhaps not accidental, because in the prooftext verse the word *tselem* (image) appears. It would therefore have been natural to declare 'diminish the *tselem* (image).' Support for this thesis is found in the famous statement of R. Akiva in Avot that is based on this very verse: 'who was created in God's image.' He uses the term *tselem* and not *demut* when he states: 'Beloved is man who was created in [God's] image (*tselem*).' Miller, 'Image,' makes the interesting claim that in Genesis 9:6, the appearance of *tselem* is discordant. In view of the poetic nature of the verse's opening clauses, which plays on the terms *dam* [blood] and *adam* [man], the reader would expect the term *demut*. The choice of the term *tselem* is deliberate, reflecting a polemical intent to break the poetic rhythm.

(*Exodus* 20:2; *Deuteronomy* 5:6) [on one tablet] and parallel to it [on the second tablet] it is written: 'You shall not murder' (*Exodus* 20:12; Deuteronomy 5:16). The scripture teaches that regarding anyone who spills blood, it is as if he diminishes the King's image.'[100] Like R. Akiva's interpretation, this passage also blurs the demarcation between God and human beings and consequently the distinction between the commandments regarding relations with God (the first tablet) and those regarding relations among human beings (the second tablet).[101] Murder is depicted in these Midrashic passages as negative theurgy.[102]

The effects of the act of murder in the divine realm are given expression in another passage from *Mekhilta de-Rabbi Ishmael*.[103] According to this passage, 'the ox that is [to be] stoned [i.e., an ox that has gored a person to death and is therefore to be stoned] defiles the land and causes the Shekhinah [Divine Presence] to depart.'[104] The departure of the Shekhinah here cannot be interpreted as a metaphor for a (volitional) response to the immoral act of the ox or the owner.[105] This passage should be read in the context of the connection that R. Akiva makes between the presence of the Shekhinah in human beings and the fact that human beings are made in God's image.[106] The 'ox that is [to be] stoned,' like all murderers, causes the Shekhinah to depart not so much because of the Shekhinah's disappointment in the immoral character of the murderer, but because of the fact that the Shekhinah dwells in the human being who was murdered and his or her murder brings about its 'diminishment.' The conception that murder causes the Shekhinah to depart is also found in the passage from the *Sifre Numbers* 161 (ed. Horovitz-Rabin p. 222) that we examined previously. There it serves as the reason for the law that requires the execution of the murderer who was caught after the heifer's neck was broken.

It is possible that the conception imbedded in R. Akiva's interpretation is shared, at least partially, with the passage from *Avot de-Rabbi Natan* that was cited previously. The two passages relate to the same Biblical verse (*Genesis* 9:6), R. Akiva explicitly and the *Avot de-Rabbi Natan* passage implicitly. In

---

[100] Ba-Hodesh, Parasha 8, Horovitz-Rabin, ed., p. 233.

[101] To exemplify his view, the sage brings the parable of the king's icon (= the ritual of the idols of the Roman Caesar). On the meaning of this parable see Lorberbaum, 'Image,' Ch. 6, section 2:1.

[102] On the term 'theurgy,' see Lorberbaum, 'Image,' pp. 87-95.

[103] Nezikin 10, Horovitz-Rabin, ed., p. 282.

[104] Therefore, one cannot benefit from it. On spilling of the blood that causes the Shekhinah to depart, see *Sifre Numbers* 160, Horovitz-Rabin, ed., pp. 220, 222.

[105] Compare with N. Zohar, 'Animals as Moral Beings,' [Hebrew] *Mahshevet Hazal* (Haifa 1990) pp. 67-83 [henceforth: Zohar, 'Animals']. For the Biblical context, see Greenberg, 'Criminal Law' pp. 23-24.

[106] See *Genesis Rabbah* 22:2 (Theodor-Albeck, ed., p. 206) on the phrase 'I have gained a male child with the help of the Lord' (*Genesis* 4:1); and see Lorberbaum, 'Image,' Ch. 6, section 2:6.

addition, both make a strong connection between man and God: according to R. Akiva they share an 'image' and *Avot de-Rabbi Natan* declares: 'Adam was the blood of the Holy One.'

It is easy to connect the interpretation of R. Akiva in *Genesis Rabbah* (and its parallels) with his demurral regarding capital punishment in the tractate *Makot*. For if the result of spilling of the blood is lessening the image and the departure of the Shekhinah, there is no difference between a 'permissible' killing (by the court) and a 'prohibited' killing (by the murderer). That is, the execution of the wicked and the killing of the righteous are identical. Any killing of a human being who is constituted in God's image 'chips away' at God and consequently, one should refrain from it.[107] According to this thesis, the roots of the conception that motivates R. Akiva to undermine the death penalty are present in the Bible. The paradox implicit in the justification the Pentateuch provides for capital punishment in the case of murder—creation in the image of God—contains within it the seed for the opposite conclusion. The recognition that one who commits murder 'diminishes the image' leads to the conclusion that 'murder' conducted by the court will also bring about the same effect.

3. Diminishing the Image and Expiation through Blood: Conflict & Resolution

If this conclusion is correct, a profound tension is imbedded in the tractate of *Sanhedrin-Makot*. On the one hand, the Mishnah maintains that the murderer receives death by sword. This death, which, unlike the other types of execution, produces a relatively large amount of corporeal damage, is grounded in the religious demand of expiation for the blood that was shed in the act of murder. In other words, according to the Pentateuch and seemingly according to the tannaim, killing the murderer—and specifically by spilling his blood—is a necessary ritual for purifying the pollutant through the act of murder. Renouncing this ritual prevents the cleansing of the impure 'stain of blood.' The tannaim derive this demand from the language in *Genesis 9:6*: 'Whoever sheds the blood of man by man shall his blood be shed.'

But, on the other hand, the continuation of the tractate includes laws that are grounded in a different, and in certain respects opposite, ideational tendency. The Mishnah records statements according to which one should refrain from capital punishment in general and the execution of murderers in particular. It also creates a penal procedure that prevents the implementation of the death penalty. This legal tendency is based on the notion of *Imago Dei*: in God's image.

If our analysis of the relationship between expiation through the blood of the murderer and the *Imago Dei* according to the tannaim is correct, the conflict is even intensified, because these ideational tendencies and the contrasting laws that are derived from them draw upon interpretations of the

---

[107] On other sources that indicate such a relationship see Lorberbaum 'Image' Ch. 7; *idem*, 'Murder.'

very same notion. The concept of *Imago Dei* establishes a dimension of holiness in the human being, so that any damage inflicted upon that human being necessitates a ritual of expiation. But this notion, according to the tannaim, also necessitates the prohibition of spilling the blood of the murderer, even to the extent of refraining from cleansing the stain that resulted from the act of murder.

Even if we ignore the possible relationship between the ritual demand for expiation with blood and *Imago Dei*, the tension that I have outlined remains. Even if the source of these motifs is located in diverse ideational structures, the Mishnah still combines them into one set of laws—the laws of capital crimes in the Mishnaic tractate of Sanhedrin. In my analysis above, I have refrained from drawing conclusions regarding the meaning that the tannaim have attributed to the stain of blood: is it derived from the Bible? Or has it undergone changes and it is understood as a symbol rather than an objective evil?[108] Whatever the Mishnah's conception of blood and its relationship to God's image, in the struggle between the approach that requires expiation of the victim's blood with the murderer's blood and the conception that the spilling of the blood—even by the court—lessens the image, the latter prevailed.

F. Conclusion

I shall conclude with some preliminary remarks about the relations between the structures of thought reconstructed above from the Hebrew Bible and especially from early rabbinic literature and the modern idea of human dignity. In these remarks I will return in part to some of the observations with which this article began. As I have argued, both the formulation of beheading as a form of capital punishment, which is based on a demand for expiation through the murderer's blood for the shed blood of his victim, and the reticence to perform capital punishment in general—and in the case of a murderer in particular—are outcomes of hermeneutic moves applied to the very same verse (*Genesis* 9:6). It seems to me that these normative inferences are really—despite the contrast between them—two sides of the same coin. As Moshe Greenberg has argued, the concept that human life is sanctified—a concept he views as having originated in the opening chapters of *Genesis*—leads to the normative conclusion that the sole punishment appropriate in response to an act of murder is death.[109] This religio-ethical insight, though, can lead to a conclusion that is its reverse: if human life is sanctified, then capital punishment is ruled out in advance and is not to be applied even to those who commit acts of bloodshed, since even the murderer's life is sanctified.

---

[108] See Zohar, 'Rituals;' *idem*, 'Animals.' In my mind, it is not necessary to assume that the development that we have depicted was possible due to parallel changes in their conception of blood from mythic-objective to symbolic.

[109] M. Greenberg, 'Criminal Law.'

It is easy to see how these two opposite normative responses spring from the very same insight. It is also easy to see how other anthropological perceptions—such as those common in the ancient Near East and the Greco-Roman world—give rise to normative conclusions that are entirely different.[110]

However, it is not only that these opposite normative conclusions embody the concept of the sanctity of life; the mythic structures of thought on which they are founded bear this basic idea within them. Blood, according to the Bible and early rabbinic sources, is unique in comparison to any other earthly element or material: it is identified in these literary sources with life itself. This is the source of its dangerousness and of its power to cleanse and atone. The unique status of blood in these ancient sources can easily be translated into a claim for the supreme value of human life, a value that has, in Kant's terms, no market price. Can the outlook not be seen as an ancient mythic stratum from which there developed, centuries later, the concept of the sanctity of life that is at the core of the idea of human dignity? As for the idea of *Imago Dei*, this argument is even clearer. It would be reasonable to argue, then, that the understanding upon which the idea of the sanctity of life and the idea of human dignity are founded lies at the base of these mutually intertwined structures of thought.

It can be argued, of course, that the modern idea of human dignity has nothing at all in common with these ancient thought structures. According to this line of thought, the idea of human dignity is an ideational revolution that has its origins in modern anthropology, metaphysics, and ethics of the school of Kant and other Enlightenment thinkers. This idea represents a new beginning. The apparent similarity that links the concepts of the sanctity of blood and *Imago Dei* with the modern idea of human dignity should not deceive us; it is merely superficial. It seems to me that the justification for such a stance is primarily that the arguments (a term inappropriate, of course, for ancient mythic thought structures) underlying these worldviews are entirely different. Therefore, the claim that they are somehow linked is baseless.

On this point, however, we can have recourse to the outlook developed by Paul Ricoeur, with which we began. Ricoeur, it will be recalled, argued that 'the symbol gives rise to thought.'[111] He explains:

> Understanding of symbols can play a part in the movement towards the point of departure (...) This does not mean that we could go back to a primitive naivete. In every way, something has been lost, irremediably lost: immediacy of belief.(...) But we modern men can aim at a second naivete in and through criticism. (...) It is by *interpreting* that we can *hear* again. Thus

---

[110] See the articles by M. Weinfeld cited in notes 2, 6 above, and those of M. Greenberg cited in notes 5, 6 above.

[111] Paul Ricoeur, *Symbolism of Evil* [see note 7 above], p. 348.

> it is in hermeneutics that the symbol's gift of meaning and the endeavor to understand by deciphering are knotted together.[112]

If philosophy needs myth to serve as a starting point for reflection and speculation, myth too, for its part, does not entirely lack theoretical foundations. Myth, Ricoeur emphasizes, is always a symbol as well. The symbol, he claims, 'aims at something beyond itself and stands for that something.... It is by living in the first meaning that I am led by it beyond itself. The symbolic meaning is constituted in and by the literal meaning which effects the analogy in giving the analogue.' Yet 'unlike a comparison that we *consider* from outside,' continues Ricoeur, 'the symbol is the movement of the primary meaning which makes us participate in the latent meaning and thus assimilates us to that which is symbolized without our being able to master the similitude intellectually.'[113] After offering a basis for these arguments, Ricoeur tries to point to the connection among the various forms taken by concepts and symbols of evil from the dawn of Western civilization to the modern era.

Ricoeur's philosophical hermeneutics, if it is valid, can serve as a reply to the counter-argument presented above. Through it, we can point to connections of a similar sort between the structures of thought we have reconstructed in this study and the modern idea of human dignity. This philosophical-hermeneutic process will show that a central component of the modern idea of human dignity is precisely a conceptualization of an ancient mythic, theological, and ethical insight that has its roots in the culture represented in the literary sources treated above. This conceptualization may bring about deep changes in that insight. It may, among other things, cause its normative implications to be different. Nonetheless, the conceptualization is *of* the ancient insight, and the two therefore share a common element. As I noted at the outset, the full and detailed development of this philosophical-hermeneutic process is a subject for another work. It is my hope that the basis for such a study, reconstructing ancient structures of thought in detail, has been appropriately laid out here.

---

[112] *Ibid.*, pp. 348-351.
[113] *Ibid.*, pp. 15-16.

CAN ETHICAL MAXIMS BE DERIVED FROM THEOLOGICAL CONCEPTS OF HUMAN DIGNITY?

Dietrich Ritschl

In the following I shall argue that 'human dignity' is not a legal concept (it is this at best in a figurative sense), nor, strictly speaking, is it an ethical concept. Moreover, I want to show that derivations from broad concepts in theological and philosophical ethics as well as in jurisprudence present special difficulties. The difficulties are of a logical nature. The problem, however, is that these difficulties can be ignored and, in fact, they usually are disregarded by authors in Jewish and Christian thought as well as by lawyers when they use broad concepts such as Human Dignity in a merely appellative sense, claiming nonetheless, that derivations from them are possible.

On the other hand, it cannot be denied that Human Dignity as a concept—regardless whether its roots are seen primarily in the Hebrew Bible, in Stoic philosophy, in Hobbes, Locke or in the later Enlightenment—plays an enormously important role in ethics, both socio-political and medical, in constitutional law and in every-day-language statements and appeals concerning their value, inexchangeability and autonomy of the individual human being.[1] In such general appeals the term is frequently used parallel to 'sanctity of life' which—contrary to wide-spread opinion—is not of theological origin. Admittedly the term is broad and encompasses a variety of values and rights, all of which have received new relevance and significance after the horrors of World War II and the atrocities of the Nazi period. It governs implicitly the United Nations Declaration of Human Rights and a large number of conventions and pacts since 1948 and it appears in the preambles of ever so many constitutions. This history need not be recapitulated here. Our point is merely this: how do concepts such as Human Dignity

---

[1] M. Hailer, D. Ritschl, 'The General Notion of Human Dignity and the Specific Arguments in Medical Ethics,' *Philosophy and Medicine*, vol. 52, K. Bayertz, ed., (Dordrecht 1996) pp. 91-106.

function in theological and philosophical ethics if it is the case that a derivation of ethical maxims from mere concepts is difficult or impossible? And correspondingly, does the concept of Human Dignity in Jurisprudence suffer the same limitations or can genuine legal contents be attributed to it so that, in the end, it can be called a legal concept?

I. Theologians and Lawyers and Their Concepts

It has often been remarked that theologians and lawyers think in similar ways. Indeed, as distinct from philosophers, they work with given texts to which they ascribe certain degrees of normativity. Thus they both speak of 'exegesis' and 'dogmatics.' They both know of the perils of positivism or fundamentalism with regard to the interpretations of their texts. Moreover, they both work with concepts, clusters of concepts and theories. Both are interested in the practical application and usefulness of their interpretations, arguments and conclusions. But this is how far the external similarities go.

In order to understand the location and function of concepts within a system of thought one will have to distinguish between primary and secondary (even tertiary) language. Although primary, everyday language does make use of simple concepts, i.e., words which 'conceptualize,' for instance, objects with three edges as triangles or phenomena such as theft and murder as crime, it must be said that complex concepts constitute another level of language. Interrelations between concepts, not to speak of their hierarchical structures, cannot be expressed in pre-reflective, primary language. However, by frequent use within fixed groups of speakers ('language games') concepts do tend to become autonomous, i.e., they are used without the awareness of their linguistic and historical origin. The language of theology (and with it the synagogue and the church) is a telling example. Likewise, the legal profession often treats legal concepts as though they were part of a basic, primary language. (This phenomenon can be explained, but I shall not go into details here).[2]

Moreover, one will have to distinguish between different classes of concepts. Human Dignity, for instance, can be called a 'frame concept' since it embraces sub-concepts which may or may not always be part of what is meant when the term is used. In any case, concepts of any class are gained by induction from a wider context, mostly one of primary language or at least a kind of language which is prior to the inductive operation from which stem the concepts. This observation can be tested or illustrated within minutes by reflecting on concepts such as 'fear,' 'joy,' 'illness/health,' 'freedom/liberty,' 'right/obligation,' 'peace,' etc. Obviously, these concepts have in common the

---

[2] On the question of the genealogy of legal concepts and their function, see, e.g., H.L.A. Hart, *The Concept of Law* (Oxford 1967); K. Engisch, *Einführung in das juristische Denken*, 8th edition (Stuttgart 1983); K. Larenz, *Methodenlehre der Rechtswissenschaft*, 6th edition (Berlin 1991); R. Zippelius, *Einführung in die juristische Methodenlehre*, 6th edition (Munich 1994).

delineation of different states of human existence; 'Human dignity,' of course, belongs to this class. But our test also works with more formal concepts such as 'rule,' 'punishment,' 'sanction,' 'duty,' etc. Here we refer to a different class of concepts but they too depend on preceding language in form of narrations, reports, summaries of conditions or events, cited texts, and so forth. In short: concepts are gained by induction.[3] This applies in a special way to concepts concerning the '*condition humaine*,' i.e., anthropological concepts. This is not to say, however, that concepts are identical with mere summaries of what can also be said in primary language, although they have some characteristics in common with them. Nor are they abstractions, as, for instance, 'furniture' is an abstraction of the enumeration of chairs, tables, cupboards, etc. Concepts—of all classes—carry with them not merely the name of what they entail, but also the indication of what is the content and meaning of that which they entail or embrace. Thus they are the bricks with which theories can be constructed; and theories, of course, are not abstractions but rather explanatory devices with which problems can be described and solved. (This is true with regard to theology, jurisprudence and the sciences).

Mindful of Karl Popper (and many others, of course), we must remember the importance of the difference between induction and deduction when demonstrations or proofs are at stake. It is only derivations by way of deduction that provide—in 'hard logics'—unambiguous results. This is not to say that induction is a useless procedure. On the contrary, communication between human beings would be reduced to the mere exchange of signals (as between animals) if the inductive construction of concepts were not possible.

I will not venture to discuss the logics of deduction in jurisprudence. It seems to me, however, that lawyers will have to aim at logically stringent deductions although they know that their concepts were gained by induction. Subsumtion then—one of the most fascinating logical operations in the eyes of outsiders—is an 'induction backwards' in the mode of deduction. This operation presupposes, it seems to me, a legal 'system'. Here lies a fundamental difference between jurisprudence and (theological) ethics. Theology, at least in its present shape since the end of the great medieval or post-Reformation systems, does not claim to be a coherent system of this kind. In fact, it is suspicious of symmetrical interrelations and conclusions. (Jewish tradition never embraced such ideals).

Human dignity is a concept gained by an inductive operation. For biblically oriented theology, the term (*kavod*) cannot be understood as apart from the texts, narratives, memories and experiences of the authors who first

---

[3] I omit here a discussion of the medieval controversy over 'universalia': the 'realists,' of course, claimed that universal ideas precede concrete manifestations or things, e.g., the idea of a table—the 'concept'—precedes any existing table and will also survive a time when there are no tables around; by the same token, 'justice,' 'righteousness,' 'goodness,' etc., precede any concrete just or good person or situation.

used the term. In other words, the term is embedded in preceding texts (or oral traditions). Any deduction from it, disregarding this embeddedness, is in danger of a circular conclusion, i.e., of reading into it what one wants to deduce from it later.

Professor David Kretzmer[4] cites an interesting quotation from Justice Shamgar:

> Human dignity, in the constitutional context, is a legal concept, but its practical expression lies in the daily human experience and in the relationship towards the individual of the state and society, including the courts, in which he lives. (...) forge his personality freely, (...) make free choices, not to be enslaved by arbitrary compulsion, to receive fair treatment by every authority...

Three points are of interest here: (1) Human Dignity is called a 'legal concept,' provided the term (the concept) is seen in the constitutional context (i.e., the Israeli Constitution); (2) the term (the concept) has a 'practical expression,' i.e., it manifests its content in daily human experiences and relationships; and (3) therefore, Justice Shamgar can continue by listing the various dimensions of personal freedom which are enjoyed by the individual whose Human Dignity is respected.

In another quotation by Professor Kretzmer,[5] Justice Barak states, 'The contents of the term 'human dignity' will be determined on the basis of the views of the enlightened public in Israel and on the background of the purpose of the Basic Law: Human Dignity and Liberty.....' What is more, statements by other significant authors speak of 'dignity, honor and glory' (of Israel as a nation) with direct or indirect reference to *kavod*. It was not surprising, therefore, to find in Professor Kretzmer's paper, as well as in the presentation by Dr. Orit Kamir,[6] the critical observation that one can 'read into' a concept such as Human Dignity certain contents. According to her paper the Supreme Court until about 1980 has done exactly this by claiming that the word *kavod* had been filled with contents of a socio-political character that were known beforehand.

My point here is not a critique of the Israeli lawyers or Courts. I merely take the quotations as examples for what has happened to 'frame-concepts' such as Human Dignity in many countries. The procedures mentioned illustrate the problem which was discussed in the first part of my paper: after, in a first step, filling by induction the concept of Human Dignity with certain concepts, a deduction from the concept, in a second step, produces the legitimation for these contents. My point is that this operation unfortunately is found widely in

---

[4] Quoted in the draft of his paper on 'Human Dignity in Israeli Jurisprudence' for this volume.

[5] *Ibid.*

[6] O. Kamir, 'Honor and Dignity Cultures: The Case of *Kavod* and *Kvod Ha-Adam* in Israeli Society and Law' in this volume.

theological ethics, possibly also in philosophically grounded moral theory and in jurisprudence.

The theological part of the discussion among Israeli lawyers and philosophers is of special interest to me as a theologian since the emphasis on *kavod* in Jewish thought is fully paralleled by the Western and Eastern Christian reference to the *Imago Dei* concept in relation to the concept of Human Dignity. Indeed, the two are identical. The two concepts, however, have not fallen down from heaven, but require a knowledge of the context, the 'stories' in which they are embedded.[7]

---

[7] The exploration of the etymological meaning of words or their root was of great importance to scholars of past generations. Words will have to be understood primarily within the context in which they appear. Thus the root *k-v-d* does not provide much cognitive gain. It indicates weight (in a physical sense) and importance, as contrasted with *k-l-l* (lightness, unimportance). The word *kavod* is used in the Torah and in the Psalms with regard to God and less frequently, to human beings. The *kavod* of God denotes the presence of God in the midst of his people (x. 29, 45f., 40, 34). In I. Reg. 8, 10 *kavod* fills the house of God. *Kavod* can even be attached to the throne (I. Sam. 2, 8), to garments (Ex. 28, 2.40) and to the crown (Job 19, 9 with reference to the man Job, or Ps. 8, 6—one of passages important in our present discussion). The famous covenant passage Ex. 24, describes how the *kavod* of God manifests itself on Sinai and is like a consuming fire, seen by the Israelites. These and many other usages of the term are embedded in stories which can be told and retold. Another usage is found in the wisdom books. Here *kavod* can occur in a 'profane' sense as 'moderation' and 'virtue' (Prov. 20, 3; 11, 16) or 'humility' (15, 33); here it denotes the dignity of a virtuous person. However, the term is also used with reference to the office and authority of a person, the king (Prov. 25, 2), the priest (28, 2. 40), the wise man (Prov. 3, 35 as distinct from the fool, 26, 1). Ps. 8, 6—the chief text in several papers for this conference—uses *kavod* in the context of king/kingship as is clearly indicated by the regal metaphors *atar* (crown, v. 6), *mashal* (investing as ruler, v. 7) etc. The metaphors referring to the kingship in this text, refer, of course, to God. The appointment of man to the dominion over creation is, obviously a direct parallel to Gen 1, 26 *ff* and this is based upon the *Imago Dei* claim which is expressed there as well as in Gen. 5, 1 *ff* and 9, 6). The Hebrew Bible does not come back to this concept very often, rather it is in the Ancient Near East that we find numerous references to the 'image of God' – concept. Although these extra-biblical traditions may be reflected in Ps. 8, the remarkable difference is that, while in the ancient Orient kings were the bearers of the 'image of God,' Ps. 8 (as well as the other passages cited) extend the image-concept to all people; this is explicit in v. 5. Moreover, the biblical passages, especially Ps. 8, contrast this astonishing appointment or investiture with the lowliness of human beings, thus maintaining a dialectical tension, to use a modern term. What this excursus on *kavod* means to show is the fact that one must not read into it what is not contained in the narratives (and texts alluded to) on which it is based. It seems clear that one should not read into the *kavod* passage of Ps. 8 the idea of a politically definable concept of 'glory' nor of a special place of Israel among the nations. (The special destiny of Israel among the nations is, of course, referred to in many other passages, but this is not the point in Gen. 1, 26 *ff* and Ps. 8).

II. Ethics and Law – Concentric Circles

The complex question of the relation between law and morality as it is usually called,[8] can of course not be discussed here. Let it suffice to observe that it is quite moving to see how great jurists, e.g., Gustav Radbruch, toward the later decades in their lives, became increasingly aware of the ethical grounding of legal systems, of the law. This has also been reported of some great American judges who had started out with naive natural-law concepts of legal positivism in their earlier years.

In the following the relation between ethics and law will be discussed merely in connection with the question of a proper understanding of Human Dignity as a starting point for either ethical or legal statements (or both). If it is a 'concept,' as was demonstrated above, it consists of elements which stem from descriptive language, in the case of *kavod*, e.g., the creation story, the account of God's covenant with Israel, of regal metaphors transferred from God to man, etc. Now, can such a concept be an ethical concept in the strict sense of the word? Modern analytical philosophers, referring back to David Hume, reiterate that one cannot derive ought-sentences from is-sentences. And ethics—much like law—must necessarily be rooted in ought-sentences. Transgressing this rule is, as is well known, called 'naturalistic fallacy'. In rabbinic thought, it is clear that *haggada* (the telling of stories, events etc.) consists of another class of sentences than *halachic* advises, admonitions, rules etc. What now is the place of *kavod*, or, even in Stoic or Enlightenment thought, of Human Dignity in ethics?

The difficulties in finding stringent answers to this question invites the thought that Human Dignity should not be called an ethical concept. Rather it is an (theological-) anthropological frame of reference or frame-concept with which one can set up certain helpful demarcation lines within which ethics, and possibly law, can and should operate. The problem is all the more interesting when one considers that Human Dignity is a notion which precedes Human Rights, i.e., that Human Rights are a juridical concretization of the more general concept of Human Dignity. Human Dignity as a concept belongs to a pre-ethical, pre-political and pre-juridical realm.[9]

In my work in medical ethics I have experienced that, if the general character of Human Dignity as a 'frame-concept' is not seen, the following unfortunate misconceptions can emerge:

---

[8] Cf. Chs. VIII and IX in H.L.A. Hart (FN2 above); J. Rawls, *A Theory of Justice*, (Cambridge, MA 1971) chs. VII-IX; Lon L. Fuller, *The Morality of Law* (Yale Univ. Press 1969); J. Habermas, *Theorie des kummunikativen Handelns*, 2 vols., (Frankfurt 1981). The theological ethicist W. Huber has presented a voluminous work on the issue of law and ethics, *Gerechtigkeit und Recht*, (Gütersloh 1996), which deserves the attention not only of ethicists but especially of jurists.

[9] The following points are listed in the article mentioned in fn. 1.

1. The generalization of the concept as though it were not an anthropological principle but an ethical or even legal criterion from which specific conclusions can be deduced. I mention as an example the critical reactions of the media and the general public to the crash-tests with human corpses, including the corpses of babies, in simulated automobile accidents conducted by the Department of Forensic Medicine in the Univeristy of Heidelberg ('Such tests are a violation of Human Dignity').

2. The squeezing of the concept of Human Dignity into quasi legal terminology as though Human Dignity were not the platform or frame of reference for Human Rights but were a summary of Human Rights in itself. The broad concept of Human Dignity here serves as a vague substitute for legal language, when in fact the constitution or any part of positive law should have its say. One may mention as an example the often heard criticism of 'unnecessary prolongation of life' by means of modern medical technology.

3. The general emotional appeal to Human Dignity in form of a 'knock-down-argument' in socio-political and especially medical-ethical fields of problems, indicating that a rational analysis and argumentative discourse has not taken place or is avoided in favor of what seems to be a foregone conclusion and all-dominating assertion.

I take the liberty of mentioning another personal experience. Helping to set up a medical ethical institute at the Buddhist Mahidol University in Bangkok (a medical school) I had the opportunity to encounter ethical concepts within an anthropological frame of reference totally alien to us from the Jewish and Christian traditions. It was difficult to translate the karma-oriented anthropological prosuppositions into our Jewish-Christian or Western concepts of the meaning of human life, of human value and the inexchangeablity of the human individual. However, when it came to concrete answers to medical-ethical questions, we were not that far away from one another. When the leaders of Mahidol Medical School were our guests in Heidelberg on two occasions, we were able to deepen our mutual understanding. This was true despite the fact that the legal situation in Thai medical ethics is deplorable: Thailand still has a totally outdated health legislation imported from France at the beginning of this century.

Anthropological concepts, ideas or ideals, it seems, surround ethical theories and concepts without necessarily influencing them in a direct manner. And if it is true that legal systems, at least their foundations, are related to ethical principles and convictions, it follows that we can think of an—however asymmetrical—array of circles in which the outer circle represents basic anthropological (or theological-philosophical) assertions, the next circle ethical ought-sentences and thirdly (perhaps reaching in part outside the other two)—the law.

The relation between the three realms is loose largely because of the naturalistic fallacy problem; in plain language: anthropological assertions do not tell people how to behave. On the other hand, ethical as well as legal assertions have to have in common the existence of well functioning and well grounded ought-sentences. The origin of the imperative (you ought to!) lies in 'someone' who is entitled to promulgate obligations or oughts and whose authority is regarded legitimate. (I. Kant distinguished between categorical and hypothetical ought-sentences). Lawyers may and will refer to the legislature, the law-giver, even if such reference does not solve the fundamental problem of the foundation of law.[10] But what will ethicists do? Quite a number of distinctly different answers have been given to this question in Western philosophy and theology. It cannot be the purpose of this paper to enumerate and discuss them. Our interest is focussed on the question of the place of Human Dignity both in ethics and in jurisprudence. If this concept is foremost an anthropological description or assertion, (in the case of the *kavod*-concept grounded in descriptive language), how can it be turned into an imperative which is articulated in performative language? Formally speaking, the transition from anthropological to ethical language depends on an authority or institution or a society which claims: 'If this is the status of human beings, the *condition humaine*, you must (or let us) behave accordingly!' In other words, someone or something—and be it the conscience of an individual, or society as a whole—will have to establish an analogy between the description and the behaviour of those described.[11] Only then can Human Dignity operate as a frame-reference with which—by analogy—concrete ethical and, perhaps, ultimately legal statements can be measured, tested and justified. The analogy is between the description of a status and the form of a behavior. It is—logically speaking—an *analogia attributionis*, in this that the attributes of the status are transferred to the behaviour. The 'agent' instigating the analogy is the root and grounding of all ethics in general and of the applicability of the concept of Human Dignity in particular.

---

[10] I have found helpful the somewhat dated collection of classical essays on this question, A. Kaufmann, ed., *Die ontologische Begrundung des Rechts*, Wege der Forschung XXII (Darmstadt 1965).

[11] Take as an example New Testament passages in which Jesus is reported to have told stories with a clear ethical bent, describing a human situation from everyday life and concluding by: 'Go and do likewise!'

III. Four Different Notions of Human Dignity and Their Consequences

The following typology lists basic anthropological assertions which manifest themselves in distinctively different notions of Human Dignity.

1. The Physis-Concept

Typical of Stoic philosophy was the thought that the whole cosmos is penetrated by the reason and rationality of God, the *logos*. Nothing in the world is categorically alien to the rest of the world. Everything is interconnected with all the rest and it is steered and interpenetrated by the *logos*: nature, human beings, social communities and even God. The ethical task is to recognize the laws of *physis* in all the realms that constitute the world and to adapt themselves to them since they represent the unchangeable will of the godhead. In this Stoic philosophy differed from the basic ideals of Plato and Aristotle whose concepts of society were distinctly non-egalitarian. The later Roman Stoics gave classical Stoic concepts and even stronger anthropological and ethical edge. One often quotes in this connection Seneca: *homo est sacra res homini*, a program that led to the demand for the abolition of slavery. This Stoic notion of the inalienability of Human Dignity exercised a significant influence on later Western thought. One may think of Pico della Mirandola, even of Calvin (whose first published work was on Seneca) and others. But it is certainly not only individual authors who cling to the Stoic notion of Human Dignity: the *opinio communis* today is more Stoic than people realize. The average journalist or politician today unhesitatingly says that human beings have Dignity 'by nature'. It is noteworthy, however, that the *physis*-concept of Human Dignity is axiomatic in nature. The 'agent' who establishes the analogy between the status of the human to his or her behavior is presupposed but not identified.

2. The Biblical Tradition

Whatever generalizations we may justly articulate about the anthropological assertions implicit in the Bible, one cannot see any consensus with the Stoic idea that God and the world interpenetrate in an ontological or structural sense. They are distinct entities. And, what is more, as the passages Gen. 1, 2 6 and Ps. 8, referred to above, indicate, the position of human beings over against animals, plants, the air and soil of the world we live in, is one of 'domination,' mirroring in a certain way the distinction between God and the world. We can leave undiscussed here the tragic abuse of this understanding in the ruthless exploitation of our world, justified by those key-passages in the Bible (cf. The angry critique of Jean Amery). It was only recently that these passages were read in an entirely different light, namely asserting the stewardship and responsibility of humans over against the non-human parts of creation. Be it as it may, the biblical books do not conceive of Human Dignity as something inherent within the human, rather it is a dignity imparted to the human being by God, i.e., humans, made 'in the image' of God, receive his dignity (*kavod*) by being assured that it is theirs. It is a reality that does not reside automatically, as it were, within the individual. On the basis of such biblical understanding, it would be proper to say to any human being, regardless whether an accepted and successful member of society or a prisoner, a mentally disturbed or senile person: 'You are a person with Human Dignity because you are being told so and we will treat you accordingly.' Or, as Justice Elon is quoted in one of the Conference's papers: :The meaning of Human Dignity is not to shame and degrade the divine image in man'.

3. Human Dignity by Means of Treaty

Thomas Hobbes and John Locke are to be mentioned here. They tie their understanding of Human Dignity to the state and to the nature of society. But while Hobbes maintained that the natural status of human existence was cruel and that a strong, absolute state would have to be created to control the aggressiveness of humans, Locke had a more optimistic assessment of the natural status of the human and to human life prior to the existence of states and laws. Still, they both saw individual dignity and rights as prior to any social structure, agreement or set of rules, either to be watched over by the state (Hobbes) or to be safeguarded by a contract to provide such protection (Locke). In any case, the actualisation of Human Dignity is vulnerable and depends upon willful actions of society and is to be guarded by political and social institutions. Here we discover a hidden parallel to the biblical understanding that humans do not possess inherently or naturally qualities such as Dignity or Human Rights but that they depend on certain steps taken by society to have those rights imparted to them. However, both Hobbes and Locke operate with the prosupposition that the destiny of the human race is not destruction or extinction. (This, too, is a parallel to the biblical concept of covenant, and there was a kinship between John Locke and Scottish parliamentarism and later the authors of the American Constitution who recognized in his thoughts their own roots in the convenanters' tradition). In our time, it is John Rawls in his *A Theory of Justice* who reconstructs the basis of society by referring back to a hypothetical primordial state of human existence. Humans need principles, rules and structures in order to safeguard equality and a relative stability of justice.

4. 'Never only as a Means...'

I. Kant criticizes sharply the classical theological foundations of the concept of Human Dignity although in elevating the human race above nature he confirms one of its basic assertions. It is human freedom which indicates and guarantees the prominent and elevated status of the human being over against nature. The finest freedom is to follow the moral law, the second formulation of which is summarized in the well-known phrase 'act so as to treat humanity never only as a means but always also as an end' and that Human Dignity consists precisely in this freedom in which humans are different from everything non-human. The autonomy of the human being is manifest in this freedom. Kant replaces the classical theological *Imago Dei* concept with the idea of an endowment of the human being with reason, a reasoning power that enables humans to exercise freedom and to follow the moral imperative. 'Never only as a means...' does not prohibit the employment of people for work, but we must, under all circumstances and always, even if we employ or 'use' other people, see in them an end in themselves and treat them accordingly. – It is interesting to note that Kant's rather formal ethics places the weight in the discussion on Human Dignity on the one who treats others, not on those who claim rights for themselves.

This typology shows that the concept of Human Dignity is capable of receiving a remarkable variety of contents each depending on anthropological presuppositions or 'creeds.' This is why I treated with such great caution the notion of 'concept' in Part I of this paper. Thus the employment of the loaded concept 'Human Dignity' in United Nations texts and in countless pacts, constitutions and appeals presents a hidden variety of contents and therefore a disturbingly ambiguous situation. For it is quite obvious that all four types mentioned above are represented in contemporary references to Human Dignity. And it is for this reason that in one of my fields of work, in medical ethics, the notion of Human Dignity words at best as a negative demarcation line in very general terms. Ethical answers can seldom be derived from it. (There are exceptions when the problem is of such enormity and also clarity that a violation of any understanding of Human Dignity serves as an unambiguous warning; but medical ethical problems usually are not of this kind).[12]

IV. Human Dignity by Impartation

Our deliberations so far have shown that Human Dignity as a concept is not a legal one, even though it may be used as such, but that it is a frame-reference in ethics, based on an anthropological or religious creed. And it is also clear that no concept of Human Dignity exists without being grounded in a creed. The history of abuses of the idea of Human Dignity shows certain perils of some and advantages of other such groundings. It would be advantageous, it seems to me, to resort to concepts of Human Dignity which forego ontological and quasi empirical assertions about an inherent dignity of humans and of

---

[12] In a medical ethical expertise which I had to write for the Federal Ministry of Health in Bonn on a new therapy for morbus Parkinson (the transplantation of aborted fetal brain tissue in the brain of Parkinson patients in order to reactivate the Dopamin production), the concept of Human Dignity was not applicable as part of an ethical argument in any way whatsoever. On the other hand, it cannot be denied that in dealing with the fetuses as well as their mothers, Human Dignity is very much at stake!

humanity. Here the conclusion is only too tempting that humans differ in the degree of worth and value, that some have forfeited their dignity and rights— e.g., terrorists, criminals—and that certain nations or races should be elevated above others. Far more useful and philosophically tenable seems to me the contention that Human Dignity is not automatically inherent in humans, as it were, but that it is imparted by others by speaking and acting. In other words, there has to be someone who tells me that I have Human Dignity, and by telling me and by acting in accordance with this pronouncement Human Dignity is imparted. Such impartation is not left to the arbitrary decision of the person who is speaking and acting toward another human being. Nor is such impartation tied to any moral assessment of the value of another person, thus resembling the most inhumane distinction between 'life worth living' and 'worthless life' which led to the mass euthanasia and extermination practices during the Nazi time. The mere belonging of a human being to the species suffices to speak of a legitimate and necessary axiom that whoever deals with this being is to impart Human Dignity upon it. (A parallel consequence: in treating an animal cruelly, one calls into question one's own Human Dignity). One may call such an axiom a creed and, indeed, this is what adherence to the biblical tradition would hold, although, it is evident that one need not be a Jew or a Christian in order to concur with this understanding of Human Dignity by impartation. The impartation is unconditional, although this does not mean that the recipient cannot be punished in case he has committed a crime. (The punishment, however, will have to correspond to the impartation of Human Dignity). Nor does it mean that the dignity which is to be imparted upon another person automatically contributes to the solution of ethical or legal problems. It often works negatively by establishing demarcation lines not to be transgressed.

The social dimension of the concept of Human Dignity advocated here can also be called a dialogical concept. Human Dignity is, in this frame, a concept inseparably connected with the relationship between people. With this we indeed come into the vicinity of J. Rawl's or J. Habermas' concepts. Or, let us turn the question around: What would happen if we were to dispense altogether with a Human Dignity concept based on such dialogical-relational creed? We would either end up with an arbitrary situation ethics or a badly legalised system of ethics. And for jurisprudence operating with a legal system not ultimately grounded in ethics and in anthropological creeds, all that would be left is legal positivism.

HUMAN DIGNITY IN A RABBINICAL PERSPECTIVE

Chana Safrai

The Rabbinical Literature is primarily a religious corpus, committed to Divine teachings and their interpretation. At the base of its teachings and writings lies the Scripture and the convictions of those who stand in its direct line of adherence, obligated to fulfill its commandments within their communities of faith. Dignity or rather 'the Dignity' (*ha-kavod*) is one of the official attributes of God in their language.[1] Its meaning vacillates between the abstract 'dignity,' and the more concrete higher status and respect that are due to the upper hierarchical entities within any social structure. Thus, intrinsic in the Rabbinical system of thought is a concept of dignity that contradicts any attempt for the pledge of an independent, sanctified, absolute principle of human dignity. Human dignity in rabbinical perspective derives its definition of dignity from the higher divine dignity, and as such is also subordinated. Furthermore, from the very beginning, the Rabbis understood their function within the community, and presented their teachings as a communal factor, investing them with a sense of self-respect, value, right and dignity above any particular individual inclination. This created an inner ladder of rights and dignity, in which the individual—man or woman—is at least twice subordinated. *kvod ha-makom* (dignity of God) takes priority over *kvod ha-briot* (dignity of the community or the many), and thus is surely superior to *kvod ha-adam* (human dignity of the individual).

The ability to discuss human rights or human dignity in the modern sense of the words is derived from an ideology based not on a humanistic perspective, but rather from an epistemological human sensitivity found

---

[1] King of Honor *Psalm* 24:17; Cloud of Honor *Exodus* 16:10; Tabernacle of Honor Jalkut Simoni 363. This expression is biblically implied, but is found in late Rabbinic literature, Chair of Honor *Jeremiah* 17:12. For Rabbinic use of Honor as a divine concept see: Tosefta Rosh Hashanah, 2:13 AdRN I II Ch. 1, p. 1, and many others.

already in the Biblical message. The Divine mission is portrayed in His people, and, without them, He might have no standing in His own world.[2] This role of the community of believers gave many rabbis in the first centuries of the Christian Era (the founding period of the Rabbinical or Jewish tradition) sensitivity for human aspects in their religious understanding, particularly those who followed the tradition attributed to the school of Hillel. They developed tools and formulations, and articulated regulations touching upon the subjects of human rights, dignity and freedoms.

I. The Expression of Human Dignity in Rabbinical Sources

In this context, it is of interest to investigate who are regarded as candidates for dignity in rabbinical language, and whether these candidates contain any of the accepted qualities that pertain to human rights or human dignity.

Two major issues seem to present themselves. The first is a careful differentiation between respect/honor due to status or social hierarchy and human dignity. The second is religious formulas that are, in themselves, either indifferent, alien or opposed to the concept of human dignity, though they might, under certain situations, turn into proper human dignity.

1. Concepts of 'Kavod'

The obvious expression in this literature is no doubt the title chosen for this volume, *kavod*. Just as in its equivalent in English, it stands for both dignity in its most abstract and lofty meaning as well as the most degenerated hierarchical concept of status and demand for subordination. For the sake of the present discussion, expressions of *kavod* that refer to the respect of parents, teachers, elders, and high priests have been discounted. Similarly, we refrain from the concept of honor of the dead, and with it respect or honor of bones, as it is dealt with elsewhere in this volume. The respect or possibly dignity of the bride, the poor, women, the community, the majority, must be included and analyzed, as well as more religious concepts like the respect of the Sabbath or the holidays, as they pertain to human obligation.

i. *Kvod ha-Adam*—Human Dignity

When man was created he had a sting or a tail like an animal; but due to his human dignity, God took it away from him to distinguish him from all other animals,[3] claims R. Juda. Nonetheless, in previous research it has been noted that the term Adam in Rabbinical literature could mean human and humanity, but in more than thirty percent of the cases it is applied to Jewish men alone, quite often excluding females and non-Jews. Furthermore, discourse interprets

---

[2] *Exodus* 32:11-12.
[3] *Genesis* Raba 14:10.

many of the neutral texts as Jewish male exclusive, rather than inclusive.[4] As a result, it turns out to be the honor of Israel rather than a plea for human rights or human dignity. The Rabbis explain the biblical case of the fallen woman (*Sota*) as special Divine favor because 'God pays attention to the honor/dignity of Israel.'[5] In this case, however, the woman is put to shame and her basic human dignity is violated. Thus, in Rabbinical terminology, human dignity refers to Israel—the males in Israel—and it infringes on female dignity.

At the end of the Temple period, Rabban Yohanan b. Zakkai canceled the entire ritual of *Sota*. The tradition maintains once again a human cause: *Masherabu haManafim* (once there were too many adulterers). This act surely enhanced human rights and dignity, not merely for the poor suspected women, but for the entire social structure.[6]

ii. *Kvod ha-Briot*—The Dignity of Creatures/People

Surely the most common expression is the dignity of creatures/people. J. Blitzstein has analyzed it and indicated its limited role within the Halakhic tradition.[7] It remains only to draw attention to possible limitations of the expression in this present discussion. When the glory of Aharon in his priestly habit surpasses any *Kvod haBriot*,[8] one must translate it as honor or glory, rather than as human dignity.

iii. *Kvod ha-Tsibur*—Public Dignity

Public or community dignity is, as mentioned above, somewhat more complex. On the one hand, one encounters a variety of instructions to preserve and nourish public rights and dignity, to refrain from wasting the public's time, and to protect the public's interests against unsolicited religious fervor or negligence. One should not roll the Torah scroll in public to avoid infringing upon public dignity.[9] One should use proper Torah scrolls and not simply parts of it out of respect for public dignity.[10] Bad smells should not be introduced

---

[4] Ch. Safrai, *Das Bild vom Menschen in Talmudischer Tradition*, Rhein Reden 1998/1, 14-34.

[5] *Numbers* Raba 9:33.

[6] M. Halbertal, *Interpretative Revolutions in the Making* [Hebrew] (Jerusalem 1997) pp. 103-106. On p. 111, Halbertal points to the revolution, though he emphasizes the interpretive female/male mutuality component rather than the aspect of dignity.

[7] J. Blitzstein, '"Great is Human Dignity," An Analysis of the History of an Halakha' [Hebrew], *Shnaton ha-Mishpat ha-Ivri* (1982-83) p. 127-186. For further discussion see below.

[8] Pesikta Rabati, 47 [190a].

[9] *Babylonian Talmud* Yoma 70a; cf. *Babylonian Talmud* Sota 41a without the dignity explanation.

[10] *Babylonian Talmud* Gittin 60a.

into the synagogue out of respect to the place, or possibly its habitants.[11] Reading the scroll of Esther is to be postponed in the case of a funeral in order to preserve human dignity.[12] But by the same token, deformed and handicapped persons are limited in performing rituals due to k*vod ha-briot*. Their personal dignity seems to come at the expense of the dignity of the community or the general public. Similarly, one could argue for the place of women in the synagogue service. According to the Babylonian tradition, a woman should not read in order to preserve the community's dignity.[13] The same concept elaborates on the dignity of the community; and within the very same community, it plays a qualifying role in relation to 'minorities.'

iv. *Kvod ha-Nashim*—The Dignity of Women

Women's dignity occurs as an expression only twice in the rabbinical literature, both times in connection with female burial rites. Female dignity forbids a presentation of her corpse in public.[14] Also, all women regardless of their purity status, require similar burial rites, including a ritual bath.[15] What is the exact content of this dignity? It is surely part of the general theme of dignity of life, represented in the attitude toward death and burial (k*vod ha-met*). But at the same time, it is part of another problematic theme of modesty or propriety (*Zni'ut*), that more often than not infringes upon female human dignity. One might argue that females are not entitled to festive public recognition—public dignity—under the pretext of their dignity.[16]

v. *Kvod ha-Kala*—The Dignity of the Bride

A similar case is the social position of the bride. On her marriage day, she is the queen of the community. She is to be hailed and helped into her husband's house, given a fair beginning in her new life. One is permitted to praise the bride's beauty, even in the case of her being ugly.[17] One prefers her procession to a funeral procession, as life takes priority over the death; in fact, King Agripas gave an anonymous bride the honor to pass him.[18] Does the interest in

---

[11] The synagogue could be the sum of the praying persons rather than the holy building *JT* Yoma 4:5 [41d]

[12] *Babylonian Talmud* Megila 3b.

[13] *Babylonian Talmud* Megila 23a. The community's honor or dignity in light of female participation in the Synagogue is an established issue. For a recent publication with an attempt to solve this historical development, see: S & Ch. Safrai, All Are Included in the Account of Seven [Hebrew], *Tarbiz* 66/3 (1997) p. 395-401.

[14] M. Moed Katan 3:8.

[15] T Nidda 9:16.

[16] For a theoretical and detailed discussion, see O. Cohen, *Female Modesty in the Modern Era, Continuity or Change in Jewish Halakha* [Hebrew] (Israel 1997).

[17] The issue is in debate between the schools of Hillel and Shammai. Kala Rabati 9:1 and parallels.

[18] Semachot 11:6.

the bride reflect human dignity, or rather does it derive its main impetus from the presupposition that she needs support since she enters a dubious position endangering her freedom and autonomy? Is it not a social cover for a dramatic deprivation of human rights, part of a patriarchal structure, benevolent as it may be?[19]

vi. *Kvod Aniyim*—The Dignity of the Poor

The dignity of the poor is mentioned in one text concerning funeral rites and lore. The gist of the Tannaic text is that a change of customs was introduced so as not to create a difference between the rites of the rich and those of the poor. The height of this tradition is attributed to Rabban Gamliel, who reduced the funeral expenses at his patriarchal home in order to enable everybody to perform the rites at normal, equal prices.[20] Once again, legal equality is surely a basis of human rights, but the concept of *kavod* is surely here closely related to the social respect paid by the members of the community in order to glorify their own social status, rather than human dignity, *per se*.

vii. *Kvod ha-Am*—The Dignity of the People

The dignity of the people is similar in concept to public dignity. But its occurrence in the tradition is much closer to the concept of human rights than many others. It appears only in tractate *Semachot*, and is connected to mourning rites, the possible tension between strict religious customs like purity rites[21] or the Halakhic prohibition to do any work in the first week of mourning, which one might overlook under specific circumstances for the sake of the people.[22] The needs and comfort of the public have priority over rites and Halakha. However, although the tradition is careful to impress the need for privacy and secrecy, it clearly introduces the public as the leading factor in the decision. Human factors are favored over supposed divine religious custom.

viii. *Kvod ha-Shabbat, Kvod YomTov*—The Dignity of the Sabbath and Holy Days

Similarly, the dignity of the Sabbath is primarily a religious factor, until it contradicts basic human factors. At that point, it seems that Rabbinical human sensitivity wins the day. Mourning requires no washing or changing of clothes, but on Thursday one is permitted to wash the clothes in honor of the Sabbath.[23] One is permitted to use one's dishes and bedding on the last holiday of Sukkot,

---

[19] I permit myself to borrow from a book by J. Hauptman, thus expressing some reservation about her conclusion concerning benevolent patriarchy. J. Hauptman, *Rereading the Rabbis: A Woman's Voice* (Westview, New York 1999).
[20] T Nidda 9:16-17
[21] Semachot 4:9
[22] Semachot 5:7
[23] *Babylonian Talmud* Ta'anit 26b.

once they are not strictly needed in the Sukka, for the dignity of the holiday[24] and one is required to bring fruits to the market and decorate the market in honor of the holiday.[25] All are cases of holiday festivities, but at the same time provide for those celebrating the means and provisions for their personal enjoyment. The Hillel Halakhic concept that danger to human life overrules the Sabbath[26] and many other instructions are in a similar vein. These scriptural, divine, holy occasions carry with them Rabbinical understanding of a heavy interest in the celebrating public. It does not constitute human dignity as such, but it carries a serious human sensitivity, using similar expressions.

ix. Summation

In summation, no single expression found in the Rabbinical literature equals the twentieth century concept of human dignity. It would seem that it toys with the idea, but it is not as yet theoretically developed

2. Literary Expressions

Nonetheless one should turn one's attention here to three literary constructions that supposedly indicate a further abstract interest in human dignity.

i.

In various passages, the concept of human dignity is formulated in relation to another human sensitive concept, namely the golden rule. R. Eliezer says: 'Let your friend's dignity be as dear to you as your own.'[27] The golden rule has a long history in early Jewish literature and ethics; furthermore it is understood to be a basic and core concept of the entire tradition.[28] Tying it together with human dignity and articulating it in a similar fashion is a value statement. It places the concept at the center of theological existence. This literary presentation is attributed to R. Eliezer, one of the major Rabbis in the Javne generation, and a disciple of Rabban Yohanan b. Zakkai.[29] We will return shortly to a possible chronology of the interest in human dignity in the Rabbinical thought.

---

[24] M. Sukka 4:8
[25] *Babylonian Talmud* Moed Katan 13b
[26] C. Safrai, 'Sayings and Legends in the Hillel Tradition,' in: *Jesus and Hillel*, J. H. Charlesworth, L.L. Johns, eds., (Augsburg Fortress 1997) p. 313-314.
[27] M. Abot 2:1 and parallels.
[28] Gen. Raba 24:7. For a recent discussion and bibliography see: P.S. Alexander, 'Jesus and the Golden Rule,' in; *Hillel and Jesus*, J. H. Charlesworth, L.L. Johns, eds., (Fortress, Minneapolis 1997) p. 363-388
[29] His friend R. Yosi has a similar saying on money 'Let your friend's money be dear to you as yours ' Abot 2:12.

ii.

Earlier in this chapter, a literary tradition was described that attempted to build a hierarchy of commitment. In this hierarchy, human dignity in the form of taking care of the dead has priority over reading the scroll of Esther on the festival of Purim. Similarly it has priority over the main Rabbinical enterprise—the study of Torah—and for the same reason, though with opposite results, it has no priority over the bridal procession to her new home.[30] Such a priority structure is a clear literary indication of an intellectual preoccupation with human dignity. The issue is not merely mentioned here and there, but rather has an active life and articulation within the tradition and its deliberations.

iii.

The last and most famous literary formula is the saying mentioned once above 'Great is human dignity (*kvod ha-briot*), that overrules the prohibitions of the Torah.' This is no doubt a Halakhic statement, and it supposedly, articulates in clear words the role of human dignity within this tradition. As indicated above, this Halakhic concept and its development in the world of Halakha has been analyzed at length as a clear example for the mild interest in human dignity. Nonetheless, Blitzstein pointed out in his research that the origin of this concept is Tannaic—he even mentions the attribution of the saying to Rabban Yohanan b. Zakkai[31] but fails to draw any conclusions from these facts. It seems that one might benefit from these details, and gain additional insight into the development of consciousness concerning human dignity within the Rabbinical tradition.

3. *Boshet*—Shame

The opposite of dignity is the lack of it, namely, shame. Avoiding shame is surely a means of achieving dignity. But the term itself is neither moral nor ethical in character. It is a Halakhic (legal) term, found in the Tannaic literature as one of the five forms of financial compensation, paid by the aggressor to the victim of his aggression.[32] The biblical compensation includes only two items: health costs and compensation for loss of time or work—and by implication, any damages. Pain and shame are new concepts added in the Tannaic tradition.[33] Both reflect an intense human sensitivity, and shame is of

---

[30] *Babylonian Talmud* Megila 3b
[31] *Shnaton ha-Mishpat ha-Ivri*, 9-10 (1982-3) p. 132.
[32] M. Baba Kama 8:1; T Baba Kama 9:12; M. Ketubot 6:1; M. Arakhin 3:4 and parallels.
[33] Earlier Jewish sources do not know as yet of additional financial components. See Josephus, *Antiquities IV* 278, and A. Shor, *The Hebrew Translation of Josephus* (Jerusalem 1900) vol. I, note 11; Philo *Spec. Leg. III* 106. See also: B. Cohen,

particular interest in our context. Nonetheless the concept of shame in Halakhic jurisprudence is understood itself as derived from scripture, though no exact reference can be quoted.[34] The biblical interpreters attached the term to Deut. 25:11, wherein a particular case of damages, the private parts of the victimized male are called 'his shame' (*mevoshav*). They play on the similarity in form and linguistic root,[35] and derive in this fashion various legal details concerning shame compensation.

The definition of shame, or the amount of compensation, depends on both parties, the offender and the offended, as stated in biblical terminology, all depends on the offender[36] and the insulted,[37] or, 'All according to his dignity.'[38] The story of R. Akiba and the supposedly shameless woman is the main story here. R. Akiba forced a man, who exposed the hair of a certain woman, to pay her as shame compensation 400 zuzim in accordance with the halakhic ruling. The man was surprised and claimed that the woman herself had no sense of self-esteem. To prove his case, he followed her and waited for her as she stood at her own gate. He then broke a vessel with oil in front of her. The woman hastened to undo her hair and anointed her own hair. The man appointed witnesses and cames with them to R. Akiba demanding, 'Rabbi! To such a woman I should give 400 *zuzim*?' Akiba's response was short and pointed, 'You have not said anything! She abides by her sense of dignity, but nobody has the right to deprive her of her basic self-dignity.'[39]

This sense of personal dignity in the negative form is applied in the rabbinical literature to physical offenses as seen above, verbal offenses,[40] charity regulations,[41] and sexual abuse.[42] The Jerusalemites were accused of abusing this notion of equating dignity when they punished the cook for bad dinner in accordance with the dignity of the host and the dignity of his guests. They are seen as major contributors to the destruction of the city.[43]

Jewish and Roman Law, (New York 1966) p. 232 notes 285-286. Accordingly the idea of shame compensation is not known in Roman law of the second century.

[34] M. Baba Kama 8:1 quotes as its basic text *Deuteronomy* 25:11, were no compensation but rather corporal punishment is mentioned. See the Midrash Tannaim to *Deuteronomy* 25:12, clearly driving shame compensation from this verse as their own invention. Sifre *Deuteronomy* 190 has a different biblical verse *Deuteronomy* 19:19, and *Exodus* 21:24 as a base for financial compensation to shame.

[35] Sifre *Deuteronomy* 292-3.

[36] The one causing shame.

[37] M. Baba Kama 8:1; M. Arakhin 3:4

[38] M. Baba Kama 8:6.

[39] M. Baba Kama 8:6.

[40] AdRN I Ch. 9.

[41] Midrash Tannaim to *Deuteronomy* 15:8.

[42] M. Arachin 3:4.

[43] Lam. Raba 4.

i.

In the name of R. Akiba and his disciples, the Mishna and Tosefta—the Javne and Usha generations—seem to emphasize an all-embracing legislation. Poor or rich, awake or asleep, dressed or naked, sighted or blind. Both in the bathhouse and the marketplace, all have this basic, legally protected human dignity.[44] Nonetheless the following Tosefta text carries a debate between a Rabbi and the anonymous tradition concerning the eligibility of minors, mute or retarded persons to shame compensation. The Rabbis insist that at least the mute person has the right to such compensation. Similarly, R. Judah[45] argued with the Rabbis concerning the retarded person. [46] The articulated question is: Do they have shame?

ii.

It would seem that the negative formula of shame is much closer to the concept of human dignity, equally embracing men and women, insisting on regularity, and protecting the weakest in the social system.

II. A Thematic Development

The name of Rabban Yohanan b. Zakkai is mentioned twice in connection with dignity. In both cases Biblical dictums are explained in his name. In the first, there is the question of why a person who steals and sells an ox has to pay five times its value, while he who steals and sells a lamb has to pay only four times the value. 'Come and see how great is human dignity. He who has to lead the ox pays five times and he who carries the lamb on his shoulders pays only four times.'[47] Similarly, there is the question of why all the soldiers who are exempted from war return together, in order to spare those who return out of fear and not to expose them. 'Come and see how much *ha-Makom* (God) protects human dignity.'[48]

Interest in human dignity is but an example of the various traditions attributed to Rabban Yohanan b. Zakkai concerning human sensitivity and dignity. In his name, it was argued that Sacrifice regulations were introduced

---

[44] M. Baba Kama 8:1; T Baba Kama 9:12 and parallels.
[45] If Rabbi is about a generation later, R. Judah carries a different and possibly older tradition within the group of disciples of R. Akiba. Both, thus, suggest a legal system in the making. An open ended legal process, and an awakening consciousness.
[46] T Baba Kama 9:13.
[47] *Babylonian Talmud* Baba Kama 79b, see also J. Blitzstein, "'Great is Human Dignity" An Analysis of the History of Halakha' [Hebrew], *Shnaton ha-Mishpat ha-Ivri*, (1982-83) p. 127-186, note 20.
[48] Not all version attribute it to Rabban Yohanan b. Zakkai, see: Sifre *Deuteronomy* 192 (Finkelstein p. 233), see also: Blitzstein, *op. cit.*, nt. 21.

in order to redeem the transgressions of the community,[49] and that human activities have priority over the speedy rebuilding of the new Temple and the coming of the Messiah.[50] Mentioned above its his canceling of the biblical teaching concerning fallen women, based on his understanding of his contemporary society. It is in his name that the tradition explains why a Jewish slave has to pierce his ear, if he refuses to be released after seven years. 'This ear that heard on Mount Sinai: 'The Children of Israel are my slaves,' and says: 'I love my master,' should be pierced.'[51] Rabban Yohanan has a deep sense of human rights, liberation, freedom and dignity. He conceives human dignity as a divine reasoning lurking behind the commandments and directing them. He has a better sense for human righteousness than for priestly dignity. 'A priest that does not pay the Temple tax (half a shekel) is a sinner.'[52] He demands equality, and a fair distribution of responsibility and dignity.

One could explain almost all of his Halakhic decrees as propagating a religious life within the community after the destruction of the Temple. He supposedly responded to the destruction with the words, 'We have an equivalent way of redemption—charity.'[53] Charity means catering to human need in times of despair; it means being attuned to people, sensitive to their calls and requirements, and to glorifying in their human dignity. 'R. Yohanan b. Zakkai says a Man that brings peace between husband and wife, between families, between cities, between states, between nations, should encounter no disaster.'[54]

As mentioned above, the tradition attributes a further step in this direction to his disciple, R. Eliezer. He, and possibly his fellow disciple Yossi, translated this human sensitivity into the 'Golden Rule,' and thus connected this renewed notion with the long-standing human perception within the tradition.

One generation later, R. Akiba and his disciples translated these perceptions of human dignity into a concrete, formulated Halakha—*Boshet*. They are mentioned in the formulations concerning shame in the Mishna, and they probably are behind the translation of the formula, 'Great is human dignity,' into 'Great is human dignity, that overrules prohibitions from the Torah.' R. Akiba and his disciples' major interest lies in concretizing the concept of human dignity. They interpret the notion and the saying 'Great is human dignity' into a legal framework. They are concerned with concrete, detailed praxis of shame.

---

[49] JT Shekalim 2:3 [46d].
[50] AdRN II, Ch. 31 [34a].
[51] Mekhilta d'R. Jishmael, Mishpatim Ch. 2 [253/7]. And parallels though not all are in the name of Rabban Yohanan b. Zakkai.
[52] M. Shekalim 1:4 and parallels.
[53] AdRN, ch 4, p. 21; II, Ch. 8, p. 22.
[54] Sifra, Kedoshim chapter 11:8.

Who has shame, and is thus included in dignity, and who is excluded? The blind the mute and the minor are present in the latter Halakhic debate.[55]

IV. Summary

The quest for human dignity in rabbinical literature started with Rabban Yohanan b. Zakkai. He established the ideology and articulated a concept. Not all expressions of dignity are relevant in the quest for human dignity. Human dignity is applied to a variety of subjects, including some relevant social factors within the Jewish society: the poor; the handicapped; women; the dead; and, most of all, to the community itself. The concepts of community, multitude, people, nation and other such expressions all seem to indicate that one does not talk of human dignity, but rather human sensitivity of the community of believers. Typically rabbinic, the most interesting development is not in the conceptual, but rather in the legal and concrete. Hense, the regulation of shame seems to be relevant in the quest for human dignity in rabbinical writings.

---

[55] For further development of the statement 'Great is human dignity,' its application and lack of it, see Blietzstein note 6 above.

THE FOUNDING FUNCTION OF HUMAN DIGNITY IN THE UNIVERSAL DECLARATION OF HUMAN RIGHTS

Klaus Dicke[*]

Introduction

When in Wolfgang Amadeus Mozart's 'Magic Flute' it comes to the question of whether or not *Tamino* should be admitted to the 'Holy Halls,' someone voices his doubts 'because he is a prince.' Sarastro's immediate answer to this move is: 'More, he is a human being.' The question of what exactly this 'more' means and implies is the question for human dignity. The 18th century, which brought up the first declarations of human rights in history, has the merit to have asked this question, and political philosophers of the 18th century provided arguments to answer it.[1] It was, however, left to the 20th century to focus the answers to this very question by politically and legally founding human rights on human dignity. The most influential document in this respect was the Universal Declaration of Human Rights, as adopted by the General Assembly of the United Nations on December 10, 1948.[2] It is certainly not to the merit of humankind that the Declaration referred to human dignity after chasms of mankind had become visible: colonialism, imperialism, racism, and after all totalitarianism and two 'world wars.'

The concept of Human Dignity is one of the most important, innovative elements introduced into International Law by the Charter of the UN and, in a more eloborated manner, by the 1948 Universal Declaration of Human Rights.

---

[*] Research for this paper was part of a larger prject on the Universal Declaration of Human Rights which was funded by the *Volkswagen-Stiftung*.
[1] For the history of ideas of human dignity, see Franz Josef Wetz, *Die Würde des Menschen ist antastbar*, Eine Provokation (Stuttgart 1998) 14-49. cf. Klaus Dicke, *Menschenrechte und europäische Integration* (Kehl/Straßburg 1986) pp. 51-61.
[2] GA Res. 217 (III) of 10 December 1948. International documents are quoted from Louis B. Sohn, ed., *International Organisation and Integration*, (Dordrecht/Boston/Lancester 1986).

The Declaration is not only the first document in the history of declarations of rights which refers to human dignity as the foundation of human rights but—and this will be my thesis—it also develops a concept of dignity which constitutes the Declaration's universality. This argument will be developed in three parts. First, the drafting history of the Declaration will be analyzed in order to identify the sources from which its concept of human dignity was taken. Second, the concept of dignity as enshrined in the Declaration will be reconstructed. And third, its founding function or its function to constitute and to legitimize human rights will be elaborated.

I. Human Dignity Was in the Air—The Drafting History of the Declaration

Its reference to 'dignity' is one of the most significant differences between the Universal Declaration of Human Rights and the 'classic' Declarations of the late 18th century. Although the concept of *dignitas hominis* was dealt with in philosophical essays[3] and although it was a key term in Kant's philosophy of freedom,[4] there was no systematic reference to human dignity in legal language until the 1940s. In order to identify the sources from which the notion of dignity became an integral part of the international human rights language, a fresh look into the drafting history of the Declaration and into the intellectual environment of its early drafts is called for.

The purpose of drafting and codifying an International Bill of Rights as a constitutive element of a post-war international legal order goes back to the early forties of this century. The incentive, set by Roosevelt's 'Four Freedoms,' by the Atlantic Charter and by the 1942 Declaration of the United Nations[5] was picked up by individuals as well as by several European and American religious and/or political groups—nowadays we would call them 'non-governmental organizations'—who prepared drafts for such an International Bill of Rights. To differing degrees, these drafts pioneered in referring to human dignity as a background value of human rights protection. Why did they do so, and what was the respective concept of 'dignity' connected with those references?

---

[3] Cf. Hubert Cancik's paper in this volume; Wetz (note 1) seq.; 28 et Rolf Gröschner, *Menschenwürde und Sepulkralkultur in Der Grundgesetzlichen Ordnung* (Stuttgart 1995) p. 29 et seq.

[4] Johannes Schwartländer, 'Menschenwürde, Personwürde,' in *Lexikon der Bioethik*, Wilhelm Korff, Ludwig Beck, Paul Mikat, eds., (Gütersloh 1998) pp. 683-688 (685); Michael J. Meyer, 'Kant's Concept of Dignity and Modern Political Thought,' in *History of European Ideas* 8 (1987) pp. 319-332; Gröschner (note 2), pp. 35-41.

[5] For the drafting history of international human rights after the second world war, see Nehemiah Robinson, *The Universal Declaration of Human Rights*, (New York 1958); Jan Herman Burgers, 'The Road to San Francisco. The Revival of the Human Rights Idea in the Twentieth Century,' in *HRQ* 14 (1992) pp. 447-477.

In the early forties, at least three different concepts, or even conceptions, of dignity prevailed. The first was a natural law concept based upon Christian traditions. The concept rests on an onto-theological concept of 'person,' which in turn has a long tradition as far back as the melting process of ancient Greek philosophy and medieval Christian theology.[6] One draft, prepared by the Catholic Bishops of the U.S., reads as an excerpt from St. Thomas Aquinas.[7] In this context, dignity of the human person underlines a certain exceptional position of man in God's creation. 'It is a synonym for human worth, the inherent excellence of the human person as distinguished from any other living creature.'[8]

A second and quite similar concept of dignity in early drafts of an international bill of rights refers to Jewish or Old Testament traditions. In October 1944, the American Jewish Committee put forth a 'Declaration of Human Rights'[9] which was founded on the following 'creed:' 'This new world must be based on the recognition that the individual human being is the cornerstone of our culture and our civilization. All that we cherish must rest on the dignity and inviolability of the person, of his sacred right to live and to develop under God, in whose image he was created.' Again, reference is made to the concept of person, which is regarded to be the substance of dignity, and dignity points to the person's inviolability as derived from his or her godlike image.

Third, we find a natural law concept of dignity in the at-that-time almost forgotten legal tradition of (mainly French and German) enlightenment and natural law philosophy, which holds that all human beings are endowed by nature with reason and therefore are to be recognized as equals.[10] The historical roots of this tradition lead back to the Hellenistic and cosmopolitan philosophers of the Stoic school of thought.

Those drafts were more or less known to the delegates of the 1945 Conference of San Francisco. In its preamble, the UN Charter refers to human dignity to spell out one of the 'determinations' which led the delegates in the name of the peoples of the UN to establish the organization. It reaffirms:

---

[6] Adolf Trendelenburg, 'Zur Geschichte des Wortes Person,' in *Kant-Studien* XIII (1908) pp. 1-17.
[7] 'A Declaration of Rights,' Bishops of the National Catholic Welfare Conference (USA), June 1946.
[8] Haim H. Cohn, 'On the Meaning of Human Dignity,' in *Israel Yearbook of Human Rights* 13 (1983) pp. 226-251 (231).
[9] The American Jewish Committee, *Declaration of Human Rights* (October 1944). This declaration was circulated for signature.
[10] For the history of this natural law tradition cf. Hans Welzel, *Naturrecht und materiale Gerechtigkeit Göttingen*, 4th edition (Göttingen 1962).

> ... faith in fundamental human rights, in the dignity and worth of the human person, in the equal rights of men and women and of nations large and small.[11]

After the 1944 'Philadelphia Declaration' of the International Labour Organization,[12] the Charter was the second document to introduce 'dignity' into international law language. But as this chapter of the Charter's preamble leaves at least as many questions open as it answers with regard to the meaning and the function of dignity, its wording should be interpreted in the broader context of the 1948 Universal Declaration of Human Rights, which seems the more appropriate as the Declaration quotes the Charter's wording.

II. The Declaration's Concept of Human Dignity

In five different places, the Universal Declaration of 1948 refers to 'dignity:' twice in the preamble, most prominently in Art. 1, and twice in the context of social and economic rights in Arts. 22 and 23 para. 3. The wording and systematic position of these references will be analyzed in turn.

(1) The Declaration's preamble starts with the following consideration:

> Whereas recognition of the inherent dignity and of the equal and inalienable rights of all members of the human family is the foundation of freedom, justice and peace in the world.

In this wording, we find three key arguments which constitute what I call the founding function of human dignity. First, dignity is regarded as something which has to be recognized. Quoting the preamble of the UN Charter, the second reference in the preamble calls this recognition 'faith.' This is important to note because it excludes an interpretation of 'recognition' as an act which constitutes dignity.[13] Rather, the existence of dignity does not depend on recognition, which at the same time means that there is an obligation to recognize dignity. This obligation is explained by the second key argument, that recognition of dignity is the foundation of freedom, justice and peace. The third argument reads that inherent dignity is a quality owned by 'all members of the human family.' From this argument one can conclude that dignity is an expression of the unity of humankind.

With regard to the systematic position of this first reference to dignity one has to recall Dorothy Jones' thesis that one of the significant developments

---

[11] Sohn *op. cit.*, p. 15. For an interpretation of this preambula paragraph, see Klaus Dicke, '... unseren Glauben an die Grundrechte des Menschen ..,' in *Die Präambel der UN-Charta im Lichte der aktuellen Völkerrechtsentwicklung*, Stephan Hobe, ed. (Berlin 1997) pp. 47-58.

[12] Sohn *op. cit.*, pp. 480-481.

[13] Cf. Dicke *op. cit.* (note 11). This argument rejects any position whatever that holds that dignity is conditioned by either societal approval or the fulfillment of virtues, codes of conduct and other norms.

of international law since the UN Charter is what she calls the 'declaratory tradition.'[14] This tradition establishes a certain style of reasoning in international documents according to which leading principles are delineated in order to produce a common standard of understanding and interpretation of legal norms. The Universal Declaration of Human Rights is one of the earlier documents to make this style of reasoning explicit, and the first reference to dignity by the Declaration—which was quoted by Art. 1 para. 3 of the German Basic Law—is one of the most prominent cases in point. Following this observation, one can conclude that the preamble's first consideration declares that wherever freedom, justice and peace are at stake in the world, due regard to the principle of human dignity is called for. In other words: dignity is considered the fundamental principle in light of which each and every policy and lawmaking to secure freedom, to implement justice and to maintain peace must be seen.[15] But what does dignity mean in this context? Is there any definition of dignity in the Declaration?

(2) The fifth consideration of the preamble, which contains the second reference of the Declaration to dignity, quotes the UN Charter and holds that:

> The peoples in the United Nations have in the Charter reaffirmed
> their faith in fundamental human rights, in the dignity and worth
> of the human person.

Remarkably enough, the Charter's wording was 'reaffirmed their faith.' Again, this is evidence for the pre-existing character not only of human dignity, but of faith in human dignity alike, and remarkably enough both the Charter and the Declaration abstain from quoting any earlier affirmation of this faith in history. Instead, they presuppose every man's knowledge of fundamental human rights and of human dignity as well. By stressing the epistemology of 'I know it when I see it even if I cannot tell you what it is,' as Oscar Schachter put it,[16] the Declaration refers to political experience. In a recent article, Johannes Morsink showed that the Declaration, article by article, is based upon the experience of the barbarious atrocities of National Socialist practices.[17] Similar

---

[14] Dorothy V. Jones, 'The Declaratory Tradition in Modern International Law,' in *Traditions of International Ethics*, J. Nardin, D. R. Marpel, eds., (Cambridge/New York 1992) pp. 42-61.

[15] This is one of the arguments as put forth by German enlightenment philosophy. It is the leading premise of Jakob Fries, *Philosophische Rechtslehre und Kritik aller positiven Gesetzgebung* (Jena 1803).

[16] Oscar Schachter, 'Human Dignity as a Normative Concept,' in *AJIL* 77 (1983) p. 849; cf. Welz *op. cit.*, (note 1), p. 84 with reference to the German Constitutional Court.

[17] Johannes Morsink, 'World War Two and the Universal Declaration,' in *HRQ* 15 (1993) pp. 357-405; cf. Klaus Dicke, "' ... das von allen Völkern und Nationen zu erreichende gemeinsame Ideal ..." Zum Politikprogramm der Allgemeinen Erklärung,' in *Vereinte Nationen* 46 (1998) pp. 191-194.

political experiences underlie philosophical considerations with regard to human rights and human dignity in the intellectual environment of the Declaration. This is true for the anti-totalitarian approach of Hannah Arendt, who holds that there is only one human right, namely, the right to live under a rule of law;[18] it is true for H.G. Wells' draft for an international bill of rights,[19] which rests on the assumption that politics after the war had the responsibility to establish counterforces against totalitarian disposal of human beings by states and by private actors alike; it is true for Karl Loewenstein, the father of the Universal Declaration's Art. 21,[20] who held that free elections and a balance-of-power approach were necessary conditions of freedom; it is true for most of the utopian literature of the first half of the 20th century[21] as well as for protagonists of the democratic state in the 1940s and 1950s.[22]

Against this background, the Declaration's reference to political experience allows for two conclusions: first, the notion of 'dignity' needs political experience to become meaningful; and second, faith in human dignity goes along with a call for the establishment of democratic states under the rule of law.

Two other arguments are important here: first, the text combines dignity with 'worth;' and second it relates dignity to the human person. The term 'worth' explains dignity with moral or personal value, as something which is honorable or of an intrinsic value and thus which calls for unconditioned respect. The explanation of dignity by 'worth' seems to be directed at an Anglo-Saxon intellectual environment that is familiar with the difference between worth and value. The relation of dignity to the human person, on the other hand, calls upon the old and however complex European metaphysical-ontological tradition of *persona* which resulted from the amalgam of Platonism and Christianity.[23] Thus, the combination of 'dignity and worth of the human person' can be read as a compromise between Anglo-American and continental European traditions of thought.

(3) The most important and innovative reference to human dignity by the Universal Declaration, however, is made in Art. 1, which reads:

---

[18] Hannah Arendt, 'Es gibt nur ein einziges Menschenrecht,' in *Die Wandlung* 4 (1949) pp. 754-770.

[19] Herbert George Wells, *The New World Order* (London 1940) pp. 136-146. Whether it is attainable, how it can be attained, and what sort of world a world of peace will have to be. Cf. Burgers (note 5), p. 464 et seq.

[20] Markus Lang, 'Menschenrecht auf Demokratie. Artikel 21 der Allgemeinen Erklärung als Bestandsgarantie des demokratischen Verfassungsstaats,' in *Vereinte Nationen* 46 (1998) pp. 195-199, with further references.

[21] e.g., Jewgenij Samjatin, *Wir* (Köln 1984). Cf. Richard Saage, *Politische Utopien der Neuzeit* (Darmstadt 1991) pp. 234 et seq.

[22] Among others see Franz Neumann, 'Zum Begriff der politischen Freiheit,' in idem, *Demokratischer und autoritärer Staat*, (CF Frankfurt a.M. 1986) pp. 100-141.

[23] Cf. Trendelenburg, *op. cit.*, (note 6).

All human beings are born free and equal in dignity and rights. They are endowed with reason and conscience and should act towards another in a spirit of brotherhood.

First of all, the first sentence of this Article refrains from any reference to religious or philosophical traditions. There is no reference to 'person,' and the original version of the draft, which read 'all human beings are by nature free and equal' was rejected because in the view of a delegate of China it revealed the language of the French enlightenment and its commitment to natural law.[24] It was subsequently amended into 'all human beings are born free and equal.' Second, the emphasis with regard to dignity and rights goes to the equality of human beings. Third, although the triad of 'freedom, equality and brotherhood' sounds French enough and embraces the spirit of the French revolution, the Article contains one assertion which clears up a certain ambiguity in particular of the French enlightenment: not reason pure and simple, but 'reason and conscience' is regarded as the substance of human nature and thus of dignity. In other words, the Declaration is not based on a concept of man as a being that is able to produce culture by way of its technical reason, but rather refers to moral reasoning as establishing equality among human beings and thus giving the unity of mankind its ethical and moral meaning. The Declaration thus follows Rousseau and Kant rather than the Physiocratic school, Voltaire or the Encyclopedists.

From a philosophical point of view, the substitution of 'are by nature free' by 'are born free' is of utmost importance. While the Declarations of the 18th century were founded in man's nature, which was held to be eternal and unchangeable in history, the underlying concepts of nature and, consequently, of natural law lost their founding capacity under the fire of the anti-metaphysical historicism and positivism of the 19th century. Thus they had to be replaced by a concept which allowed the acknowledgement of the historical perspectiveness of human life and at the same time to the recognition and respect of the unconditionality of human existence. In the intellectual debates accompagnying the drafting of the Universal Declaration there are many hints to this very philosophical challenge.[25]

(4) Further references to human dignity are made in Arts. 22 and 23, both containing so-called social rights. According to Art. 22 everyone is entitled to the realization of economic, social and cultural rights 'indispensable for his

---

[24] For details see, Klaus Dicke, 'Die der Person innewohnende Würde und die Frage der Universalität der Menschenrechte,' in *Würde und Recht des Menschen*, Festschrift Johannes Schwartländer, H. Bielefeldt, W. Brugger, K. Dicke, eds. (Würzburg 1992) pp. 161-182.

[25] Cf. Arendt, *op. cit.*, (note 18); Hermann Broch, 'Bemerkungen zur Utopie einer 'International Bill of Rights and of Responsibilities,''' in *idem Politische Schriften*, vol. XI of *Hermann Broch's Works*, Michael Lützeler, ed. (CF Frankfurt a.M. 1986) pp. 243-277; Hannah Arendt/Hermann Broch, *Briefwechsel 1946-1951* (CF Frankfurt a.M. 1996) pp. 18, 42, 97 seq.; 244 seq.

dignity, and the free development of his personality.' And Art. 23 para. 3 bases the right to just and favorable remuneration upon the aim to ensure 'an existence worthy of human dignity.' Both references refer to dignity as a yardstick for a certain quality of life which can be brought up only by State action. Accordingly, they represent a socialist tradition of argument. Nevertheless, both articles leave the question open as to what exactly would constitute an 'existence worthy of human dignity.' Again, the Declaration abstains from definitions and leaves it to subsequent policies to agree on measures that are appropriate to establish conditions under which an existence worthy of human dignity would be possible.

To conclude this section, four observations must be kept in mind: (1) the Declaration's reference to human dignity refrains from defining dignity; (2) The Declaration refers to various European and Anglo-American traditions of thought, but at the same time it refrains from identifying dignity with a particular tradition; (3) With regard to the meaning of 'dignity,' the Declaration refers to political experience. At the same time, it calls for policies to agree on the establishment of conditions which secure a life for all human beings in dignity; (4) Theoretically, the question remains open, how an undefined concept can establish a yardstick or can establish a norm from which, to use the language of the 1966 Covenants, human rights can be derived.[26] This fourth question now calls for a functional interpretation of dignity and for a theoretical explanation of the relationship between dignity and human rights.

III. The Founding Function of Human Dignity under International Law from the Declaration's Point of View

My thesis in this regard is the following: A functional analysis shows that the dignity of human beings in the Declaration is a formal, transcendental norm to legitimize human rights claims. This means first of all that dignity is not a substantive norm which can be defined in substance and from which individual human rights claims can be derived immediately by deduction. Rather, the legitimizing function of human dignity is critical in nature: it depends on its relation to single human rights as listed by the Declaration and by instruments of human rights protection as agreed upon later. What does that mean? Each and every human rights claim bears a certain ambiguity as it (1) is conditioned by historical, economic, political, cultural or even financial circumstances of the society in which it is articulated; but (2) it nevertheless claims to be a human right and thus calls for unconditioned respect or, in other words, for universality. Schwartländer put forth the thesis that it is the legitimizing function of dignity to clear up and to reconcile this ambiguity:

> The normative validity of human rights claims is founded on the function of different human rights claims under particular historical

---

[26] Sohn, *op. cit.*, (note 1), p. 366.

circumstances to express and to represent the *a priori* unconditioned dignity of human beings. Dignity of human beings is, in other words, the source from which the validity and universal authority of human rights is derived, and at the same time dignity functions as a critical yardstick to answer the question of which historically conditioned claims shall be recognized as human rights.[27]

This legitimizing function of dignity, however, can only be translated into political or legal reasoning if a set of regulative principles governing the relationship between dignity and rights is applied.

In classical human rights texts, this regulative function was fulfilled by different triads: 'life, liberty, property' in the writings of John Locke; 'life, liberty and the pursuit of happiness' in the Declaration of Independence; 'freedom, equality and brotherhood' in the French Revolution. Those triads[28] put forth fundamental goods of humanity without which a life in dignity would not be possible. In my view, the Universal Declaration of Human Rights develops its own triad, namely, freedom, equality and participation in a political, social and international order as necessary to secure the rights that the Declaration contains.

These principles are not human rights in themselves, but rather they make the difference between political interests and human rights claims or, in other words, they are critical and regulative by nature: wherever freedom, equality and participation of human beings is endangered, respect for human dignity calls for a human rights policy. The UN General Assembly, to name but one example, acknowledged this—at least in theory, I should add—when in its resolution 'Setting International Standards in the Field of Human Rights' of December 4, 1986,[29] it stated that new instruments of human rights protection should, i.a., 'be of fundamental character and derive from the inherent dignity and worth of the human person.'

While this first critical function of human dignity is merely political, there is a second critical function of dignity that goes more into the legal field: as derived from human dignity, human rights contain at their heart unconditional inviolability. This means, above all, that physical and mental integrity as a precondition to enact freedom must not be violated under any conditions whatsoever. This hard core of fundamental human rights cannot be balanced even against the interests of the political community.

To justify this conclusion two final remarks are necessary:

---

[27] Schwartländer, *op. cit.*, (note 4), p. 687 (author's translation).
[28] Cf. Wolfgang Schild, 'Freiheit-Gleichheit-'Selbständigkeit' (Kant): Strukturmomente der Freiheit,' in *Menschenrechte und Demokratie*, Johannes Schwartländer, ed. (Kehl/Straßburg 1981) pp. 135-176; Reinhard Brandt, 'Menschenrechte und Güterlehre. Zur Geschichte und Begründung des Rechts auf Leben, Freiheit und Eigentum,' in *Das Recht des Menschen auf Eigentum*, Johannes Schwartländer, Dietmar Willoweit, eds. (Kehl/Straßburg 1983) pp. 19-31.
[29] GA res. 41/120 of December 4, 1986.

(1) As has been demonstrated in this paper, the Universal Declaration of Human Rights abstains from defining dignity and acknowledges it as a formal background value which has meaning only if referred to political experience and political claims. In a religious context we know the prohibition to draw pictures of God. I would not hesitate to apply that prohibition to human beings because freedom, understood as the underivable responsibility of human beings as citizens of the world,[30] cannot be enacted without a certain sphere of individual secrecy.[31] Dignity is another word for the secrecy of responsibility and the respect it calls for. Responsibility cannot be enacted without the full development of human personality. This development, in turn, depends on institutions that protect and promote the growth of personality: family, schools and universities, communities of culture, churches and others. It is not arbitrarily that their legal protection is part of modern human rights instruments.[32]

(2) In concluding her 1949 article on human rights, Hannah Arendt observed that after nature—i.e., the natural law tradition—and history—i.e., historicism and positivism as well as Marxism—had lost any power to convincingly put forth universal principles only mankind itself is left to fill this gap.[33] In other words, politics and policies can no longer be justified by nature or by history; instead they have to stand the test of mankind. In my view, the Universal Declaration is a prompt and clear answer to the challenge that Arendt's observation implies. Based upon political experience, it spells out a political program to establish conditions under which human beings can equally enact their responsibilities as citizens of the world. It thus gives place to the experience that behind cultural and religious pluralism and behind the conflict of interests, an ethical unity of mankind exists.

To fulfill the Declarations program, however, is a task still left to the political skills and to the political will of mankind to establish a world-wide constitutional system based upon the rule of law, human rights protection, democracy, and due regard to international law. Although those skills can be learned, they will always be uncertain and far from perfect. The will, however, gets new momentum whenever a human being is 'born free and equal in dignity and rights.'

---

[30] For this ethical concept of world citizenship, see Klaus Dicke, 'Das Weltbürgerrecht soll auf Bedingungen der allgemeinen Hospitalität eingeschränkt sein,' in *Republik und Weltbürgerrecht*, Klaus Dicke, Klaus-Michael Kodalle, eds., (Weimar/Köln/Wien 1998) pp. 115-130.

[31] Cf. Wetz (note 1), 86, again with reference to the German Constitutional Court.

[32] See, Johannes Schwartländer, 'Staatsbürgerliche und sittlich-institutionelle Menschenrechte,' in *idem, Menschenrechte—Aspekte ihrer Begründung und Verwirklichung* (Tübingen 1978) pp. 77-95.

[33] Arendt (note 18), p. 767; cf. ead., *Elemente und Ursprünge totaler Herrschaft*, 4th edition (München 1995) pp. 452 et seq.

HUMAN DIGNITY IN INTERNATIONAL LAW

Jochen Abr. Frowein

I. Introduction

Let me start with some historical remarks. It is noticeable that ideas of human dignity were present in international law very early, although we tend to forget that because of the positivist school of the late 19th century, which limited international law to interstate relations and did not protect the individual as such. In fact, the discussion of the Spanish school concerning whether it is justified to convert the Indians in Latin America to Christianity was such a discussion. Victoria, who wrote during the early 16th century, stressed that all men are of the same nature and are our next of kin.[1]

Even more remarkable is the specific treaty stipulation in Article 24 in the Treaty of Amity and Commerce, concluded between the Kingdom of Prussia and the United States on 10 September 1785. His Majesty the King of Prussia and the United States of America agreed as follows[2]:

> And to prevent the destruction as prisoners of war, by sending them into distant and inclement countries, or by crowding them into close and noxious places, the two contracting parties solemnly pledge themselves to each other and to the world that they will not adopt any such practice; that neither will send the

---

[1] See Franciscus de Victoria, 'De Indis Recenter Inventis et de Jure Belli Hispanorum,' in *Barbaros Relectiones* § 3 No. 3 (1539), reprinted in 2 *Die Klassiker des Völkerrechts*, Walter Schätzel, ed., (1952) pp. 96-97; James Brown Scott, *The Spanish Conception of International Law and of Sanctions* 3-5 (1934); Wolfgang Preiser, 'History of the Law of Nations: Ancient Times to 1648,' in *Encyclopedia of Public International Law 2*, Rudolf Bernhardt, ed., (1995) pp. 740-741, p. 722; Karl Josef Partsch, 'Individuals in International Law,' in *ibid.* pp. 957, 958.

[2] *Fontes Historiae Iuris Gentium* 2 1493-1815, Wilhelm G. Grewe, ed., (1988) pp. 566-567.

prisoners whom they may take from the other into the East Indies, or any other parts of Asia or Africa, but that they shall be placed in some part of their dominions in Europe or in America, in wholesome situations; that they shall not be confined in dungeons, prison-ships, nor prisons, nor be put into irons, nor bound, nor otherwise restrained in the use of their limbs.

Probably the most important early development concerning human dignity in international law was the development of a common rule against the trade of Negro slaves during the 19th century. In the famous Declaration of 8 February 1815, which is part of the Vienna Congress Act, the parties declare that the trade of African Negroes '*a été envisagé, par les hommes justes et éclairés de tous les temps, comme répugnant au principe d'humanité et de morale universelle.*' In the Treaty of 1841, the trade was formally prohibited and qualified in the same way as piracy. The General Act of the Berlin Conference of 1885 could declare that a principle of international law generally prohibited the trade of Negro slaves.[3] But we had to wait until the tragedies of the 20th century to have human dignity formally recognised as a value in public international law.

II. The New Texts

Not only the Universal Declaration of Human Rights, but also the United Nations Covenants, the Torture Convention, and the specific treaties concerning women and children expressly refer to human dignity as a value to be protected under public international law.[4]

It is of some interest to notice that the first express provision stems from the same time as the first drafts of the German Constitution. In fact, the famous Herrenchiemsee draft of 1947 already included human dignity almost in the same way as the present Article 1 of our Constitution. The Herrenchiemsee Conference took place in August 1948. That was shortly before the adoption of the Universal Declaration but, of course, the draft for the Universal Declaration, in all probability, was already being circulated in Germany. However, certainly before the first drafts were known in Germany, the

---

[3] See Anne M. Trebilock, 'Slavery,' in *Encyclopedia of Public International Law*, Rudolf Bernhardt, ed., (1985) vol. VIII, pp. 481-482; 3/1 *Fontes Historiae Iuris Gentium 1815-1945*, Wilhelm G. Grewe, ed., (1988) pp. 306-307, 376, 379.

[4] See 'Universal Declaratrion of Human Rights,' Dec. 10, 1948, Art. 1, in D. J. Harris, *Cases and Materials on International Law*, 5th edition (1998) p. 631; 'International Covenant on Civil and Political Rights,' Dec. 16, 1966, Art. 7, in *ibid*. p. 639; 'International Covenant on Economic, Social and Cultural Rights,' Dec. 16, 1966, Art. 13, in *ibid*. p. 693; 'Convention Against Torture and Other Cruel, Inhumane, Degrading Treatment or Punishment,' Dec. 10, 1984, Art. 16, in *ibid*. p. 714; 'Convention on the Elimination of All Forms of Discrimination Against Women,' Dec. 18, 1979, Preamble para. 2, 1249 U.N.T.S. 13; 'Convention on the Rights of the Child,' Nov. 20, 1989, Preamble para. 2, 23 I.L.M. 1457.

constitutions of the Land of Hessen, of 1 December 1946, and of Bavaria, of 2 December 1946, formally proclaimed human dignity—the Constitution of Hessen in Article 3 and the Bavarian Constitution in Article 100.[5]

One can easily see that these developments were the clear consequence of the complete negation of human dignity during the Nazi period as shown by the German measures, particularly in central and Eastern Europe, against the Jewish population and other parts of the population.[6]

Let me add one other thought on the basis of this morning's discussion. We should also recognise that the notion of human dignity was seen as a response to the notion of the 'dignity of the state,' which is very much present in recent German history, particularly in the battle against the so-called Weimar System, the first democratic constitution in force in Germany during the 1919-1933 period. National-Socialist propaganda discredited the democratic constitution with the claim that the dignity of the state should be re-established.

It seems all the more interesting, and to a certain extent not easy to understand, that the European Convention on Human Rights, the first binding international treaty that followed the Universal Declaration of Human Rights, does not expressly refer to human dignity. The Preamble only refers to human rights and fundamental freedoms. None of the specific rights mentions human dignity. It is difficult to speculate about the reasons. It may well be that at that time, the draftsmen were of the opinion that human dignity would be too wide a notion to be included in treaty language. This has not hindered the Convention Organs to interpret the European Convention on the basis of an understanding of human dignity. I would personally be of the opinion that no other way of interpretation would have been justified.

Let me also come back to President Barak's lecture. He sees human dignity as the source of all fundamental rights. On the other hand this must mean that human dignity is subject to limitations through balancing, as President Barak explained.

There seem to be advantages and disadvantages in this theory. Israel, in fact, then has a full catalogue of rights not listed expressly in the Basic Law. That is certainly an important advantage. As a disadvantage, one may point to the fact that the fundamental concept of human dignity as an absolute limit for state action can easily be blurred. In German Law and in the system of the European Convention on Human Rights, human dignity is generally seen as an absolute limit to state action, although what human dignity requires may be dependent on the context.

Is it possible to avoid the danger just explained? I see a possibility of making distinctions between secondary rights flowing from the concept and subject to limitations, and the fundamental right of human dignity as an

---

[5] See Adalbert Podlech, Art. 1, in 1 Reihe Alternativkommentare – *Kommentar zum Grundgesetz Für Die Bundesrepublik Deutschland* 2nd edition, Rudolf Wassermann, ed., (1989) pp. 202-203.

[6] *Ibid.*

absolute limit. I believe that the absolute nature of human dignity is very important as a concept, even if President Chaskalson is certainly right that it will be a long time before every human being around the globe can enjoy human dignity in the full sense. In that respect, one should also see the important distinction between the different sorts of rights. Torture inflicted by state organs can never be justified. The fulfilment of the right to housing may for some time be beyond the possibilities of the state.

III. Human Dignity as an Element in Interpreting the European Convention on Human Rights

It has become clear through the case law of the Commission and Court that human dignity is an important element when interpreting the European Convention. Indeed, referring to Article 3 of the Convention, which prohibits inhuman and degrading treatment, it would seem to be impossible to interpret that rule without taking into account what human dignity requires.

This became very clear in the famous Tyrer Case, where birching by police officials on the basis of a formal court judgment was at issue. The European Court of Human Rights referred particularly to the institutionalized use of force through judicially imposed birching as an assault upon the dignity of the human person and upon his or her physical integrity. This was seen to be a violation of Article 3. Let me quote from the Court's judgment:[7]

> The very nature of judicial corporal punishment is that it involves one human being inflicting physical violence on another human being. Furthermore, it is institutionalised violence, that is in the present case violence committed by the law, ordered by the judicial authorities of the state and carried out by the police authorities of the state (...) Thus, although the applicant did not suffer any severe or long lasting effects, his punishment—whereby he was treated as an object in the power of the authorities—constituted an assault on precisely that which is one of the named purposes of Article 3 to protect, namely a persons dignity and physical integrity. Neither can it be excluded that the punishment may have had adverse physiological effects.
>
> The institutionalised character of this violence is further compounded by the whole aura of official procedure attending the punishment and by the fact that those inflicting it were total strangers to the offender.

It would seem that the Court, in the Tyrer Case, has very well interpreted Article 3 on the basis of human dignity. To treat a human being in such a way as an object, even without lasting consequences, must be seen as an attack on human dignity.

---

[7] Tyrer v. United Kingdom (1978) 26 Eur. Ct. H.R. (ser. A) p. 16.

Certainly less obvious is the possible relationship between human dignity and the length of court proceedings. This relationship was established in the Bock case concerning Germany. In this case, a divorce procedure lasted for nine years. This was clearly a violation of Article 6 according to which a civil case must be determined 'within a reasonable time.' However, there was a very peculiar element essential in this case. The procedure lasted so long because the wife, as defendant, questioned the mental health of her husband, the plaintiff. During most of the nine years, different experts were heard by the different courts involved, finally arriving at the conclusion that no grounds existed for questioning the mental and procedural capacity of the plaintiff.

The Commission and Court expressly referred to this element of the case. The Commission stated that the examination of the capacity to take part in proceedings involves particular problems with regard to an individual's dignity, and to his right to respect for his private life under Article 8 § 1 of the Convention:[8]

> The Commission observes that under the German Code of Civil procedure the courts shall, ex officio, consider a lack of the capacity to take part in proceedings. In general, the courts will proceed on the assumption of a party's capacity to take part in proceedings. Furthermore, section 607 of the Civil Code provides that even persons with a limited capacity to enter into legal transactions may take part in matrimonial proceedings. In case of doubt, the courts have to take expert evidence. However, German law does not provide for coercive measures to secure a party's examination by a medical expert in this kind of proceedings. The question of a party's capacity to take part in proceedings forms part of the plaintiff's burden of proof, in default of proof the action being inadmissible.
>
> In the present divorce case, altogether four experts were involved before the issue of the applicant's capacity to take part in the proceedings was settled in his favour. The Düsseldorf Regional Court appointed the second expert, Dr. Ba, although it was doubtful from the very beginning that the applicant would accept to be examined by him. However, the Court does not seem to have considered appointing as expert the public health officer Dr. L. In this respect, the Commission notes that, after the applicant lodged his divorce action, his wife brought— ultimately unsuccessful—guardianship proceedings against him, in the course of which he was committed to a mental hospital.
>
> The Commission understands that the German courts took the issue of the applicant's capacity to take part in proceedings seriously. However, especially where a person is finally found

---

[8] Bock v. Germany (1989) 150 Eur. Ct. H.R. (ser. A) pp. 36-37.

not to be mentally ill, proceedings of the kind in question raise serious problems. The High Contracting Parties are, therefore, obliged to provide under their domestic procedural laws, for appropriate means to have this issue determined speedily so as to permit the main proceedings on the divorce to be terminated within a reasonable time. In the present case, however, the matter of the applicant's capacity to take part in the proceedings was finally settled only after more than nine years.

The Commission finds that, as a result of the delays for which the courts must be held responsible, viewed together and cumulatively, the applicant's case was not heard within a reasonable time, as required by Article 6 § 1 of the Convention.

The Court was even clearer:[9]

In the present case, the Court notes first that, one after the other, proceedings based on Mr Bock's alleged mental ill-health failed. A guardianship application was dismissed in 1975; a further action for a declaration of his incapacity was turned down in the following year. Yet doubts still persisted in the national courts as to his soundness of mind, although, by the time of the final divorce judgment, there was a total of five reports attesting Mr Bock's soundness of mind against one whose author had been disqualified. Moreover, this case concerned matters central to the enjoyment of private and family life, namely relations between spouses, as well as between the parents and their children.

Finally, the Court cannot disregard the personal situation of the applicant who, for some nine years, suffered by reason of the doubts cast on the state of his mental health subsequently proved unfounded. This represented a serious encroachment on human dignity.

IV. Human Dignity and Torture

In the famous case of Ireland against the United Kingdom, one of the main issues was whether the application of the so-called five techniques amounted to torture or not. The European Commission of Human Rights saw them as torture, the European Court of Human Rights only as inhuman treatment. The Court, to avoid the consequence of torture, relied particularly on the severity of the treatment. You will recall that the so-called five techniques consisted of at the same time hooding a prisoner, putting him into a very uncomfortable position against the wall, exposing him to very high noise continuously and

---

[9] Bock v. Germany (1989) 150 Eur. Ct. H.R. (ser. A) p. 23.

depriving him of food and sleep. The system was also explained as a sensory deprivation technique. The Commission reasoned as follows:[10]

> In the present case, the five techniques applied together were designed to put severe mental and physical stress, causing severe suffering, on a person in order to obtain information from him. It is true that all methods of interrogation that go beyond the mere asking of questions may bring some pressure on the person concerned, but they cannot, by that very fact, be called inhuman. The five techniques are to be distinguished from those methods.
>
> Compared with inhuman treatment discussed earlier, the stress caused by the application of the five techniques is not only different in degree. The combined application of methods that prevent the use of the senses, especially the eyes and the ears, directly affect the personality physically and mentally. The will to resist or to give in cannot, under such conditions be formed with any degree of independence. Those most firmly resistant might give in at an early state when subjected to this sophisticated method to break or even eliminate the will.
>
> It is this character of the combined use of the five techniques which, in the opinion of the Commission, renders them in breach of Article 3 of the Convention in the form not only of inhuman and degrading treatment, but also of torture within the meaning of that provision.
>
> Indeed, the systematic application of the techniques for the purpose of inducing a person to give information shows a clear resemblance to those methods of systematic torture which have be known over the ages. Although the five techniques—also called disorientation or sensory deprivation techniques—might not necessarily cause any severe after-effects the Commission sees in them a modern system of torture falling into the same category as those systems which have been applied in previous times as the means of obtaining information and confessions.

I am aware of the specific sensitivity this issue has in Israel. I remain convinced, however, that the Commission was right. I do not believe that it is compatible with human dignity to bring this sort of physical and mental pressure on a person to force him or her to confess.

We should not forget that the world-wide definition of torture, as included in Article 1 of the United Nations Torture Convention, particularly refers to the term torture as meaning any act by which severe pain or suffering,

---

[10] Ireland v. United Kingdom (1976) Y.B. Eur. Conv. on H.R. pp. 792-794 (Eur. Comm'n H.R.).

whether physical or mental, is intentionally inflicted on a person for such purposes as obtaining from him or a third person information or a confession.

V. Prisoners and Dignity

In many cases human dignity has been an important element in interpreting the rights of prisoners under specific circumstances. Probably the most severe situation faced by the Commission was during the Interstate Case, brought by several countries against Turkey when delegates of the Commission visited military detention houses in Turkey. The threatening behaviour of the soldiers vis-à-vis prisoners for the purpose of intimidation was something that very much concerned the delegates.

A Greek Case, which was finally settled, concerned the situation of a young Dutch woman who did not speak a word of Greek in a Greek prison together with a group of women prisoners with whom she could not communicate except by signals. I have no hesitation in saying that the Commission would have found that to be a degrading treatment in the extreme.[11]

In British prison cases, the lack of sufficient toilet facilities was a phenomenon which finally did not come to a Commissions' report because of technical procedural reasons. Again, I would have no difficulty in describing these situations as violating human dignity and constituting inhuman treatment.[12]

A full article 31 report was put forth by the Commission before the Court in the case of Hurtado against Switzerland. The case was settled before the Court. The matter concerned a prisoner who was suspected of being a very dangerous drug dealer. He had been overpowered by a special police unit in a very violent attack. The Commission found that to be fully justified because he was suspected of being armed and police feared that he would use his firearms immediately. However, the person was then not given proper medical treatment, although one rib had been broken during the attack. He was not

---

[11] See Van Kuijk v. Greece, App. No. 14986/89 (1991) 70 Eur. Comm'n H.R. Dec. & Rep. 240 and (1992) Y.B. Eur. Conv. on H.R. 82 (Eur. Comm'n H.R.).

[12] The report by the Committee for the Prevention of Torture from its 1990 visit to England dealt with the severely inadequate conditions in British prisons and designated the combination of overcrowding, lack of hygiene and poor regime as inhuman and degrading treatment: see CPT Report, UK (CPT/Inf (91)15), para. 57; Roland Bank, 'International Efforts to Combat Torture and Inhuman Treatment: Have the New Mechanisms Improved Protection?' *European Journal of International Law* 8 (1997) pp. 613, 626. At the time of a follow-up visit in 1994, the situation had not materially improved: see CPT Report, UK (1994), para. 95; Roland Bank, *Die Internationale Bekämpfung von Folter unmenschlicher Behandlung auf den Ebenen der Vereinten Nationen und des Europarates* (1996) p. 305-306.

given fresh underwear, although the attack had resulted in his spoiling himself. The Commission, for this reason saw a violation of Article 3.[13]

VI. Identity and Dignity

The problem of personal identity and human dignity had to be confronted by the European organs under different circumstances. One area concerned the problem of sexual identity. Another concerned the question of early childhood and personal identity.

As for sexual identity, the European Commission of Human Rights, in the case of Dudgeon, for the first time came to the conclusion that discriminatory treatment of homosexuals was a violation of Article 8 of the Convention. The case concerned the criminal prosecution of somebody of homosexual orientation who had had homosexual contacts, and had been warned by the police without a formal prosecution being started. He was an adult and his contact persons were adults as well.[14]

The Commission was more careful than the Court. It did not decide the case on the criminality of homosexual contact as such, but found it to be essential that while in practice prosecutions did not happen, the threat of prosecutions always existed. The Court came to the conclusion that under present circumstances it is a violation of Article 8 if adults are prosecuted for normal homosexual behaviour in private. The Court particularly referred to the development of criminal laws in the member countries of the Council of Europe.[15] The Northern Irish legislation was immediately amended. The same was held in a case concerning the Republic of Ireland and Cyprus.[16]

Much more difficult were the cases concerning so-called transsexuals. In all developed medical systems, transsexual operations are permitted under very rigorous circumstances. This happens in all the Western countries. The issue then arises as to what extent personal documents, identity cards, passports, etc. should show the new identity. The Commission first had an oral hearing on these matters in 1978. A Belgian and a German case were heard orally. The Belgian case went before the Court and was declared inadmissible due to the lack of exhaustion of local remedies.[17] The German case was very impressive, indeed, because the woman explained her regular treatment by the GDR border police when driving from West Berlin to the Federal Republic of Germany. It did not lead to an Article 31 report because the Federal Constitutional Court, in a parallel case, had intervened before and the German law had been changed.[18]

---

[13] See Hurtado v. Switzerland (1994) 280 Eur. Ct. H.R. (ser. A) pp. 10-16.
[14] See Dudgeon v. United Kingdom (1981) 45 Eur. Ct. H.R. (ser. A) pp. 7-16.
[15] See Dudgeon v. United Kingdom (1981) 45 Eur. Ct. H.R. (ser. A) pp. 23-25.
[16] See Norris v. Ireland (1988) 142 Eur. Ct. H.R. (ser. A) pp. 20-21; Modinos v. Cyprus (1993) 259 Eur. Ct. H.R. (ser. A) pp. 10-12.
[17] See Van Oosterwijck v. Belgium (1980) 40 Eur. Ct. H.R. (ser. A) pp. 13-20.
[18] See BVerfGE 49, 286; X. v. Germany, App. No. 6699/74 (1977) 11 Eur. Comm'n H.R. Dec. & Rep. 16.

Then came the case of Rees, concerning the United Kingdom. In this case the Commission drafted a report and put it before the European Court of Human Rights. The Commission's report dated 12 December 1984. The important § 43 of the Commission's report, which bears my signature, states the following:[19]

> § 43. The Commission accepts the applicant's view that sex is one of the essential elements of human personality. If modern medical research into the specific problems of transsexualism and surgery as effected in the present case has made possible a change of sex as far as the normal appearance of a person is concerned, Article 8 must be understood as protecting such an individual against the non-recognition of his/her changed sex as part of his/her personality. This does mean that the legal recognition of a change of sex must be extended to the period prior to the specific moment of change. However, it must be possible for the individual after the change has been effected, to confirm his/her normal appearance by the necessary documents.

This would seem to be a case where human dignity in the most essential way is affected. It was a sad experience, therefore, that the Court was not willing to follow the Commission. In a later French case, the Court in 1992 came to a violation of Article 8 because the applicant in this case was not allowed to choose a female first name and was described in many documents as male, although she appeared as a woman.[20] It is certainly correct that this situation in France was more severe than the one in Britain, but it is regrettable that the Court could not come to the same conclusion for Britain. In a more recent case, again, the Court did not follow the Commission in a British case.[21]

The same specific connection with personal identity occurred in the famous case of Gaskin, where the applicant claimed information concerning his very early childhood. He had been taken into care by the British authorities and apparently lived in several foster families and public institutions. He wanted to be sure about his first deals of existence. The authorities refused information on a general principle that childcare institutions did not give out information on foster families. The Commission and Court concluded that there had been a violation. The Court held as follows:[22]

> In the Court's opinion, persons in the situation of the applicant have a vital interest, protected by the Convention, in receiving the information necessary to know and to understand their childhood and early development. On the other hand, it must be

---

[19] Rees v. United Kingdom (1986) 106 Eur. Ct. H.R. (ser. A) p. 25.
[20] See B. v. France (1992) 232-C Eur. Ct. H.R. (ser. A) pp. 47-54.
[21] See X., Y. and Z. v. United Kingdom (1997) II 35 Eur. Ct. H.R. (ser. A) pp. 628-635.
[22] Gaskin v. United Kingdom (1989) 160 Eur. Ct. H.R. (ser. A) p. 20.

borne in mind that confidentiality of public records is of importance for receiving objective and reliable information, and that such confidentiality can also be necessary for the protection of third persons. Under the latter aspect, a system like the British one, which makes access to records dependent on the consent of the contributor, can in principle be considered to be compatible with the obligations under Article 8, taking into account the State's margin of appreciation. The Court considers, however, that under such a system the interests of the individual seeking access to records relating to his private and family life must be secured when a contributor to the records either is not available or improperly refuses consent. Such a system is only in conformity with the principle of proportionality if it provides that an independent authority finally decides whether access has to be granted in cases where a contributor fails to answer or withholds consent. No such procedure was available to the applicant in the present case.

Accordingly, the procedures followed failed to secure respect for Mr Gaskin's private and family life as required by Article 8 of the Convention. There has therefore been a breach of that provision.

It would seem clear that here, again, personal dignity in a very essential way is affected by the procedure.

VII. The Treatment of Young Persons

The Strasbourg organs have had to deal with several cases concerning young offenders. Let me mention the two cases of Bouamar and Bulus.

In the case of Bouamar, the issue concerned the repeated detention of a young Moroccan for short periods of time by the Belgian authorities. This repeated detention occurred because the law did not make it possible to detain him for longer periods. Such repetition clearly showed a complete lack of respect for the young person, who at the same time certainly behaved illegally. The Commission and Court found a violation of his rights under Article 5, but in fact the human dignity issue was also very much present.[23] In the case of Bulus, a ten-year-old child was to be deported alone without his parents by the Swedish authorities. The Commission intervened and the person was, in fact, not deported.[24]

---

[23] See Bouamar v. Belgium (1988) 129 Eur. Ct. H.R. (ser. A) pp. 21-22 and 34-35.
[24] See Bulus v. Sweden, App. No. 9330/81 (1984) 39 Eur. Comm'n H.R. Dec. & Rep. 75.

VIII. Conclusion

The Strasbourg system has created a specific understanding of human dignity in vulnerable situation. This is an important development of international law.

HUMAN DIGNITY AS A CONSTITUTIONAL VALUE

Arthur Chaskalson

The United Nations was established at a time of widespread revulsion against the holocaust and other evils associated with the Second World War. Within Germany and the occupied territories, Jews and other victims of Nazi terror such as Gypsies and homosexuals, had been treated as people of no worth, who needed to be isolated and excluded from society. As the war progressed, some were used as slave labor in support of the German war effort, others, including those whose who could no longer labor, were eliminated in death camps established for this purpose. We all know that this happened. But on the occasion of the 50th anniversary of the Universal Declaration of Human Rights, these are facts that need to be stated. It was against this background that the United Nations was established and the Universal Declaration of Human Rights adopted.

The Charter of the United Nations called upon member states to reaffirm 'faith in human rights, in the dignity and worth of the human person, in the equal rights of men and women and of nations large and small.'[1] In a sense this was a radical move. Before the war, human rights and dignity had been protected by the domestic law of some countries, but not by international law. Positivism was then the dominant legal theory, and practices inconsistent with respect for fundamental rights and human dignity were sanctioned in many parts of the world. Colonialism, discrimination and exploitation were widespread. And this was so even where the legal order was rights based. In the United States of America, for instance, fundamental rights had been entrenched in the constitution for more than 150 years, yet racial segregation was practiced, particularly in the South, and racial and gender discrimination existed throughout the country.

The UN Charter, reacting to the horrors of the recent war, articulated aspirations for a new world order in which things would be different. It went

---

[1] Preamble to the Charter.

beyond affirming faith in human rights and dignity. It required, also, from all member states that adopted the Charter, a pledge to promote 'respect for, and observance of, human rights and fundamental freedoms'[2] and to take joint and separate action in cooperation with the United Nations for the achievement of this purpose.[3]

The Universal Declaration of Human Rights was the first major step taken in pursuit of this goal. The General Assembly of the United Nations adopted it on 10 December 1948. The preamble to the Declaration records that 'disregard and contempt for human rights' had 'resulted in barbarous acts which have outraged the conscience of mankind,' that the 'peoples of the United Nations have in the Charter reaffirmed their faith in fundamental human rights, in the dignity and the worth of the human person and in the equal rights of men and women and have determined to promote social progress and better standards of life.' It records, also, the pledge made in the Charter to promote 'universal respect for the observance of human rights and fundamental freedoms' and goes on to proclaim the Universal Declaration of Human Rights 'as a common standard for all peoples and all nations' for the attainment of this goal.

Respect for human dignity is implicit in the rights of personality, and in the social and economic rights set forth in the Universal Declaration and other human rights instruments. It is inherent in any legal order based on freedom and human rights. Yet it is not entrenched as a discrete right in all human rights instruments. It is not, for instance, referred to as a right in the Universal Declaration of Human Rights, the International Covenant for the Protection of Civil and Political Rights, the European Convention for the Protection of Human Rights and Fundamental Freedoms or in the United States, Canadian or Indian[4] constitutions. I could not even find 'dignity' or 'human dignity' listed in the indexes of books on Canadian, Indian, United States and European constitutional law that I consulted, and the only legal dictionary in English that I could find that listed dignity, was the 1990 edition of Black's Law Dictionary which refers to dignity as a term in English law, and gives as its meaning, 'an honour; a title, station or distinction.'

In a broad and general sense, respect for dignity implies respect for the autonomy of each person, and the right of everyone not to be devalued as a human being or treated in a degrading or humiliating manner. The reluctance to give dignity the status of a discrete right in human rights instruments may be due to the breadth of its meaning and the difficulty of defining its limits. Greater certainty is achieved by enumerating the rights of personality to be

---

[2] Article 55(1) of the Charter.
[3] Article 56.
[4] The preamble to the Indian Constitution does, however, make a commitment to secure for all its citizens justice, liberty, equality and 'fraternity, assuring the dignity of the individual.' The Indian Supreme Court has held that the preamble may be invoked to determine the ambit of the fundamental rights: Keshavananda v. State of Kerala (1973) SC 1461.

protected. Where this has been done, the entrenchment or implication of a residual right of dignity might be thought to have an open-ended quality which would be unmanageable. The same is, however, true of the right to life, which appears more often than dignity does, as a discrete right in human rights instruments.[5] But in India, where dignity is not an enumerated right, the Supreme Court has said that Article 21, which provides that 'no person shall be deprived of his life or personal liberty except according to procedure established by law,' includes the right to live in human dignity and all that goes along with it. Every act which offends against or impairs human dignity would constitute deprivation *pro tanto* of the right to life.[6]

To legal systems based on Roman law, the concept of dignity as a right is not strange. Roman law treats dignity as a right of personality, and provides civil and criminal remedies for its infringement.[7] But respect for dignity is also a value, and these two aspects of dignity—as a right and as a value—are sometimes conflated.

In the Declaration of Human Rights dignity is treated as a foundational value for the enumerated rights. Article 1 of the Declaration states that:

> All human beings are born free and equal in dignity and rights.
> They are endowed with reason and conscience and should act towards one another in a spirit of brotherhood.

Article 2 then deals with entitlement to the rights, making it clear that they vest in everyone without distinction of any kind. The remaining articles enumerate rights to which 'everyone' is entitled. All of these rights can be analyzed and defended as being necessary for the protection or promotion of human dignity.

Dignity is also given a foundational role in the International Covenant on Civil and Political Rights whose preamble asserts that fundamental rights 'derive from the inherent dignity of the human person.' So too, in the preamble to the International Covenant on Economic, Cultural and Social Rights there is a reference to the recognition given in the UN Charter of the 'inherent dignity and of the equal and inalienable rights of all members of the human family,' and the assertion that 'these rights derive from the inherent dignity of the human person' is repeated.

Treating dignity as a foundational value of a human rights order may give it greater weight than if it were treated merely as an enumerated right. This is the case in Germany. The Basic Rights set out in the German Constitution begin with the provisions of Article 1 that:

---

[5] The right to life is protected by section 7 of the Canadian Constitution, section 21 of the Indian Constitution, and Article V of the US Constitution. In Canada the right is formulated as a positive right, in the USA and India as a negative right.

[6] Bhagwati J. in Francis Coralie v. Union Territory of Delhi A.I.R. (1981) SC 746 p. 753.

[7] The civil remedy was the *actio injuriarum* and *crimen injuria* was a crime.

1) The dignity of man shall be inviolable. To respect and protect it shall be the duty of all state authority.
2) The German people therefore acknowledge inviolable and inalienable human rights as the basis of every community, of peace and justice in the world.
3) The following basic rights shall bind the legislature, the executive and the judiciary as directly enforceable law.

The German State has a duty to respect and protect human dignity, which is regarded as the central value of the Basic Law. The basic rights set out in the articles following Article 1 are all interpreted and applied by the German Federal Constitutional Court in the context of this central value, and the decisions of the German courts provide a prodigious jurisprudence of dignity.[8]

Dignity has also been recognized as having a foundational role in jurisdictions in which it is entrenched as a discrete right. The Hungarian and South African Constitutions both include the right to dignity amongst the enumerated rights entitled to protection.[9] In both countries, however, the Constitutional Courts give special weight to dignity.[10] The Hungarian Constitutional Court has described the right to life and the right to dignity as the source and the essential content of all other human rights.[11] Similar views have been expressed by the South African Constitutional Court.[12] And even in constitutions in which dignity is not mentioned either as a right or a foundational value, the connection between human dignity and a human rights order has been recognized. In the United States of America, the Supreme Court has said that the foundation for the privilege against self-incrimination 'is the respect a government must accord to the dignity and integrity of its citizens,'[13] and that the basic concept of human dignity is at the core of the prohibition of

---

[8] The role of human dignity in German jurisprudence is discussed by Kommers, *The Constitutional Jurisprudence of the Federal Republic of Germany*, Ch. 7 (Duke University Press 1997); Currie, *The Constitution of the Federal Republic of Germany* (University of Chicago Press 1994) pp. 314-316; Eberle, 'Human Dignity, Privacy, and Personality in German and American Constitutional Law,' *Utah Law Review* 963 (1997); Fletcher, 'Human Dignity as a Constitutional Value,' *Western Ontario Law Review* 22 (1984) p. 171.

[9] Section 54(1) of the Hungarian Constitution and section 10 of the South African Constitution.

[10] See below for a discussion of the importance of human dignity in the evolving human rights jurisprudence in South African.

[11] Per Solyom P. in the capital punishment case, Decision No. 23/1990 of 24 October 1990. Two of the judges of the Hungarian Constitutional Court, Dr. Labady and Dr. Terstyanszky, were of the opinion that human life and dignity are . . . included in the list of human rights in modern constitutions as the sources of rights or values beyond the reach of law, which are inviolable, rather than as fundamental rights.

[12] S. v. Makwanyane (1995) 6 BCLR 778(CC), par. 144: see page 12 below.

[13] Miranda v. Arizona (1966) 384 US 436, p. 460.

cruel punishments.[14] In Canada it has been said that the genesis of the rights and freedoms in the Canadian Charter include 'respect for the inherent dignity of the human person,'[15] and that 'The idea of dignity finds expression in almost every right and freedom guaranteed by the [Canadian] Charter.'[16]

Over the past fifty years human rights jurisprudence has developed rapidly, and human dignity has come to be accepted as a core value of this jurisprudence. By 1983 Professor Schachter could rightly say:

> Political leaders, jurists and philosophers have increasingly alluded to the dignity of human persons as a basic ideal so generally recognised as to require no independent support. It has acquired a resonance that leads it to be invoked widely as a legal and moral ground for protest against degrading and abusive treatment. No other ideal seems so clearly accepted as a universal social good.[17]

But when we enquire whether this universal good has been achieved in the course of the past fifty years, each part of the world has its own story to tell. These stories include accounts of oppression, inhumanity and suffering. Apartheid, the cultural revolution, ethnic cleansing, state terror, torture and disappearances, children removed from their parents and homes and forced to take up arms, and refugees driven from their homes and country as a consequence of war or oppression in different parts of the world, and left homeless in strange and foreign countries, are but some of these stories. And all of them involve accounts of oppression and of victims being subjected to degrading and abusive treatment.

There are also stories of poverty and famine, of millions of people living in abject conditions in underdeveloped parts of the world and elsewhere, including the slums of great cities. Unable to sustain themselves in ways that permit them to meet the basic necessities of life, they too experience degradation and humiliation.

A question that cannot be ignored is how did these things happen, when the nations of the world have pledged themselves to promote human rights, social progress and better standards of life? Why do they continue to happen, if respect for human dignity is indeed a universal social good?

These are questions we need to address to our own countries. Has our country lived up to the pledge made fifty years ago in the UN Charter? Has our country sought since then to promote human dignity within its own borders? How does our country treat its minorities, its prisoners, and people living in poverty? How has our country met its pledge to cooperate with other countries

---

[14] Trop v. Dulles (1958) 356 US 86 p. 100; Gregg v. Georgia (1976) 428 US 153 p. 182 (Stewart, Powell and Stevens JJ) and p. 230 (Brennan J).

[15] Dickson CJC in R v. Oakes (1986) 19 CRR 308 pp. 334-335.

[16] Wilson, J., in In v. Morgenthaler (1998) 31 CRR 1 p. 82; see also, Cory J., in Kindler v. Canada (1992) 6 CRR 193 pp. 237-8.

[17] *The American Journal of International Law*, 77 (1983) p. 848.

and with the UN to achieve the purpose of the Charter and the Universal Declaration of Human Rights? Has it met the pledge that it made when it adhered to the Charter? And what has the international community done during the past fifty years about these matters?

I will try to answer the questions I have raised as far as my country, South Africa, is concerned. Our history before the Second World War was one of colonialism and white political and economic domination. After the war, when the countries of the world committed themselves to the principles contained in the Universal Declaration of Human Rights, South Africa declined to do so. Instead it adopted apartheid as state policy. Apartheid affected all aspects of life in South Africa. It institutionalized racial discrimination through statutes and regulations that sought to classify, define, control and regulate the lives of all South Africans, advancing the interests of the already powerful and dominant white community and marginalizing blacks who are the great majority of the population. It was enforced by the application of harsh and unjust laws, including draconian security laws, which were condemned by the international community as being gross violations of basic human rights. Apartheid itself was declared a crime against humanity.[18]

Apartheid caused poverty, degradation and suffering on a massive scale, denying to the overwhelming majority of the population access to the ownership and occupation of most of the land, to proper education, to mobility and work opportunities other than in menial occupations, and to fundamental rights and freedoms which are essential for self esteem. It forced those who were not white into inferior positions in society, and required them to live in degrading and humiliating conditions. Through the use of pass laws it brought about the separation of black families and had a devastating impact on their family life. It led to great disparities which still exist between blacks and whites in relation to economic power, wealth, skills and living conditions.

After a long and debilitating struggle, a crucial decision was taken by political leaders who accepted that the best hope for our country lay neither in oppression nor war, but in a commitment to reconciliation and the reconstruction of our society. A new constitution was adopted to give effect to this decision. The constitutional order, which has taken the place of apartheid, is totally different from that which previously existed. It is based on respect for human rights and democracy. The legal system is one in which the Constitution is supreme and adherence to the rule of law is demanded. According to the Constitution all law must be consistent with the Bill of Rights. The Constitution calls for a coherent system of law built on the foundations of the Bill of Rights, in which the common law and customary law will be developed and legislation will be interpreted in a manner consistent with the Bill of Rights and with our obligations under international law. The core values are democracy, human dignity, equality and freedom.

---

[18] The relevant resolutions and other authorities are referred to in the report of the Truth and Reconciliation Commission, published for the Commission by Juta & Co. Ltd. (1998), vol. I, pp. 94-102.

In the light of our history, the importance of dignity in the interpretation and application of the Bill of Rights has been stressed.[19] According to the Constitutional Court:

> Respect for the dignity of all human beings is particularly important in South Africa. For apartheid was a denial of a common humanity. Black people were refused respect and dignity and thereby the dignity of all South Africans was diminished. The new Constitution rejects this past and affirms the equal worth of all South Africans. Thus recognition and protection of human dignity is the touchstone of the new political order and is fundamental to the new Constitution.[20]

In decisions dealing with punishment and discrimination, the Constitutional Court has given particular weight to the underlying constitutional value of dignity. In the capital punishment case,[21] a unanimous court of 11 judges held that capital punishment was inconsistent with the values of our Constitution and the rights entrenched in it, including the right to dignity.[22] The main judgment, with which none of the members of the Court disagreed, referred to the rights to life and dignity as the most important of all human rights and the source of all other personal rights in chapter 3. By committing ourselves to a society founded on the recognition of human rights we are required to value these two rights above all others. And this must be demonstrated by the state in everything it does, including the way it punishes criminals.[23]

The importance of dignity as a constitutional value was reaffirmed in the corporal punishment case,[24] where the court held that corporal punishment of juvenile offenders was not justifiable under our constitution, saying:

> The simple message is that the state must, in imposing punishment, do so in accordance with certain standards; these will reflect the values which underpin the Constitution; in the present context, it means that punishment must respect human dignity.

---

[19] Section 1 of the 1996 Constitution sets out the founding values of the constitutional order, which include, 'human dignity, the achievement of equality and the advancement of human rights and freedoms.' In the interim Constitution of 1993, the founding values were not expressly recorded, but the Court attached special significance to dignity as a constitutional value.

[20] O'Regan, J., in S. v. Makwanyane, n. 11 above, para. 329.

[21] S. v. Makwanyane, n. 12 above. The case was decided under the interim Constitution of 1993.

[22] Rights regarded as relevant were the right to life (section 9), the right to human dignity (section 10) and the right to equality (section 7), as well as the commitment in the constitution to 'ubuntu.' Ubuntu 'recognises a person's status as a human being, entitled to unconditional respect, dignity, value and acceptance from the members of the community such person happens to be part of.' (Langa J. at para. 223).

[23] Ibid. Para.144; see also para. 225, and 326-328.

[24] S. v. Williams (1995) 7 BCLR 861(CC), para. 38.

Dignity is also at the heart of the approach to privacy. A breach of privacy might occur through an unlawful intrusion into the personal privacy of another, or by way of an unlawful disclosure of private facts about another person.[25] The scope of the right to privacy is related to the concept of identity:

> Rights, like the right to privacy, are not based on a notion of the unencumbered self, but on the notion of what is necessary to have one's autonomous identity ... In the context of privacy this means that it is ... the inner sanctum of the person ... which is shielded from erosion by conflicting rights of the community ... Privacy is acknowledged in the truly personal realm, but as a person moves into communal relations and activities ... the scope of the personal space shrinks accordingly.[26]

In interpreting the equality and anti-discrimination clauses of the Constitution the Court has linked discrimination with the impairment of dignity, saying:

> Given the history of this country we are of the view that 'discrimination' has acquired a particular pejorative meaning relating to the unequal treatment of people based on attributes and characteristics attaching to them. We are emerging from a period of our history during which the humanity of the majority of the inhabitants of this country was denied. They were treated as not having inherent worth; as objects whose identities could be arbitrarily defined by those in power rather than as persons of infinite worth. In short they were denied recognition of their inherent dignity.[27]

Discrimination is thus said to exist if there has been differentiation based on attributes and characteristics that have the potential to impair the fundamental human dignity of persons as human beings or to affect them adversely in a comparably serious manner.[28]

Dignity and equality are interdependent. Inequality is established not simply through group-based differential treatment, but through differentiation, which perpetuates disadvantage and leads to the scarring of the sense of dignity and self-worth. Conversely, an invasion of dignity is more easily established when there is an inequality of power and status between violator and victim.[29]

---

[25] Bernstein v. Bester (1996) 4 BCLR 449(CC), para. 68, citing Financial Mail (Pty) Ltd. v. Sage Holdings Ltd. (1993) 2 SA 451(A), at 462F.
[26] Ibid. paras. 65 and 67.
[27] Prinsloo v. van der Linde (1997) 6 BCLR 759(CC), para. 31.
[28] Harksen v. Lane NO (1997) 11 BCLR 1489(CC), para. 53.
[29] Sachs, J., in The National Coalition for Gay and Lesbian Equality v. The Minister of Justice (CCT11/98, judgment delivered on 9 October 1998; to be reported in (1998) 12 BCLR).

The past hangs over us and has had a profound effect on the environment in which we live. It is seen most obviously in the disparities of wealth and skills between those who benefited from colonial rule and apartheid and those who did not. Although recent economic indicators show that the disparities are very gradually beginning to grow less, there are still millions of people without adequate housing, health facilities and proper education, without access to clean water and with limited employment opportunities. There can be little dignity in living in such conditions. These realities of our society are sobering but in the light of our history not surprising. The process of transformation was always going to be difficult.

This has implications for the way in which our courts approach questions of social and economic rights. The Constitution makes provision for persons to 'have access to' adequate housing, health care, food and water, and social security.[30] The state is required to take reasonable legislative and other measures, within its available resources, to achieve the progressive realization of these rights.[31] This imposes a positive obligation on the state. It does not have the resources to meet all these needs at once, and so the Constitution enjoins it to take steps progressively to do so within its available resources. The only case yet to come before the Constitutional Court in respect of these social and economic rights, concerned a claim by a hospital patient suffering from chronic renal failure, to be provided with dialysis treatment. The hospital had refused to do so because the patient did not meet criteria which had been prescribed for such treatment. The criteria were rational and directed to making the best use of the available resources. The Constitutional Court declined to interfere with the hospital's decision, saying:

> The state's resources are limited and the appellant does not meet the criteria for admission to the renal dialysis program. Unfortunately this is true not only of the appellant but also of many others who need access to renal dialysis units or to other health services. There are also those who need access to housing, food and water, employment opportunities, and social security. These too are aspects of the right to 'human life: the right to live as a human being, to be part of a broader community, to share in the experience of humanity.' The state has to manage its limited resources in order to address all these claims. There will be times when this requires it to adopt a holistic approach to the larger needs of society rather than to focus on the specific needs of particular individuals within society.

At this stage of the development of our country the shortage of resources has a material bearing on what the state can be expected to do:

---

[30] Sections 26(1) and 27(1).
[31] Sections 26(2) and 27(2).

> Society ... must regulate what is to be given so that it has the resources to honour claims, and to honour all similar claims in a similar way.[32]

The courts cannot do much more in any given case that may come before them than this. First, to satisfy themselves that the state acknowledges and is genuinely seeking to give effect to its constitutional obligation to meet these basic needs, and secondly, to ensure that decisions are taken rationally and implemented fairly.

Transformation takes time. Resources are scarce and competition for available resources can lead to conflict and tension. We need to acknowledge this. We need also to recognize, however, that material progress has been made in South Africa, that relationships within the country have improved, and that there is a genuine commitment to transforming our society so as to achieve the aspirations set out in our Constitution. South Africa is a far better place today than it was five years ago. We are beginning to restore dignity to our people.

Let me return to the larger picture. What has the international community done and what can it do about the gross impairment of human dignity of so many people in so many different parts of the world? The examples of the gross impairments of dignity to which I have referred earlier can frequently be traced to two causes, conflict and underdevelopment, and not infrequently, they go together.

The causes of conflict are often complex and subject to contradictory constructions depending upon the side that is taken. The conflict may be fanned by nationalism, ethnicity, religion or ideology where the participants believe passionately in the justice of their own cause and of the actions taken to support it. Sometimes there is simply naked oppression—the marginalization and exclusion of persons who do not belong to a dominant group within a particular society, or the crude abuse of power exercised to put down dissent against arbitrary rule. But they usually have this in common. The victims are treated as persons of little worth, whose death or indignity is justified as being necessary for, or incidental to, the achievement of an end more important than their welfare.

The causes of underdevelopment are equally complex. They embrace factors such as the history of a particular country (most of the poorest countries were once colonies of the richest countries), the country's economic policies, lack of the capital needed for development, obligations to make massive debt repayments, the imposition of adverse terms of trade, lack of natural resources, lack of skills, corruption and mismanagement, and pillaging of natural resources and the environment, often by powerful foreign corporations.

Because of the complexity of the causes, multiple strategies are required to deal with such matters. The United Nations is the organization through which the international community expresses itself and takes the action that is

---

[32] John A. Most, 'Autonomy and Rights: Dignity and Right,' *Journal of Contemporary Health Law and Policy* 11, pp. 473-477.

necessary to address these issues. It has not been effective in preventing the many gross abuses of human rights that have occurred during the past fifty years. Governments of states are naturally reluctant to become involved in the affairs of other states, partly because of concerns for the principle of national sovereignty, and partly because of the financial and human cost of doing so. This reluctance was heightened for most of the past fifty years because of the cold war and the conflicting national interests that had to be accommodated in addressing any particular issue. The various agencies of the UN are able to provide assistance to impoverished countries as a contribution to their social progress and an improvement of the their standard of living. These activities are of importance, but the problems of poverty and underdevelopment call for much more than this, and are not likely to be alleviated in material respects in the foreseeable future.

The international community is better placed to take action against the commission of gross abuses of human rights. Paul Sieghart[33] has commented on the importance of treaties entered into since the adoption of the Universal Declaration, saying they:

> (...) impose obligations on many governments as to what they may or may not do to individuals over whom they are able to exercise state power. To the extent of those obligations the strict doctrine of national sovereignty has been cut down in two crucial respects. First, how a state treats its own subjects is now the legitimate concern of international law. Secondly, there is now a superior international standard, established by common consent, which may be used for judging the domestic laws and the actual conduct of sovereign States within their own territories and in the exercise of their internal jurisdictions, and may therefore be regarded as ranking in the hierarchy of laws even above national constitutions.[34]

Although there are difficulties in enforcing treaties and international agreements, a breach of their provisions offers a basis for intervention. If the views of the majority of the House of Lords which heard the first Pinochet case[35] stand when the case is reargued,[36] and become the international standard, high officials responsible for the gross abuses of human rights will be at risk. Lord Nicholls, who was one of the majority, referred to the judgment of the Nuremberg International Military Tribunal, which held that:

---

[33] Sieghart, *The International Law of Human Rights*, (Clarendon Press, Oxford 1983).
[34] *Ibid.* p. 15.
[35] Regina v. Bartle and the Commissioner for the Metropolis and others, Ex parte Pinochet (decision of the House of Lords delivered on 25 November 1998).
[36] On 17 December 1998, the House of Lords set aside the judgment because one of the Law Lords who had participated in the hearing was disqualified from sitting in the case.

> The principle of international law which under certain circumstances, protects the representatives of a state, cannot be applied to acts condemned as criminal by international law. The authors of these acts cannot shelter themselves behind their official position to be freed from punishment.

He went on to point out that a resolution passed unanimously on 11 December 1946 by the UN General Assembly affirmed the principles of international law recognized in the charter of the Nuremberg Tribunal and its judgment:

> From this time on, no head of state could have been in any doubt about his potential personal liability if he participated in acts regarded by international law as crimes against humanity.

And this applies also to other international crimes, such as torture and hostage taking, for as Lord Nicholls says,

> It is not consistent with the existence of these crimes that former officials, however senior, should be immune from prosecution outside their own jurisdiction.

The failure of the international community to prevent ethnic cleansing in the former Yugoslavia and genocide in Rwanda demonstrates the reluctance of governments to involve their countries in conflicts which do not directly affect their national interests. But even allowing for this reluctance, if the political will to do so exists, there are steps short of armed intervention which can be taken, and which may serve as a deterrent. Although diplomatic pressure and sanctions may not be effective to deter acts such as those which were committed in Rwanda and the former Yugoslavia, prompt responses from the international community to prevent action that is imminent, and a determination to penalize those responsible for the commission of gross abuses of human rights, may cause leaders who sanction such activities to have second thoughts before doing so. And if, as was decided last year at Rome, an International Criminal Court is established to deal with gross abuses of human rights, there will be an additional deterrent.

As we enter the new millennium there can be no issues of greater importance to the international community than the promotion of peace, the avoidance of war and the fight against poverty and underdevelopment. Societies in which there is respect for life and dignity are bulwarks against war and poverty. By building societies in which there is respect for life and dignity, we accordingly become actors in the struggle to end war and poverty. That is a struggle worth joining.

HUMAN DIGNITY IN GERMAN LAW*
Eckart Klein

It is a moving moment to be here at a place that means so much to such a vast part of mankind. I feel the burden and the responsibility to lecture on human dignity as a German in Israel. There is a saying that the lessons of history are in vain. This, unfortunately, may often be true. However, the goal of the Basic Law to make the dignity of man the cornerstone of the German State and legal order, and the way that this basic constitutional momentum has been understood and applied for nearly fifty years, give hope that at least sometimes history's lessons are learned.

I. Some Introductory Remarks

In this context, it is very understandable that a provision on the inviolability of human dignity heads the text of the German Basic Law.[1] In most cases, the

---

* Public speech, delivered in Jerusalem on 18 November 1997.

The following notes are mainly restricted to references to the jurisprudence of the Federal Constitutional Court. This does not mean that the relevant literature has not been taken into account. In particular, I wish to point to the following books and articles: Ulrich Becker, *Das Menschenbild des Grundgesetzes* (1996); Ernst Benda, 'Menschenwürde und Persoenlichkeitsrecht,' *Handbuch des Verfassungsrechts*, Benda, Maihofer, Vogel, eds., 2nd edition (1995) p. 161 et seq.; Winfried Brugger, *Menschenwürde, Menschenrechte, Grundrechte* (1997); Horst Dreier, in: *Grundgesetz Kommentar*, Dreier, ed. (1997) Art. 1; Günter Dürig, in: *Grundgesetz-Kommentar*, Maunz, Dürig, eds. (1958) Art. 1; Christoph Enders, 'Die Menschenwürde in der Verfassungsordnung. Zur Dogmatik des Art. 1,' *GG* (1997); Peter Häberle, 'Die Menschenwürde als Grundlage der staatlichen Gemeinschaft,' *Handbuch des Staatsrechts*, 2nd edition, Isensee/Kirchhof, eds. (1995) vol. I, p. 815 et seq.; Wolfram Hoefling, in: *Grundgesetz Kommentar*, Sachs, ed. (1996) Art. 1; Wolfram Hoefling, 'Die Unantastbarkeit der Menschenwürde—Annaeherungen an einen schwierigen Verfassungsrechtssatz,' *Juristische Schulung* 35 (1995) p. 857 et seq.; Philip Kunig, *Grundgesetz-Kommentar*, 4th edition, (1992) vol. I, Art. 1; Christian Starck, in: *Das Bonner Grundgesetz, Kommentar*, 3rd edition, v. Mangoldt, Klein, Starck, eds. (1985) Art. 1, p. 24 et seq.

first articles attempt to express a specific feature of a constitution, to underline what seems to be of particular importance for the whole community. Article 1 of the Bismarck Constitution of 1870 stressed the newly created unity by defining the territorial components of the federal State. Article 1 of the Weimar Constitution proclaimed the German Reich a republic. The Basic Law had to face different needs. Its first article was supposed to address the past as well as the future, to give an answer as well as a promise. The degeneration of State power after 1933 into a barbarian, murderous apparatus should be clearly condemned. The Federal Republic of Germany should be firmly founded upon the perception that the State exists for the benefit of the human being, and not the human being for the benefit of the State. Though this wording, which was contained in a first draft of the new constitution[2] and was similar to the text of the French Declaration of Human Rights of 1789 (Art. II), was not accepted for the final version, article 1 retains this very idea. The dignity of man is the legitimizing basis of the State and its legal order. The State's respect for and protection of human dignity constitute its purpose. The State's failure to serve this purpose would raise the question of the citizens' right to resistance (art. 20 para. 4 BL).

Before taking a closer look at the elements of the concept of human dignity, we have to deal briefly with the architecture of art. 1 BL.

II. Architecture of Article 1 BL

1. Two fundamental statements and conclusions

Article 1 contains two fundamental statements. Both of them are enforced by normative conclusions.

The first declaration is: 'The dignity of man shall be inviolable' (art. 1 para. 1 cl. 1). The second declaration reads, 'The German people therefore acknowledge inviolable and inalienable human rights as the basis of every community, of peace and of justice in the world' (art. 1 para. 2).

The two statements are interrelated. The idea of human rights is linked with the idea of the constitution as such. The constitution adopts the view that dignity of man means the recognition of the human being as a bearer of rights, as 'a person before the law' (see art. 16 CCPR).[3] Dignity of man requires the

---

Many English quotations of the Federal Constitutional Court's decisions are taken from Donald P. Kommers, *The Constitutional Jurisprudence of the Federal Republic of Germany*, 2nd edition (1997) Ch. 7 'Human Dignity and Personhood,' p. 298 et seq.

[1] Starck, loc. cit., p. 29.
[2] Art. 1 para. 1 of the Herrenchiemsee draft (1948).
[3] For the impact of the idea of human rights on the *pouvoir constituant* see Christian Tomuschat, 'Die staatsrechtliche Entscheidung für die internationale Offenheit,' *Handbuch des Staatsrechts*, J. Isensee and P. Kirchhof, eds. (1992), vol. VII, pp. 483, 522.

attribution of rights to the individual which enable him or her to defend his or her own design of life. It has been aptly said recently that human dignity is a 'right to rights.'[4]

The conclusions drawn from these statements are the following: first, to respect and protect the dignity of man shall be the duty of all State authority (art. 1 para. 1 cl. 2); second, 'The following basic rights shall bind the legislature, the executive and the judiciary as directly enforceable law' (art. 1 para. 3). These conclusions contain normative commands addressed to the State, which make the dignity of man the corner stone or, as the Federal Constitutional Court has put it, the constitutive principle in the system of basic rights.[5]

2. The human dignity clause—a basic right in itself

Art. 1 para. 1 includes more than an essential assertion with regard to the State, its purpose and duties. It also embodies a right, a basic right. It is true that this opinion has always been disputed, but the mainstream of legal thinking and, particularly, the jurisprudence of the Federal Constitutional Court have upheld this view.[6] The Court expressly qualifies the phrase 'the dignity of man shall be inviolable' as a legal right,[7] meaning that this clause may also be interpreted as 'Everybody has the right to his or her inviolable dignity.' Seen in the whole context, it would be strange to deny the character of a legal right only in terms of the conceptional basis of all the fundamental rights. The reference to the term 'the following basic rights' in art. 1 para. 3 is not convincing to the contrary. There was no need to include the right to human dignity in para. 3, since the State's duty to respect and to protect it is already clearly expressed in art. 1 para. 1 itself.

Both elements, the objective legal norm and the individual basic right, have a comprehensive impact on the entire legal order. The Federal Constitutional Court, already early in its Lüth decision (1958), has held that the constitution, in particular the basic rights headed by the declaration on human dignity, constitute an order of values that radiate to the whole body of law.[8] Therefore not only the relations between the individual and the State but also the relations between the individuals themselves have to be seen in the light of these values. The implications for the legislative power are that it must respect these values while enacting or amending provisions of private law, and for the executive and judiciary that they must respect these values while

---

[4] Enders, loc. cit., p. 501.
[5] BVerfGE (collection of decisions of the Federal Constitutional Court/FCC) 87, 209, 228 (1992).
[6] See, e.g., Benda, loc. cit., p. 165.
[7] BVerfGE 61, 126, 137 (1982).
[8] BVerfGE 7, 198, 204 et seq. (1958).

applying and interpreting such laws.[9] Directly by the constitution, or indirectly secured by law, human dignity is protected against encroachment by anyone.

3. Special features of art. 1 para. 1

Turning more closely now to art. 1 para. 1 cl. 1, we have to consider what the guarantee of inviolability may mean. Of course, it does not mean that human dignity cannot be violated. But it does say that dignity of man must not be violated, and it further says that a loss of dignity does not necessarily follow its violation. Human dignity may be violated but not taken.[10] It is not lost by an undignified act of the individual himself. There is no self-deprivation of dignity seen from the perspective of the law. A mere moral judgment may come to a different conclusion.

Equally, a waiver of dignity is not acceptable under art. 1. The Federal Constitutional Court has held that human dignity means not only the individual dignity of the person but the dignity of man as a species. Dignity is therefore not at the disposal of the individual.[11] It is another question as to whether specific ways of acting (e.g., the transmitting of the files of a divorce proceeding to a person in charge of instituting disciplinary proceedings against a civil servant) would amount to a violation of the right to personality, which is based in German law on art. 2 para. 1 in conjunction with art. 1 para. 1 BL, if it is done with the consent of the person concerned.[12] We have to address this issue later in more detail.

At this stage it might be useful to point to two other special features that distinguish the dignity clause from most other basic rights. The first characteristic is that its scope of protection is not limited to a certain area of action or behaviour, as is the case with other fundamental rights like the rights to life, to express opinion, to assemble or to associate.[13] Only the right to the free development of the personality (art. 2 para. 1) and the right to be equal before the law (art. 3 para. 1) have a similarly broad scope, but their meaning may become more easily elucidated by other provisions of the Constitution.

The second peculiarity of the dignity clause is that any encroachment upon human dignity means a violation. This is not the case with other human rights, where interference with the protected rights may be justified by the limits which are, expressly or implicitly, provided for by the Constitution.[14] By

---

[9] Eckart Klein, 'Grundrechtliche Schutzpflicht des Staates,' *Neue Juristische Wochenschrift (NJW)* 42 (1989), pp. 1633, 1640.
[10] BVerfGE 87, 209, 228 (1992).
[11] BVerfGE 45, 187, 229 (1977).
[12] Cf. BVerfGE 27, 344, 352 (1970).
[13] See Hoefling, *JuS* 35 (1995), p. 858.
[14] Peter Lerche, 'Grundrechtsschranken,' *Handbuch des Staatsrechts*, Isensee and Kirchhof eds. (1992), vol. V, p. 780 et seq.

contrast, human dignity has an absolute effect.[15] There is, according to the jurisprudence of the courts, no way to balance other legal interests, be they of other individuals or of the community, with the dignity of a person. The principle of proportionality does not come into play as long as an intrusion upon human dignity has been established. It is only a further consequence from the absolute effect of art. 1 para. 1 that art. 19 para. 2 does not apply;[16] this provision generally prohibits encroachment upon the essential content of a basic right.

III. The Substantial Meaning of Art. 1 Para. 1 BL

1. The objective scope of protection

It is evidently difficult to get a clear picture of the meaning of human dignity. The famous German philosopher Immanuel Kant found that means dignity has no price.[17] In order to deal legally with human dignity, one has to develop criteria or standards for its interpretation. The difficulty is that these standards inevitably depend on value judgments.[18] For the law applying authorities the problem is easier if the legislature has transformed the general rule into clear cut provisions, e.g., into those of the penal law or criminal procedure code.[19] This, however, does not solve the problem, since the legislature may have failed to interpret the human dignity clause correctly. Sometimes the laws merely include the term 'human dignity' in the text of the provision. Then the law applying bodies have to refer back to the constitutional norm itself.

Something that may help clarify the understanding of human dignity is the fact that art. 1 para. 2 refers to the concept of inalienable human rights, and accordingly, to the relevant achievements of the Great Revolutions at the end of the 18th century. It proceeds from the assumption that individuals are reasonable beings, autonomous and capable to decide for themselves their own paths to happiness. Even if there might be doubts concerning the correctness of this finding on the grounds of anthropological deliberations, the Basic Law closes the door on any attempt to fall back behind this line of philosophical assessment.[20]

---

[15] BVerfGE 75, 369, 380 (1987) 93, 266, 293 (1995). Fundamentally different Brugger, loc. cit., p. 12 et seq.: Art. 1 para.1 BL neither is a basic right nor presents an absolute value, being instead a constitutional principle which must be balanced with other constitutional principles.

[16] See also Starck, loc. cit., p. 40 et seq.

[17] Immanuel Kant, *Grundlegung zur Metaphysik der Sitten*, Weischedel, ed., (1956) vol. IV, p. 67 et seq.

[18] Norbert Hoerster, 'Zur Bedeutung des Prinzips der Menschenwürde,' *JuS* 23 (1983) p. 93 et seq.

[19] e.g., Art. 81 a Criminal Procedure Code.

[20] Enders, loc. cit., p. 171 et seq.

The most famous approach to developing such standards has become the so-called 'theory of object.' According to this concept, which also traces back to Kant[21] and has, at least in principle, been adopted by the Federal Constitutional Court: 'The State violates human dignity when it treats persons as mere objects.'[22] Another formulation would be that 'It is contrary to human dignity to make persons the mere objects in the State'[23] or 'of the State.'[24]

Though the Federal Constitutional Court applies this theory,[25] it held in the famous tape judgment of 1970, where an amendment to art. 10 BL (privacy of mail and telecommunication) was be examined, that the object theory may indicate only the right direction; every case must still be judged on its own merits.[26] Of course, the individual is very often the object not only of the general living conditions and social developments but also of the law he or she has to abide. Therefore the word mere, in 'to treat a person as a mere object' must be stressed. It means to treat a person in such a way that calls his quality as a person (a subject) principally into question.[27] The treatment of the individual must be the expression of disdain, must be qualified as contemptuous treatment.[28]

Before giving some examples I would like to draw your attention to another legal argument that is, to some extent, linked with the concept of human dignity. The Federal Constitutional Court has developed the image of a human being, which is supposed to be reflected in the Basic Law and, in particular, in its basic rights provisions.[29] The definition reads: 'The image of man in the Basic Law is not that of an isolated, sovereign individual; rather, the Basic Law has decided in favour of a relationship between individual and community in the sense of a person's dependence on and commitment to the community, without infringing upon a person's individual value.'[30] The connection with human dignity lies in the argument that restrictions and limitations to freedoms, as such, do not interfere with human dignity and do not make persons mere objects of the State.[31] Let me quote the Federal Constitutional Court: 'On the contrary: citizens are members of and bound to society.'[32]

---

[21] Hoerster (note 18).
[22] BVerfGE 27, 1, 6 (1969). See also Dürig, loc. cit., para. 28.
[23] BVerfGE 45, 187, 228 (1977).
[24] BVerfGE 87, 209, 228 (1992).
[25] For a closer look at this theory see Becker, loc. cit., p. 35 et seq.; Enders, loc. cit., p. 20 et seq., 156 et seq.
[26] BVerfGE 30, 1, 25 et seq. (1970).
[27] BVerfGE 87, 209, 228 (1992).
[28] BVerfGE 30, 1, 26 (1970).
[29] See Peter Haeberle, *Das Menschenbild im Verfassungsstaat* (1988); Becker, *op. cit.*
[30] BVerfGE 4, 7, 15 (1954).
[31] Cf. Bundesverwaltungsgericht (Federal Administrative Court), *Deutsches Verwaltungsblatt (DVBl.)* 109 (1994) p. 527 et seq.
[32] BVerfGE 27, 344, 351 (1970).

As the object formula does not always suffice, sometimes the intention of a contemptuous treatment is put forward as argument.[33] It is true that this also may be indicative. However, a bad intention alone hardly amounts to a violation of human dignity, and the lack of negative intent is not enough to qualify an act as not violating human dignity, if this act is qualified for objective reasons as an encroachment on the dignity of man.[34]

What does follow from this? The elements just discussed may help, but they do not automatically offer a convincing result. Human dignity is too important an idea to be wasted on trivialities, like changing titles for civil servants or judges,[35] spelling a name by 'oe' instead of 'ö,'[36] addressing a woman by 'Frau' Meier instead of 'Dame' Meier and so on. The Bavarian Constitutional Court has tried to give some examples that seem to be generally recognized as violations of human dignity: 'defamation, discrimination, humilation, stigmatizing, proscription and cruel punishment.'[37] The Federal Constitutional Court has added the maxim *'nulla poena sine culpa;'*[38] it has further held that the expulsion to a country where the individual reasonably fears being tortured would violate art. 1.[39] In a famous decision, the Court found that the penalty of life imprisonment, as such, is not prohibited by the Constitution, but that life imprisonment without at least a concrete and realistically attainable chance to regain the freedom at some later point in time would be a violation of art. 1.[40] Dignity means hope; and the imposition of severe punishment for the sole reason of general crime prevention would also be contrary to art. 1, since here the offender would be made a mere tool of the State's struggle against crime. However, the Court has approved that general crime prevention may be taken into account, among other considerations.[41]

Three further examples can be added to show where the Court did not find that the individual had been placed in the position of a mere object. In the second abortion case, the Court held that a pregnant woman who is obliged to take part in the counselling procedure with a view to avoid abortion does not suffer a violation of her dignity, because the law treats her as a partner, recognizing her autonomy and responsibility.[42] In the second case, a constitutional complaint of the former chief of the Ministry of State Security ('Stasi') of the GDR Erich Mielke was not accepted, since the Court held that

---

[33] See BVerfGE 30, 1, 26 (1970); but see also the dissenting vote, BVerfGE 30, 33, 40 (1970).
[34] Hoefling, JuS (1995) p. 860.
[35] BVerfGE 47, 253, 270 (1978).
[36] BVerwGE (Collection of Decisions of the Federal Administrative Court) 31, 236 et seq. (1969).
[37] Bayerische Verwaltungsblaetter 28 (1982) 47, 50.
[38] BVerfGE 45, 187, 228 (1977); 95, 96, 131 (1996).
[39] BVerfG, *Neue Zeitschrift für Verwaltungsrecht (NVwZ)* 11 (1992) p. 660 et seq.
[40] BVerfGE 45, 187, 245 (1977).
[41] BVerfGE 50, 166, 175 (1979).
[42] BVerfGE 88, 203, 281 (1993).

the finding of the trial court on Mielke's mental and physcial ability to follow the criminal procedure was well founded. As long as the accused is able, through the advice of his counsel, to exercise his procedural rights by himself or by his counsel, the proceedings may go on and the accused is not treated as a mere object of criminal prosecution.[43] Lastly, the constitutional complaint of a person who had been convicted of support of an agent provocateur was also not accepted.[44]

Summing up the results we have achieved so far, one might say that the right to human dignity is the right not to be treated in specific ways. It is a modal right.[45]

2. The personal scope of protection

The personal scope of protection under art. 1 is very broad. It includes not only human beings between birth and death, but also the unborn child since nidation and the dead person.[46] While, according to the Court, other basic rights no longer apply to a dead person, human dignity does, at least for a while, with decreasing tendency. One may wonder whether this assessment is convincing. I think that it would be more reasonable to attribute to the dead person some after-effect of the right to personality instead of human dignity. If we turn later to the famous Mephisto case,[47] I shall explain why I think so.

Some authors suggest that those who do not possess the intellectual capacity to make autonomous decisions have no right to human dignity.[48] This approach would, of course, not only exclude the unborn and the dead, but also small children and mentally ill people. The Federal Constitutional Court has rightly repudiated this opinion, arguing that human dignity belongs to the species of human beings, notwithstanding their mental and intellectual state.[49]

3. The relationship between human dignity and other basic rights

Having established that the dignity of man is the constitutive principle of the whole basic rights system, we now turn to the question of the relationship between human dignity and other fundamental rights.

A first and more general response to this question would be that all basic rights are in the service of human dignity.[50] I quote from the Federal Constitutional Court's judgment in the Census Act Case (1983): 'The focal

---

[43] BVerfGE, *Europaeische Grundrechte Zeitschrift* 22 (1995) p. 138, 140.
[44] BVerfG, *NJW* 48 (1995) p. 651 et seq.
[45] Hoefling, *JuS* 35 (1995) p. 859.
[46] BVerfGE 39, 1, 36 (1975); 88, 203, 251 (1993); 30, 173, 194 (1971).
[47] BVerfGE 30, 173 (1971).
[48] e.g., Norbert Hoerster, 'Haben Föten ein Lebensinteresse?' *Archiv für Rechts-und Sozialphilosophie* 77 (1991) p. 385.
[49] BVerfGE 87, 209, 228 (1992).
[50] Haeberle, loc. cit., p. 844; Kunig, loc. cit., p. 136.

point of order established by the Basic Law is the value and dignity of the individual, who functions as a member of a free society with free self-determination. The general personality right, as laid down in art. 2 (1) in tandem with art. 1 (1) serves to protect these values—along with other, more specific guarantees of freedom.'[51] This means that the dignity clause puts all basic rights in a conceptual order without establishing, however, a hierarchy among the basic rights—with the sole exception of the human dignity clause itself, which is at the top of the basic rights system.[52] The establishment of this conceptual order does not mean that all basic rights themselves have a hard dignity core that would automatically prevent them—as far as this core is concerned—from being balanced against other legal interests or would put them under the shelter of art. 79 para. 3, which restricts constitutional changes. The conceptual relationship to art. 1 is not a sufficient basis for such conclusions.[53]

It is true that, in this respect, the Court's remarks are not always very clear. In its decision concerning the restitution of property seized under the Soviet occupation regime, the Court held that the basic rights cannot be restricted 'as far as they are indispensable for the maintenance of an order consistent with art. 1 para. 1 and 2 Basic Law.'[54] But this statement points to art. 1 itself, and it might be better to deal in these cases directly with art. 1 instead mixing up the different basic rights.

Actually, we do find some unnecessary and sometimes even confusing, rhetoric in the jurisprudence of the Court—for example when the Court acknowledges a particularly close relationship between various basic rights and human dignity. In this respect, the Court is not over-scrupulous. Many basic rights share this lofty qualification, e.g., the right to life, equality, freedom of faith and creed, freedom of information, art, family, profession and so on.[55] However, the Court does not draw specific consequences from this assessment. I shall try to explain this assertion in terms of the right to life, the right to personality, and the freedom of art.

On several occasions, in particular in its abortion judgments, the Court has qualified human life as 'the vital basis of the dignity of man,'[56] or as 'a supreme value.'[57] Despite this very close relationship with human dignity, the Court did not seriously attempt to argue that human life is absolutely protected

---

[51] BVerfGE 65, 1, 41 (1983).
[52] See Eckart Klein, 'Preferred Freedoms-Doktrin und deutsches Verfassungsrecht,' in: *Grundrechte, soziale Ordnung und Verfassungsgerichtsbarkeit, Festschrift für E. Benda*, E. Klein, ed. (1995) p. 135, 139 et seq.
[53] Kunig, loc. cit., p. 135 et seq.
[54] BVerfGE 84, 90, 121 (1991).
[55] See Kunig (note 50).
[56] BVerfGE 39, 1, 42 (1975).
[57] BVerfGE 49, 24, 53 (1978).

under the Basic Law, like human dignity is. Rather, the disengagement of both rights in the course of the deliberation is inevitable.[58]

In many cases the State must ask people to risk their lives,[59] or it even deliberately takes the lives of individuals.[60] This understanding is also reflected by art. 2 para. 2 cl. 3 BL, according to which the right to life, as well as the right to corporal inviolability 'may only be encroached upon pursuant to a law.' Actually, the Court's reasoning in the abortion cases shows, though with different results, that the Court is, in fact, balancing the right to life of the unborn child with the right to self-determination of the mother.[61] If art. 1, be it on the side of the unborn or on the side of the mother, would have been applied, no balancing of conflicting rights and no arguing with the principle of proportionality would have been appropriate. It is inconceivable that the Court could have been satisfied, on the basis of art. 1, with a solution which inevitably leads to the death of hundreds of thousands embryos if the mothers, after a mandatory counselling procedure, nevertheless decide, according to their own free will, to proceed with an abortion.[62]

What, then, is the sense in introducing art. 1 in the abortion judgments at all? I think it is twofold: first, the argument helps to define the life of the unborn child as a life distinguished from that of the mother; and second, it helps to rest the duty of the State to protect human life on a safer basis. The legal basis of this duty is still in dispute.[63] While some find, as I do, that the duty to protect is implied in any basic right, others base it on the general task of the State to ensure peace and security, or fall back to art. 1 where the duty to protect life in terms of human dignity is expressly provided for.

The result is that in the abortion cases, as well as in other famous cases involving the right to life—like the case of Schleyer[64] and the case concerning the blocking of contacts between terrorists and their counsels[65]—the right to life and the State's duty to protect it, are 'to be determined by weighing (their) importance and need for protection against other conflicting legal values.'[66]

---

[58] See Horst Dreier, 'Menschenwürde und Schwangerschaftsabbruch,' *Die Öffentliche Verwaltung (DÖV)* 48 (1995) pp. 1036, 1037.

[59] e.g., policemen, soldiers.

[60] e.g., criminals who are killed to protect the lives of hostages.

[61] BVerfGE 39, 1 (1975); 88, 203 (1993).

[62] BVerfGE 88, 203, 264 et seq. (1993).

[63] See Johannes Dietlein, *Die Lehre von den grundrechtlichen Schutzpflichten* (1991) p. 34 et seq.; Hans H. Klein, 'Die grundrechtliche Schutzpflicht,' *DVBl.* 109 (1994) p. 489; Josef Isensee, 'Das Grundrecht als Abwehrrecht und staatliche Schutzpflicht,'in: *Handbuch des Staatsrechts*, Isensee and Kirchhof, eds. (1992) vol. V, p. 145, 181 et seq.; *E. Klein* (note 9), p. 1635 et seq.

[64] BVerfGE 46, 160, 164 (1977).

[65] BVerfGE 49, 24, 53 (1978).

[66] BVerfGE 88, 203, 254 (1993).

In a huge number of cases, the Federal Constitutional Court has addressed the right to personality.[67] While the Court is interpreting the right to freely develop one's own personality, as contained in art. 2 para. 1, in a very broad sense as the general guarantee of the right to liberty and freedom—including, e.g., gathering flowers or horse riding[68]—the right to personality has been developed as a special guarantee of privacy as a distinct right based upon art. 2 para. 1 in conjunction with art. 1 para. 1.[69] Although the right to personality is distinguished by this qualification, like in the life cases, the Federal Court has to balance it with legal interests of other individuals or of the community. Whether the right to personality prevails or not depends of the importance of these conflicting rights. Thus, the Court found that the right to personality should prevail in favor of a transsexual, who had undergone an irreversible operation, against the interest of the State not to change the recorded sex in the birth register.[70] On the other hand, if certain standards are met, census laws providing for the collection of data prevail over the right of a person to be left alone.[71] How difficult this balancing process is can be illustrated by the judgment of the Federal Constitutional Court in the diary case.[72]

The key issue was whether diary records of a person accused of murdering a woman after raping her could be used in the criminal proceedings. The Court was equally divided; hence no violation of the Constitution could be established.[73] While four judges held that the right to personality had to yield to the interest of the State to prosecute such serious crimes,[74] the four other judges argued that this would constitute a violation of art. 2 para. 1 and art. 1 para. 1.[75] Methodically, both parts argued conclusively. The first four judges did not qualify the recorded thoughts and sentiments of the accused as belonging to the absolutely protected area of privacy under art. 1. The reason for this was found in the close connection between the recorded thoughts and the criminal act, transcending the personal sphere of the author. Therefore the conflicting interests had to be balanced. The other judges found that the records had highly personal character, and would therefore belong to an area which must never be encroached upon. Consequently, no balancing test could take place.

---

[67] See, e.g., Enders loc. cit., p. 444 et seq.; latest example BVerfGE 95, 220, 241 (1997).
[68] BVerfGE 6, 32, 36 (1957); 80, 137, 152 (1989).
[69] See, e.g., BVerfGE 27, 344, 350 et seq. (1970).
[70] BVerfGE 49, 286, 298 et seq. (1978).
[71] BVerfGE 27, 1, 6 (1969); 65, 1, 41 et seq. (1983).
[72] BVerfGE 80, 367 (1989).
[73] According to Art. 15 para. 3 of the law on the FCC.
[74] BVerfGE 80, 367, 376 et seq. (1989).
[75] BVerfGE 80, 367, 380 et seq. (1989).

The approach of the Court can also be explained by the following case. An artist had portrayed a well-known politician as a pig copulating with another pig wearing the robe of a judge. The satire was meant to show the immoral interplay between politics and the judiciary. The artist had been convicted for an insult. His constitutional complaint was not successful. A unanimous court held that, though the picture had to be qualified as art, the artist's right was limited by the right of the politician to his personality, because in the circumstances this right had to be seen as a direct emanation of human dignity. In this case the limit placed on freedom of art has absolute effect, without offering any possibility for the balancing of conflicting values.[76]

This brings us to the Mephisto Case.[77] The novel *Mephisto* sketches an opportunistic actor during the Nazi regime, in a rather rough portrayal of the famous actor Gustaf Gründgens. After the death of both the author and the portrayed, the book was to be published in Germany. The adopted son of Gründgens succeeded in convincing the civil courts to stop the publication of the book, claiming that it violated the human dignity of his father. The Federal Constitutional Court dismissed the constitutional complaint of the publisher, who invoked art. 5 para. 3 (freedom of art).

The Court used art. 1 (human dignity) at two stages. First, it underlined the connection between freedom of art and the dignity of man.[78] The stressing of this link is certainly meant to be an answer to the defamation of so-called 'degenerated art' during the Third Reich. Its concrete function in the context of the decision is to explain the broad interpretation of freedom of art.

In this case, human dignity comes into play again, but this time opposed to freedom of art. Had Gründgens still been alive, his right to personality would have been the right balanced against the right of the publisher. But Gründgens was dead. The Court did not accept the view that a dead person is still entitled to basic rights, with the exception of human dignity. Since art. 1 para. 1 has absolute effect, the Court consequently should have abstained from balancing the freedom of art with human dignity. Nevertheless, the Court did so and found that the dignity of Gründgens prevailed and had been violated.[79] A minority of two judges ruled to the contrary.[80] However, all of the judges failed to apply art. 1 as an absolute right excluding any balancing interests test.

In my opinion, the Court should have decided the case from the perspective of a conflict between freedom of art and the right to personality, which for some time after the death is still effective. Then, the balancing of conflicting rights, taking into account the principle of proportionality, would

---

[76] BVerfGE 75, 369, 380 (1987); the Court consequently did not mention Art. 2 para. 1 at all, but only Art. 1 para. 1 BL, though speaking of the right to personality.
[77] BVerfGE 30, 173 (1971).
[78] BVerfGE 30, 173, 193 (1971).
[79] BVerfGE 30, 173, 194 et seq. (1971).
[80] BVerfGE 30, 200, 202 et seq. (1971).

not have presented any particular difficulties; the freedom of art should have prevailed.

As I have tried to show, art. 1 has, in most cases, an auxiliary function. Sometimes it helps in interpreting the scope of other basic rights, and sometimes it supports the understanding of their limitations and restrictions.

There are, however, cases where art. 1 functions on its own. A case in point is the life imprisonment case where, deducing from the human dignity clause, the Court has held that it would amount to a violation of the dignity of man if a person had no realistic chance to be free again.[81] In another case, art. 1 likewise proved to be the only constitutional yardstick for a law ordering the detention of a debtor who refused to take an oath, and making the averting of the detention dependent on an application of the debtor.[82] In a recent case, the Court had to examine an order of a judge asking a former drug addict not to take any drugs during his time of probation, and to pass ten supervised urine tests. The Court examined all questions, applying, one after the other, the arts. 2 para. 1, 1 para. 1, and 2 para. 1 in conjunction with art. 1 para. 1. The end result was that no violation was found.[83]

IV. Specific Issues

In my last chapter, I would like to address two specific issues. The first is the impact of voluntary behaviour on the assessment of a violation of human dignity.[84] The second relates to the problem of whether it is true that, under all circumstances, human dignity must not be encroached upon.

1. Does voluntary action exclude a violation of art. 1 para. 1?

Sometimes the protection under art. 1 depends on the fact that the relevant conduct belongs to the private sphere of an individual. But if privacy is the reason for protection, then the protection is lost when the individual himself voluntarily opens the door separating his private life from the public sphere. It is likely that no court would have a problem using a diary recording intimacies after the author has consented to its use. The same would be true concerning the harvesting and transplantation of organs.

However, other cases are less clear. Could a person be extradited according to his own wishes to a country where he would probably be subjected to torture? Certainly not.[85] The individual cannot lift the State's

---

[81] BVerfGE 45, 187, 245 (1977).
[82] BVerfGE 61, 126, 137 (1982).
[83] NJW 46(1993) p. 3315.
[84] See Starck, loc. cit., p. 131.
[85] See BVerfG, NVwZ 11 (1992) p. 660; Ralf Alleweldt, *Schutz vor Abschiebung bei drohender Folter oder unmenschlicher oder erniedrigender Behandlung oder Strafe* (1996) p. 106.

objective duty to protect; he may, if at all, forfeit the possibility to invoke his subjective right before the authorities of the State.

German administrative courts have had to deal with cases where the individuals concerned had expressly maintained the voluntariness of their conduct. The owner of a peep show establishment instituted proceedings against an order of the competent authority prohibiting the performance of such shows. It was undisputed that the women involved participated in the show on a clearly voluntary basis. The Federal Administrative Court, however, held in a first judgment (1981) that shows like this one may be prohibited on the ground of public morals, which must be interpreted in light of human dignity. Under these circumstances, women would be humiliated and treated as mere objects, taking into account the whole mechanism of peep shows, the small cells of the spectators, etc. The voluntary co-operation of the participating women was of no avail because of the objective value of human dignity, which cannot be disposed of.[86] A later decision (1990) upheld this result, but, in view of harsh criticism in the legal literature,[87] changed the line of reasoning. Now, the term 'public morals' is no longer interpreted by drawing arguments from human dignity but the reasoning was founded on the moral judgment of the public. Needless to say that in this case, there is no clear judgment of the public.[88] One can only assume that the decision of the Court is based on the moral judgment of the judges themselves.

Allow me to give another example. In some countries, a rather macabre performance is seen on stage—so-called dwarf throwing. Little handicapped persons are hurled by others, mostly spectators, in a kind of competition. The administrative courts have prohibited these performances, notwithstanding the argument that the handicapped people are willing participants; nor did the courts accept the argument that these performances enable the dwarfs to earn money.[89] The main reason again was human dignity. The dwarfs are used as projectiles, as mere objects, stirring mean instincts in the participants and other spectators. Human dignity cannot be waived. It is interesting to note that the French Conseil d'Etat, in a parallel case, reached quite a similar conclusion.[90]

2. Can human dignity be balanced against other values in extreme cases?

Some years ago, an article was published by a law professor who shed some doubts on the firmly founded opinion that encroachments upon human dignity

---

[86] BVerwGE 64, 274, 277 et seq. (1981).

[87] For references see Starck, *op. cit.*, p. 63.

[88] BVerwGE 84, 314, 317 et seq. (1990); see also Federal Administrative Court decision of 23.08.1995, NJW 49 (1996) p. 1423.

[89] See Verwaltungsgericht Neustadt, decision of 21.05.1992, NVwZ 12 (1993) 98.

[90] Judgment of 27.10.1995, Recueil Dalloz Sirey (1996) p. 177; see Peter Raedler, 'Die Unverfügbarkeit der Menschenwürde in Deutschland und Frankreich,' *DÖV* 50 (1997) p. 109 et seq.

would always be violating the Constitution. He used a case that was fabricated, but not beyond all reality. The question was whether a terrorist who had been arrested could be compelled to confess where he had concealed a chemical weapon that would explode at a certain time and create the loss of countless lives and terribly suffering for the population. As the time ran short and all other possibilities were exhausted the question was raised whether physical force, perhaps even torture, could be applied.

The case was discussed in a journal of legal education.[91] The author proposed two alternative solutions. The first one followed the traditional view that any intrusion on human dignity is a violation of the Constitution; no exception is admissible. The second one argued in favor of the balancing of the conflicting legal rights and interests in those cases where human dignity is at stake on both sides. The author suggested that in such circumstances, physical force could be applied against the person.

It is probably true that extreme cases make bad law. But they have the advantage that they start us thinking and make us reflect on firmly established convictions. However, I am of the opinion that the Constitution cannot open this door.[92] The executive would have to act under its own responsibility.

V. Conclusion

In concluding, one might say that it was a fortunate decision of the pouvoir constituant to make the dignity of man the focal point of the whole constitutional and legal order, to commit the Federal Republic of Germany to the idea of human rights and to underscore the direct effect of all basic rights on all powers of the State.[93] This decision has set Germany on the right track. At the end of the day, however, it will all depend on how much the values enshrined in the Constitution become rooted in the people of the present and future generations.[94] The Constitution is expected to help a great deal in this process of sowing and growing.

---

[91] Winfried Brugger, 'Würde gegen Würde,' *Verwaltungsblaetter für Baden-Württemberg*, 16 (1995) p. 414 et seq.; *ibid.*, 'Darf der Staat ausnahmsweise foltern?' *Der Staat* 35 (1996) p. 67 et seq.

[92] In BVerfGE 49, 24, 64 (1978) the FCC expressly made clear that the specific precaution measures taken against terrorists are not violative of Art. 1 para. 1 BL.

[93] See Kunig, *op. cit.*, p. 138.

[94] Cf. BVerfGE 45, 187, 229 (1977): 'Thus any decision defining human dignity in concrete terms must be based on our present understanding of it and not on any claim to a conception of timeless validity.'

HUMAN DIGNITY
IN ISRAELI JURISPRUDENCE
David Kretzmer

I. Place of Human Rights in Israel's Legal System

Israel was for a long time regarded as one of the few countries that have neither a formal constitution nor a bill of rights. The 1948 Declaration of Independence stated that the new state's constitution would be drawn up by an elected constituent assembly, but after its election the constituent assembly transformed itself into the Knesset, Israel's parliament, and adoption of the constitution was delayed. Under a Knesset resolution passed in 1950 it was decided that the State's formal constitution would be drawn up in a piecemeal fashion by a series of basic laws. Pursuant to this resolution basic laws were enacted covering virtually all aspects of Israel's system of government, but until 1992 a basic law on civil liberties or human rights was not included among them.

Lack of a basic law on human rights was not accidental. Attempts made over the years by members of the Knesset, the Knesset Constitution and Law Committee and Ministers of Justice to further passage of such a basic law met with political opposition, mainly from the religious political parties. In the final session of the outgoing Knesset before the 1992 elections two basic laws dealing with human rights were at last enacted: the Basic Law: Freedom of Occupation and the Basic Law: Human Dignity and Liberty.[1] Enactment of these basic laws grew out of the realization that if it were impossible, for political reasons, to enact a general bill of rights, it might be possible to get through a bill that deals with those rights that are not considered controversial on the political level. Thus two basic laws on human rights were enacted, which deal with some of the rights that are protected in modern constitutions and international instruments. The first basic law deals with 'freedom of occupation,' i.e., the freedom to follow the vocation of one's choosing. The

---
[1] A translation of the Basic Laws appears in the annex.

second basic law deals with a whole range of rights under the general rubric of 'human dignity and liberty.' It includes the right to life and bodily security, property, personal freedom, the right to enter and leave the country, and privacy. It also includes 'man's dignity as a human being.' Significantly, however, the Basic Law does not mention many of the fundamental rights that are protected under most constitutions and international human rights instruments, such as the ICCPR and ECHR. The most blatant exclusions are equality, freedom of religion and conscience and freedom of speech.

Exclusion of the above rights was not the result of an oversight. On the contrary, as explained above, the Basic Laws were passed because of the political constraints that prevented passage of a general bill of rights that would protect all fundamental human rights, including equality, freedom of religion and conscience and freedom of speech. It is important in the present context to explain the background to these constraints.

Since no political party has ever commanded an absolute majority in the Knesset, Israel's political system is based on a coalition system in which various political parties take part. In virtually every case the coalition has been comprised of one of the two large parties (Labor or Likud) and a number of smaller parties that invariably include one or more religious parties. Thus the religious parties have held the balance of power and have been able to use this strategic position to pass legislation that is religiously motivated, or to prevent changes in existing legislation that has a religious basis.

The most important legislation that has a religious basis is the legislation regulating marriage and divorce in Israel. The system of marriage and divorce is still based on the Ottoman millet system, under which personal status is regulated by the law of the religious communities. There is no provision for secular marriage in Israel. This system not only prevents people who do not wish to have a religious marriage from having a secular marriage, but also to prevent marriage of persons who are not able to marry under the religious laws. Examples of such cases are marriage between persons of different religious persuasions and marriage of persons who may not marry under religious law (such as a divorcee and a '*kohen*' (person of priestly descent) under Jewish law).

Many of the laws enforcing religious practices are clearly incompatible with basic concepts of human rights. Thus, the lack of non-religious marriage would appear to be incompatible with freedom of religion and conscience.[2] The objection of the religious parties to including protection of freedom of religion and conscience in a bill of rights rests of the realization that this could be used as a mechanism for undermining the supremacy of Knesset legislation. This would be the case especially if the courts could strike down legislation that is incompatible with basic rights. The objection to including equality among the protected rights was based on similar considerations. Some of the laws of marriage and divorce enforced by the religious courts (whether Jewish

---

[2] See Rogosinsky v. State of Israel (1970) 26 P.D. (1) 129.

of Muslim) discriminate on the basis of gender. Constitutional protection of equality could open the path to judicial intervention in these laws.

II. The Status of Human Rights Prior to the Basic Laws

A bill of rights fulfils at least one of three normative functions in a legal system. Its first, and most obvious, function is to define those basic rights that are recognized and protected by the system. The second function is to define the scope of protection of recognized rights by setting standards for deciding if, and when, they may legitimately be restricted. The final function is to establish the constitutional status of the recognized rights, by determining whether a court or some other constitutional body may invalidate legislation that is inconsistent with individual rights.

The lack of a formal constitution or bill of rights did not mean that prior to enactment of the Basic Laws human rights had no status in Israel's legal system. In a long line of decisions, starting with Justice Agranat's landmark decision in the *Kol ha-Am* case,[3] the Supreme Court created what may be termed a 'judicial bill of rights.' Fundamental rights, as recognized in other democratic countries, enjoy the status of what I have elsewhere termed 'soft legal principles.'[4] They are legal principles because government authorities may not restrict them without express statutory authority, all authorities must be guided by them in interpretation of statutes, and governmental authorities must give them appropriate weight when exercising administrative discretion. They are soft principles because they do not limit the legislative power of the Knesset. The Supreme Court has refused to invalidate primary legislation that places restrictions on those basic rights that are recognized as legal principles.[5]

III. Human Dignity: The Period before the Basic Laws

The notion of 'human dignity' appears in the human rights jurisprudence of the Supreme Court that preceded the Basic Laws. The main use of this concept was in dealing with the conditions of detainees or prisoners. Thus, in the case of *Darwish v. Prison Authority*,[6] a person who had been convicted of a serious security offence complained that security prisoners did not have beds and were required to sleep on mattresses on the floor. The authorities explained that if provided with beds the prisoners could dismantle them and use parts as weapons. The majority accepted this explanation. However, Justice Haim Cohn dissented. He took the view that even if the fear of the authorities was well-founded they had to provide beds to the prisoners. The reason was that

---

[3] See Kol ha-Am v. Minister of Interior (1953) 7 P.D. 871.
[4] See D. Kretzmer, 'Demonstrations and the Law' (1984) 19 *Israel Law Review* 47.
[5] See, e.g., Rogozinsky v. State of Israel note 2 *supra*; Tnuat Laor v. Speaker of the Knesset (1990) 44 P.D. (3) 529.
[6] (1980) 35 P.D. (1) 536.

'the human dignity of prisoners must be protected. Every prisoner in Israel is entitled to his own bed for the whole period of his imprisonment.'[7]

In *Katlan v. Prison Authority*[8] the issue was whether the prison authorities could force a prisoner returning from a furlong to undergo a stomach pump. The authorities explained to the Court that they had to take strong action to prevent introduction of drugs into the prison. They knew from experience that prisoners on furlong would swallow drugs wrapped in nylon before returning to the prison and then remove the package with a bowel movement. The Court accepted that the prison authorities had a legitimate interest in keeping drugs out of the prison, and that the stomach pump was an effective means of preventing prisoners returning from outside from bringing in drugs. However, the Court held that every person in Israel enjoys the right to bodily integrity and to protection of his human dignity and that using a stomach pump without the prisoner's consent violated these values. The statutory power of the authorities to search a prisoner did not include the power to search in his body. Absent any other specific statutory power the authorities were acting illegally if they used a stomach pump without the prisoner's consent.

It should be noted that as this case was decided before the Basic Laws were enacted, the legal framework in which the Court analyzed the issue was one that accepted the notion of parliamentary supremacy. In other words, the Court assumed that if the Knesset were to enact a statute empowering the authorities to use a stomach pump without the prisoner's consent that statute would be valid, despite the violation of human dignity involved. It would be interesting to see how the Court would decide a parallel case today, when it has assumed the power of judicial review of parliamentary legislation.

On the basis of the *Katlan* case the Court decided that a distinction must be made between searches on a person's body, and searches in a person's body. If carried out without consent the latter involves a violation of human dignity.[9]

Another prisoner context in which the Court referred to the notion of human dignity related to notification of an arrest to members of the arrestee's family. In a petition submitted by Palestinian residents of the Occupied Territories against the military commander, the petitioners complained that they were not informed of the arrest and whereabouts of family members. The Court held that the right of an arrestee that his family be informed of his arrest was derived from his right to human dignity and from general principles of justice.[10]

---

[7] *Ibid.* Also see Yussef v. Director of Central Prison (1984) 40 P.D. (1) 567.
[8] (1979) 34 P.D. (3) 294.
[9] See Khouri v. State of Israel (1981) 36 P.D. (2) 85. The Court decided in this case that requiring a detainee suspected of drug offences to dip his hands in a solution did not involve invasion of his bodily integrity and was therefore not a violation of his human dignity.
[10] See Uda v. IDF Commander (1989) 43 P.D. (4) 515.

In summarizing the decisions given in the era that preceded the Basic Laws we can see that human dignity is used as term that protects vulnerable individuals against treatment which denigrates them as human beings. It would seem that the term 'violation of human dignity' is used as one that is synonymous with the term 'inhuman treatment.'[11]

IV. The Basic Law: Human Dignity and Liberty

1. The Constitutional Revolution

The Basic Laws on Human Dignity and Liberty and Freedom of Occupation opened the door to judicial review of primary legislation. For this reason they are widely regarded as laws that ushered in a 'constitutional revolution.' The architecture of the Basic Laws is based on a wide definition of the protected rights and a general limitation clause. Under this clause protected rights may be limited by a statute that befits the values of the State of Israel as a Jewish and democratic state, that serves a worthy purpose and that meets the proportionality test. The Supreme Court has made it quite clear that the courts have the power to invalidate legislation that violates protected rights and does not meet the requirements of the limitation clause. It has so far used this power on two occasions: 1. to strike down part of a statute that violated the freedom of occupation and did not meet the proportionality test;[12] and 2. to strike down a statutory provision that gave military police the power to detain a soldier suspected of an offence for 72 hours before bringing him or her before a judge.[13]

The power of judicial review over legislation that is inconsistent with the demands of the Basic Laws means that the question of whether a right is protected by the Basic Laws or not can be of major significance. If the right is not protected by the Basic Laws, the courts cannot strike down Knesset legislation that is incompatible with the right, even if the said right is part of the 'judicial bill of rights' created before enactment of the Basic Laws.

The actual impact of the Basic Laws has not been confined to judicial review of parliamentary legislation. The Basic Laws have transformed the rhetoric of the courts in general, and the Supreme Court in particular, and have promoted a 'discourse of rights' that pervades the Court's decisions. In this discourse the concept of 'human dignity' plays a major role.

2. Human Dignity in the Basic Laws

As stated above, since the enactment of the *Basic Law: Human Dignity and Liberty*, there has been a radical change both in the frequency with which the

---

[11] Cf. Article 10 (1) of the International Covenant on Civil and Political Rights: All persons deprived of their liberty shall be treated with humanity and with respect for the inherent dignity of the human person.
[12] See Investment Brokers in Israel v. Minister of Finance (1997) 51 P.D. (4) 367.
[13] See Tzemach Sagi v. Minister of Defense (1995) 99 Takdin-Elyon (3) 1400.

Court refers to the concept of 'human dignity' and the meaning ascribed to the concept. Before examining the decisions of the Court it is important to review the use of the term 'human dignity' in Israel's Basic Laws.

The Basic Law: Human Dignity and Liberty mentions the concept of human dignity, *kvod ha-adam*, four times:

1. The term appears in the name of the Basic Law;
2. Section 1a., which defines the purpose of the Basic Law, states:

> The purpose of this Basic Law is to protect human dignity and liberty, in order to entrench in a Basic Law the values of the State of Israel as a Jewish and democratic state.

3. Section 2 states:

> There shall be no violation of the life, body or the dignity of any person as a person.

4. Section 4 provides:

> All persons are entitled to protection of their life, body and dignity.

The term human dignity is also used in the Basic Law: Government. This Basic Law provides that during a state of emergency the executive branch of government has the power to promulgate emergency regulations that may change or cancel any law. There are a number of restrictions on this power. The one that interests us here is contained in section 50 (d) of the Basic Law that states:

> Emergency regulations may not prevent recourse to legal action, prescribe retroactive punishment or allow violation of human dignity.

Looking at the above provisions it is hard to discern a clear picture of what the term *kvod ha-adam*, human dignity, means. On the one hand, from the name of the Basic Law: Human Dignity and Liberty and section 1a that defines its purpose, one could deduce that the Basic Law deals with two types of rights: those that fall under the heading 'human dignity' and those that fall under the heading 'liberty.' Thus, for example, one could deduce that when the Basic Law protects the right to privacy and to the confidentiality of one's conversations, writings and notes, it does so under the umbrella of human dignity. When it protects the right to leave the country it does so under the umbrella of liberty. When one turns to articles 2 and 4, however, the term human dignity seems to refer to a specific interest that must be ensured and protected, alongside one's interest in life and bodily security.

If the right to human dignity were regarded as a right that exists alongside the other rights protected in the Basic Law, it would seem to enjoy only limited protection. Under the general limitation clause in section 8, the protected rights may be limited if the limitation meets the conditions laid down therein. This principle would seem to apply to the right to human dignity. But when one turns to the Basic Law: Government, use of the term would seem close to the meaning of the term in German jurisprudence, that is the kernel of every person's essence as a human being that may not be violated in any circumstances.

In interpreting the term *kvod ha-adam,* human dignity, in the Basic Law one can discern a few strands in the jurisprudence of the Supreme Court. I shall now discuss each of these strands.

3. Human Dignity as a General Value

In its initial decisions interpreting the term 'human dignity' the Court adopted universalistic concepts based on the essence of the individual personality. Thus in a leading judgment, the former president of the Court, Justice Shamgar, described the term as follows:

> Human dignity, in the constitutional context, is a legal concept, but its practical expression lies in the daily human experience and in the relationship towards the individual of the state and society, including the courts, in which he lives. Human dignity is reflected, inter alia, in the ability of the human being as such to forge his personality freely, as he wishes, to give expression to his aspirations and to choose ways to fulfill them, to make free choices, not to be enslaved to arbitrary compulsion, to receive fair treatment by every authority and by every other individual, to enjoy equality between human beings, to receive the proper attention of the society in which he lives and to accept or reject ideas, as he wishes.[14]

In describing the concept the present president of the Court, Justice Barak, stated:

> The contents of the term "human dignity" will be determined on the basis of the views of the enlightened public in Israel and on the background of the purpose of the Basic Law: Human Dignity and Liberty. Underlying this concept lies recognition of man as a free being, who develops his body and spirit according to his will within the social framework with which he is connected and on which he is dependent.[15]

The reference to the 'enlightened public in Israel' provoked a response from Justice Elon, a justice who regarded introduction of Jewish law and tradition into the jurisprudence of the Court as a mission in life. Even before the above decision of Justice Barak, Justice Elon had tried to base the concept of human dignity on religious sources when he stated:

---

[14] See Ploni v. Almoni (1992) 48 P.D. (3) 837, 843.
[15] See Vickselbaum v. Minister of Defence (1992) 47 P.D. (2) 812, 827.

> The meaning of human dignity is not to shame and degrade the divine image in man.[16]

In response to Justice Barak's reference to the enlightened public, Justice Elon declared:

> Since we have benefited from the entrance of the Basic Law: Human Dignity and Liberty into the world of our legal system, we have no need, and it is improper, to introduce into our legal system an element and a definition like "the enlightened public in Israel." It is not proper, since this Basic Law is entirely made up of values the interpretation of which is soaked in world outlook and fundamental attitudes, and a concept as vague as "enlightened" will only add uncertainty to the uncertainty in the difficult art of interpretation. It is not needed, since the Basic Law contains an express provision relating to its purpose, and thereby as to its interpretation, i.e., entrenchment of the values of a Jewish and democratic state.[17]

The perception of human dignity as a general value has enabled the Court to resort to the concept in order to create rights in various situations. Thus, it has held that human dignity implies one's right to know the identity of one's parents,[18] the right of a man to grow a beard,[19] the right of a person not to be subject to sexual harassment,[20] the right of a detained person that his family be informed of his whereabouts,[21] the right of the family of a deceased person to hold a decent funeral[22] and to determine the inscription on the tombstone,[23] the right to parenthood,[24] the right of a spouse to maintenance,[25] and the right of an adult to be adopted by a family with whom he has a special relationship.[26] Furthermore, as human dignity relates to the person's essence as a human being it does not pass with his death. Thus, the Court may protect the right of a deceased to human dignity after death.[27]

---

[16] See State of Israel v. Goata (1992) 46 P.D. (5) 708.
[17] Shefer v. State of Israel (1988) 48 P.D. (1) 87, 101.
[18] Ploni v. Almoni note 14 *supra*.
[19] Nof v. State of Israel (1994) 50 P.D. (5) 449.
[20] State of Israel v. Ben-Asher (1996) 98 Takdin-Elyon (1) 1.
[21] Uda v. IDF Commander note 10 *supra*.
[22] Barkaat v. Officer Commanding Central Command (1992) 46 P.D. (5) 1.
[23] Chevra Kadisha v. Kastenbaum (1991) 40 P.D. (2) 464.
[24] Nachmani v. Nachmani (1993) 49 P.D. (1) 485.
[25] Solomon v. Solomon (1993) 51 P.D. (2) 577.
[26] Ploni v. Attorney General (1996) 51 P.D. (1) 160.
[27] Chevra Kadisha v. Kastenbaum (1991) 40 P.D. (2) 464; Hagar v. Hagar (1992) 47 P.D. (2) 793; Barkaat v. Officer Commanding Central Command, note 22 *supra*; Shefer v. State of Israel, note 17 *supra*.

Human dignity also enters the picture as a constraint on other rights. In *Station Film Co.*[28] the Court considered the decision of the Film Censorship Board to demand deletion from a film of sections that were regarded as degrading to women. Justice Cheshin mentioned that the grounds for restrictions on pornographic films were, inter alia, that they may degrade human dignity (especially of women). The artistic value of the film was important but equal importance should be attached to conflicting values, such as prohibiting violence and protecting human dignity. In another case, the Court held that racism harms human dignity and racist speech may therefore be prohibited.[29]

4. Human Dignity as a Separate Right

Another stream of decisions regards the right to human dignity as a specific right that exists alongside other classic rights, such as the general right to personal liberty, the right to property, freedom of movement, and the right to privacy. This would seem to be the function of sections 2 and 4 of the Basic Law: Human Dignity and Liberty, which speak of protection of life, body or dignity.[30]

Whether one regards human dignity as a general value or as a specific right, under the Court's jurisprudence it may be limited so as to accommodate other interests and rights. When categorized as a specific right, the acceptability of limitations may be regarded as a function of the Basic Law: Human Dignity and Liberty, which contains a general limitation clause that applies to all the protected rights. However, by categorizing human dignity as a general value that expresses the fundamental right of every individual not to be treated in a degrading or inhuman manner, rather than as a specific right, the Court could have avoided the need for balancing. It could then have taken an approach, similar to the German approach, that human dignity is inviolable. It seems to me that such an approach is inherent in section 50 (d) of the Basic Law: Even when demanded by security needs, the government may not implement emergency regulations that violate human dignity.[31] Unfortunately,

---

[28] See Station Film Co. v. Public Council for Film Censorship (1994) 50 P.D. (5) 661.

[29] Alba v. State of Israel (1995) 50 P.D. (5) 221.

[30] It should be noted, as my colleague, Dr. Orit Kamir, shows in her paper, that the Hebrew term *kavod* means both dignity and honor. It seems quite clear that in the title of the Basic Law and in section 1a, which defines its purpose, the term *kvod ha-adam* means human dignity. It is not self-evident, however, that when sections 2 and 4 refer to *kavod* the intention is to dignity, rather than honor. I shall, however, assume that the reference is indeed to dignity.

[31] It must be noted that under section 50 (e) of the Basic Law, emergency regulations may not be promulgated beyond the extent demanded by the emergency. The prohibition on regulations that violate human dignity is an additional constraint. This surely means that human dignity may not be violated even if demanded by the emergency.

such an approach would have been out of tune with the pervasive role of balancing in the Court's jurisprudence.

The notion of balancing is featured both in decisions dealing with human rights, and in all other spheres of the Court's decision-making. In the sphere of human rights the Court has repeated time and again the theme that human rights do not enjoy absolute protection, but must be balanced against competing interests and rights. In making this statement no distinction is made between different rights, some of which enjoy absolute status under international law,[32] or in the jurisprudence of other countries.[33] Thus, for example, in a recent case Justice Barak stated:

> Freedom of vocation—*like other human rights*—is not an absolute right. It gives the person a relative right.[34] (emphasis added).

Given the general commitment to the notion of balancing it is not surprising that the Court has applied the notion to the concept of human dignity. In the *Bank ha-Mizrahi*[35] case Justice Barak stated:

> Human dignity, liberty, property, movement, privacy and freedom of occupation are not absolute rights. They may be limited in order to protect the social framework.

In a later case Justice Barak developed this notion even further, when he stated:

> Among the values of the State of Israel human dignity is the supreme value. But this is the dignity of man as the member of a community, which is entitled to protect its existence and security. Only in this way may the human dignity of all its sons and daughters be maintained. Therefore it is permissible to violate human dignity in order to maintain the social framework that protects human dignity.[36]

Similarly, Justice Shamgar explained that:

---

[32] The right against torture is regarded as an absolute right in international law that may not be limited in any circumstances. So is the right against slavery.

[33] Under the German system the right to human dignity must not be violated in any circumstances.

[34] See Investment Brokers in Israel v. Minister of Finance (1997) note 12 *supra*. Also see Ben Hur v. Tel Aviv Municipality (1997) 51 P.D. (4) 625, 642: 'The freedom to demonstrate is indeed a fundamental right, and it belongs to the applicants, as is does to every other person. However, like every fundamental right, it is not an absolute right.'

[35] Bank ha-Mizrahi v. Migdal Kfar Shitufi (1993) 49 P.D. (4) 221.

[36] Klingberg v. Parole Committee (1995) 96 Takdin-Elyon (1) 192, 197.

Like every other right, in examining human dignity care must be taken to consider the rights of others.[37]

As we see, then, whether perceived as a specific right or a general value the Court regards human dignity as a relative value that must be balanced against societal interests and other rights. The notion that a certain form of state action violates human dignity is not a trump card. The state may concede that an action does indeed violate human dignity and still try to justify it.

The pernicious implications of this line of thought became apparent in a recent case dealing with administrative detention. Under the Israeli emergency law dealing with administrative detention, the Minister of Defense may issue an order for the detention of a person if the security of the state or public security demands it. The Supreme Court has ruled time and again that the purpose of such detention is preventive. It may only be used when it is necessary to limit the freedom of a person who endangers state security and no less drastic means are available.

In the case of *Ploni v. Minister of Defense*,[38] the detainees were Lebanese nationals who had been held in Israeli jails for long periods.[39] The state did not argue that the detained individuals themselves would threaten security were they to be released, but that they were being held as bargaining chips in negotiations for the return of Israeli soldiers who had disappeared in Lebanon. The majority in the Supreme Court held that this constituted valid grounds for holding the detainees under administrative detention. Writing for the majority Justice Barak stated:

> Administrative detention violates the individual's freedom. When the detention is carried out in circumstances in which the detainee constitutes a "bargaining chip," indeed this entails a severe violation of human dignity, since the detainee is perceived as a means for achieving an end and not as the end itself. In these circumstances, the detention violates the autonomy of will, and of a human being controlling his actions and being responsible for the outcome of his actions. The detention of the Appellants is nothing other than a situation in which the key to the prison of persons is in the hands of others, not in their own hands. This is a grave situation. Indeed, as was stated by Judge Vinograd in the lower court, "I am on the horns of a dilemma. However, after thoroughly studying the material before me and the arguments of the sides, I am satisfied that this violation—harsh and painful as it may be—is necessitated by the

---

[37] Ploni v. Almoni, note 18 *supra*, 843.
[38] *Dinim-Elyon* (1994) vol. LVI no. 921.
[39] Most of the detainees were tried and convicted a belonging to a terrorist organization and sentenced to short terms of imprisonment. They were not released after serving their sentences. Others were captured in Lebanon, brought to Israel and held without trial ever since.

security and political reality, and reflects the proper balance point in the circumstances of the case, between individual freedom and the necessity to protect State security."

While Justice Barak concedes that detaining a person as a 'bargaining chip' entails a severe violation of human dignity, he nevertheless legitimizes that detention which 'reflects the proper balance...between individual freedom and the necessity to protect state security.' It is not clear at all what significance there is in categorizing behavior as a severe violation of human dignity, if such behavior can still be acceptable. This apparently later became clear to Justice Barak himself. In a further hearing of the case before an expanded bench of nine judges, the original decision was reversed.[40] Justice Barak conceded that he had been mistaken in his original decision. He stated that in the case of persons who have committed no crime, and who do not themselves endanger state security, holding them as bargaining chips is a violation of human dignity so great and deep that it cannot be justified even if grounds of state security favor the measure.

In the Israeli political context, in which it is all too frequently claimed that certain rights must be limited on grounds of security, adoption of an approach according to which the core value of human dignity must never be violated is sorely needed. It is to be hoped that the Court will reconsider it's commitment to balancing, and that it will adopt a line of thought that will prevent further decisions, such as the original *Plonim* decision, which fly in the face of international human rights standards. Two recent decisions of the Court seem to suggest that this process of reconsideration has indeed begun and that it has already had an effect on the Court's jurisprudence.[41]

5. Human Dignity as a Super-Right

As I explained above, the Basic Law: Human Dignity and Liberty was based on a minimalist approach. Only those rights on which political consensus could be gained were entrenched in the Basic Law. Freedom of religion and conscience, equality and freedom of speech were intentionally omitted from the rights mentioned in the Basic Law. Nevertheless, in a series of decisions the Court has mentioned rights omitted from the Basic Law as rights that are in fact part and parcel of the notion of human dignity and that are, as such, protected under the Basic Law.

In the *Meatrael* case[42] Justice Barak was prepared to assume, without ruling on the matter, that equality and freedom of conscience are protected as

---

[40] See Plonim v. Minister of Defense, *Dinim Elyon* (1997) vol. LVII no. 755.
[41] The one decision is the Plonim decision, *ibid*. The other decision is Public Committee Against Torture in Israel v. State of Israel, Dinin Elyon (1994) vol. LVI no. 774, in which the Court held that the General Security Service has no power to use force in interrogation of suspected terrorists.
[42] Meatrael v. Knesset (1994) 40 P.D. (5) 15. Also see Chevra Kadisha v. Kastenbaum, note 27 *supra*.

part of human dignity under section 2 of the Basic Law; in the *Re'em* case[43] he stated quite clearly that freedom of expression could be deduced from human dignity, and in the *Dayan* case[44] he extended this to include the right to hold demonstrations.

In the *Hupert* case,[45] Justice Orr declared that since the enactment of the Basic Law: Human Dignity and Liberty, the right to equality may be derived from the notion of human dignity. It therefore enjoys a constitutional, supra-legislative, status. This approach was adopted by Justice Barak in the *Danilewitz* decision,[46] and by Justice Matza in the *Women's Network* case.[47] In a number of cases, justices have expressed the view that freedom of religion is also included in the concept of human dignity.[48] It has also been suggested that the right to strike,[49] the right to fair trial,[50] the right of minors not to be subject to corporal punishment[51] and a patient's right to know[52] derive from the right to human dignity. On the other hand the Court has refused to accept the argument that the right to education,[53] or the right of a imprisoned offender to rehabilitation,[54] are derived from human dignity

The problematic nature of the above approach, that uses judicial interpretation to include within the Basic Law specific rights that were intentionally omitted, was raised by Justice Dorner in two decisions. In the *Alice Miller* case the issue before the Court related to discrimination against women in recruitment for pilots' training courses in the Israel Air Force. Justice Dorner voiced the opinion that given the legislative background to the Basic Law and its internal construction, it was not possible to include the right

---

[43] Re'em Engineers and Constructors Ltd v. Upper Nazareth Municipality (1992) 47 P.D. (5) 189.

[44] See Dayan v. Commander of Jerusalem Police (1993) 48 P.D. (2) 456. Also see Meretz Faction v. Commander of Jerusalem District, Israel Police (1996) 50 P.D. (2) 822.

[45] Hupert v. Yad Vashem (1992) 48 P.D. (3) 353.

[46] El-Al Airlines v. Danilewitz (1994) 48 P.D. (5) 749.

[47] See Israel Women's Network v. Minister of Transport (1994) 48 P.D. (5) 501. It should be noted that one of the three justices in this case, Justice Zamir, stated that he was not expressing an opinion whether the right to equality is indeed to be deduced from human dignity, as there was no need for the Court to decide the question in the instant case.

[48] See, e.g., Manning v. Minister of Justice (1993) 47 P.D. (3) 282; Jabareen v. Minister of Education (1993) 48 P.D. (5) 199.

[49] See Attorney General v. National Labor Court (1993) 49 P.D. (2) 485. It must be noted that the two justices on the bench were not prepared to express an opinion on the question.

[50] See The Movement for the Quality of Government v. Attorney General (1996) 51 P.D. (2) 757.

[51] See Plonit v. State of Israel (1998) 2000 Takdin-Elyon (1) 764.

[52] See Hadassah Medical Organization v. Gilead (1996) 99 Takdin-Elyon (2) 1381.

[53] See Amutat Shocharei Gilat v. Minister of Education (1995) 50 P.D. (3) 2.

[54] See State of Israel v. Abu Rabia (1997) 51 P.D. (5) 470.

to equality as such as part of the notion of human dignity. However, this did not mean that aspects of the right to equality were not covered by human dignity. In her mind, the essence of a violation of human dignity is degrading treatment. If discrimination is degrading it involves a violation of human dignity. Furthermore, in her view, when discrimination is on the grounds of gender or race it is necessarily degrading and therefore involves a violation of human dignity.[55]

In the *Golan* case Justice Dorner once again pursued this line of thought and applied it to the question of freedom of expression.[56] It is clear that not every limitation on freedom of expression involves harm to human dignity. Thus, for example, limitations on commercial expression can hardly be seen as violations of the human dignity of the commercial enterprise. On the other hand, when the limitation relates to the essence of the individual's right to express himself or herself it involves degrading treatment that violates human dignity.

It seems to me that the principles of Justice Dorner's approach should be accepted. The Court should not ignore the political background to the Basic Law, nor its internal construction that is based on specifying the protected rights and not laying down a general super-right to human dignity. On the other hand, the mere fact that conduct involves violation of a right that is not specifically protected in the Basic Law should not mean that that conduct does not violate human dignity. Conduct which violates the essential humanity of every individual and turns him or her into a mere object to serve the interests of society or of others must be regarded as a violation of human dignity, even if it also involves violation of an unprotected right. Thus I would agree that most, if not all, cases of discrimination on the grounds of gender or ethnic origins should be regarded as a violation of human dignity. So would conduct that violates rights that enjoy absolute protection under international law, such as the right to be free from torture or slavery.

Conclusions

Inclusion of human dignity in the Basic Law: Human Dignity and Liberty has spurred the Supreme Court to refer to this concept in numerous contexts. The concept serves as a general value of the legal system from which specific forms of behavior may be required, as a specific right that exists alongside other classic rights and as a super-right, from which other classic rights such as equality and freedom of religion may be derived.

It is hoped that the Court will now start refining the concept so as to prevent its use as a catch-all phrase, which, if it means everything, may also

---

[55] Alice Miller v. Minister of Defense (1994) 49 P.D. (4) 94. Also see Reknat v. National Labour Court (1995) 51 P.D. (3) 289, in which the Court regarded discrimination on grounds of age as degrading and therefore as on offence to human dignity.

[56] Golan v. Prisons Service 50 P.D. (4) 136.

mean nothing. As a general value it should be restricted to the kernel of the 'essential humanity' of every individual that may not be violated in any circumstances. It should not be used so as to import all the classic rights that were intentionally omitted from the Basic Law into the list of constitutionally protected rights, lock, stock and barrel, but should be employed to prevent gross violations of such rights which are degrading or involve breach of rights granted absolute protection under international law.

Annex

Basic Law: Human Dignity and Liberty

Fundamental principles
1. Fundamental human rights in Israel are founded on recognition of the value of the human being, the sanctity of human life, and the principle that all persons are free; these rights shall be respected in the spirit of the principles set forth in the Declaration on the Establishment of the State of Israel.

Purpose
1a. The purpose of this Basic Law is to protect human dignity and liberty, in order to entrench in a basic law the values of the State of Israel as a Jewish and democratic state.

Respect for life, body and dignity
2. No one's life, body or human dignity shall be violated.

Protection of property
3. No one's property shall be violated.

Protection of life, body and dignity
4. Everyone is entitled to protection of his life, body and dignity.

Personal liberty
5. No one's liberty shall be denied or restricted by imprisonment, detention, extradition or in any other way.

Entering and leaving Israel
6. (a) Everyone is free to leave Israel.
(b) Every Israeli citizen who is abroad is entitled to enter Israel.

Privacy and personal confidentiality
7. (a) Everyone is entitled to privacy and to confidentiality of his private life.
(b) No one's private domain shall be entered without his consent.
(c) No search shall be carried out of a person's domain, on or of his body, or of his personal effects.
(d) The confidentiality of a person's conversations, writings or records shall not be violated.

Violation of rights
8. The rights according to this Basic Law shall not be violated except by a statute that befits the values of the State of Israel and is directed

towards a worthy purpose, and to an extent that does not exceed what is necessary, or by regulation promulgated by virtue of express authorization in such a statute.

Exception for security forces
9. The rights according to this Basic Law may not be restricted, qualified or waived for those serving in the Israel Defence Forces, the Israel Police, the Prison Service or in other security services of the State, except according to law and to an extent that does not exceed what is required by the nature and character of the service.

Preservation of laws
10. Nothing in this Basic Law affects the validity of laws that existed prior to this Basic Law's coming into force.

Application
11. All governmental authorities are obligated to respect the rights under this Basic Law.

Stability of the Law
12. Emergency regulations shall not have the power to change this Basic Law, to suspend its force temporarily, or to set conditions upon it; however, when there exists a state of emergency in the country by virtue of a proclamation under section 9 of the Law and Administration Ordinance, 5708-1948, emergency regulations may be promulgated under the aforesaid section which deny or restrict rights according to this Basic Law, provided that the denial or restriction are for a worthy purpose, and for a period and to an extent that do not exceed what is necessary.

Basic Law: Freedom of Occupation

Fundamental principles
1. Fundamental human rights in Israel are founded on recognition of the value of the human being, the sanctity of human life, and the principle that all persons are free; these rights shall be respected in the spirit of the principles set forth in the Declaration on the Establishment of the State of Israel.

Purpose
2. The purpose of this Basic Law is to protect freedom of occupation in order to entrench in a basic law the values of the State of Israel as a Jewish and democratic state.

Freedom of occupation
3. Every citizen and resident of the State may engage in any occupation, profession or business.

Violation of freedom of occupation
4. Freedom of occupation shall not be violated except by a statute that befits the values of the State of Israel and is directed towards a worthy purpose, and to an extent that does not exceed what is necessary, or by regulation promulgated by virtue of express authorization in such a statute.

Application
5. All governmental authorities are obligated to respect the freedom of occupation of every citizen and resident.

Stability
6. Emergency regulations shall not have the power to change, temporarily suspend or place conditions on this Basic Law.

Entrenchment
7. This Basic Law shall not be changed except by a basic law enacted by a majority of Knesset members.

Validity of exceptional law
8. A provision in a law that violates freedom of occupation shall be valid even if it is not compatible with section 4, if it was included in a law passed by a majority of Knesset members in which it was expressly stated that it would be valid notwithstanding this Basic Law; the validity of such a law shall terminate four years after it came into force, unless it is stipulated therein that it will terminate sooner.

9. (Revocation of previous version of the Basic Law).

Temporary provision
10. Legislative provisions that were in force prior to the coming into force of this Basic Law shall remain in force for two years from the day this Basic Law comes into force, unless they are revoked sooner; however, such provisions shall be interpreted in the spirit of this Basic Law.

THE RELIGIOUS AND PHILOSOPHICAL BACKGROUND OF HUMAN DIGNITY AND ITS PLACE IN MODERN CONSTITUTIONS

Christian Starck

I. Religious and Philosophical Background

1. The Problem

The constitutional guarantee of human dignity poses a central doctrinal problem, which can only be grasped by examining the development of law in Western society. The guarantee of human dignity is one of the central components of the German Basic Law:[1] Art. 1(1) represents the highest source of law that gives positive expression to human dignity in the German Constitution. It determines the position of human beings in the community and in the state: 'Human dignity is inviolable. All state power must respect and protect it.'[2] Reference to human dignity may be found in the preamble to the Irish Constitution of 1937. Art. 41 of the 1947 Italian Constitution provides that human dignity shall set the limit to the scope of private economic initiatives. Art. 1 of the 1948 Universal Declaration of Human Rights recognizes the 'inherent dignity and ... equal and inalienable rights of all members of the human family.' Four of the constitutions which have been enacted in Western European states since 1975—those of Sweden, Portugal, Spain and Greece—and the draft for a complete revision of the Swiss

---

[1] Günter Dürig, 'Der Grundrechtssatz von der Menschenwürde,' *Archiv des öffentlichen Rechts*, (1956), vol. LXXXI, p. 117; Hans Carl Nipperdey, 'Die Würde des Menschen,' in Neumann, Nipperdey and Scheuner, eds. (1954), vol. II, p. 8.

[2] Similarly, the following West German Land Constitutions: the Preamble to the Constitution of Baden-Württemberg (1953); the Preamble and Art. 100 of the Constitution of Bavaria (1946); Art. 5 § 1 of the Constitution of Bremen (1947); Art. 3 of the Constitution of Hesse (1946); the Preamble to the Constitution of Rhineland-Palatinate (1947); Art. 1 of the Constitution of the Saarland (1947).

Constitution either describe human dignity as the basis of the political order[3] or place the guarantee of human dignity at the head of a catalogue of basic rights.[4] The Israeli Basic Law 'Human Dignity and Liberty' of 1992 makes similar reference to human dignity. Human dignity is, then, a particularly current concern in constitutional thought. That the most recent European constitutions have incorporated it certainly provides us with reasons enough to investigate its roots.

The issue is, at heart, historical: to what extent has Christianity, with its biblical and classical roots, influenced the formation of modern law, whether directly or mediated by humanism, the Enlightenment and revolution? Human dignity is of fundamental importance to modern constitutional thought. Since it determines the relationship between individuals and the state, the guarantee of human dignity allows us to draw inferences regarding the very basis of the state itself. This, in turn, has legal implications for the organization of the organs of state and the tasks with which they are entrusted; moreover, it has considerable impact on the way in which civil liberties are practiced and understood.

2. The Philosophical Roots of Human Dignity

The recent affirmation of human dignity in constitutions and international declarations is a product of a relatively secular age. Yet the development of the underlying idea—the concept of what a human being is—closely parallels the development of Christian thought. Both the Old and New Testaments state that the basis of human dignity is the fact that humans were created in the image of God (Gen. 1, 27; Eph. 4, 24).[5] It follows that every human being has inalienable value in his or her own right, which is why no human being may be treated as a mere object or as a means to an end.

A second strand of the concept of human dignity finds its origins in classical antiquity. Philosophers in this period recognized characteristics of human beings that distinguish them from animals, namely their capacity for rational thought and free will, and from this starting point, began to recognize human dignity in citizens. Later, their theory was extended in a more cosmopolitan context to all human beings.[6]

A strong social component characterizes the classical and Christian concepts of freedom which the notion of human dignity underpins: human beings were always seen as interdependent, social creatures. This is evident

---

[3] Chap. 1 § 2 phrase 1 of the Constitution of Sweden; Art. 1 of the Constitution of Portugal; Art. 10 § 1 of the Constitution of Spain.

[4] Art. 2 of the Constitution of Greece; Art. 8 of the draft Constitution of Switzerland.

[5] See Ernst Wolf, 'Die Freiheit und Würde des Menschen,' in *Recht, Staat, Wirtschaft* (1953) vol. IV, pp. 27, 32; Alfred Verdroß, 'Die Würde des Menschen als Grundlage der Menschenrechte,' in *Europäische Grundrechte-Zeitschrift* (1977) p. 207.

[6] Felix Flückiger, *Geschichte des Naturrechts* (1954) vol. I, pp. 127, 163, 191, 215; Hans Welzel, *Naturrecht und materiale Gerechtigkeit*, 4th edition (1962) p. 41.

from the concepts of the *polis*, of the community of believers, of general fraternity and of solidarity. Human freedom was anchored in divine law, in natural law and in moral law.

Christian life and belief, in which human beings depend (*religio*) on God, on Jesus Christ as intercessor and savior and on the Christian community, led by the Holy Spirit, transcend the physical world. In this context, it is usual to speak of metaphysics. Thus, human beings have a metaphysical anchor, which provides the basis for their freedom, and for their equality and fraternity: all human beings are, in equal measure, the image of God. Human dignity does not mean unlimited self-determination, but self-determination which is exercised on the basis that everyone—not simply the person claiming the right to self determination—is of value in his or her own right.

One might, of course, raise historical objections to the statement that human dignity can be traced to Christianity: the separation of society into estates, which the church accepted and encouraged; the theory of slavery adopted by medieval theologians from classical antiquity, and the church's use of secular power to persecute heretics and other opponents. Yet violations of human dignity through the church—including violations because of a failure to exercise proper toleration—do not gainsay the assertion that the concept of human dignity originated in Christianity. Certainly, the church was involved with the division of society into estates. This is a historical form of human community, however, which does not necessarily contradict the tenet of human dignity. As far as the church's attitude to slavery, its lack of toleration and its persecution of 'heretics' is concerned, they show, if anything, that the historical development of the concept of human dignity needed certain further historical events and intellectual advances in order to develop fully. It is not necessary to consider whether, as Hegel stated, the concept of human dignity should nowadays be seen as a development of Christianity,[7] or whether it represents a new philosophical movement, because neither alternative alters the fact that it owes its genesis to Christian thought and to classical antiquity.

3. Political Philosophy

Political philosophy and law approach human dignity differently. The law gave early recognition to dignity: it formed the basis of civil liberties, especially, in earlier centuries, of the pacts and statutes which gave effect to the habeas corpus rule.[8] Political philosophers, on the other hand, tended to advance general arguments, in which the Christian heritage of human dignity was particularly evident. The concept of human dignity was central to the political

---

[7] Georg Wilhelm Friedrich Hegel, 'Philosophie der Weltgeschichte,' 1. *Hälfte: Die Vernunft in der Geschichte*, J. Hoffmeister, ed. (1955) p. 47; Gerhard Ritter, *Ursprung und Wesen der Menschenrechte*, R. Schnur, ed. (1949); *Zur Geschichte der Erklärung der Menschenrechte* (1964) p. 205.

[8] Ernst Wolf (note 5), pp. 27, 34; Bertrand de Jouvenel, *Über die Staatsgewalt*, (1972) p. 279.

thought of Samuel Pufendorf, for example: he derived it from the social character of human nature, which he believed was divinely determined.[9] According to Pufendorf, human dignity provides the basis for morally anchored freedom[10] and equality.[11]

By contrast, Kant emphasized the individual nature of human freedom. His understanding of human dignity follows from his theory of moral autonomy,[12] according to which human beings, while free, are bound to the duties imposed by moral law, in which the tradition of natural law can be found. Human beings are themselves law-giving members of a moral empire, enabled by freedom and represented by practical reason (*praktische Vernunft*). While human beings belong to this empire and enjoy the power to legislate within it, they do not dominate it, but are subordinate to it. The Christian roots of Kant's concept of human dignity are evident, notwithstanding the concept's immediate basis in moral autonomy. Our hubristic refusal to recognize that, having been created, we are necessarily subject to a higher law is, according to Kant, an apostasy.[13]

Since the Renaissance, the discipline of anthropology has gradually freed itself from a theologically oriented metaphysical tradition. Nonetheless, it is rich with descriptions and experience of human nature (*doctrina humanae naturae*) in which the Christian concept of human beings is evident.[14] This is not uniformly the case, of course: we need only think of Hobbes, who derives the equality of human beings from the fact that we have the potential to destroy each other,[15] and who equates human dignity with the individual's value as a citizen[16].

4. Secularization

According to Hegel,[17] only under Christianity '... did the Germanic nations become aware that human beings themselves are free.' Initially, this recognition was theological, but, according to Hegel, there followed a painful 'secularization' process. He saw history as a progression in the awareness of

---

[9] Samuel Pufendorf, *De iure naturae et gentium*; lib. 1 cap. III § 1; lib. 2 cap. III § 20; lib. 3 cap. II § 1; see Hans Welzel, *Die Naturrechtslehre Samuel Pufendorfs* (1958) p. 47.

[10] Pufendorf (note 9), lib. 2 cap. I § 2.

[11] Pufendorf (note 9), lib. 3 cap. II §§ 1, 2.

[12] Immanuel Kant, *Grundlegung zur Metaphysik der Sitten*, K. Vorländer, ed. (1920) p. 56.

[13] Immanuel Kant, *Kritik der praktischen Vernunft*, K. Vorländer, ed. (1929) p. 96.

[14] Udo Marquard, Art. 'Anthropologie,' in: *Hist. Wörterbuch der Philosophie I* (1971) column 363 ff.

[15] Thomas Hobbes, *Leviathan*, cap. XIII; Vom Bürger, cap. I 3.

[16] Hobbes, *Leviathan*, cap. X.

[17] Hegel (note 7), p. 62.

liberty from Reformation[18] through Enlightenment[19] to Revolution.[20] The modern world together with modern law had, according to Hegel, blossomed from the seeds of Christianity. Hegel understood Christianity, not as the brake-shoe of historical progress, but as the wellspring of the modern world. This theory is incompatible both with the argument that the modern world was wrest from Christianity and with the belief that the Christian heritage must be defended against the depredations of the modern age.[21] Secularization is, in effect, shorthand for the process whereby the seeds of Christianity germinate and flourish in the temporal world.

Yet Christianity also sowed the seeds for later philosophical and practical individualism. Individualism, whose theological basis is the individual's direct relationship with God, permeated all aspects of society, culminating in declarations of human rights. These declarations assumed a distinction between human beings and the state. Ernst Wolf correctly describes human rights declarations as a 'product of the Christian Occident.'[22] We may add that it is a product of the process of secularization in the classical sense. An exclusively theological postulate of individualism on the basis of a direct relationship between the individual and God began to inform attitudes in the secular sphere, even though, from a theological point of view, fraternal compassion, not individualism, ought to have followed. Human rights catalogues were conceived as rights which the individual could bring to bear against the state: they do not, of course, give complete expression to the complex tapestry of social relationships which characterize human society. Demarcating the spheres of individual and state activity does not delimit relationships among individual human beings. Nonetheless, the extent to which individualism now characterizes both the civil law and civic life can scarcely be overlooked.

5. Liberalism and Positivism

Nineteenth century legal and political commentators still clearly assumed human dignity as the basis of human freedom; nonetheless, they do not mention human dignity explicitly. Carl von Rotteck[23] posits an ability, inherent in every human being, which enables him to choose freely between sensuality and reason. The radical democrat Gustav von Struve, in the *Staatslexikon*,[24] saw the first seeds of the understanding of human rights in the teachings of

---

[18] Hegel, *Philosophie der Weltgeschichte*, 2nd half, 2nd edition, Lasson, ed., original reprint (1976) p. 877.
[19] Hegel (note 7), p. 915.
[20] Hegel (note 7), p. 920.
[21] See Hermann Lübbe, *Säkularisierung*, 2nd edition (1975) p. 38.
[22] Wolf (note 5), p. 27.
[23] V. Rotteck/Welcker, eds., *Staatslexikon*, 2nd edition (1847) vol. V, p. 180; similar for instance Karl Salomo Zachariä, *Vierzig Bücher vom Staate* (1820) vol. I, pp. 33.
[24] V. Rotteck/Welcker eds., *Staatslexikon*, 2nd edition (1847) vol. IX, p. 65.

Christ, which rest upon the principle of the equality of all human beings.... These teachings removed the obstacles which stood in the way of the recognition of eternal, inalienable human rights; at the same time, they contained a powerful imperative to research and investigate these rights. Difficulties and drawbacks notwithstanding, the seed had been sown. According to Struve, Christianity, working hand in hand with history and philosophy, had pulled humanity another rung up the developmental ladder.

If human dignity could still be detected among the sources of human rights in the age of liberalism, it disappeared altogether in the positivist movement which followed. Positivism displayed a pointed disregard for the philosophical and moral dimension of the law. Paul Laband believed that the proper task for the law was constructing legal institutions, tracing the clauses of statutes back to general principles, and, conversely, deducing consequences from those principles. Thus, according to Laband, historical, political and philosophical considerations were all irrelevant to the proper doctrinal analysis of concrete positive law: generally, they served only to hide a lack of constructive work.[25] Statements like this are evidence of a self-confident generation's disinterest in the intellectual basis of the law; nonetheless, while that basis was not of interest, it was not denied, either.[26] We should also recall that positivism provided support and justification for the legal protection of basic rights, for the rule of law and for due process. Examples are the so-called fundamental rights statutes, which bound the executive. We can observe the same development in France and in other European countries. The great pity is that, in perfecting these legal safeguards, their purpose was forgotten;[27] worse, there developed a general belief that rights were granted by the state and, thus, were at its disposal.

6. Metaphysical Dimension to Human Beings Rejected

A radical denial of any religious or metaphysical basis to human dignity is particularly evident in the writings of Karl Marx, whose analysis of religion centered on the conviction that man is the highest being for man.[28] This is—at least in theory—a wholesale rejection of human self-alienation, with the serious consequence that human beings are defined exclusively by social relationships.[29] These, according to Marx, flow from the economic order,

---

[25] Paul Laband, ed., *Das Staatsrecht des Deutschen Reiches*, preface to the 2nd edition (1887) quoted from 5th edition, vol. I, p. IX.

[26] Franz Wieacker, *Privatrechtsgeschichte der Neuzeit*, 2nd edition (1967) p. 441.

[27] Luis Legaz y Lacambra, 'Das Recht aus religiöser Perspektive,' in: *Festschrift für E. Voegelin* (1962) pp. 343, 354.

[28] Karl Marx, 'Zur Kritik der Hegelschen Rechtsphilosophie' (1844) in: *Karl Marx, Frühschriften*, V.Landshut, ed. (1964) p. 216; Adam Schaff, *Marxismus und das menschliche Individuum* (1970) p. 28; Karel Kosik, *Die Dialektik des Konkreten*, (1967) pp. 23, 215, 231.

[29] Schaff (note 28), p. 24.

which can itself be analyzed and explained. The consequences of this premise should not be underestimated. Denuded of a moral and metaphysical dimension—and, I need scarcely add, of human dignity—the individual is reduced to a scientific problem awaiting a scientific solution.[30] In Marx' eyes, human rights are regarded—and rejected—as a product of Christianity which simply protect human egotism.

This philosophy has been well received by behavioural scientists. Skinner's book (entitled, tellingly, *Beyond Freedom and Dignity*) expresses the author's hope for a 'technology of behavior,' which would render superfluous concepts like freedom, value and dignity.[31] According to Skinner, freedom and dignity are not operational concepts, but metaphysical or quasi-religious ideas. Science, he believes, has advanced to the point where it can describe and alter (!) those individual human circumstances which freedom and dignity describe only imprecisely. In 1973, Skinner acknowledged the consequences of his world-view for the constitutional protection of human dignity, noting that he trusted to Communist China for the future, after initially placing his hopes on the Soviet Union.[32]

Not every opinion is as clearly expressed, however; not every commentator is as ready as Skinner to follow a pet theory to its logical conclusion. Yet human dignity collapses if human beings can be scientifically explained. Why should dignity inhere in a collection of nerves, which respond predictably (or can be trained to respond predictably) to stimuli? Such a philosophy lets us recognize human dignity or deny it, quite as we like, but it does not allow us to justify dignity if we do choose to recognize it. I do not intend to attack the scientific value of psychology, medicine or the behavioural sciences, but I do criticize the philosophical school to which certain of their adherents belong and its consequences for the legal order.[33]

Atheist humanism denies the metaphysical dimension to human existence, claiming to be something original, 'a completely new association of materialism and spiritualism, of pessimism and optimism' (Merleau-Ponty). Whatever this might mean, it is not clear how we should measure what is particularly human in this strand of humanism, which categorizes both God and nature as negations of humanity.

Clearly, none of these theories offers assistance in understanding the constitutional guarantee of dignity: if it is not perfectly clear what requires respect and protection, the guarantee is simply a hollow phrase, able to provide an alibi for any given political ideology.

---

[30] Critically Martin Kriele, *Befreiung und politische Aufklärung* (1980) pp. 53, 250.
[31] See German edition: *Jenseits von Freiheit und Würde* (1973) p. 28.
[32] Burhuss Frederic Skinner, *Futurum II*, (1972), p. 16.
[33] Also critically Ralf Dahrendorf, *Homo Sociologicus*, 15th edition (1977) pp. 83, 85, 88, 92.

7. Metaphysical Dimension to Human Beings Downplayed

In the process of secularization and the concomitant focus on temporal things, we can observe the liberation of a considerable part of society, and hence also of the law, from Christianity. This 'process of liberation' does not mean that Christianity is irrelevant for our society or our law today: rather, it requires re-examination, adaptation and development.[34] Christianity is, thus, still relevant to modern law. A humanistic rationale for the guarantee of dignity cannot lag behind the standard of dignity which we have inherited from the Christian tradition.[35]

The attempt to find a secular justification for law and society should not be seen as a search for the polar opposite to the Christian basis of either. It would be quite wrong to see any such search as a great struggle to free either law or society from the clutches of Christianity. There is simply no evidence that such a fundamental opposition exists. It is not present where humanists, upbraiding Christianity for not having done enough to protect human dignity, claim that humanism is a development or even a completion of the concept of freedom and dignity. And it is certainly not present where the secular activity of the Church is restricted and the separation of church and state is upheld. After all, the metaphysical, religious justification for freedom, which provided the ground in which humanism took root,[36] is not affected by this kind of criticism.

The Christian basis of human dignity is clearly evident even where a secular, temporal justification is sought,[37] for dignity is understood as a quality which vests in each individual human being. Accepting this concept, humanism is precluded from embracing any ideology in which human beings are reduced to a means by which a collective or technocratic community accomplishes its ends. Attempts have been made at a non-metaphysical justification for human dignity, rejecting a wholly empirical explanation for human beings. The non-metaphysical justification for human dignity simply masks a value judgment, expected in response to the leading question: 'Why should human freedom, dignity, conscience and responsibility exist, and how can we prove that they are true?'

H. L. A. Hart says, in his criticism of natural law:[38] 'Indeed, the continued reassertion of some form of Natural Law doctrine is due in part to the fact that its appeal is independent of both divine and human authority, and to the fact that despite a terminology, and much metaphysics, which few could now accept, it contains certain elementary terms of importance for the understanding of both morality and law. These we shall endeavor to disentangle from their metaphysical setting and restate here in simpler terms.'

---

[34] Lübbe (*supra* note 21), pp. 34, 109.
[35] For criticism to Skinner see Dahrendorf (note 33), p. 95.
[36] Jacques Maritain, *Gesellschaftsordnung und Freiheit* (1936) p. 64.
[37] Werner Maihofer, *Rechtsstaat und menschliche Würde* (1968) p. 26.
[38] H. L. A. Hart, *Law and Morals*, (Oxford, Clarendon Press 1961) p. 184.

This is an attempt to drive out metaphysics with the weapons of language. Analytical legal theory treats natural law as a fact, simply because certain scholars advocate it or—in other words—because 'discourse' leads us in that direction. But what follows if this conclusion is not reached—if not equality and freedom of human beings are denied? The truths concealed by natural law must be understood in advance: clearly, they follow from the understanding of human beings which we have inherited from the Judeo-Christian tradition.

II. Human Dignity in the German Basic Law

The human dignity clause, which heads the German Basic Law, was enacted in reaction to the atrocities of the National Socialist regime. It recalls the regard in which European law has historically held human beings, as is evident in the 1789 French Declaration and the various American bills of rights of the same era. It is one of the essential planks upon which our civilization rests.

1. Beneficiaries

The dignity clause takes every human being—or, more specifically, every entity conceived by a human being—within its compass.[39] It confers a certain amount of protection beyond death.[40] This is the most inclusive definition possible: it is imperative that dignity be framed so that no one is excluded by definition. According to our biological knowledge of DNA, all genetically determined characteristics of a human being are completely present in the fertilized ovum. With fertilization, a continuous process of gradual development of individual human life begins. No further turning-point is evident. In particular, eligibility does not depend upon the capacity for mental or physical experience. Thus, dignity extends to teratological products of human conception, to the mentally handicapped and the mentally ill. As the 1975 and 1993 decisions of the Federal Constitutional Court on the termination of pregnancy confirm, human dignity also vests in the unborn child.[41]

2. Validity, Nature and Status of the Guarantee

Before I turn to the particulars of the dignity clause, I must briefly describe its constitutional context, the structure within which it operates.

The dignity clause opens the Basic Law; it stands at the head of a catalogue of basic rights. Art. 1(3) states that 'the following basic rights bind the legislature, the executive and the judiciary as directly enforceable law.' Since the dignity clause is contained in Art. 1(1), it cannot be counted among

---

[39] Starck, in: v. Mangoldt/Klein/Starck, *Das Bonner Grundgesetz*, 4th edition (1999) vol. I, Art. 1 marg. no. 17 ff.
[40] BVerfGE 30, 173, 194 (= Decisions of the Federal Constitutional Court, vol. XXX, pp. 173, 194).
[41] BVerfGE 39, 1, 41; 88, 203, 251.

the 'following' rights mentioned in paragraph 3. Some early commentators argued that the dignity clause was not directly enforceable law. Rather, they said, it was merely a guideline for the interpretation of the catalogue of rights which followed.

However, it is now generally accepted by the Federal Constitutional Court and by constitutional scholars that the word 'inviolable' and the 'duty to respect and protect' do indicate that the dignity clause is directly enforceable law.[42] Moreover, Art 79(3) provides that no constitutional amendment to the Basic Law may touch the core of Arts. 1 and 20. If the dignity clause is beyond the reach of a Parliament amending the constitution, it can scarcely be within the grasp of the ordinary legislature.

Finally, we must consider whether the dignity clause is an individual right, which can be enforced by means of a constitutional complaint. Because the dignity clause protects human beings as individuals, both an examination of the context of the Basic Law as a whole and a purpose-based approach to Art. 1, lead inexorably to the conclusion that the dignity clause gives positive expression to a right. Thus, individuals can file a constitutional complaint against constitutional amendments which do not respect human dignity.

3. The Inviolable Character of the Guarantee

Art. 1(1) states: 'Human dignity is inviolable.' The German word, *unantastbar*, is unusually powerful: it might equally well be translated as 'unassailable,' or even 'sacrosanct.' An unamendable constitutional provision that dignity is 'inviolable' is extremely forceful: it means that dignity ought not to be infringed. It means that infringements of Art. 1(1), like infringements of the other basic rights, may not be justified by reference to any common good.

This is a significant difference to the concept of human dignity in the Israeli Basic Law, at least according to the jurisprudence of the Supreme Court. But we must add that human dignity is defined very narrowly in German constitutional law as the final essence of what constitutes a human being. The human being may not be treated as a means to an end or as a mere object. This narrow definition harmonizes with the fact that the catalogue of fundamental right in the German Basic Law is exhaustive. In particular, the Basic Law contains a general freedom clause which reads: 'Everyone shall have the right to free development of his personality insofar as he does not violate the rights of others or offend against the constitutional order or against morality.' This clause encompasses all new fundamental right issues—e.g., data protection—which can be treated under Art. 2 in the normal way and can be balanced with the rights of others and common goods.

---

[42] BVerfGE 6, 32, 36; 45, 187, 227; 61, 126, 137.

4. The Duty to Respect and Protect

Who is subject to the duty to respect and protect human dignity? All state functions, which is to say the legislature, the executive, the judiciary and all other public law authorities (local government, universities and public law authorities) share this obligation.

The state's duty to respect human dignity requires that it refrain from taking measures which would infringe upon human dignity. Public law must be structured to preclude violations of human dignity. The dignity clause provides a guideline for the drafting of legislation. Furthermore, legal norms are to be interpreted in such a way that human dignity is not violated.

The requirement that the state protect human dignity imposes a twofold duty. First, the state must take positive action, often by providing a financial safety net, to safeguard human dignity. As the Federal Constitutional Court has twice confirmed, the state must make sure that those who are physically or mentally disabled and are unable to support themselves have the minimum necessities to live in dignity.[43]

Second, the state must prevent individuals from infringing upon one another's dignity. The protection must be adequate to ward off the type, the scope and the intensity of potential violations. This is accomplished by attention to three fields: substantive law, especially criminal and private law; procedural law, especially criminal and civil procedure; and the enforcement of judgments. The protection of human life, the basis of human dignity, requires the bulwark of the criminal law. Other measures—for example, protection from defamation to the extent mandated by dignity—can be achieved by the civil law.

One final aspect of protection deserves mention here. The Federal Constitutional Court has ruled that protection requires information. If the state is to protect dignity effectively, it must gather information about factors which might endanger dignity in order to be able to react in time.[44] This new 'duty to inform' is particularly important in light of technological developments, particularly in the field of nuclear energy.

This systematic approach to the dignity clause, which can be derived from the text of Art. 1 para. 1, is based on several decisions of the Federal Constitutional Court.

A review of the case law on human dignity discloses a particular emphasis in two areas: the state's duty to respect dignity and to refrain from infringing it (5 a-g); the state's duty to protect human dignity against violation by third parties (5 h).

Since the latter duty is discharged chiefly within the sphere of the civil law, it is one of the ways in which the Federal Constitutional Court influences the interpretation and application of the civil law.

---

[43] BVerfGE 40, 121, 133; 45, 187, 228 f.
[44] BVerfGE 49, 89, 132; 56, 54, 78; 88, 203, 309 f.

5. Case Law

a. Criminal Law

Art. 102 of the Basic Law abolishes capital punishment, giving direct effect to the dignity clause. Human life is the basis of human dignity: the state does *not* have the right to dispose of it. Because there is no direct relationship between capital punishment and the protection of other human life, capital punishment violates the dignity clause.[45] Human dignity may only be violated where human dignity is at stake. For example, a police officer may, to save the life of X, use force—in a worst-case scenario, lethal force—against Y. Finally, the guarantee of human dignity forbids extradition where capital punishment is a threat.

The constitutionality of life imprisonment has been challenged before the Federal Constitutional Court. In the Court's opinion, dignity requires that a convicted person retain the prospect of eventually regaining his or her liberty. I believe that this decision is correct; its implementation falls to the institution of clemency. Yet the Federal Constitutional Court goes further, requiring legal regulation of the conditions and procedures under which a sentence of life imprisonment may be commuted.[46]

Cruel and disproportionate punishments violate the guarantee of dignity.[47] Torture and inhumane punishment also violate Art. 3 ECHR.

In itself, using the general principle of crime prevention to justify the length of a prison sentence does not violate the dignity clause: the imprisoned person does not become a mere instrument for the policing responsibility incumbent upon the state. He or she is treated as a member of the community, and general crime prevention within that community is a legitimate goal.[48]

Within the general context of the criminal law, the Federal Constitutional Court has certainly been asked to rule on peculiar questions. It has been claimed that the offence of leaving the scene of an accident is a violation of the dignity guarantee. The Court has rejected this argument: the legal order requires that individuals take responsibility for their actions, and, at the very least, that they not hinder the investigation of the causes of an accident.[49]

b. Criminal Procedure

Most cases which raise issues of criminal procedure are not dealt with under the dignity clause, but under Art. 2(1) of the Basic Law, quoted under II 3.

The Federal Constitutional Court has developed a general right of liberty from Art. 2(1), which has been used as the basis for regulation of the use of

---

[45] BVerfGE 18, 112, 117; 60, 348, 354.
[46] BVerfGE 45, 187, 238; 50, 5, 9; 54, 100, 108 f; 114 f; 86, 288, 312.
[47] BVerfGE 28, 386, 391; 72, 105, 116; 75, 1, 16.
[48] BVerfGE 50, 166, 175 f.
[49] BVerfGE 16, 191, 194.

medical records, diaries and tape recordings as evidence in criminal trials.[50] Other cases have concerned the right to physical integrity, which Art. 2(2) of the Basic Law guarantees.[51] Cases involving human dignity are rare. Legal texts do discuss hypothetical cases, most of which concern methods of interrogation and the prohibition on hypnosis or on so-called 'truth drugs.'

c. Remand Detention & Imprisonment Following Conviction

Whether hunger-striking prisoners may be force-fed is an issue with which German courts have wrestled. I do not believe that the dignity clause requires force-feeding where a prisoner freely decides to refrain from eating.[52]

Observation peepholes in prisoners' cell doors are only permissible to protect prisoners' life or physical integrity. Constant observation of a prisoner in order to investigate his or her personality is a violation of human dignity.[53]

d. General Procedural Law

The right to a hearing in accordance with law, which is guaranteed by Art. 103(1) of the Basic Law, is a direct consequence of the guarantee of human dignity in Art. 1.[54] Procedural law must be structured so that no one becomes merely the object of a procedure. Before a decision affecting anyone's rights is made, that person must be given the opportunity to be heard by the courts.

e. Compulsory Military Service

Compulsory military service does not violate the guarantee of human dignity.[55] While Art. 26 of the Basic Law declares wars of aggression unconstitutional, the state may call upon its citizens in its own defense. The duty to risk one's life in a conflict of that nature reflects the duty to put one's own life at risk to protect the dignity and freedom of one's fellow citizens.

The right to refuse to participate in military service involving the use of arms, which is explicitly granted by Art. 4(3) of the Basic Law, does not flow automatically from the dignity clause. As this example shows, the ambit of the dignity clause is narrower than the spheres of protection of the other basic rights.

---

[50] See Starck (note 39), Art. 2 marg. no. 88 *ff*, 160 *ff*.
[51] Starck (note 39), Art. 2 marg. no. 201 *ff*.
[52] Starck (note 39), Art. 1 marg. no. 60.
[53] Starck (note 39), Art. 1 marg. no. 61.
[54] BVerfGE 7, 275, 279; 57, 250, 275; 63, 322, 337.
[55] BVerfGE 12, 45, 50.

f. Police Action

Police officers may only use firearms to prevent attack or escape. If it is virtually certain that a shot will kill an aggressor, it may only be fired in order to prevent a clear and present danger to life, or severe harm to physical integrity. Placing a higher value on the life of the victim than on the life of the aggressor is consistent with the dignity clause.

g. Data Protection

Data protection falls within the scope of the general liberty clause in Art. 2(1) of the Basic Law. Nonetheless, the dignity clause restricts the state's efforts to gather and use personal data. For example, any attempt to treat an individual like a physical object by registering the whole of his or her personality violates the guarantee of human dignity.[56] Similarly, the dignity clause is violated by the collection of data concerning the most private aspects of human life or the sphere of changing opinion.

h. Duty to Forbid and to Sanction

Like public law, private law is influenced by the dignity clause. It must be structured and interpreted so that human dignity is protected from infringement by third parties. While the other basic rights have traditionally required the state to refrain from taking action, the dignity clause mandates that the state take positive steps to ensure that dignity is protected. The Federal Constitutional Court has, in consequence, had a certain impact on the civil law and on the jurisprudence of the federal courts. I am not concerned, here, with increasing the influence of the Federal Constitutional Court by enlarging the concept of state duties of protection on the basis of other fundamental rights whose wording does not specifically provide for such a duty.[57] I should note, too, that the issue of a constitutional court's influence on the civil law is irrelevant in legal systems such of that of the United States, where the supreme court is both the highest court in civil, criminal and administrative cases and a constitutional court capable of reviewing—and striking down—statutes. When a Supreme Court interprets and applies statutes, it does so with the constitution in mind, but without any further control by a constitutional court.

Where statutory interpretation alone is insufficient to give effect to the requirements of the dignity clause, the statute cannot be applied. It must be treated as null and void.

Often, however, a court is not confronted with a provision which, being incompatible with the constitution, must be declared null and void. More frequently, the legislature has omitted to grant protection when required to do so by the Basic Law. The judge may add to the statute by interpretation, whether by the Continental technique of the analogous application of statutory

---

[56] BVerfGE 27, 1, 6; 65, 1, 41 *ff.*
[57] See Christian Starck, *Praxis der Verfassungsauslegung*, (1994), p. 46.

provisions to situations not expressly covered by a statute, or by creating genuine judge-made law on the basis of constitutional provisions. Where this is impossible, a declaratory judgment is rendered.

The Federal Constitutional Court frequently discusses whether protecting human dignity in a given situation requires the intervention of the criminal law, or whether the matter can be regulated by the norms of private law. The German Civil Code, or BGB, contains a general right to redress where life, physical integrity, liberty, property or any other right is violated. The Court has decided that human life, having paramount value and being the basis of human dignity, must be protected by the criminal law.[58] This, the Court has said, requires a police force to counteract danger to human life. Two decisions of the Federal Constitutional Court argue that the criminal law must normally also extend its protection to unborn human life.[59] At a minimum, abortion must be considered illegal in the absence of serious justification, excluding the so-called social indication.

The artificial production of human embryos outside the female body for biomedical research violates the dignity guarantee, because it treats human life as a means to an end, not as an end in itself. The eugenic alteration of human gametes might one day give a physician (or his or her client) total power over the individual character of a human being. This is a violation of human dignity, which must be forbidden by the criminal law.[60]

The right to have one's personal honor respected, which Art. 5(2) of the Basic Law names as one of the limits to freedom of expression, does not derive solely from human dignity. Nonetheless, the dignity clause protects the basic core of the right.[61] Human dignity is violated by an incitement to violence and to arbitrary action against any group of the population, whether expressed in speech or in writing. In the absence of specific criminal offences, human dignity could be protected in this context by the offence of criminal insult.

Third-party interference in the core of the right to privacy, whether through recording private conversations, through listening devices or data collection, must be prevented by statute.

Final example: Art. 6(2) of the Basic Law states that 'the care and upbringing of children is a natural right of, and a duty which is primarily incumbent upon, their parents.'

Where parents abuse their right of upbringing, violating their children's dignity, the state has a duty to intervene in order to protect the children against their parents. That duty is regulated by the fourth book of the Civil Code, which deals with family law.[62]

---

[58] BVerfGE 45, 187, 254; 46, 160, 164.
[59] BVerfGE 39, 1, 42; 88, 203, 251 f.
[60] See Starck (note 39), Art. 1 marg. no. 89, 90.
[61] BVerfGE 30, 173, 194; 75, 369, 380.
[62] Starck (note 39), Art. 1 marg. no. 98.

DIGNITY AS A (MODERN) VIRTUE
Michael J. Meyer

I. Introduction

Any discussion of the place of the idea of human dignity, within a modern regime of human rights, like the Universal Declaration of Human Rights, might consider dignity as either a moral 'minimum' (typically a kind of moral status) or a moral 'maximum' (typically a kind of moral ideal). This paper takes the latter, less traveled, road. The renewed philosophical interest in 'the virtues' has, in addition, tended to focus largely on virtues first identified in the ancient world like courage, temperance, or justice;[1] however, an essential supplement to any viable contemporary discussion of virtue would be some detailed consideration of particular virtues that are ascendant in the modern world. What might be called the virtue of dignity—roughly understood as a disposition grounded in the idea of 'human dignity—is a valuable candidate for such an investigation. The absence of dignity from more traditional lists of the virtues itself seems a reason to consider the virtue of dignity as one candidate for an updated catalog of modern virtues. Moreover, though often central to contemporary moral discourse, the idea of human dignity is rarely associated with the virtues. Finally, the main reason for considering dignity as a virtue is perhaps most clearly seen with an example. While Martin Luther King's marching at Selma or Mahatma Gandhi's marching for the Salt Satyagraha might be understood as exemplifying an ancient virtue, like courage, they seem best understood as an expression of the virtue of dignity. This paper will investigate this claim, focusing at first on various aspects of the

---

[1] See, for example, Peter Geach, *The Virtues*, (Cambridge University Press 1977) especially Ch. 5-8; Phillipa Foot, *Virtues and Vices*, (University of California Press 1978) especially pp. 1-18; Bernard Williams, 'Justice as a Virtue,' in *Moral Luck* (Cambridge University Press 1981) pp. 83-93; Alasdair MacIntyre, *After Virtue*, (University of Notre Dame Press 1984), especially Ch. 17, pp. 227-237; Gregory E. Pence, 'Recent Work on the Virtues,' *American Philosophical Quarterly* (1984) vol. XXI, no. 4 pp. 281-97; John Casey, *Pagan Virtue* (Oxford University Press 1990) *passim*.

concept of dignity (section II) especially this conception of the virtue of dignity (section III). I will conclude with discussion of the basically modern character of the virtue of dignity (section IV).

II. The Concept of Dignity

The idea of dignity is a complex notion. At one level of appraisal, animals or even objects may be said to have dignity. A thoroughbred racehorse or some Rembrandt self-portraits may be said—perhaps due in part to a certain nobility of style—to have great dignity. Yet, the normative use of the concept of dignity is typically, if not exclusively, reserved for human beings. Within these bounds it is useful to recognize four senses in which human beings may be said to have dignity. First, and perhaps least common in contemporary discussions, a person may have dignity simply in virtue of occupying a position of high rank in an established social hierarchy. Having what I will here call 'social dignity'—or the dignity of office—is typically limited to persons of some social rank. In this sense only those who have social rank (e.g., earls, bishops, or kings) are said to have dignity.[2] This conception of 'social dignity' (the idea that only persons of some social rank have dignity) provides an important backdrop for the generally modern idea of human dignity.[3]

It is considerably more common at present to suggest that human beings, those within every social rank, have 'human dignity.' The more egalitarian idea of human dignity can be seen as a response to the suggestion that only those of a certain social rank have dignity. Kant's discussion of dignity is perhaps the most important philosophical account of the grounds of such an egalitarian notion of human dignity. Roughly put, in the paradigm case human dignity is that special moral worth and status had by a human being.[4] One has human dignity regardless of not only (hereditary) social position, but also race, gender, nationality, ethnicity or other markers of social hierarchy. This egalitarian account of 'human dignity' is arguably a moral high-water mark of modern ethical and political thought.

---

[2] The cognate idea here is the notion of a 'dignitary.' Samuel Johnson defined 'dignity' as 'rank of elevation' and a 'dignitary' as a 'clergyman advanced to some dignity, to some rank above that of a parish priest.' *A Dictionary of the English Language*, [1746-55] (Philadelphia 1819), I sig. 3x2, 3v. The *New Shorter Oxford English Dictionary*, (1993) continues to note one meaning of 'dignity' as 'a person who holds a high or official position.'

[3] On the general topic of 'social dignity' see Michael J. Meyer, 'Kant's Concept of Dignity and Modern Political Thought,' *History of European Ideas* (1987) vol. VIII no. 3 pp. 319-332.

[4] One obvious way to read Kant is that for him dignity is a kind of moral status grounded on a fundamental type of moral worth (Kant uses *Würde* for both) which is in turn grounded on a basic normative capacity (viz., practical deliberation). See, for example, *Groundwork of the Metaphysic of Morals*, Academy edition, trans. H.J. Paton (Harper 1964) p. 434 *ff.*

Having dignity can also be understood as having a 'sense of dignity.' A person with a proper sense of his (human) dignity will most likely resist humiliation and dehumanization by others. However, it is important to recognize that a person who does not have a *sense* of own dignity does not lack dignity altogether. For example, the individual lacking a proper appreciation of his human dignity still retains his human dignity in the sense that he retains his status as deserving of basic moral respect.

The final conception of having dignity is the primary focus here: one may have the *virtue* of dignity. To simplify a bit: a virtue of character is a more or less settled disposition, and attendant attitudes, that over time contributes to the constitution of a good moral or ethical temperament. I will not offer a general theory of the virtues here—for example, an account of the ultimate moral grounding of the virtues or of the relationship (unity? hierarchy?) between the various virtues—although a few related matters will be considered below. It is worth emphasizing that the virtue of dignity is not a conception of moral status. Furthermore, I do not wish to suggest that having the moral status of 'human dignity' is grounded upon a person actually acting in a virtuous way in general or by possessing the more specific virtue of dignity. The first two conceptions of having dignity (having social dignity and having human dignity) intersect with the second two conceptions of having dignity (having a sense of dignity and having the virtue of dignity). In short, a person might have a sense of his human dignity, or a sense of his social dignity, or both. Likewise the virtue of dignity might be tied to either a person's social dignity, or his human dignity, or both. In the analysis to follow I will take the 'virtue of dignity' to have its conceptual home within the notion of 'human dignity.'

III. The Virtue of Dignity

One classic way to explicate any virtue is to locate the opposing vices. Following Aristotle in thinking of a virtue as a mean between extremes of character, consider the contrasting vices: 1) misplaced or submissive humility (roughly, a deficiency in regard to the virtue of dignity), and 2) misplaced or haughty nobility (roughly, an excess in regard to the virtue of dignity).[5] The man of misplaced humility is deflated by the idea that he is less than the equal of others. The man of haughty nobility is, on the contrary, inflated by the notion that he is superior to those who lack his nobility. The haughty man is disposed to comport himself as an elite individual; the submissively humble man has instead a disposition derived from his attitude about his general insignificance. To explore this notion of elitism, I will consider first some issues related to the exercise of rights.

---

[5] For a thoughtful account, from which I have benefited, of similar but distinct vices see 'Servility and Self-Respect,' 'Self-Respect Reconsidered,' and 'Social Snobbery and Human Dignity,' in Thomas E. Hill Jr., *Autonomy and Self-Respect* (Cambridge University Press 1991).

The elitism of the haughty man is not only, or even primarily, a question of which moral or legal rights he actually possesses. The elitism of the noble man is instead most clearly revealed by the dispositions (and attitudes) he has regarding his rights. And so, too, for the submissive man. The submissive man is, for example, disposed to put the convenience of 'his betters' before that of his own. For example, if pressing what are in fact his legitimate rights would be a source of frustration to his superiors, he will be loath to do so. Here the man of misplaced humility exhibits an over-generalized inclination to please his superiors. For the man of misplaced humility the actual *possession* of rights is not sufficient to ensure a victory against humiliation.

The haughty man, on the other hand, expects the habitual deference of others to his rights. He is disposed to enjoy his rights without the need for any overt agitation to insure that they be respected. Suppose the noble man actually had the right to board the bus before what he regards as 'the rabble' and to ride up front so as to have the honor of the best view. Now it would already be a problem for him if the noble man had to stand up and agitate for this right. Such agitation would suggest that others had not spontaneously taken their subordinate positions. This is not to say that there is ultimately any unwillingness on behalf of the noble man to claim his legitimate rights. It is rather that there is already some dishonor involved in the necessity of publicly, or privately, pressing for the recognition of his rights.

Compare these examples of the vices of misplaced nobility and misplaced humility with the virtue of dignity exemplified by Mahatma Gandhi or Martin Luther King. Gandhi and King are disposed to claim their rights publicly, forcefully (as is called for), and they do so without any exaggeration or underestimation about how their rights should be seen by others. Gandhi and King are not, like the haughty man, in any way dishonored by the fact that they may be called upon to stand up and publicly agitate for their legitimate rights. They are not, like the submissive man, at all disinclined to press their rights, even if doing so inconveniences those alleged to be their superiors. Gandhi and King see the activity of claiming their legitimate rights as a sometimes necessary and sometimes even distinguished practice. They do not imagine that they are in any way above (or not up to) the public insistence that their legitimate rights be respected. I do not, however, wish to suggest here that the activity of claiming rights is the sole, or always the best, exemplification of the virtue of dignity. Indeed, exemplars like Gandhi and King are able to command respect (for their rights) merely by the way they carry themselves, as though they expect respect without the need to claim it.[6]

Perhaps it seems obvious in the above examples how a trait of character like misplaced humility is a vice in direct opposition to the virtue of dignity. But some might suppose that the noble man does not in fact fail to have the virtue of dignity because he does not fail to recognize, even if he does

---

[6] The very activity of claiming rights can also be undignified for character types other than the haughty man. See Michael J. Meyer, 'Dignity, Rights, and Self-Control,' *Ethics* (April 1989) vol. XCIX, especially pp. 525-27.

exaggerate, his importance relative to others. One might claim that the alleged vice of nobility is quite dissimilar to the actual vice of misplaced humility and further suggest that misplaced humility alone should be taken as the paradigm case of the absence of the virtue of dignity. Put otherwise, if misplaced nobility is a vice at all, perhaps it is not a vice opposed to the virtue of dignity.

In reply, however, note first of all how the haughty man's nobility has telling similarities to the humiliations of the submissively humble man. They are both, albeit in different ways, disinclined to press their rights. Moreover, they both lack the attitude that doing so is in any way morally distinguished. If it is too strong to say that the noble man is actually humiliated by a public or private protest on behalf of his rights, he nonetheless does lack the attitudes and the dispositions of the individual with the virtue of dignity who sees that when such protest is called for it is surely admirable. In this sense then both misplaced humility and haughty nobility are undignified traits—the sometimes self-defeating pride of the nobility having some ironic similarity with the self-defeating shame of the man of misplaced humility.

Secondly, note how one of the exemplars of the dignified person displays the link between the noble and the humble person. This is prominently demonstrated by Gandhi's story of his encounter with Balasundaram, a Tamil indentured laborer in South Africa, who having been beaten severely by his master had sought Gandhi's legal assistance:

> Balasundaram entered my office, head-gear in hand. There was a peculiar pathos about the circumstance ... A practice had been forced upon every indentured labourer and every Indian stranger to take off his head-gear when visiting a European, whether the head-gear were a cap, a turban or a scarf wrapped round the head. A salute even with both hands was not sufficient. Balasundaram thought that he should follow the practice even with me ... I felt humiliated and asked him to tie up his scarf. He did so, not without a certain hesitation, but I could perceive the pleasure on his face. It has always been a mystery to me how men can feel themselves honoured by the humiliation of their fellow-beings.[7]

Several features of Gandhi's account merit comment as they bear on the present sketch of the virtue of dignity. First of all, Gandhi sees with utter clarity both the fact of and the reasons for the humiliation of the Tamil man. Furthermore, as it is within his power, Gandhi acts promptly to end the man's humiliation. Gandhi's clarity of observation and action in this case is a prime assertion of that sense of human equality at the heart of the idea of the virtue of dignity. Moreover, not only does Gandhi further assert this equality by, for one, noting that in general is there no honor in the humiliation of fellow human beings; but the Tamil man's need to humble himself before Gandhi actually

---

[7] Mohandas K. Gandhi, *Autobiography: The Story of My Experiments with Truth*, (Dover 1983) [1948] p. 135.

humiliates Gandhi because he is here taken to play the role of a superior. The disposition to share the humiliation of the Tamil laborer in a situation like this lies deep at the core of the virtue of dignity. This is then a disposition whereby a traditional hierarchy is overthrown not only for the sake of some its most obvious victims but also for the sake of those who are commonly considered its benefactors. Gandhi manifests the realization that it is a false nobility, and, if you will, a humiliating form of dignity, that is built on a practice requiring the belittling of fellow human beings.

It is surely worth emphasis that not every trait of character that might best be described as humility is a vice related to the virtue of dignity. It is my claim that as a matter of interpersonal relations misplaced humility (roughly, an over-generalized tendency to try to please ones 'betters') is a paradigm case of a vice opposed to the virtue of dignity. Other forms of humility—humility before God or nature—may be virtues of character that can operate in harmony with the virtue of dignity because here one can be humble without a general habit of deference to one's betters.[8] This discussion of the vices of misplaced humility and haughty nobility—vices born of quintessential considerations of social hierarchy—simply highlights one especially central aspect of the virtue of dignity (in section IV, they will be called upon again to help clarify how dignity is a modern virtue of character). As it is not my goal here to catalogue all of the possible vices related to the virtue of dignity in its most general form I pass by, for example, cases of what is often called 'dying with dignity.'[9] As noted above I am focusing on the virtue of dignity within the context of the more specific conception of human dignity. The primary goal here is to highlight dignity *as a virtue*, not to give that virtue a complete analysis. In pursuit of this end consider yet a different kind of problem.

Some critics might think that they detect a paradox within the very idea of dignity as a virtue. If a virtue is a trait of character, which is in turn a kind of excellence—that is, the kind of trait that should be perfected—then there may be a lack of coherence in the normative recommendations issuing from this virtue. The complaint is that an individual is here presented with the paradoxical task of perfecting the attitude that she is equal to others.[10] Put a different way: it is incoherent to try to perfect the attitude that one is equal to others who in all likelihood have (perfected) this very attitude to a different

---

[8] Of course, even in the socio-political sphere one may well feel humility before someone of great accomplishment; such a disposition may or may not be regarded as a virtue (or a vice) depending on further details of such cases—e.g., how do one's own accomplishments compare? Generally the moral value of deference is highly context dependent. When the rich man shows deference to the poor man, or the powerful to the powerless, it is likely to be seen as morally different from the reverse case.

[9] See, however, Michael J. Meyer, 'Dignity, Death and Modern Virtue,' *American Philosophical Quarterly* (1995) vol. XXXII, no. 1, pp. 45-55, especially 50-52.

[10] To simplify matters I focus on attitudes, rather than both attitudes and dispositions; but perhaps one might say much the same, *mutatis mutandis*, about perfecting dispositions.

degree. What drives this worry is the doubt that attitudes about one's equality with others can be combined with attitudes that one should be perfecting oneself—and thereby outdistancing or being outdistanced by others. This is the doubt, found for one in Nietzsche, that perfectionism and egalitarianism can be joined as commensurable aspects of a disposition or a plan of life.[11]

One solution to this problem would be to reject the general claim that the virtues require perfectionist thinking. Since this reply is only adequate if one wishes to embrace a non-perfectionist account of the virtues—or of this virtue in particular—consider a further, two-point reply to the alleged paradox. First, the virtue of dignity only requires those attitudes grounded in the idea that one is equal in basic moral worth and status with others. Roughly speaking, on such a view of equality individuals irrespective of social hierarchies possess: i) the capacities for practical deliberation, moral or ethical choice, and virtuous action; and ii) whatever moral, and legal, rights are necessary to fairly protect the employment of these capacities. This notion of equality does not entail that individuals are equal with respect to their moral, ethical, or rational efforts or accomplishments. Avoidance of the elitism or snobbishness destructive of the virtue of dignity is fully consistent with concerted attempts to perfect one's attitudes because any inequality of accomplishment, or effort, is simply irrelevant to the applicable account of equality.[12] Second, the suggestion that in perfecting one's virtues one is engaged in equality-upsetting competition with others makes little sense of the nature of virtue-based aspirations. In the senses that virtue-based aspirations are comparative, they tend not to be competitive with others but rather exercises in self-evaluation.[13]

Finally, yet another critic might suggest that dignity is not a true virtue because it is not a single, distinct virtue. This critic might distinguish between: i) 'the virtue of dignity' as a single, distinct idea like the virtue of courage; and ii) 'the virtues of dignity' as a loosely organized collection of admirable traits. Perhaps the 'virtue' of dignity, unlike a classic virtue like courage, is only a collection of loosely related traits like self-respect, self-control and self-discipline. In reply, I think that the discussion so far already offers a suggestive—if not absolutely complete—account of the integrity of the virtue of dignity. The discussion of the next section will supplement this account. Furthermore, one might set out to 'deconstruct' any seemingly integrated

---

[11] See, for example, Nietzsche's *Beyond Good and Evil* trans. W. Kaufmann (Vintage 1966), especially part 9, pp. 201-237.

[12] Hill's notion of 'moral snobbery' (in loc. cit. 'Social Snobbery and Human Dignity') offers an interesting point of comparison. While eschewing 'moral snobbery' is not necessary to avoid acting from what might be called the vice of social snobbishness, as I understand it here, it seems true that the avoidance of 'moral snobbery' is a moral excellence.

[13] While one aspect of virtue-based aspirations may well be comparisons with others, the point of such interpersonal comparisons is surely not to see how one has improved—and not only because a moving point of comparison makes this point difficult to assess. The goal of most virtue-based interpersonal comparisons is, more likely, to discover new methods for self-improvement.

virtue. Perhaps even a traditional virtue like courage is a complex concatenation of various disparate traits including—but perhaps not limited to—emotional bravery, military valor, and political fortitude. In short, the preceding critique provides no more of a case against the existence of dignity as an integrated virtue than against the coherence of any traditional virtue.

At this point, the conception of dignity as a virtue has been, at least in a preliminary way, both explicated and defended. In this section I have attempted to provide enough detail to at least make clear the general outlines of how the virtue of dignity meets the standard account of a virtue of character. It should now be helpful to discuss why I have suggested that dignity is best understood as a modern virtue.

IV. Dignity as a Modern Virtue

The idea of modernity is at best enormously complex.[14] The present focus suggests attending to only one aspect of modernity: the general tendency to reject what I will call the ideology of aristocracy. Otherwise put, modern thought generally tends to reject (natural or hereditary) moral and political hierarchies as normative ideals. This aspect of modern thought is, for example, displayed in Kant's moral philosophy as opposed to, say, Aristotle or Burke; it is also displayed in the democratic provision for universal adult franchise under the rule of 'one citizen, one vote.'[15] I will simply assume that some tendency to reject the ideology of aristocracy is generally emblematic of modernity. Yet in doing so I mean to suggest neither that all who might rightly be seen as modern do reject it, nor that all who are not modern must embrace it.

Given this narrowing of what I will consider modern, a further clarification may be helpful. The choice of Kant—and not, say, Aristotle—as a focal point for analyzing the virtue of dignity is not meant to suggest that (Kantian) morality is generally superior to (Aristotelian) ethics. Indeed I do not wish to offer an unequivocal endorsement for a Kantian account of morality, in spite of my focus on the Kantian tradition's quite admirable attention to human dignity. In short, I do not wish to endorse any hegemony of moral concerns (understood roughly as a tendency within Kantian morality to overemphasize

---

[14] Charles Taylor's impressive account of modernity in *Sources of the Self: The Making of the Modern Identity*, (Harvard University Press 1989), suggests (pp. 15-16) that the range of notions concerned with dignity is one of the three axes of moral thinking. The present treatment of the virtue of dignity, and the related account of the ideology of aristocracy, would track with much of what Taylor says about modern 'inwardness' (pp. 111-207) as well as the 'affirmation of ordinary life' (pp. 211-233).

[15] Kant's political philosophy—in Part II of *The Metaphysics of Morals* trans. J. Ellington (Hackett 1983)—is, of course, not so egalitarian. For Burke, see *Reflections on the Revolution in France* (Harmondsworth 1969) passim. For Aristotle, see the *Politics*, trans. E. Barker (Oxford University Press 1946) especially Books 1, 3, 7.

impartiality or other-regarding normative principles).[16] So, for those who observe the distinction, the virtue of dignity can be described as a virtue of character rather than a 'moral' virtue.

Considering dignity as a *modern* virtue of character will help highlight the main objection to the suggestion that dignity as here outlined should be on any adequate contemporary list of 'the virtues.' The objection is, in general, that 'traditional virtues'—which do not include dignity as presently outlined[17]—are sufficient for a complete account of the virtues. Put another way, such critics would suggest that the virtue of dignity as outlined here has fully adequate non-modern substitutes.

One way to begin to make out the traditionalist's objection to the present account of the virtue of dignity is to consider the dignity of a butler. As an example I have in mind Kazuo Ishiguro's novel (and James Ivory's film adaptation) *The Remains of the Day*.[18] Whatever his other shortcomings, the quintessential butler of the story, Mr. Stevens, does manifest an undeniable dignity. The problem for my account of the virtue of dignity is that Mr. Stevens possesses his dignity not in spite of the ideology of aristocracy but for reasons directly related to it. He has the virtue of dignity in so far as he acts in accord with the complex social hierarchy of his day.

Even though it is Stevens's job, indeed his whole life, to bow and scrape before the stately guests of his Lord Darlington, he displays a certain dignity in so doing. Moreover, behind the scenes Mr. Stevens further displays the virtue of dignity by standing in for the aristocracy. Here as 'the gentleman's gentleman,' the butler manifests the virtue of dignity as accorded to his station. He does so by taking his privileged place at the top of a humble but vigilantly ranked class of underbutlers, footmen, maids, and cooks who are all necessary to make a 'great house' like Darlington Hall run as expected.

Now some critics of my account of the virtue of dignity—following a line of thought which can be found among other places in Burke—would suggest that the dignity of the butler provides a fully adequate model for our general understanding of the virtue of dignity. In response to this critique consider first that it can be acknowledged that Stevens does in one sense possess the virtue of dignity. Because of his social position Stevens has what I have previously called 'social dignity' or the 'dignity of office' (understood in direct contrast with 'human dignity'). And the virtue of dignity manifested by the good butler is most clearly understood in terms of this conception of the dignity of office. As Stevens puts it, the butler has a 'dignity in keeping with his position.'[19] Yet, the butler's version of the virtue of dignity is hardly a satisfactory paradigm case for our best understanding of the virtue of dignity.

---

[16] For one critique of the 'hegemony of moral concerns' see Michael Slote, *From Morality to Virtue* (Oxford University Press 1992) especially Chs. 1-4.

[17] For a popular example, see William J. Bennett, *The Book of Virtues* (Simon and Schuster 1993).

[18] Kazuo Ishiguro, *The Remains of the Day* (Knopf 1990).

[19] *Ibid.*, pp. 35, 169.

The dignity of the butler is a conspicuously inadequate substitute for the virtue as manifested by Martin Luther King or Mahatma Gandhi. For example, while marching at Selma, King better represents common intuitions about the virtue of dignity than does Stevens's unrelenting deference to 'his superiors.' Now to be fair to the critics here, Stevens's deference is not necessarily a constant source of humiliation, although there are moments where the upshot of his humble role is clearly a kind of political humiliation.[20] However, we should also be clear about the burden of this portion of the present argument. The incessant deference of the butler need not be a (full-blown) case of the vice of misplaced humility to be a clearly inadequate model for the virtue of dignity.[21]

Putting this last point another way, the good butler's instinctive habit of deference to 'his betters' simply makes this exemplar an unsuitable model for our basic understanding of the virtue of dignity when compared to that of King or Gandhi. This does not mean that the good butler fails to express dignity altogether, but rather that the conception of social dignity, or the dignity of office, is not well suited to ground our best prevailing understanding of the virtue of dignity. Generalizing somewhat, the pre-modern world of natural and hereditary hierarchy represented by the butler of Darlington Hall—which includes practices of enforced obsequious behavior like the requirement that humble folk address their superiors with averted eyes, bowed head, or cap in hand—will not provide a suitable ground for our understanding of the virtue of dignity.

It is not the point of the present argument to offer a critique of the justice of such a social hierarchy. Nor, on the other hand, do I wish to celebrate every aspect of the modern world. Even less do I wish to suggest that service to others, or even a life of such service, is somehow lacking the virtue of dignity as presently proposed. The point here is simply to show how our understanding of the virtue of dignity—or for that matter, a general practice of service to others—is best served by the exemplars of King or Gandhi. This is so, in part, because their service was grounded in a vision of both human liberty and equality that was not generally available in the pre-modern world, which is represented by the butler and the Lord of Darlington Hall. Even the important ancient or pre-modern predecessors of the idea of human dignity—say the democracy of Pericles or the religion of the early Christians—did not generally inform the ancient or the pre-modern world.[22]

---

[20] Consider, for one, the scene when Stevens is questioned by a 'gentleman' on politics and economics and Stevens' reserve (and his likely ignorance regarding complex questions of fiscal policy) are taken to be evidence against the claim of common men to vote, *ibid.*, pp. 194-201.

[21] While it provides an interesting point of comparison here, I do not wish to be taken to endorse without qualifications in each case Tocqueville's suggestion that in the modern world what were once vices are now in a sense virtues, see *Democracy in America* (Vintage 1990) vol. I, p. 296.

[22] See, for example, Casey, *Pagan Virtue*, Ch. 1.

The good butler represents the institutionalization of deference on demand. In this respect the butler's dignity is only possible because of the deference of the underbutler. In roughly the same way, the dignity of the entire aristocracy is only possible because of the deference of the lower orders. This last point may well suggest a Hegelian understanding of the story of Lord Darlington's world whereby the master/servant interdependency inevitably results in some considerable disadvantage, including a loss of dignity, for them both. (This understanding might also help illuminate Gandhi's exemplary reaction to the humiliated Tamil servant). Thomas Jefferson's remarks about the moral price of owning slaves comes to mind when considering how the institutionalization of deference on demand tends to undermine the master's possession of the virtue of dignity:

> The whole commerce between master and slave is a perpetual exercise of the most boisterous passions, the most unremitting despotism ... Our children see this, and learn to imitate it ... The parent storms, the child looks on, catches the lineaments of wrath, puts on the same airs in the circle of smaller slaves, gives a loose to his worst of passions, and thus nursed, educated and daily exercised in tyranny, cannot but be stamped by it with odious particularities. The man must be a prodigy who can retain his manners and morals undepraved by such circumstances.[23]

The 'odious particularities' that undermine the master's dignity—for instance, his overbearing manner, his meddlesome supervision, his self-centered hostility—are likely to have an explicit, if diverse, manifestation in a variety of particular historical practices of the institutionalization of deference. Moreover, the master's susceptibility to such 'odious particularities' clarifies how the rejection of the ideology of aristocracy is crucial to the personal possession of the dispositions and attitudes that constitute the virtue of dignity.

Consider yet another version of this general critique that some set of 'traditional virtues' obviates the need to embrace the virtue of dignity as a significant virtue of character. Traditionalists might press the point that King or Gandhi display familiar virtues like courage or perseverance; and, moreover, that such ancient virtues are sufficient to explain those cases where I have suggested the characteristically modern virtue of dignity is in play. I have, of course, already acknowledged that Martin Luther King's march at Selma or Mahatma Gandhi's march on behalf of the Salt Satyagraha do exemplify traditional virtues like courage or perseverance. My point here is that there is something about their virtuous deeds—and their moral or ethical characters—that is not fully understood in the absence of the present account of the virtue of dignity.

The life work of King and Gandhi is emblematic of the virtue of dignity in large part because it was work on behalf of the liberty and equality of human beings as against the ideology of aristocracy. (Recall that at Selma,

---

[23] Thomas Jefferson, *Writings* (The Library of America 1984) p. 288.

King was marching for voting rights and the end of legally imposed racial segregation; and that the Salt Satyagraha was part of the 1930-31 civil disobedience movement which had the goal, beyond the removal of the Salt Acts, of complete independence of India from unrepresentative, colonial control). This recognition of the equal moral and political standing of all human beings independent of traditional or imposed hierarchies is also essential to the present account in two further ways: 1) it differentiates the virtue of dignity from the related, but more purely self-regarding, modern virtues like self-respect, self-reliance, and self-determination, and 2) as an ineliminable component of the virtuous deeds of King and Gandhi here highlighted, it differentiates the virtue of dignity from ancient virtues like Aristotle's *megaloprepeia* and *megalopsychia*.[24]

As part of an effort to explain away the need for the modern virtue of dignity in cases like those of King and Gandhi, traditionalists may gather together the collective explanatory power of all of the virtues in their preferred catalogue of the virtues of character. But for King and Gandhi, something essential is missing from the traditionalist account. The shortcomings of the traditionalist account can be made even clearer if one considers the suggestion that a virtue like pride is an adequate replacement for the virtue of dignity. Even if pride is in some ways related to the virtue of dignity—and hence might be seen by some traditionalists to be a 'rival' virtue—in the end the best account of moral exemplars like King and Gandhi resists eliminating the virtue of dignity.[25]

The reason to not reduce the virtue of dignity to the virtue of pride is that for King or Gandhi the most plausible full description of their pride itself suggests that it is necessarily informed by the virtue of dignity. Since King and Gandhi lived lives on behalf of the view that some substantial liberty and equality should be enjoyed by persons irrespective of positions in traditional or imposed socio-political hierarchies, they possess kindred virtues like pride, or self-respect, in direct relation to attitudes about their human dignity. For one, King and Gandhi are particularly proud of their moral and political equality, especially their equality in basic liberty, with others.

Moreover, the ways the pride of an exemplar like King or Gandhi becomes manifest in particular circumstances are contrary to someone like Mr. Stevens. Stevens' pride in being a good, and a dignified, butler is inexorably

---

[24] Aristotle, *Nichomachean Ethics*, trans. M. Ostwald (Bobbs-Merril 1966) Book 4 Chs. 2 & 3, pp. 89-99.

[25] The present issue (which virtues are necessary or jointly sufficient to explain a certain virtuous action or a particular trait of character) is quite a bit more complex than is necessary to delve into for the purposes of this argument. My goal here is not to offer a full analysis of the conditions for the possession of a virtue but to give a credible general account of the virtue of dignity. I simply claim that if virtuous acts are identified in part by motives [see Robert Audi, 'Acting From Virtue,' *Mind* (July 1995) vol. CIV, no. 415] as well as attitudes (see Philippa Foot, 'Virtues and Vices,' *op. cit.*, p. 5*ff*), then the examples of King and Gandhi will not easily be explained away by a typical set of traditional virtues.

marked by his disposition to defer to his 'betters'—for example, in the presence of his 'superiors' any real pride will likely be covert lest it be mistaken for insolence. Likewise, the butler's pride may well be hidden from his 'inferiors' lest it be taken for arrogance. On the other hand, in fully public ways the pride of the modern man possessed of the virtue of dignity will reveal how he takes himself to have equal moral and political status with all. The pride of standard-bearers of modern virtue like King and Gandhi will be suffused with the egalitarian dispositions at the root of the modern virtue of dignity. Given this, in the final analysis not even pride can replace dignity in an adequate account of exemplars of modern virtue.

E. Conclusion

This essay has had two goals. First of all, I have tried to elucidate the idea of dignity as a virtue as it develops under the influence of the notion of human dignity. If the analysis and the arguments of sections II and III have by in large been successful, then this goal has been advanced even if it is not yet fully complete. The analysis and the arguments of section IV—that the most adequate model for our general understanding of the virtue of dignity is characteristically modern—are a further attempt to carry forth this primary goal. Secondly, I have tried to show, especially in section IV, how the virtue of dignity is a generally modern virtue. I hope the point has been advanced even if more could also be said on this score.

It does seem that the now quite sustained, contemporary interest in 'the virtues' will only be fully viable when combined with some detailed consideration of particular virtues that are ascendant in the modern world. Moreover, we need such an investigation into characteristically modern virtues—to set alongside the now well-advanced study of ancient and Judeo-Christian virtues—in order to understand fully the moral fabric of our time and our lives. The present account of the virtue of dignity is therefore, finally, a preliminary attempt to help articulate a catalog of modern virtues.[26]

---

[26] I would like to thank Robert Audi, Stephen Darwall, Philip Kain, Tom Powers, William J. Prior, Mark Ravizza, and Lori Zink for helpful comments on the general issues and the earlier drafts of this paper, and the conference participants at the Hebrew University Conference on Human Dignity for stimulating discussion of a variety of related issues.

HUMILIATION, DIGNITY AND SELF-RESPECT[*]
Daniel Statman

That an intimate connection exists between the notion of human dignity and the notion of humiliation seems to be a commonplace. Humiliation is seen as first and foremost an injury to the dignity of its victims, an injury usually described in figurative language: in humiliation one 'is stripped of one's dignity,'[1] one is 'robbed of' dignity,[2] or simply 'loses' it.[3] This close connection between dignity and humiliation has brought some writers to argue that we face a strictly conceptual connection here. In Avishai Margalit's words, 'If there is no concept of human dignity, then there is no concept of humiliation either.'[4]

I believe, however, that rather than making our notion of humiliation clearer, this assumed connection creates difficulties. Tying the concept of humiliation to that of human dignity makes the former too 'philosophical,' so to say, and too detached from psychological research and theory. The purpose of this paper is to modify this connection and to offer a more down to earth account of humiliation that does not depend on metaphysical and axiological question concerning the unique dignity enjoyed by all human beings *qua* human beings.

In Section I, I explore the difficulties in the idea that humiliation should be understood in terms of (violation of) human dignity. I then turn, in Section II, to examine whether these difficulties can be overcome by replacing the notion of dignity by that of self-respect, i.e., by defining humiliation as injury

---

[*] This article was originally published in *Philosophical Psychology*, 13:4 (2000). It is reprinted with the permission of Taylor & Francis Ltd.—www.tandf.co.uk.

[1] Paul Gilbert, 'The Evolution of Social Attractiveness and Its Role in Shame, Humiliation, Guilt and Therapy,' *British Journal of Medical Psychology* 70: 113-147 (1997) p.133.

[2] Robin S. Dillon, 'Self-Respect: Moral, Emotional, Political,' *Ethics* 107:226-249 (1997) p.1.

[3] Avishai Margalit and Gabriel Motzkin, 'The Uniqueness of the Holocaust,' *Philosophy and Public Affairs* 25: 65-83 (1996) p.115.

[4] *Ibid.*, p. 149.

to self-respect. Following Massey, I distinguish between an objective-normative and a subjective-psychological notion of self-respect and show how taking the former as a basis for understanding humiliation leads us back into trouble. In Section III, I explain in what sense a distinction between justified and unjustified feelings of humiliation can be retained even in a subjective-psychological account of humiliation. In Section IV, I elaborate on the connection between humiliation and exclusion and on the evolutionaary basis for this connection. Section V concludes the argument by clarifying the conceptual and normative implications.

I. Humiliation and Dignity

In this section, I point to several reasons against making the concept of humiliation dependent on that of human dignity. I refer, first, to the effect of Darwinism, which has undermined notions of the sanctity of human life, and has blurred the metaphysical and moral boundaries between humans and animals. In his 1990 book, *Created from Animals*, James Rachels explains the notion of of human dignity as follows:

> The idea of human dignity is the moral doctrine what says that humans and other animals are in different moral categories; that the lives and interests of human beings are of supreme importance, while the lives of other animals are relatively unimportant. That doctrine rests, traditionally, on two related ideas: that man is made in God's image, and that man is a uniquely rational being.[5]

According to Rachels, Darwinism forces us to give up both of these ideas, hence:

> The traditional supports for the idea of human dignity are gone. They have not survived the colossal shift of perspective brought down by Darwin's theory.[6]

Therefore, if Margalit is right in assuming that without a concept of human dignity, there is no concept of humiliation, and if Rachels is right in arguing that the idea of human dignity must be abandoned, then we are left with no concept of humiliation, a result which is unacceptable. One could, of course, suggest a different understanding of dignity than the one suggested by Rachels. However, as Rachels's definition reflects a common understanding, I suspect that other definitions would be somewhat stipulative and would not advance our understanding of humiliation.

Second, even granting the idea that humans are unique in some way, what exactly is meant by the term 'human dignity' is far from clear. According to Rachels, the basis for this notion has to do either with the idea of man being

---
[5] *Ibid.*, p. 171.
[6] *Ibid.*, p. 171.

created in the image of God or with the idea of man being a uniquely rational being. But both these ideas are ambiguous and open to different interpretations. Are all human beings made in the image of god, including, for example, very defective fetuses? By virtue of what properties exactly are they said to be his image? Can human beings be ever said to lost these properties? Regarding the unique rationality enjoyed by human beings, it is again unclear what exactly is referred to. Is it some basic rationality shared by all members of the human species, including babies and the retarded? Is it a mere capacity for rationality or is it rationality actualized? Indeed the philosophical and the legal literature on dignity is full of disagreements about its nature, hence it seems rather unpromising to turn to this notion in order to clarify the notion of humiliation.

Third, the imprecision and unclarity of the notion is especially troubling when one asks whether dignity is a descriptive or a normative notion. To understand it in a descriptive way is to refer to some given feature that all humans possess and by virtue of which they enjoy privileged status in the world.[7] This feature belongs to all members of the human species, irrespective of their rational or moral capacities, and irrespective of the exercise of these capacities.[8] To understand the expression 'human dignity' in a normative way is to refer to obligations incumbent on oneself or on others with regard to oneself. Such a normative use is assumed, for example, by Feinberg, when he argues that:

> Respect for persons may simply be respect for their rights, so that there cannot be the one without the other; and what is called "human dignity" may simply be the recognizable capacity to assert claims. To respect a person then, or to think of him as possessed of human dignity simply is to think of him as a potential maker of claims.[9]

Without going into the details of these two different approaches, I want to raise a problem for both with respect to the relation between dignity and humiliation. As I said earlier, humiliation is thought of as a behavior that strips its victims of their dignity. If we hold a descriptive account of dignity, it is difficult to see how such a loss can occur, especially when we bear in mind

---

[7] Some philosophers, such as Kant, contend that dignity is not restricted to the human race but extends to all rational beings (whatever their nature might be). Yet hardly anybody claims that dignity is enjoined by sub-human beings such as animals. For an exception, see Sapontzis (1981, 1982), and the criticism by Nelson (1982).

[8] For such understanding, see, for example, Charles R. Tremper, 'Respect for Human Dignity of Minors: What the Constitution Requires,' *Syracuse Law Review* 39 (1988) p. 1321. In Tremper's view, the idea that one has human dignity merely by virtue of belonging to the species is required, if we want to use this language with respect to minors.

[9] Joel Feinberg, 'The Nature and Value of Human Rights,' *Journal of Value Inquiry* 4:243-261 (1970). pp. 252-3.

that the feature that entitles humans to dignity belongs to all members of the species, irrespective of their individual capacities or behavior. If human beings with limited rational capacities nevertheless possess dignity, then one cannot rob human beings of their dignity by injuring their rational capacities. Similarly, if even the wicked possess human dignity, one cannot rob a human being of his dignity by injuring his moral character or behavior. In short, if mere belonging to the human race in sufficient for having dignity (whatever this term denotes), then, necessarily, no human beings can exist who have lost, or have been stripped of, their human dignity. So, paradoxically, if humiliation is injury to dignity, then precisely because dignity is a fixed feature of all human beings, humiliation is impossible.

One might respond by saying that dignity does not belong to all members of the human species, but only to most of them. But apart from its departure from our common understanding of dignity, according to which the notion of dignity os needed to protect precisely those who are humanly underprivileged, this response invites the following objection. We humiliate either those who have dignity or those who do not. If the latter are the intended objects of humiliation, then their dignity cannot be violated, simply because they don't have dignity. Hence – if one assumes a connection between humiliation and dignity – they cannot be humiliated either. If the former are the intended objects of humiliation, i.e. those human beings who are endowed with dignity, then the only way to strip them of their dignity would be be to strip them of the relevant feature(s) by virtue of which they have dignity, e.g. their rationality. But physically incapacitating some person's rationality would not ordinarily be thought of as a case of humiliation. Such incapacitation would turn its object into an entity with no dignity and, thus, into an entity that (conceptually) cannot be humiliated.

These considerations could be put forward in the form of the following paradox. Assuming that it is by virtue of an entity's having a particular quality, q, that it is wrong to humiliate it, then one of two paradoxical conclusions results: either humiliation is impossible, since everyone has q by virtue of being human, or, in a case where q is a quality that not everyone enjoys and that can be lost, humiliating people makes it less wrong to humiliate them, as it strips them of the very condition for being humiliated.

If, instead, we hold a normative account of dignity, emphasizing rights, claims and obligations, it is again hard to see how dignity might be lost. If, as Feinberg puts it, to have human dignity *is* to have rights or to be a potential maker of claims, then nothing we might do to a human being can rob her of these rights or this potential. One can treat another human being *as if* she had no rights, or *as if* she had no dignity. But one cannot make it the case that she loses her rights or her dignity. Thus, in either account of dignity it is hard to see what it would mean to lose, or cause the loss of, dignity. Therefore, it would be unhelpful to bind the concept of humiliation to such a loss.

II. Humiliation and Self-Respect

The above difficulties concerning the connection between the notions of humiliation and dignity seem to be avoided if we focus instead on the notion of self-respect, that is, if we define humiliation as an injury to self-respect. This is the definition offered by Avishai Margalit in his book *The Decent Society* (1996).[10] Though I disagree with it, the book contains one of the most thorough and insightful analyzes of humiliation. Margalit defines humiliation as:

> [A]ny sort of behavior or condition that constitutes a sound reason for a person to consider his or her self-respect injured.[11]

However, the notion of self-respect is ambiguous too. The ambiguity concerns a fundamental question about self-respect explicated by Stephen Massey, namely: is it a psychological or a moral concept? According to the psychological, or the subjective concept of self-respect, 'a person who respects himself believes that he acts in accord with his conception of worthy behavior and has confidence that he will continue to do so.'[12] The crucial point about the subjective concept of self-respect is that 'the self-respecting person's beliefs about and attitudes toward himself need not have any particular content, nor must his actions meet any independent standards of worthiness or appropriateness.'[13] Self-respect is a subjective attitude each individual has toward him or herself, based on standards for worthiness and excellence endorsed by the individual. On this account, self-respect can characterize slaves and masters, chauvinist men and servile women, moral saints and moral monsters—provided the slaves, servile women and moral monsters believe that their behavior accords with what *they* regard as the true conception of worthy behavior.[14]

By contrast, the moral or objective concept of self-respect contends that a self-respecting person's behavior and attitudes must satisfy independent standards of worthiness. Self-respect is not merely valuing oneself, but valuing oneself *properly*, the criteria for propriety being a matter of dispute between different objective accounts. A well-known account of this sort emphasizes the importance of moral equality, arguing we can have self-respect only if we treat

---

[10] See also Honneth 1995, who regards humiliation as a form of disrespect which leads to injury to self-respect.

[11] Margalit, p. 9.

[12] Stephen Massey, 'Is self-respect a moral or psychological concept?' *Ethics* 93 (1983) pp. 246-61.

[13] *Ibid.*, p. 249.

[14] The concept of self-respect is hardly to be found in the psychological literature which subsumes the phenomenon of psychological self-respect under the heading of self-esteem. Cf. Robin S. Dillon, 'Self-Respect: Moral, Emotional, Political' *Ethics* 107 (1987) p. 235, note 20: 'Many of the psychological studies define 'self-esteem' in ways that overlap with self-respect.'

ourselves as morally equal to all other human beings. On this account, Uncle Tom does not have proper respect for himself, as he fails to take seriously his moral rights.[15]

What concept of self-respect, then, is assumed when we define humiliation in its terms? Does humiliation injure one's subjective-psychological self-respect, or one's moral-objective self-respect?[16] Does humiliation undermine the way its victims actually value themselves, or the way they ought to value themselves? To connect humiliation to subjective self-respect would mean that humiliation is any behavior that makes a person think she is unworthy, or less worthy, of respect, according to her own standards. By contrast, to connect humiliation to objective self-respect would mean that humiliation is any behavior that makes a person unworthy, or less worthy of respect, according to independent standards of worthiness, standards not necessarily acknowledged by the object of humiliation. Thomas Hill's famous example of the servile woman can illustrate this distinction. The servile woman sees it as her duty to serve her husband, take care of his needs and advance his career, and the fulfillment of these tasks brings her great pleasure and satisfaction. On the psychological-subjective concept of self-respect, her husband's behavior and demands do not injure her self-respect, hence they are not humiliating. On the moral-objective concept, however, the husband's behavior is humiliating, as it reflects and fosters improper self-respect by the servile woman.[17]

The moral concept of self-respect is of course tightly connected to the notion of human dignity. It is by virtue of this dignity that human beings are assumed to deserve special respect both in their own eyes and in the eyes of others. Hence it comes as no surprise that Margalit who thinks, 'If there is no concept of human dignity, then there is no concept of humiliation either,'[18] also utilizes an objective-moral notion of self-respect. In his analysis, self-respect has to do with attitudes such as 'insistence on one's basic rights, a mad refusal to compromise one's personal honesty ... or readiness to endanger oneself in a struggle against people who insult or humiliate one, even if they

---

[15] A distinction similar to that between psychological and normative self-respect is made by Richard Keshen, *Reasonable Self-Esteem* (McGill-Queen's University Press, Montreal 1996) Ch. 6, between, respectively, self-esteem and self-respect.

[16] Logically speaking, these notions are not mutually exclusive and one might adopt both to the effect that for a person to have self-respect he or she needs both subjective self-respect and objective self-respect. I find it hard, however, to see the basis for such a view, particularly as the grounds for subjective self-respect might be different and even contradictory to those for objective self-respect.

[17] Arguments against sexual behavior which is regarded improper are often based on its damage to the practitioners' self-respect. See, for example, Kupfer' argument in this vein against prostitutes, Joseph Kupfer, 'Prostitutes, Musicians, and Self-Respect' *Journal of Social Philosophy* 26 (1995) pp. 75-88.

[18] Margalit, p. 149.

are stronger than oneself.'[19] If one is indifferent to one's rights or to personal honesty, then one lacks self-respect and one's dignity is injured, even if on a subjective-psychological level, one has a positive attitude toward the self.[20]

We are now in a better position to understand Margalit's definition quoted earlier, according to which humiliation 'is any sort of behavior or condition that constitutes a sound reason for a person to consider his or her self-respect injured.' To determine whether A's behavior toward B is humiliating we need to know nothing about B's actual feelings as a result of A's behavior or about her subjective standards of self-valuation. All we need to know is whether the behavior under question constitutes a 'sound reason' for B to feel humiliated, or a sound reason for B to feel that her self-respect has been injured.

This normative understanding of self-respect and of humiliation leads Margalit to think that the notion of humiliation depends on the idea that human beings are worthy of respect. The argument to this conclusion is simple: Sound reasons for thinking that one's self-respect is *injured* exist only if sound reasons exist to think that such respect is warranted in the first place. If there is nothing to respect in human beings *qua* human beings, then there is no room for *self*-respect either, and thus no room (i.e., no conceptual room) for injuring it. Hence, to justify the notion of humiliation we must take aboard the most powerful Kantian artillery—concepts like dignity, unconditional value, and (transcendental, or 'radical')[21] freedom. This is indeed the project which engages Margalit in the second part of his book (entitled 'Grounds for Self-Respect') the purpose of which is to find 'what aspect of human beings, if any, justifies respecting all human beings just because they are human.'[22]

Finding this aspect, however, is not sufficient—on Margalit's view—to establish the rationality of humiliation, which faces a further challenge, one drawn from the Stoic view on autarky and well-being. That other people can hit me, put me in jail and ridicule me publicly is beyond question. But why should such behaviors be taken as constituting a reason for me to respect myself less? How could it ever be rational to consider my *self*-respect injured because of the disrespect *other* people express toward me? These questions, which constitute what I shall call 'The Autarky Problem,' are logically distinct from the question we just posed about the grounds for respect (hereafter: 'The

---

[19] *Ibid.*, p. 46.

[20] It is not entirely clear to me whether Honneth is assuming a psychological-subjective or a moral-objective notion of self-respect. On the one hand he quotes Feinberg's argument mentioned above (Section I), to the effect that having self-respect is thinking of oneself as a holder of rights (Honneth, p. 120) and all his discussion is very much Kantian in its spirit. On the other hand, he repeatedly emphasizes the psychological effects of self-respect or disrespect (see especially Ch. 6), which seems to deny the possibility mentioned above of having psychological self-respect without moral self-respect.

[21] Margalit, p. 70.

[22] *Ibid.*, p. 57.

Grounds Problem'). If we deserve respect by virtue of our humanity, then, indeed, nothing our tormentors do to us can provide us with a sound reason to think we deserve less respect, hence nothing they do to us can provide us with a sound reason to feel humiliated. But the same holds true if the standards by which we value ourselves are subjective. If a person has a firm sense of her value, a secure conviction that her conception of her good, her plan of life, is worth carrying out—to utilize Rawls's definition of self-respect[23] —then there seems to be no sound reason to think otherwise just because she is beaten or sexually abused by some villain. This assumed irrationality of humiliation is strengthened by the way the tormentor is perceived by his victims as evil and wicked. Precisely because victims of humiliation distance themselves from the values and standards of the tormentor, it is unclear why they should assign any weight in their own eyes to the humiliating behavior and experience any loss in their self-respect.

The distinction between these two problems can easily be confused and it is worthwhile to recapitulate. The Grounds Problem derives from the assumption that humiliation is rational only if a common human trait exists that makes all human beings worthy of respect. If no such trait exists, then, supposedly, it is false that human beings deserve respect solely on the basis of their being human, hence self-respect is ungrounded, hence there can be no sound reason to consider it injured. The Autarky Problem derives from the assumption that self-respect ought to be independent of the respect of others. Accepting this assumption implies that the disrespectful behavior of others can never constitute a sound reason to consider one's *self*-respect injured, hence, again, a sound reason can never exist for feeling humiliated.

The impression one gets from Margalit is that solving these problems is necessary to establish the possibility of humiliation. But this seems wrong to me. Suppose that human beings do not possess the supreme value often ascribed to them. Maybe the humanistic idea is just a futile attempt to take a religious idea, i.e., that man was created in the image of God, and translate it into secular terms. Or, suppose that we fail to offer a convincing reason for self-respect being injured by the behavior and the attitude of others. What then? Would these suppositions imply that, conceptually speaking, one cannot be humiliated? It is hard to see what such a claim would even amount to. Maybe it would mean that though people often *feel* humiliated, they don't have a sound *reason* for feeling this way, hence humiliation makes sense only as a psychological concept, not as a normative one. But such a result is hard to accept. In fact Margalit himself seems to reject it when, concluding his discussion on the paradoxes of humiliation, he says:

> The attempt to find a general justification for this fact is ludicrous. That's the way it is, that's life .... To ask why the Jews in the Viennese square considered themselves degraded when

---

[23] J. Rawls, *A Theory of Justice* (Harvard University Press, Cambridge, MA 1971) p. 440.

their Nazi tormentors forced then to scrub the pavement is absurd. If that is not humiliation, then what is?[24]

I take it that when Margalit refers to the Nazi behavior as self-evidently humiliating, he is referring not only to the psychological sense of humiliation (who would ever deny that the Jews *felt* humiliated?), but to the normative sense too. He wants to say that the Jews in this dreadful situation had a sound *reason* to feel humiliated, though reasons like this call for no further philosophical justification. And this self-evident fact is immune to both skeptical challenges mentioned above: it does not require an answer to the Stoic paradox, neither does it need justification in terms of a theory of human worth.

Yet this is only a beginning towards an answer and much more needs to be said. Though no general justification is needed to establish the possibility of humiliation, sometimes asking for a justification for feelings of humiliation does make sense. When, then, is humiliation immune to charges of irrationality, and when is humiliation susceptible to rational evaluation? What sort of reasons might prove feelings in general, and humiliation in particular, to be unjustified, and what sort of reasons might prove them to be justified, to be *reason*able? To answer these questions we need to make some brief claims about emotions and rationality in general, which will be the task of the next section.

III. The Rationality of Emotions: A Multi-Layer Model

If a wild dog is released and the dog runs in my direction, the effect on me will be a strong feeling of fear. We would say that releasing the dog is the *cause* of my fear, that the releasing of the dog frightened me. We would also say that in these circumstances I have a good *reason* to feel afraid, that my fear is justified, that it is rational. By contrast, some people get frightened by the sight of mice. For them, the sight of a mouse is the cause of their fear, though in their case they have no sound reason to feel afraid; their feeling is irrational, or inappropriate. What makes the first fear rational and the second irrational? It is the soundness of the beliefs that underlie them. In both cases the emotion under discussion includes the belief that the object of the feeling poses a real treat to the subject. This belief is correct in the case of the dog, while it is false in the case of the mouse. The cognitive aspect of emotions is one obvious source (not the only one) for evaluating the rationality of a given emotion.

Note, however, that these considerations do not apply to the rationality of fear in general, but to the rationality of particular instances of it. Is the very feeling of fear rational? It is not easy to see how to understand this question. Here is one suggestion. Fear of wild beasts, like fear in the battlefield, is first and foremost fear of being killed, fear of one's death. But, as Epicures and other philosophers have argued, fear of one's death is irrational, as death is not

---

[24] Margalit, p. 127.

a state of the subject. So one might think that in order to justify the feeling of fear, i.e., in order to demonstrate that fear might be based on sound reasons, we must first establish the evil of death, otherwise such fear could never be rational and would be a mere psychological fact. Furthermore, one might argue that we must climb to a higher order of justification and establish the rationality of emotions in general, not only that of particular emotions such as fear or humiliation. The Stoics who raised the most troubling questions about the rationality of humiliation, raised similar questions about the rationality of emotions in general. As Martha Nussbaum[25] explains at length, the Stoics advocated the extirpation of emotions altogether because they believed that emotions attach the person possessing them to externals, which is a denial of the self-sufficiency of virtue. The idea of self-sufficiency which poses a challenge to the rationality of humiliation poses a much wider challenge to the rationality of emotions in general.

Thus, when we talk about reasons for emotions, we must bear in mind that this is a complicated and multi-layered issue. One's fear might be irrational because one's beliefs about a particular danger are false; one's fear might be irrational because, ultimately, there is never a sound reason to be afraid, and one's fear might be irrational because all emotions are irrational and ought to be extirpated. These various levels of rationality or irrationality are logically independent. Even if all emotions are irrational, or even if death is not an evil and hence fear of it is unjustified, a valid distinction between fear of a wild dog and fear of a mouse remains. Furthermore, the fact that human beings, just like other animals, get frightened by the sight of wild beasts running in their direction has clear advantages for survival. These advantages point to another sense of rationality here, rationality in the sense of serving vital interests of the human race, or of other species in the animal world.

How, then, would we define *frightening* behavior? Using a definition analogous to the one suggested by Margalit for humiliation, we would say that frightening behavior is any sort of behavior that constitutes a sound reason for a person to consider his life, property or vital interests to be in danger. The crucial point to notice is that the sound reason required here refers to the *first* level of justification, not to the higher levels of justification concerning fear in general, or emotions on an even more general level.

Let us return now to humiliation. Like with fear and other emotions, the rationality (justification, appropriateness) of humiliation is a multi-layered issue. On the first level, just as we respond by fear to events that threaten our vital interests, we respond by humiliation to behaviors that injure or threaten to injure our self-respect. When the behavior of others conveys a message of subordination, rejection or exclusion (see below), we have a perfectly good reason to feel humiliation. We not only *feel* humiliation as a matter of psychological fact, but have a sound *reason* to feel so and our emotional

---

[25] Martha Nussbaum, *The Therapy of Desire*. (Princeton University Press, Princeton, NJ 1994).

response is rational. Although on higher levels one might challenge the rationality of humiliation, using, e.g., the Grounds and Autarky problems mentioned earlier, these challenges, powerful as they might be, are not strong enough to blur all distinctions regarding first level rationality of humiliation. We do not need to rebut Epicures' skepticism about the evil of death in order to judge some cases of fear (e.g., of a wild dog) more rational than others (fear of a mouse), and similarly we do not need to solve the Grounds and Autarky problems in order to make helpful distinctions between more and less rational cases of humiliation. Note that I am not arguing that these skeptic challenges cannot be rebutted,[26] only that doing so is not necessary for establishing the (first-level) distinction between rational and irrational instances of a given emotion.

What might be a case of irrational humiliation? To take a trivial example, if one feels humiliated because one misinterprets a comic comment by one's superiors, then one's humiliation is obviously groundless. In a less trivial manner, there is a direct relation between the justification for humiliation and the humiliating intention of the humiliator. The pure cases of humiliation are those in which the humiliator explicitly seeks by his actions to reject the victim, to humble and degrade him, to exclude him from a specific group or from the family of man altogether. The weaker these evil intentions are, the weaker the justification is for feeling humiliated.[27] When no such intention exists, humiliation is often out of place.

The analogy between humiliation and fear helps to bring to light one further point about the former. With regard to fear, a behavior that constitutes a sound *reason* to feel fear need not necessarily result in that person actually *feeling* fear. A behavior that would make most people extremely frightened might leave others quite indifferent (e.g., when one is a dog-trainer and feels completely safe in the face of a released bull-mastiff). To be more accurate, then, we should say that for A to frighten B, A must engage in behavior that constitutes a sound reason for B to consider her life in danger, and B must actually sense fear (as a result of A's behavior). When we refer to sorts of behavior as frightening without presupposing the 'success' of such behaviors, we really refer to behaviors that *tend* to cause fear, i.e. behaviors that result in fear for most people in normal circumstances. So when I say to Jim, 'Let's frighten Tom,' I really mean to say 'Let's *try* to frighten Tom,' as we have no way of enforcing this feeling. Though we can provide Tom with a strong

---

[26] With respect to the Epicurean view about death, see Nagel (1979). As for the Stoic challenge, see Nussbaum (1994) and Harris (1997).

[27] Here I again find myself in disagreement with Margalit who contends that the humiliators need not have any humiliating intent (1996, p. 10). This contention seems to me inconsistent with Margalit's claim that only humans can produce humiliation (*ibid.*, 9). It seems to me that the only basis for this last claim is the human capacity to form humiliating intentions, otherwise I see no justification to assume that only humans can humiliate.

reason to feel fear, he can nevertheless refuse to succumb. Ultimately for the success of frightening behavior, one needs the cooperation of its object.

The same holds true for humiliation. To humiliate a person is not only to provide her with a reason to feel humiliated but actually to produce this painful feeling.[28] In this respect, the structure of humiliation is different from that of betrayal. As a well-known anti-hedonistic argument shows,[29] the evil of betrayal is independent of its painful discovery by the betrayed person. You can betray a person behind her back, thereby wronging her. By contrast, you cannot humiliate a person without her knowing it and, furthermore, without her accepting it, i.e., experiencing a loss in her self-respect and acknowledging you as its source.[30]

One can see how this understanding of humiliation presupposes a subjective-psychological notion of self-respect rather than an objective-moral one (see Section II above). If humiliation must end up in the victim actually *feeling* humiliation, then the reasons to consider one's self-respect injured that produce this feeling must be of a sort with which the victim identifies, otherwise she would be untouched. The servile woman whose (subjective) self-respect depends on her success in serving her husband and on watching his achievements wouldn't feel humiliated by behaviors of her husband that would definitely be regarded as providing sound reasons to consider her self-respect injured on an objective-moral notion of self-respect.

In closing this Section, I wish to clarify the significance of the claims made here to morality. No doubt a valid distinction obtains between the very feeling of an emotion and the appropriateness or rationality of this feeling. But at least from a moral point of view, placing too high constraints on rationality here would lead to unreasonable results. The moral rules governing the relations between humans must refer to human beings as they actually are, not to human beings as they ideally ought to be, according to some philosophical theory of rationality. And as human beings are emotional creatures, as they tend to suffer painful feelings due to other people's actions, our moral and political rules should be drawn accordingly. Hence, in the moral-political context, questions regarding the rationality of emotions are relevant only on the first level of justification mentioned above, i.e., that concerning the rationality of particular instances of a given emotion. If a particular instance of

---

[28] The same holds true for shaming, i.e., you cannot shame a person without him feeling shame, or feeling ashamed. This explains one of the problems with shame sanctions (see *supra* note 40), as noted by Stephen Garvey (1998, p. 749): If a criminal is "shameless," then subjecting him to a shaming penalty will have little retributive bite.

[29] See, for instance, Nagel 1979, p. 5.

[30] That humiliation requires the cooperation of the victim creates a Hegelian master-slave dialectic, as argued by Margalit & Motzkin (1996) in their discussion of the unique role of humiliation in the Holocaust. The humiliator seeks to dehumanize the victims, but his dependence on the victims' acceptance of the humiliation forces him to re-acknowledge their humanity.

fear or of humiliation is irrational, or unreasonable, it would not suffice to establish a normative demand to others (or will establish only a weak one). If it is rational, or reasonable, then it would establish such a demand, even if on some higher level of justification this type of emotion, or the emotions in general, can be shown to be irrational. In the next section, I try to connect this rationality to our strong need for inclusion in a social group.

IV. Humiliation and Fear of Exclusion

I mentioned earlier that one way to understand the notion of rationality with regard to the emotions is to refer to their advantages in serving vital interests, in other words to their evolutionary benefits. Fear is definitely rational in this sense. Is humiliation too? I believe the answer is in the affirmative, and exploring it will enable us to advance our general understanding of humiliation. The point is that the chances of survival are much higher when one is part of a group, hence one has a strong interest in becoming part of a group and a sound reason to fear being excluded. But to be accepted as a member of a group one needs to conform to the standards of worthiness set by the group, and the best strategy to achieve that goal is to internalize those standards as one's own. At times the standards of worthiness are relative to a particular group, while at other times they apply to membership in any human community. If an individual is made totally powerless, if he is forced to depend on others for the most mundane aspects of life, if he is left with no private area, then he might feel that he has lost the most basic social skills and is therefore in danger of being excluded from the human family altogether.[31]

The tight connection between subjective-psychological self-respect, or self-esteem (to use the common psychological term),[32] and feelings of social inclusion is established by Leary and Downs.[33] In their view, a motive as pervasive and potent as self-esteem must serve a very important function, yet this function has been rather neglected in the psychological literature. According to Leary and Downs, the function that self-esteem serves is the need to belong. Human beings are unlikely to survive in isolation, hence they have a powerful interest to be included in a group. But as such inclusion is never guaranteed unconditionally, and as it is, at any rate, a matter of degree, human beings need a ready way to (1) monitor the social environment for cues indicating rejection or exclusion, and (2) be alerted to them via affective reactions when such cues are detected.[34] Empirical studies indeed reveal that the events that enhance self-esteem typically also enhance feelings of social inclusion and vice versa, while events that diminish self-esteem also lead to

---

[31] On the importance of powerlessness in humiliation, see especially Silver et al. (1986).
[32] See note 31 above.
[33] M. R. Leary and D. L. Downs, 'Functions of the Self-Esteem Motive,' In M.H. Kernis, ed., *Efficacy, Agency, and Self-Esteem*, (Plenum Press, New York 1995).
[34] *Ibid.*, pp. 128-9.

perceived social exclusion. To illustrate this point, let me mention one of these studies, conducted by Tambor & Leary.[35] In this laboratory experiment, subjects were assigned to work as part of a group (i.e., to be included) or to do work alone (i.e., to be excluded) and were told that this assignment was based either on the preferences of the other participants or on a random procedure. Subjects then rated themselves on a self-esteem scale: The results indicated that inclusion or exclusion greatly affected subjects' feeling about themselves, but only when the inclusion or exclusion was due to perceived acceptance or rejection by the group. Leary & Downs contend that the need to belong is understood from an evolutionary perspective, as no other motive is so essential for survival and reproduction.

The need to belong is so strong that its protective monitor, that is, self-esteem, alerts one to perceived threats of exclusion in an automatic manner which does not depend on rational reflection, though such reflection might sometimes be able to turn off the alarm, so to say, if found to be ungrounded. Some diminishing of our self-esteem occurs automatically even when an insult comes from people who pose no real threat to our social status.[36]

An evolutionary framework for the understanding of shame and humiliation is also developed by Paul Gilbert,[37] who suggests that social attractiveness, rather than fighting, has become the most salient strategy for humans to gain status and to develop useful relationships in groups.[38] That is why the experience of being degraded, devalued, unattractive, 'not worth bothering with,' is so threatening for humans, an experience common to both shame and humiliation.

This connection between humiliation and social exclusion helps realize how such exclusion might entail humiliation irrespective of other moral aspects of the situation at hand. First, humiliation is independent of the overall moral justification of the humiliating behavior. For many years it was believed that retributive justice permits, maybe even requires, the humiliation of wicked criminals.[39] Some still hold this view nowadays.[40] They regard the humiliation

---

[35] Tambor, E.S. & Leary, M. R., Perceived Eclusion as a Common Factor in Social Anxiety, Loneliness, Jealousy, Depression, and Low Self-Esteem,' Unpublished Manuscript (Wake Forest University, Winston-Salem, NC 1993).

[36] Leary and Downs, pp. 134-5.

[37] Gilbert, Paul, 'The Evolution of Social Attractiveness and Its Role in Shame, Humiliation, Guilt and Therapy' *British Journal of Medical Psychology* 70 (1997) 113-147.

[38] For minor differences between the Leary & Downs' model and Gilbert's model, see Gilbert 1997, 130.

[39] For a brief survey and references, see Whitman 1998, 1055-1056, and accompanying notes.

[40] For the revival of shame sanctions in the United States, see Wooler 1997; Whitman 1998, 1056; and Garvey 1998, 734-37. The desirability of such sanctions is under dispute. See Kahan 1996 who endorses them and Massaro 1991 and Whitman 1998 who oppose them.

of criminals as a way of meting out to criminals the punishment they deserve, of doing justice. But, obviously, even if humiliating sanctions—exposing criminals publicly, beating them up in front of a watching crowd, etc.—are just, they are nevertheless humiliating due to their message of rejection and exclusion.[41]

Second, the possibility of humiliation is not contingent on the moral views held by the perpetrators or the victims of humiliation, in particular their views about the equal or unequal worth of all human beings. The victims of humiliation need not believe (implicitly or explicitly) in the equal value of all human beings in order to feel humiliated. All they need assume is that *they* are worthy of respect, while the 'they' can refer to numerous groups; nations, religions, even SS officers.[42] An SS officer might be humiliated by his commander and comrades for not being cruel enough in a murder mission. His assumed misbehavior might be announced publicly on the parade grounds, followed by the officer being declared unworthy to serve in the SS. To judge this situation as humiliating for this SS officer seems to me rather obvious, and this judgment need not make any assumptions about the equal respect due to all human beings, nor of course about the beliefs of the humiliators or the victim in such equal respect.

The fear of being rejected is so strong[43] that it cannot be evaded even when the signals of rejection are sent by people with whom the victim strongly disassociates herself, which is typical to many cases of humiliation.[44] Though the victim of humiliation often does not value the standards of worthiness and of social success assumed by the humiliator, the humiliator manages to shatter

---

[41] Humiliation might be viewed positively not only in the context of punishment and not only by masochists. Many anthropologists contend that humiliation is part of all rites of passage, in particular the liminal stage of the rite (see, for instance, Turner 1979). As participation in such rites is often desirable from the point of view of the participants, especially in initiation rites, they accept them with no resistance. Levy et al. (1986) explain in this way the relatively weak resistance of patients in closed psychiatric wards to the humiliation they undergo. Such humiliation indicates to the patients that some change is in process, and hence that there is a possible end to their suffering.

[42] That one might feel rejected from many groups is expressed in an analysis of the degradation reported by many clients in psychotherapy. Bergner (1987, 25) characterizes this degradation as being 'subjected to treatment by others which has given them reason to conclude that they were not fully entitled, coequal members of their communities.' The identity of the communities varies from one individual to another.

[43] It is stronger than the wish to *improve* one's social status. Empirical studies show that people are more concerned about avoiding exclusion, with its lowered self-esteem, than about facilitating inclusion, with its higher self-esteem. See Leary & Downs 1995, 133.

[44] The fact that in some cases the victims come to adopt the point of view of their tormentors and to identify with it is no objection to this thesis. Such identification is not the victims' state at the time of the humiliation but one of its unfortunate results.

the victim's self-respect, to make her feel unworthy, diminished in stature, devalued. This involves presenting the victim's claim for status as a pretense,[45] often by making her appearance or behavior seem contrary to the requirements of this status. Such appearance or behavior makes it hard for the victim to retain the desired status even in her own eyes.

Our understanding of the inescapable damage to self-respect in humiliation is advanced by Robin Dillon's recent distinction between what she coins 'basal self-respect' and other, more superficial modes of self-respect. On Dillon's view, basal self-respect concerns our primordial interpretation of self and self-worth, 'the invisible lens through which everything connected to the self is viewed and presumed to be disclosed ... The heart of basal self-respect is our most profound valuing of ourselves.'[46] Basal self-respect is a nonpropositional attitude to oneself and it is not just a matter of fitting some subjective criteria of worthiness. Often, and this is the case with women in sexist societies, though the individual believes she is doing fine according to such criteria, she still suffers from a damaged basal self-respect, as result of systematic oppression and devaluation in the social, political and cultural reality.[47] One cannot then avoid damage to basal self-respect by critically reflecting on the reasons for such damage, because the damage affects the very lens through which one assesses reality and weighs reasons.[48]

---

[45] Cf. Miller 1993, 145: 'Humiliation is the consequence of trying to live up to what we have no right to,' and also Taylor 1985, 67-8, who says that the humiliated person 'will think of herself as being thought presumptuous in having allotted to herself such a high position... It is this thought, that she is regarded as presumptuous, which is essential to humiliation.'

[46] Dillon 1997, 241-242. As Dillon notes (241, note 29) the notion of basal self-respect is congruent with a number of analyzes in psychology. In addition to the sources she quotes, see also the distinction made by Deci & Ryan (1995) between contingent self-esteem and true self-esteem. The former refers to one's achievements according to some specific criteria of excellence, while the latter reflects 'a solid sense of self,' to a large extent independent of one's failure or success in any specific task.

[47] These brief remarks about the low basal self-respect of women in sexist societies suggest a need to modify the use I made earlier of Hill's example (1991) of the servile woman (see section II). I argued that the servile women is satisfied and enjoys a rise in her (subjective) self-respect when she realizes what good care she takes of her husband and how helpful she is in advancing his career. Now, however, we can see that this rise in self-respect might be rather superficial, while deep inside this woman might have a basal low self-respect. The notion of self-respect is thus multi-leveled, even within the subjective- psychological notion.

[48] Failure to appreciate the importance of basal self-respect is at the root of the illusion that by acquiring various techniques one can improve one's self-esteem and, consequently, solve all of one's problems. Self-esteem, as Brown & Duton put it, has become 'the panacea of modern life... no matter what ails you today, self-esteem is the cure' (1995, 712). This is an illusion because there is no easy way to transform one's basic view of oneself by 'learning how to be assertive,' or practicing 'taking no notice of what others think.' Dillon shows that as basal self-respect is structured by society, the only way to prevent damage to it is to transform society so that all

Despite the Stoics, the Epicureans and a long philosophical tradition, our self-respect—and our well-being in general—is fragile and vulnerable to many types of contingencies, some produced by Mother Nature and others by our fellow humans.[49] People with whom we might strongly disassociate ourselves have the power to injure our selves, at times to the point that we regard our lives as not worth living. To the cold philosophical mind this might not make sense, but it is a sad and unfortunate fact of life. Very few people, if any, are immune to humiliation, especially when it is severe and systematic.[50] The trauma caused in such circumstances is unavoidable, as argued by Judith Herman in her book *Trauma and Recovery*; no one is immune to post-traumatic damage if the traumatic exposure is severe enough.[51] With all respect to the philosophical reflections and personal merits of people like Epictetus, Marcus Aurelius and Diogenes, I suspect that even they would fail to remain indifferent to the systematic humiliation in a place like Auschwitz.[52] *Pace* Aurelius,[53] there is no inner citadel inside of which human beings are totally safe from the effects of humiliation.[54] People might indeed hope to recover from such experiences, and one therapeutic method is to bring them to refuse to succumb to the degradation, i.e., to maintain a personal conviction of their innocence and the undeservedness of their demotion. The Stoic approach, which is rather limited in its power to give immunity to humiliation, might turn out as more efficient in the *post* trauma recovery process.[55]

Let me conclude this section by trying to clarify how the foregoing arguments help respond to the charge that humiliation is irrational. First, as a result of a long evolutionary process, our self-respect depends crucially on the respect or disrespect shown to us by others. In other words, it is a given fact about human nature that self-respect is vulnerable to injury by others, i.e., to humiliation. Second, this is not just an unfortunate fact about human nature,

---

individuals can grow up valuing themselves unconditionally. The prospects for such transformation are not high and, hence, from the point of view of the individual, there is room for pessimism (Dillon 1997, 248-9).

[49] The question of whether, and to what extent, our well-being might be immune to luck has been discussed in the last two decades as part of the moral luck problem. See Statman 1993a. For a recent argument against the possibility and the desirability of such immunity, see Harris 1997.

[50] Even anti-social personalities are vulnerable to humiliation. As Millon and Everly argue, one cause for their aggressive pattern of behavior is their fear of being humiliated (1985, p. 263). I do not, however, wish to rule out the possibility that some severe personality disorders result in total apathy to humiliation.

[51] Judith Lewis Herman, *Trauma and Recovery* (Basic Books, 1992) Ch. 3.

[52] For a philosophical exploration of the essential role of humiliation in the Holocaust, see Margalit & Motzkin 1996.

[53] *Meditationes*, 8th bk., 48, III

[54] On how even 'lifeless stones' are vulnerable to day-to-day humiliation, see Miller (1993, p. 148).

[55] See Bergner 1987 who illustrates the use of this therapeutic method with victims of sexual abuse.

but one that has clear evolutionary advantages. We have a strong interest in belonging to society and a strong interest in not being excluded. Humiliation reflects this fundamental interest and also alerts us to possible threats of exclusion coming both from our limited social circles as well as from the family of man altogether.

V. Summary and Conclusions

It is a plain fact about human beings that their sense of personal worth is shaped to a large extent by what other human beings think about them, and the treatment they receive. That individuals are sufficient to bestow self-respect on themselves is an illusion. Humiliation takes advantage of this fact and seeks to injure self-respect by sending painful messages of subordination, rejection and exclusion. No normal human being is immune to the devastating effects of these messages. It is this injury to (subjective) self respect that explains the moral wrongness of humiliation.

This vulnerability to humilation is the flip side of the human urge for social inclusion and recognition. Since this urge—and the vulnerability to humiliation that comes with it—has obvious evolutionary advantages, it is not irrational. Nor is further philosophical justification required to render humiliation rational. In particular, the concept of humiliation does not presuppose a Kantian notion of human dignity, the idea that human beings are all equally worthy of respect. Neither our theory of humiliation, nor the actual victims of humiliation, need presuppose these ideas.

The independence of the concept of humiliation from a theory of human dignity leaves open the possibility that certain higher level primates can also be humiliated.[56] The only way to block this possibility is to point to some human feature relevant to humiliation that these animals lack. But most probably this feature would be absent in some human beings too, with the unwanted implication that they too would conceptually disqualify as objects of humiliation.

Particular feelings of humiliation can have sound or unsound reasons of various types. A strong reason for feeling humiliated exists when the humiliating behavior is explicitly intended to degrade its victim. When there is no intent to humiliate, or when one simply misunderstands the message of the assumed humiliator, the reason for feeling humiliated is much weaker, or does not exist.

---

[56] A few years ago, the Supreme Court of Israel prohibited an entertainment show which included a fight between a man and an alligator, on the basis, *inter alia*, of the claim that the show humiliated the alligator. See Justice Heshin's opinion in CA 1684/96 *The 'Let Animals Live' Association v. Entertainment Projects Hamat-Gader Ltd.*, section 41. For a recent discussion on personality dimensions in nonhuman animals, see Gosling & John 1999.

This last conclusion accords well with the conclusions of a separate study I published recently[57] on the nature and the normative strength of claims about hurt feelings. I argued that the normative power of hurt feelings to enforce limitations on behavior or expression exists mainly when the hurt is intentional. When the hurt is incidental, it usually cannot ground a demand for such limitations. The same is true of humiliation; claims about humiliation are typically weighty claims from a moral point of view, as humiliation is one of the worst evils. However, this negative status applies mainly to cases of intentional humiliation. The weaker the intention to humiliate and to hurt feelings, the weaker the normative demand on behalf of the hurt person to limit the behavior of others.

I argued that the ambiguity of the notion of human dignity makes this notion rather unhelpful in explicating the notion of humiliation. It might, however, be helpful to explore the argument the other way round, namely, to use the notion of humiliation to interpret the notion of dignity. The down to earth understanding of humiliation suggested here might provide us with a more down to earth understanding of dignity too. This result might be especially useful for legal discourse, in which, on the one hand, dignity is assigned supreme importance, but, on the other, it has no clear reference. Defining violations of dignity as behaviors that humiliate—in the sense alluded to here—might help to give our constitutional concept of dignity a clearer and more practical meaning. This suggestion has significant normative implications, but developing them lies beyond the scope of the present paper.

Acknowledgements

For helpful comments on earlier drafts I am deeply indebted to Eve Garrard, Amihud Gilead, Susan James, Saul Smilansky, Jim Whitman and two anonymous referees for *Philosophical Psychology*.

---

[57] Statman 1998. An English version is forthcoming in *Democratic Culture*.

Bibliography

Bergner, Raymond M. 'Undoing Degradation.' *Psychotherapy* 24 (1987) pp. 25-30.

Brown, J.D. & Dutton, K.A. 'The Thrill of Victory, the Complexity of Defeat: Self-Esteem amd People's Emotional Reactions to Success and Failure.' *Journal of Personality and Social Psychology* 68 91995) pp. 712-722

Deci, E.L. & Ryan, R.M. 'Human Autonomy: The Basis for True Self-Esteem.' *Efficacy, Agency, and Self-Esteem.* M.H. Kernis, ed. New York: Plenum Press 1995.

Dillon, Robin S. 'Self-Respect: Moral, Emotional, Political.' *Ethics* 107 (1987) pp. 226-249.

Feinberg, J. 'The Nature and Value of Rights.' *Journal of Value Inquiry* 4 (1970) pp. 243-261.

Garvey, Stephen. 'Can Shaming Punishments Educate?' *University of Chicago Law Review* 65 (1998) pp. 733-794.

Gilbert, Paul. 'The Evolution of Social Attractiveness and Its Role in Shame, Humiliation, Guilt and Therapy.' *British Journal of Medical Psychology* 70 (1997) 113-147.

Gosling, S.D. & John, O.P. 'Personality Dimensions in Non-Human Animals: A Cross-Species Review.' *Current Directions in Psychological Science* 8 (1999) pp. 69-79.

Harris, George W. *Dignity and Vulnerability: Strength and Quality of Character*. Berkeley: University of California Press 1997.

Herman, Judith Lewis. *Trauma and Recovery*. Basic Books 1992.

Hill, T.E. Jr. 'Servility and Self-Respect.' *Autonomy and Self-Respect.* T. Hill, ed. New York: Cambridge University Press 1991.

Honneth, A. *The Struggle for Recognition.* Cambridge, MA: Polity Press 1995.

Kahan, Dan M. 'What Do Alternative Sanctions Mean?' *University of Chicago Law Review* 63 (1996) pp. 630-653.

Keshen, Richard. *Reasonable Self-Esteem.* Montreal: McGill-Queen's University Press 1996.

Kupfer, Joseph. 'Prostitutes, Musicians, and Self-Respect.' *Journal o Social Philosophy* 26 (1995) pp. 75-88.

Leary, M.R. & Downs, D.L. 'Functions of the Self-Esteem Motive.' *Efficacy, Agency and Self-Esteem.* M.H. Kernis, ed. New York: Plenum Press 1995.

Levy, Amichai, Cooper Simon and Elitzur Avner. 'Degradation and Degradation Rituals in a Closed Psychiatric Ward: An Alternative to Goffman' (in Hebrew). *Sihot-Dialogue, Israel Journal of Psychotherapy* 1 (1986) pp. 42-47.

Margalit, A. *The Decent Society.* Cambridge, MA: Harvard University Press 1996.

Margalit, Avishai, and Motzkin, Gabriel. 'The Uniqueness of the Holocaust.' *Philosophy and Public Affairs* 25 (1996) pp. 65-83.

Massaro, Toni M. 'Shame, Culture and American Criminal Law.' *Michigan Law Review* 89 (1991) pp. 1880-1944.

Massey, S.J. 'Is Self-respect a Moral or a Psychological Concept?' *Ethics* 93 (1983) pp. 246-61.
Miller, William Ian. *Humiliation, and Other Essays on Honor, Social Discomfort, and Violence.* Ithaca: Cornell University Press 1993.
Millon, T. & Everly, G.S. *Personality and Its Disorders.* New York: Wiley 1985.
Nagel, T. 'Death.' *Mortal Questions.* T. Nagel, ed. New York: Cambridge University Press 1879.
Nelson, J.A. 'A Review of Sapontzis' Recent Work on Animal Rights." *Ethics and Animals* 3 (1982) pp. 117-123.
Nussbaum, Martha. *The Therapy of Desire.* Princeton, N.J.: Princeton University Press 1994.
Rachels, James. *Created from Animals: The Moral Implications of Darwinism.* Oxford: Oxford University Press 1990.
Rawls, J. *A Theory of Justice.* Cambridge, MA: Harvard University Press 1971.
Sapontzis, S. 'A Critique of Personhood.' *Ethics* 91 (1981) pp. 607-618.
Sapontzis, S. 'On Being Morally Expendable.' *Ethics and Animals* 3 (1982) pp. 58-72.
Silver, M., Conte, R., Miceli, M., & Poggi, I. 'Humiliation: Feeling Social Control, and the Construction of Reality.' *Journal of the Theory of Social Behavior* 16 (1986) pp. 269-283.
Statman, Daniel, ed. *Moral Luck.* New York: SUNY Press 1993a.
Statman, Daniel. 'Self-Assessment, Self-Esteem and Self-Acceptance.' *Journal of Moral Education* 22 (1993b) pp. 55-62.
Statman, Daniel. 'Hurting Religious Feelings' (in Hebrew). *Multiculturalism in a Democratic and Jewish State.* M. Mautner, A. Sagi & R. Shamir, eds. Tel-Aviv: Ramot Publishing House 1998.
Tambor, E.S. & Leary, M. R. *Perceived Eclusion as a Common Factor in Social Anxiety, Loneliness, Jealousy, Depression, and Low Self-Esteem.*' Unpublished Manuscript. Winston-Salem, NC: Wake Forest University 1993.
Taylor, G. *Pride, Shame and Guilt: Emotions of Self-Assessment.* Oxford: Clarendon Press 1985.
Tremper, Charles R. 'Respect for Human Dignity of Minors: What The Constitution Requires.' *Syracuse Law Review* 39 (1988) pp. 1293-1349.
Whitman, James Q. 'What Is Wrong with Inflicting Shame Sanctions?' *Yale Law Journal* 107 (1998) pp. 1055-1092.
Wooler, Ann. 'Despite Its Unknown Impact, Shaming Makes a Comeback.' *New Jersey Law Journal*, vol. 150, n. 4 (October 27, 1997).

HONOR AND DIGNITY CULTURES: THE CASE OF *KAVOD* AND *KVOD HA-ADAM* IN ISRAELI SOCIETY AND LAW[*]

Orit Kamir

Introduction

For decades, the theoretical distinction between honor and guilt cultures, if often criticized, has served to analyze dynamics, sentiments, tensions, conflicts and developments in societies around the world.[1] In an attempt to offer yet

---

[*] I am deeply grateful to the devoted, hard-working, students who assisted me in the research of historical and legal materials as well in discussion and conceptualization of the results: Dan Arad, Adi Avraham, Itay Baranes, Gur Blay, Galit De-Yung, Yair Eldan, Tamar Krickly, Yasmin Piamenta, Noya Shamir, Guy Shani and Tamar Weiner. Warm thanks to the attendants of the Fawley Lunch Series at the University of Michigan Law School, to the friends and colleagues who read previous drafts and gave me helpful advice, and especially to David Chambers, Hanoch Dagan, Ruth Gavison, Rebecca Johnson, Deborah Malamud, Bill Miller, Yoram Shachar, Marc Spindelman and J. B. White. Special thanks to Nita Schechet and Maya Steinitz for their consistent help and support throughout the writing process, and to the Minerva Center for Human Rights at the Hebrew University in Jerusalem and David Kretzmer for generously sponsoring much of the research and encouraging the publication of this essay.

[1] For a brief presentation of honor cultures, see Part I below. In a word, members of honor cultures are said to be publically 'shamed' into conforming with social 'honor codes,' whereas members of guilt cultures are said to internalize guiding notions of guilt and sin. For obvious examples of honor cultures, think of Saga Iceland and western films; for guilt cultures, think of traditional Western, monotheistic socialization. For a brief presentation of honor cultures, see Part I below. In a word, members of honor cultures are said to be publically 'shamed' into conforming with social 'honor codes,' whereas members of guilt cultures are said to internalize guiding notions of guilt and sin. For obvious examples of honor cultures, think of Saga Iceland and western films; for guilt cultures, think of traditional Western, monotheistic socialization.

another angle from which to pursue such purposes, I suggest an additional, four-headed distinction, between cultures that are honor-based, dignity-based, glory-based and respect-based (or, more accurately, a distinction between honor-based, dignity-based, glory-based and respect-based socio-cultural tendencies and drives). Like the distinction between honor and guilt cultures, this proposed distinction may be useful and allow insightful socio-cultural analysis only if taken as suggestive and tentative, and it is as such that I propose it.

The distinction between honor, dignity, glory and respect as values and principles that may be used to read value structures and cultural codes has risen out of my particular analysis of Israeli, Hebrew culture. It is within that specific cultural and linguistic scope that the theoretical categories emerged and took on meaning. Like many, I believe that socio-cultural theoretical distinctions are most valuable when rooted in concrete culture and language. Nevertheless, concepts derived from the close study of a particular culture, if generalized without compromise of their authentic, specific origins, may be more useful for comparative purposes than strictly abstract ones. It is in this context that I look at the dynamics of Israeli society, culture and law through the lenses of the Hebrew terms that roughly correspond with the English honor, dignity, glory and respect. I attempt to establish a useful point of view of Israel's specific socio-cultural dynamics through the theoretical concepts, while developing these concepts through their manifestation in the Israeli case study.

Overview of the Argument

History demonstrates that, at a historical turning point, a society may choose to declare a certain value or set of values as its fundamental constitutional core. Within Western contemporary civilization, the first examples that come to mind are the US choice of equality and liberty in 1776, followed, in 1789, by the French choice of these same values, augmented with comradeship. In more recent times, post-World War (Western) Germany chose human dignity and post-apartheid South Africa—dignity and equality (in 1949 and 1992 respectively). In each of these cases, the chosen fundamental value, or set of values, was established as the cornerstone of the respective state's new constitution.

As these familiar examples indicate, such dramatic moral-legal choices typically coincide with times of fundamental revolutions, when a society's deepest structure is questioned, revisited and redefined. The collective declaration of a new fundamental value is, therefore, indicative of a dramatic socio-cultural transformation. The symbolic act of establishing the chosen value in a new constitution is a legal manifestation of the socio-cultural shift. It both mirrors and enhances the new collective ideology, instituting it as the foundation of public order. It is in this context that I look at the particular case of Israeli society, culture and law, and the fundamental concept and value *kavod*, which is at the heart of Israel's new, 1992, bill of rights.

Due to complex historical circumstances and political constraints, Israel has no formal constitution. Instead, Israel's parliament, the Knesset, has legislated sporadic 'Basic Laws,' which can be regarded as fragments of a constitution. Most of these regulate the separation of powers; only in 1992, after long and dramatic deliberations, did the Knesset finally succeed in passing a basic law that has some features of a charter of human rights, and which is often considered to be the country's bill of rights: *hok yesod kvod ha-adam ve-heruto*, officially translated to 'Basic Law: Human Dignity and Liberty.'[2]

The 'official stand' (voiced by Knesset members and Supreme Court justices) is that human dignity and liberty have always been fundamental values underlying Israel's society and law. In declaring dignity and liberty as Israel's fundamental values, the Basic Law is said to have merely proclaimed an existing socio-legal reality, awarding it a formal, constitutional status. In fact, this official stand is at least arguable.

First, while the Hebrew *herut* is easily translated to 'liberty,' the translation of *kvod ha-adam* to 'dignity' is substantially inaccurate, concealing the Hebrew term's full range of meanings. The translation of *kvod ha-adam* to 'human dignity' conveniently associates the Basic Law with the 1948 Universal Declaration of Human Rights. But in fact, although the combined phrase *kvod ha-adam* does connote 'human dignity,' the word *kavod* is also the only Hebrew term for 'honor,' 'glory' and 'respect.'[3] In Israeli culture and society, as well as in Israeli law, human dignity (*kvod ha-adam*) is, therefore, inseparable from—while sometimes at variance with—these other values, representing distinct sentiments and value systems. The Basic Law's 'dignity-honor-glory-respect' is not exactly the Universal Declaration's 'dignity.' Rather than ignoring this complexity, it seems imperative to investigate the exact meaning of each of the concepts associated with *kavod* in Israeli culture, society and law, as well as the interactions between them and the unique multi-layered concept *kvod ha-adam*.

Second, it is highly questionable whether any of the mentioned values was ever a fundamental value of Israel's society or law. Significantly, up to 1992, neither this set of values nor any other was ever declared as Israel's ideological foundation. The State of Israel was established in 1948, an historical turning point, at which the founding fathers, representing the Zionist community in Palestine, composed and signed the new state's Declaration of Independence. Pronouncing the new state's moral principles, the Declaration named a whole list of values, some specifically Zionist and others, dictated to the emerging state by the United Nations, more universalistic. Among the listed values are, above all others, the Zionist values of Jewish settlement in the Land of Israel. Next come liberty, justice and peace, all 'in accordance

---

[2] SH for the year 5752, p. 150. The Basic Law's status as a bill of rights is controversial in many ways. I assume that despite severe deficiencies, the Basic Law does constitute a bill of rights, if partial and unsatisfactory.

[3] For explication of these terms, see Part I below.

with the vision of the Hebrew Prophets;' complete civil and political equality for all citizens, with no discrimination based on religion, race or gender; freedom of religion, conscience, language, education and culture. None of these values was awarded a superior status, although the particularistic, Zionist values were more enthusiastically emphasized in the Declaration of Independence than others. Human dignity, honor, glory and respect were not listed among the Declaration's values.[4]

Furthermore, Israel's Declaration of Independence has not been treated as a formal constitution and the Supreme Court determined that it had no compelling legal force. The Declaration did, allegedly, inspire the judiciary in its creation of Israel's 'judicial bill of rights.' Freedom of speech and other human rights established by the Supreme Court as part of the state's common law, were often rhetorically derived by the justices from the Declaration. Human dignity was not one of these human rights (at least not until the 1980s).

I suggest that, although unacknowledged, it is *kavod*-honor rather than *kavod*-dignity that has been a predominant, fundamental feature of the Zionist movement and the Zionist state. *Kavod*-honor, in the Jewish-Israeli context, implies a set of Zionist values stressing national Jewish power and 'masculine' militant honor. This ideology views the long Jewish Diaspora (and especially the Holocaust) as a stain of shame and humiliation on collective Jewish identity. The only means of overcoming this acute national degradation is a firm insistence on Jewish honor, mainly through the military power of the Jewish state. *Kavod* as honor, therefore, implies a zealous protection of the rights of individual Jews as well as those of the Jewish collective. This particularistic, nationalistic *kavod*-honor is very different from the universalistic *kavod*-dignity suggested by the official translation of the Basic Law's title. They are both distinct from *kavod*-glory, which, in the Israeli context, bears a religious, orthodox connotation.[5]

The significance of the distinction between *kavod*-honor, *kavod*-dignity and *kavod*-glory is not merely linguistic or cultural but also social and political. Using *kavod* terminology, the Israeli society on the brink of the 21st century, can be (roughly) described as divided into three feuding camps. The first, and perhaps largest camp consists of those who remain devoted to Israel's Zionist *kavod*-honor culture. The other is made up of those who wish to shift emphasis from the Zionist honor mentality towards a more universalistic human dignity (*kvod ha-adam*) oriented culture. In varying degrees, members of this camp are associated with the view that Israel should reformulate its 'Jewishness' and become 'a state of all its citizens,' Jews and Arabs alike, as well as a secular political entity, where state and church are separate and women enjoy full legal equality. This ideology, which, in its extreme forms, is sometimes referred to as 'post-Zionist,' can, in this context, be labeled a 'post *kavod*-honor' worldview. The third camp is composed of Israeli Jews for

---

[4] For further reference to this point see Part II.

[5] In this paper I merely mention *kavod*-respect in passing, focusing on *kavod*-honor and *kavod*-dignity.

whom *kavod* is above all glory. Glory, in this context, implies a rabbinical, religious, ('pre-Zionist') Jewish ideology, which attributes Man's glory to his heavenly creation in the divine image of God. According to this worldview, Man's glory is the source not only of certain human rights, but also of Man's duties to his creator. As 'glory,' the word *kavod* does not entail such rights as to end a pregnancy and to die at will; rather, it implies a person's duties to live and multiply. Clearly, each of these camps assigns a different meaning to the root *k-v-d*, the word *kavod* and the phrase *kvod ha-adam*. The tension between the three camps is considered by many in Israel as a 'culture war,' which may break into a civil war of some sort.

This paper is a part of a larger project, aimed at addressing a variety of social, cultural, legal questions, as well as developing the theoretical concepts of honor, dignity, glory and respect cultures. Taking seriously the challenge presented by Israel's constitutional choice, I venture a look at certain developments, tensions and conflicts in Israeli society and culture through the prism of the value that, in 1992, was chosen as Israel's fundamental (socio-legal) value. Through the rhetoric and logic of *kavod* and the theoretical distinction between honor, dignity, glory and respect I propose to get at socio-cultural subtexts that may be overlooked when Israeli society is analyzed through other, more familiar formulas and keywords, such as 'a Jewish and democratic state.' At the same time, I conduct the analysis of Israeli society, culture and law as a case study in the development of the general categories of honor, dignity, glory and respect.

The scope of the present paper does not allow for a discussion of all or even most of the components of the larger project. Here, I merely outline one of that study's themes. Concentrating on *kavod*-honor and (*kvod ha-adam*) dignity and focusing on the honor and dignity logic and rhetoric of Israel's Supreme Court, I trace the recent shift, in the Supreme Court's decisions, from 'honor' to 'dignity' talk, highlighting the shift's social context as well as its problematic ideological/political implications.

My line of argument in this paper is as follows: in enacting the Basic Law *kvod ha-adam ve-heruto*, the Knesset (can be understood to have) signaled a socio-cultural shift of emphasis from the logic of *kavod*-honor to the logic of (*kvod ha-adam*) human dignity. In the Israeli context, I argue, this shift, clearly an issue within the scope of the Israeli culture war, is sufficiently fundamental to be viewed as an ideological revolution. The symbolic change of emphasis, the move away from Israel's *kavod*-honor mentality and in the direction of embracing the universalistic value of human dignity, is no less than a new conceptualization of the premises underlying the self-definition of the state of Israel. Yet this dramatic shift of emphasis was not explicitly declared, publicly acknowledged nor widely embraced. Furthermore, it was completely obscured by the Knesset's choice of the multi-layered root *k-v-d*, containing the fraught inter-relations between the incohesive values dignity, honor, glory and respect. Each fragment of the Israeli society uses *kavod* to mean something else, not fully admitting the many faces of the root, which correspond with the deep political conflict. The choice of the term *kvod ha-*

adam, therefore, allows the Israeli society to deny, ignore and suppress both the issue of an ideological shift of emphasis and the conflict behind it.

The Knesset's choice of the (multiple) Janus-faced root *k-v-d*, accompanied by the legislature's vague references to the Basic Law's exact ideological meaning, left the potential dignity revolution in an ambiguous, embryonic state. In this delicate state of affairs, the legal form and status of the Basic Law imposed the implementation of the revolution on the Israeli legal system, to be executed through its courts' decisions. The legal system, led by the Supreme Court, responded to the challenge by beginning to develop (*kvod ha-adam*) dignity discourse that would balance, if not overshadow the ruling *kavod*-honor discourse. (To be exact: the Supreme Court had begun to develop a dignity discourse as early as the 1980s. This development took on new dimensions with the legislation of the Basic Law).

I suggest that the legal response to the constitutional challenge is creating a discrepancy between the new legal rhetoric and logic of (*kvod ha-adam*) dignity and the prevailing social notions of *kavod*-honor (as well as between the dignity talk and the *kavod*-glory frame of mind). I pose the question whether fundamental ideological shifts, such as the one from honor to dignity, can and should be led or executed by the legal system, when significant portions of the population are either unaware or unaccepting of the new premises.

Focusing on honor and dignity, I begin this discussion by substantiating the four distinct meanings of the word *kavod*, thus also portraying the conceptual distinction between the four categories of honor culture, dignity culture, glory culture and respect culture. Next, in part II, I flesh out the argument that the Zionist movement and state chose an honor rhetoric (rather than a dignity oriented one). Finally, in part III, I show how the Israeli Supreme Court, which was as honor-oriented as the rest of the Israeli society, has begun to replace its honor rhetoric with a new dignity one, thus executing the Knesset's supposed intention.

I. The Many Faces of *K-V-D*: Honor, Dignity, Glory and Respect

In contemporary, Israeli Hebrew, the root *k-v-d*, the word *kavod* and the phrase *kvod ha-adam* are fraught with meanings and connotations, assimilated together beyond clear distinction. A native speaker of Hebrew, operating within that language, I could not fully identify the distinct components linked together in the root *k-v-d*, as Hebrew does not offer the terminology and concepts to do so. I, therefore, stepped outside the boundaries of my own, examined language and culture, to see more clearly the ingredients that make up the meaning of *k-v-d*. I turned to English because it is the foreign language I am most comfortable with and also one of the most commonly used in cross-cultural comparisons in the humanities and social sciences. I was looking for English terms and concepts that would help me define the components of *k-v-d*, unspecifiable within contemporary Hebrew.

The older (and more popular) of my two Hebrew-English dictionaries (Alcalay, 1965) translates *kavod* as 'honor, respect, glory, splendor, majesty, reverence, distinction, importance, wealth, riches, ambition.' The other (Levy, 1997), composed thirty years later, translates the Hebrew *kavod* as 'honor, respect, dignity' (translating the English 'dignity' into the Hebrew '*kavod, mekuvadut, hadar*'). A thorough examination of several (Christian and Jewish, old and new) translations of the Hebrew bible into English revealed that dozens of words deriving from the root *k-v-d* were translated into 'honor,' 'glory' and 'respect.' The translations vary greatly: the same word in the same context is sometimes translated differently by different translators; the same translator sometimes chooses different English terms for the same *k-v-d* word in different contexts.[6] Nevertheless, 'glory' and 'honor' are the most prevalent English terms used to capture the essence of the biblical *k-v-d* words. 'Honor' is more commonly used when a *k-v-d* word refers to humans, whereas 'glory' is more often used to translate *k-v-d* words relating to god. Although my own translation of biblical *k-v-d* words would sometimes differ from existing translations, I agree that 'glory,' 'honor,' 'respect' and maybe 'dignity' are the most appropriate English words that capture the essence of the Hebrew root *k-v-d* both in both biblical and modern Hebrew. I would argue that in many cases, a more accurate translation would consist of more than one of these English words.

The intuitive differences between the English 'honor,' 'glory,' 'respect' and 'dignity' indicate the complexity of the Hebrew root *k-v-d*. Clearly, none of the English terms, nor any artificial combination thereof can fully capture the exact, specific meanings of *k-v-d* in biblical or modern Hebrew contexts. Yet, the existence of these distinct terms in a different language helps differentiate aspects in the Hebrew root, which cannot be fully verbalized within the Hebrew language itself. The use of English terminology in this context is far from perfect, but may be as much as we can hope for.[7] It is, therefore, meant to be taken as suggestive rather than definitive.

The proximity of 'honor,' 'glory,' 'respect' and 'dignity' is similarly interesting. A quick look in any English language dictionary reveals that each of these terms is often defined using one or more of the others. The proximity of these words' meanings illustrates that the connection between different aspects of *k-v-d* is not unique to Hebrew. In English, as in Hebrew, each meaning of *k-v-d* is related to the others, and any attempt to separate them completely would be arbitrary. If I stress the differences between the concepts encoded in these terms it is for didactic reasons and because within Hebrew these differences go unverbalized and undistinguished.

Despite the proximity of 'honor,' 'glory,' 'respect' and 'dignity' they are not interchangeable and each consists of a distinct, definable core. Of these

---

[6] A close analysis of these variations is beyond the scope of this paper, and I pursue it elsewhere.

[7] Of course the use of any other language would have rendered slightly different insights; I cannot say that one language would have been better than others.

four terms, 'honor' is the most distinctively defined and conceptualized in academic literature, which associates it with a specific pattern of cultural codes.

Honor Cultures

As has been shown by many writers, honor cultures differ greatly in many of their specifics, as well as in the linguistic terms they use to denote honor and shame.[8] My distinct interest is in the Hebrew root *k-v-d* and in what I perceive as the Zionist-Israeli honor culture, which differ greatly from Mediterranean and north European honor cultures. Nevertheless, I side with those who find it worthwhile to examine a particular honor culture against general characteristics of honor cultures as a category. Whether a particular behavior is 'shameful' may be viewed differently by different honor cultures, but the use of 'shame' as a fundamental criterion to determine worthiness and social rank is typical of them all. Pitt-Rivers suggests likening honor 'to the concept of magic in the sense that, while its principles can be detected anywhere, they are clothed in conceptions which are not exactly equivalent from one place to another.'[9] The following brief general reference to the logic of honor cultures is meant to supply the fundamental background for the understanding of Zionism as an honor culture. (In turn, the analysis of Zionism as a particular honor culture may contribute to the understanding of honor cultures in general).

To use Miller's words, '[t]he well-known distinction between shame and guilt cultures, though rightly and roundly criticized, still captures a fundamental difference ... between a culture in which reputation is all and one in which conscience, confession and forgiveness play a central role.'[10] Members of historical and contemporary honor cultures derive their social rank and sense of worthiness by measuring up to well-defined social norms of honorable behavior and avoiding or avenging behaviors and situations which are conceived as inflicting shame. Sketching a basic, general definition, Miller suggests that:

---

[8] Michael Herzfeld, 'Honor and Shame: Problems in the Comparative Analysis of Moral Systems,' *Man* (1980), vol. XV, p. 339. The literature on honor cultures, mostly anthropological, is too voluminous to be surveyed here. Most of the literature I am relying on is cited in William Ian Miller, *Humiliation and Other Essays on Honor, Social Discomfort and Violence* (Cornell University Press, Ithaca 1993). For some of the most classic writing see Gerhard Piers and Milton B. Singer, *Shame and Guilt: A Psychoanalytic and Cultural Study* (Norton, New York 1971) and Julian Pitt-Rivers, *The Fate of Shechem or the Politics of Sex: Essays in the Anthropology of the Mediterranean* (Cambridge University Press, Cambridge 1977).

[9] Julian Pitt-Rivers, 'Honor and Social Status,' in *Honor and Shame: The Values of Mediterranean Society*, J. G. Peristiany, ed. (Chicago University Press 1966) p. 21.

[10] William Ian Miller, *Humiliation: And Other Essays on Honor, Social Discomfort and Violence* (Cornell University Press, Ithaca 1993) p. 116.

> [H]onor is above all the keen sensitivity to the experience of humiliation and shame, a sensitivity manifested by the desire to be envied by others and the propensity to envy the successes of others. To simplify greatly, honor is that disposition which makes one act to shame others who have shamed oneself, to humiliate others who have humiliated oneself. The honorable person is one whose self-esteem and social standing is intimately dependent on the esteem or the envy he or she actually elicits in others. At root honor means 'don't tread on me.' But to show someone you were not to be trod upon often meant that you had to hold yourself out as one who was willing to tread on others. ... In the culture of honor, the prospect of violence inhered in virtually every social interaction between free men... For shame and envy are quickly reprocessed as anger, and anger often is a prelude to aggression.[11]

This description elucidates why a culture that demands of its members to 'turn the other cheek' is not an honor culture. Traditional Jewish and Christian cultures are usually defined as guilt oriented: rather than publicly measuring behaviors as 'honorable' or 'shameful,' their members are said to internalize a strong sense of moral obligation, sin and guilt.

Stressing honor cultures' typical linkage of social status, social rights and self esteem, Pitt-Rivers defines honor as 'the value of a person in his own eyes, but also in the eyes of his society. It is his estimation of his own worth, his *claim* to pride, but it is also the acknowledgment of that claim, his excellence recognized by society, his *right* to pride.'[12] Adding the 'honorable impulse' expected of members of honor cultures, the formula becomes this: 'the sentiment of honor inspires conduct which is honorable, the conduct receives recognition and established reputation, and reputation is finally sanctified by the bestowal of honors. Honor felt becomes honor claimed and honor claimed becomes honor paid.'[13]

Analyzing the emotional economies of honor cultures, Miller claims that:

> [A] culture in which honor is a dominant organizing principle is very likely to make certain emotional dispositions more salient than they would be in an American upper-middle-class suburb. We might expect emotions that depend on relative standing in the community, such as shame and envy, to be more prevalent than those that depend on self-evaluation independent of the

---

[11] Miller, p. 84. Miller often suggests that in order to sympathize with members of honor cultures we need simply recall our own adolescent social experiences.
[12] Pitt-Rivers (1966) p. 21.
[13] *Ibid.*, p. 22.

views of others, such as guilt or remorse, or those that accompany alienation, such as angst and ennui.[14]

In honor cultures, honor serves as an effective disciplining tool, and the honor-code is, therefore, a structure of social power. In order to achieve and maintain honor, an honor culture offers its members specific behavior codes, demanding complete obedience. Failure to detect an insult which taints one's honor, or failure to respond to an offense to one's honor at the right time, in the right fashion, in the right degree result in costly consequences, i.e., in loss of honor. Honor cultures are local and particularistic in the sense that they only apply to their own members, demanding thorough mastery of the most nuanced specific norms and expectations. (Foreigners and outcasts are honorless and honor norms very often do not apply to them). Such cultures are ritualistic in the sense that they demand very specific responses to offensive behaviors. (A slap on the face is the only right response for some people in certain situations, whereas for other people in other situations the preservation of honor demands a duel or a killing in the context of a feud). Honor cultures are individualistic in that each member is responsible for his or her honor, and will suffer the consequences of a wrong social move. They are collectivist in the sense that each person's honor also influences the honor of his or her clan, and sometimes that of the whole group. They are also class oriented, in the sense that a person's honor and the means of maintaining it vary greatly depending on social class. The most obvious class difference is gender based.

> The honor of a man and of a woman ... imply quite different modes of conduct. This is so in any society. A woman is dishonored ... with the tainting of her sexual purity, but a man [is] not. While certain conduct is honorable for both sexes, honor=shame requires conduct in other spheres, which is exclusively a virtue of one sex or the other. It obliges a man to defend his honor and that of his family, a woman to conserve her purity ... [R]estraint is the natural basis of sexual purity, just as masculinity is the natural basis of authority and the defense of familial honor ... Masculinity means courage whether it is employed for moral or immoral ends ... The honor of a man is involved ... in the sexual purity of his mother, wife and daughters, and sisters, not in his own ... [T]he honorable woman: locked in the house with a broken leg.[15]

Another central class distinction distinguishes those who are honorable by birth from all others. To use Pitt-Rivers' terms, in leaders and members of reputable, distinguished families, honor is simultaneously 'precedence' as well as 'virtue.'[16] *Being* honorable, anything such people do is assumed to be

---

[14] Miller, p. 116.
[15] Pitt-Rivers (1966) pp. 42-45.
[16] *Ibid.*, p. 36.

honorable and therefore also virtuous. Thus, for some people in honor cultures, 'the possession of honor guarantees against dishonor, for the simple reason that it places a man (if he has enough of it) in a position in which he cannot be challenged or judged. The king cannot be dishonored. What he *is* guarantees the evaluation of his actions.'[17] Pitt-Rivers rightly notes that 'honor which derives from virtuous conduct and that honor which situates an individual socially and determines his right to precedence' are and should be conceptually distinct, yet in many honor cultures an honorable person's conduct is always honorable and beyond reproach.

Dignity v. Honor

In this discussion, 'dignity' is the contemporary, liberal, post-World-War II, minimalist, 'legalistic' concept. It is the fundamental, egalitarian, humanistic value celebrated in Article 1 of the 1948 Universal Declaration of Human Rights, which proclaims that '[a]ll human beings are born free and equal in dignity and rights.'

Despite much contemporary reference to dignity, writers typically refrain from offering precise, comprehensive definitions, sometimes claiming that it is 'intuitively' self-explanatory. Often discussed from legal and legalistic perspectives, dignity tends to be treated instrumentally rather than theoretically. 'When it has been invoked in concrete situations, it has been generally assumed that a violation of human dignity can be recognized even if the abstract term cannot be defined. "I know it when I see it even if I cannot tell you what it is."'[18] Thus, there seems to be no standard, widely accepted definition of dignity which could serve as a basis for discussion.

Like honor in honor cultures, dignity relates to the core of a person's worth as a human being. It is viewed as an axiomatic human quality, the source of social acknowledgment and rights and the organizing principle of humanistic value systems. Like honor, the concept of dignity confuses 'human nature,' noble sentiment, claim to social treatment and legal rights and actual 'natural,' social and legal rights. Dignity is generally treated as simultaneously empirical and normative, source and consequence, natural and social, absolute and tentative. The discussion of dignity manifests much ambiguity in crucial points: is dignity inherent and equal in all persons under all circumstances? does a person's moral behavior influence his or her dignity? is a person's dignity dependent on social recognition? can a person be deprived of human dignity, and if so—how?[19] I do not address these issues here. Rather, I try to

---

[17] *Ibid.*, p. 37

[18] O. Schachter, 'Editorial Comment—Human Dignity as a Normative Concept,' *American Journal of International Law* (1983), vol. LXXVII, p. 849.

[19] For discussion of these issues, see, for example, Alan Gewirth, 'Human Dignity as the Basis of Human Rights,' in *The Constitution of Human Rights* Michael J. Meyer and W. A. Paret, eds. (Cornell University Press, New York 1992), and George P. Fletcher, 'Human Dignity as a Constitutional Value,' *University of Western Ontario Law Review* (1984), vol. XXII, pp. 171-182.

sketch a rough outline of dignity by highlighting the ways in which it differs from honor. For this purpose, I use simplistic portrayals of both honor and dignity, avoiding ambiguity and complexity within each term and value system.

Whereas, for most members of honor cultures, honor is earned and maintained through careful, painful observance of a specific cultural code, many define dignity as an essential human quality obtained at birth. All persons are 'worthy' of dignity and/or posses it merely by being humans. Honor is both 'precedence' and 'virtue' for the few 'honorable' persons of high social rank; dignity is 'precedence' and 'virtue' for all human beings. Whereas for most people honor is easily lost by a person's slightest social error or by another's sometimes honorable behavior, a person's dignity is only lost through grave, extreme behavior, which is deemed negative. Furthermore, many argue that one cannot lose or be deprived of his or her human dignity under any circumstances. Honor is socially and culturally specific, and each person's honor varies greatly, in both type and degree, depending on his or her class and behavior. Dignity is universal and many claim that, except for extreme cases, all human beings are entitled to and/or posses it equally. Honor dictates specific, daily (sometimes ritualistic) behavior; dignity merely precludes very extreme, unusual conduct (such as torture and mutilation). Honor implies both self worth and social status; dignity does not convey social status. Honor demands that an individual measure him or herself against social norms and other members of the community; dignity demands equal basic concern for and treatment of all humans. Honor encourages competition and sometimes aggression, whereas dignity begs consideration and constraint. Honor is complimented by fear of shame and humiliation; dignity—by empathy, solidarity, humanistic obligation (and maybe disgust with the thought of human violation). In an honor culture, an offense to one's honor burdens him or her with the duty to remove the stain, purify the honor, avenge the offense and humiliate the offender. Within the logic of dignity, an attack on a person's dignity is an attack on society and its fundamental values; it does not burden the offended party, but challenges the social order. Honor, like a commodity, a valuable possession, a trophy, can be accumulated; dignity is often portrayed as merely the most essential human asset. In this sense dignity inspires a 'minimalist' social code, whereas honor promotes ambition. An honor culture, therefore, offers higher stakes and higher risks, whereas dignity secures the minimum.

Miller asserts that 'the mathematics of honor usually meant that you could never be just like someone else without taking what he had, appropriating his status to yourself. For the most part, people acted as if the mechanics of honor had the structure of a zero-sum or less-than-zero-sum game.'[20] Pitt-Rivers documents that in some honor cultures 'one who gave an insult thereby took to himself the reputation of which he deprived the other.'[21]

---

[20] Miller, p. 116.
[21] Pitt-Rivers (1977), p. 4.

Dignity, on the other hand, like a parent's love, 'expands' with every newborn human being; no matter how many humans there are, there is always enough dignity to be equally shared by all. In contrast with the logic of honor, the logic of dignity links a person's own dignity with the dignity he or she allows others. By offending another's dignity, a person loses his or her own. This logic motivates all humans to secure each other's dignity.

Defining an honor culture, Campbell claims that '[s]elf regard forbids any action which may be interpreted as weakness. Normally this would include any altruistic behavior to an unrelated man. Co-operation, tolerance, love, must give way to autarky, arrogance, hostility.'[22] In clear contrast, dignity promotes tolerance, love and sometimes altruism, renouncing vengeance and hostility.

I, therefore, agree with Bourdieu's observation that:

> [T]he ethos of honor is fundamentally opposed to a universal and formal morality which affirms the equality in dignity of all men and consequently the equality of their rights and duties. Not only do the rules imposed upon men differ from those imposed upon women, and the duties towards men differ from those towards women, but also the dictates of honor, directly applied to the individual case and varying according to the situation, are in no way capable of being made universal. This is so much the case that a single system of values of honor establishes two opposing sets of rules of conduct—on the one hand that which governs relationships between kinsmen, and in general all personal relations that conform to the same pattern as those between kinsmen; and on the other hand, that which is valid in one's relationships with strangers. This duality of attitudes proceeds logically from the fundamental principle ... according to which the modes of conduct of honor apply only to those who are worthy of them.[23]

Glory, Honor, Dignity and Respect

'Glory' is used in most English translations of the Hebrew bible to translate *k-v-d* qualities attributed to god. In other words, the biblical god's glory is the English version of his Hebrew *kavod*. Associated with divinity, this particular *kavod*-glory, although surely related to honor, took on divine, theistic characteristics. God's *kavod*-glory is supreme honor adorned with splendor, majesty, reverence and distinction (to use the English terms suggested by the Alcalay dictionary mentioned above). This *kavod*-glory, inseparable from

---

[22] J. K. Campbell, 'Honor and the Devil,' in *Honor and Shame: The Values of Mediterranean Society*, J. G. Peristiany, ed. (Chicago University Press, Chicago 1966) p. 151.

[23] Pierre Bourdieu, 'The Sentiment of Honor in Kabyle Society,' in *Honor and Shame: The Values of Mediterranean Society*, J. G. Peristiany, ed. (Chicago University Press, Chicago 1966) p. 228.

godly essence, is clearly inherent, absolute, eternal and indestructible. Sun-like, its brilliance is both natural and good, empirical and normative, 'is' and 'ought to be,' 'precedence' and 'virtue.' Its mere existence constitutes god's 'rights' and his worshippers' duties and required behavior. It is both the source and manifestation of god's 'worth,' 'status' and 'privileges.'

Relying on the biblical portrayal of Man as created in the image of god, Rabbinical Judaism attributes some of god's *kavod*-glory to mankind. As an earthly reflection of god's glorious image, Man, too, and the community of men, are said to possess and be entitled to a fragment of the divine *kavod*-glory, together with the rights and obligations it implies.

Many characteristics of the divine *kavod*-glory resemble those of both honor and dignity. In fact, within western, monotheistic culture, glory may have inspired the development of both these notions. Yet glory differs, in spirit and in specifics, from both honor and dignity. As this essay focuses on honor and dignity, I will merely mention the most significant aspect in which glory is distinct from honor and dignity.

Whereas honor and dignity (although often associated with 'human nature') are social, non-metaphysical values, glory is inherently metaphysical. Associated with a monotheistic organized religion, it is also absolute and unchangeable. When applied to humans, it is attributed to them not on the sole basis of their self-determined humanity, but rather due to their alleged resemblance to an external, super-human entity. In contrast with dignity, glory does not refer to people's human essence, but to the godly element within them. Glory, therefore, does not establish human worth in its own right, but as deriving from an external, metaphysical source. This distinction has deep psychological significance as well as practical, worldly implications. The logic of glory dictates that the divine godly glory in each person be acknowledged, cherished and treated not according to that person's—or even society's—self perception and determination, but according to god's unchangeable, inexplicable rules. In Rabbinical Judaism, Man's glory was used to preclude methods of execution that distort the human body and practices that would allow human bodies to rot. But it was also the basis for commanding people to wash, feed, treat and conceal their own bodies with the care and reverence due to god's glory, as interpreted by the organized religion. Man's glory precludes suicide, abortion, homosexual intercourse and masturbation among other 'unglorified' treatments of a person's body. The sentiment associated with violation of glory is not shame or pride but rather sin and awe. In this sense, a glory culture has much in common with a guilt culture.

Duties imposed in the name of glory may be at odds with the liberal implications of human dignity. Furthermore, unlike dignity, all humans take part in the divine glory—but not equally. Men are more glorious than women and Jews than non-Jews. Glory, thus, cannot be the basis of women's rights that are not acknowledged by Rabbinical Judaism, such as the right to pray or sing in public or to dress as they please.[24]

Although I discussed glory in the context of Rabbinical Judaism, I believe that Christian formulations may be close enough to justify some Judeo-Christian notion of glory.

Respect is the least researched and, to date, most illusive of *kavod*'s four faces. As it has no determined meaning, it is flexible and open to experimentation. To me, respect is of the same essence as dignity, but less minimalistic. Whereas dignity only invites protection of the most fundamental components of any human existence, I suggest that respect correlates with a demand for active tolerance and acceptance of different patterns of human existence, as determined by human agents and groups. Both socially and legally, respect can be the basis for a celebration of diversity and plurality of human existence. In my view, it is the preferred value for the conceptualization of women rights, as well as for the accommodation of cultural differences. Respect correlates with the sentiments of empathy and acceptance.

As their brief presentation demonstrated, honor, dignity, glory and respect can constitute four partially overlapping value systems, compatible in some respects and less so in others. In this sense, some cultures, or periods in the histories of cultures, or tendencies within cultures may be identified as honor-based, dignity-based, glory-based or respect-based. Societies may shift emphasis from one value system to another, or use more than one of these principles simultaneously. In fact, as many societies manifest both honor and guilt mentalities, it stands to reason that some societies are motivated by combinations of these four principles.

In the following sections I look at Zionism and contemporary Israeli society as struggling with socio-cultural shifts to honor (from glory) and from honor to dignity.

II. The Zionist Adoption of *Kavod*-Honor

I suggest that Zionism is, inherently, an honor discourse. Zionism transformed pain, widely felt by European Jews as a result of the continuous assault on their dignity and human rights, into anger in the context of national honor. The honor code, eagerly adopted from European and especially from German culture by Zionists and presented as authentically Hebrew, made it possible to present Jewish life in Europe as degrading and humiliating to the collective entity. The national state in Palestine was presented as an honorable solution to a dishonorable existence in exile. In Palestine, the honor rhetoric also seemed to bridge the gaps between European Jews and 'Oriental Jews' (i.e., Jews from Middle-Eastern honor culture societies) as well as those between all Jews and

---

[24] Speaking of 'Rabbinical Judaism,' I refer to Orthodox Judaism, which is both historical and the most relevant to Israeli social reality. Reform, Conservative, Reconstructionist and many other branches of Judaism, more popular in the U.S than in Israel, currently view women's rights differently.

the local, 'Oriental' (Palestinian and Bedouin) culture. This frame of thought proved highly effective, but it neglected discourse on dignity in favor of that on honor. Let me elaborate.

In the 19th-century, the majority of Jews, living in Eastern Europe, were subjected to harsh, undignified living conditions. Confined to restricted territories and to limited occupations, prevented from participating in the societies within which they lived, deprived of equal economic and cultural opportunities, and often facing severe danger to both life and property, many Jews suffered overwhelming violations of their human dignity. Traditional, Rabbinical, 'pre-Zionist' Judaism often conceptualized these abuses as manifestations of a heavenly ordeal and of a cosmic, purifying punishment; the victims were often thought of as martyrs, patiently doing the Almighty's work and glorifying his name. Zionism denounced this attitude and declared it passive, submissive, cowardly, feminine and disgraceful.[25] In its stead, the Zionists embraced Europe's 19th-century national and nationalistic ideas, as well as its honor discourse.[26] Both violations of Jews' human dignity and the

---

[25] For the Zionist renunciation of the Jewish Diaspora, its culture and mentality see Yehezkel Koifman, *Diaspora and Foreign Land: An Historical Sociological Study on the Destiny of the Jewish People from Antiquity to this Day* [in Hebrew, *Gola Ve-Nechar: Mechkar Histori Sotziologi be-She'elat Goralo Shel Am Yisrael Miymei Kedem ve-Ad ha-Zman ha-ze*] (Dvir, Tel Aviv 1971); Pnina Lahav, 'Israel's Supreme Court: The Formative Decade (1948-1955),' [in Hebrew 'ha-Oz ve-ha-Misra: Beit ha-Mishpat ha-Eliyon ba-Asor ha-Rishon le-Kiyumo'] *Iyunei Mishpat* (1989) vol. XIV; Anita Shapira, *Land and Power* [in Hebrew, 'Herev ha-Yona: ha-Zionut ve-ha-Koach 1881-1948'] (Am Oved, Tel Aviv 1992); George L. Mosse 'Max Nordau, Liberalism and the New Jew,' *Journal of Contemporary History* (1992) vol XXVII; Amnon Raz-Krakotzkin, 'Exile Within Sovereignty: Towards a Critique of the 'Negation Of Exile in Israeli Culture,' *Theory and Criticism - An Israeli Forum* (1993) vol. IV; Ze'ev Sternhall, *Nation-Building or a New Society? The Zionist Movement (1904-1940) and the Origins of Israel* [in Hebrew, *Binyan Uma o Tikkun Hevra?*] (Am Oved, Tel Aviv 1995), pp. 62, 64; Oz Almog, *The Sabra: A Profile* [in Hebrew, *ha-Tzabar: Profil*] (Am Oved, Tel Aviv 1997), p. 127; Adi Ofir, 'The Declaration of of Independence: A User's Manual,' *The Declaration of State: 21 Tablets*, D. Tartakover, ed., (Modan, Tel Aviv 1988) vol. LXV [In Hebrew 'Megilat ha-Atzmaut: Horaot Shimush]; Daniel Boyarin, 'Colonial Drag: Zionism, Gender, and Mimicry' [in Hebrew, 'Neshef ha-Maseckot ha-Kolonialy'] *Theory and Criticism – An Israeli Forum* (1997), vol. XI; Orit Kamir, 'The Declaration of Israel's Independence Has Two Faces: The Strange Case of the Zionist Declaration and the Democratic Declaration' [in Hebrew, 'la-Megila Yesh Shtei Panim: Sipuran ha-Muzar Shel ha-Hachraza ha-Zionit ve-ha-Hackraza ha-Democratit'] *Iyunei Mishpat* (2000) vol. XXIII.

[26] For one portrayal of a German honor culture see Ute Frevert, *Men of Honor: A Social and Cultural History of the Duel* (Polity Press, Oxford 1995). For the Zionists' yearning for and adoption of European honor codes see Amos Eylon, *Herzl* (Am Oved, Tel Aviv 1976) pp. 56-61; Mosse; Jacques Kornberg, *Theodor Herzl: From Assimilation to Zionism* (Indiana University Press, Bloomington 1993) pp. 1, 35; Raz-Krakotzkin, p. 24; Idith Zertal, 'The Sacrifice and the Sanctified: The Construction of a National Martyrology,' *Zmanim – An Historical Quarterly* (1994),

victims' responses were reformulated and presented as a national humiliation and disgrace. Zionism's unique, revolutionary contribution was, thus, in translating behaviors which could be viewed as assaults on the dignity of Jewish persons, and the Jewish acceptance of such behaviors, into a disgrace to Jewish national honor. Within this framework, the infringement of human and civil rights of Jews was neither a cosmic, heavenly trial, nor a humanitarian issue; it tarnished Jewish honor, and was, therefore to be avenged within the ritualistic, masculine logic of the European honor code.

Theodor Herzl, an assimilated German Jew, founder and leader of the Zionist movement, was deeply disturbed by the undignified conditions of Eastern Europe's Jews.[27] Herzl had internalized the Jewish stereotypes of the European enlightenment. He saw Jews as inferior: cowardly, unmanly, preoccupied with money, bereft of idealism; but he also identified with their history of victimization.[28] But it was the dishonorable treatment of Dreyfus that inspired his political activism.[29] His writings reveal him obsessively concerned with issues of honor, and Dreyfus' humiliation surely touched a nerve.

The first solution Herzl devised for the problem of Europe's Jews was a public duel between a leading anti-Semite and himself, or another Jewish leader.[30] According to the honor logic, which he whole-heartedly embraced, this was a 'win-win' solution. The Jew's victory, he wrote, would restore Jewish honor and clear the nation of its disgrace. The Jew's death would achieve the same result, proving to the world that Jewish men are as brave, masculine and honorable as all others. Herzl cast himself in the role of a modern-day David, proudly challenging contemporary Goliath. This fantasy is the backbone of his 1897 play, *The New Ghetto*,[31] in which the Jewish protagonist, Jacob, is fatally wounded in a duel he initiated. Jacob's honorable conduct reestablishes his honor, which was tarnished when, on a previous occasion, he had failed to challenge an offender. Dying in the arms of his family, he calls them to leave the ghetto and start a new life.

Herzl was fascinated with the honorable practice of dueling since his days in the radical, national fraternity *Albia* in the early 1880s in Vienna.[32] 'In 1878, *Albia* adopted the dueling practices of the German student fraternities,

---

vol. XII, p. 35; Boyarin, pp. 129, 132, 136; Michael Gluzman, 'Longing for Heterosexuality: Zionism and Sexuality in Herzl's *Altneuland*' [in Hebrew, 'ha-Kmiha le-Hetrosexualiut'] *Theory and Criticism – An Israeli Forum* (1997), vol XI, pp. 145, 148.

[27] Eylon; Kornberg, p. 115; Theodor Herzl, *Herzl's Writings in Ten Volumes* [in Hebrew, *Kitvey Herzl be-Asra Krahim*] (Ha-Sifriya ha-Tzionit, Jerusalem 1960).

[28] Kornberg, p. 2.

[29] Herzl, 'Matters in France' *Herzl's Writings in Ten Volumes* (1960) vol. VII, p.184.

[30] Herzl, *Herzl's Writings in Ten Volumes* (1960) vol. I, p.5.

[31] Theodor Herzl, *Books of Days* [in Hebrew, *Sifrey ha-Yamim*] (Mizpeh, Tel Aviv 1939) vol. I, p. 177.

[32] Kornberg, p. 41.

introduced in Austria in the 1860s. This included an obligatory code of honor, according to which conflicts and insults were to be settled or vindicated through duels.'[33] Upon initiation to the fraternity, Herzl:

> [...] began preparations for the fencing bout that would make him a senior member (*Bursch*), attending fencing classes daily from one to three in the afternoon and from five to seven in the evening, and in addition taking a special course with a fencing master. In view of his idealization of dueling as a manly recourse for Jews, it is noteworthy that his duel, fought on 11 May 1881, was a disappointment by *Albia* standards. [...] As a result of Herzl's weak performance, some were opposed to his acceptance.[34]

Kornberg documents that even after his *Albia* days 'Herzl continued to admire the duel as a test of honor. He was involved in three challenges in the mid-1880s and was ready to launch another after he became a Zionist statesman.'[35] In fact, on one of these occasions he failed to pursue a duel in a manner very similar to that depicted in The New Ghetto. 'That the affair filled him with shame, that he feared he was a coward, Herzl acknowledged himself. That Herzl saw his cowardice as a Jewish trait and that this fed his Jewish self-contempt, can be concluded from his play.'[36]

Herzl's carried his self-doubt, yearning for honor and preoccupation with dueling over into his Zionist vision. In a diary entry dated June 9th, 1895, sketching guidelines for his Utopist Zion, Herzl writes: 'I need the duel to create decent officers and improve noble society in a French manner. Sword dueling will go unpunished, under all circumstances, provided that the seconds do their best to achieve honorable peace. A sword-duel will only be legally investigated after-effect.'[37] Not surprisingly, Kornberg observes that Herzl's 'Zionist politics was to transform Jews from wary, calculating survivors lacking physical courage, into 'real men.' Political Zionism was in some ways a re-creation of *Albia*, writ large.'[38]

Herzl's second, and slightly more realistic, idea regarding the solution of the Jews' problem was that all Jews be baptized as Christians.[39] This proposed solution reveals Herzl's concern for the real-life suffering of the Jewish masses, which he believed would cease once Jews were Christians (i.e., once they ceased to be an identified minority). Nevertheless, he was very conscious of the effect this act might have on Jewish honor. In his vision, therefore, not only would the baptism ceremony be performed with great splendor and

---

[33] *Ibid.*, p. 42.
[34] *Ibid.*, p. 41.
[35] *Ibid.*, p. 67.
[36] *Ibid.*, p. 70.
[37] Herzl (1939) vol. I, p. 58, my translation from Hebrew.
[38] Kornberg, p. 53.
[39] Herzl (1939) vol. I, p.7-8.

grandeur, but, most importantly, the leaders of the Jewish community would remain Jewish, explicitly proclaiming and vindicating Jewish honor.[40]

Political Zionism was Herzl's third option. It too was motivated by compassion for the undignified conditions endured by most Jews. At the same time it aimed to remedy these indignities by restoring and constructing Jewish national honor. Accordingly:

> Herzl was to oppose the Zionist policy of incremental settlement in Palestine. Instead, Jews were to aim for Jewish sovereignty immediately. Jews were to think big, to practice bold and risky self-assertion, to seek sweeping solutions that would alter their situation in one fell swoop. They were to be direct, to openly state their aims, proclaim them to the world no matter what the risk to the fragile Jewish infrastructure in Ottoman Palestine. As well, they were to develop physical strength and beauty, ridding themselves of their blighted physiognomy. The Jewish state would nurture physical courage by rewarding its outstanding adepts with medals and prizes.[41]

Herzl's independent Jewish state was to be inherently a display of Jewish honor. Every element of Herzl's plan was carefully designed to serve and enhance the honorable effect. So, for example, Herzl envisioned a special committee whose task would be to ensure that, upon leaving Europe on their way to their new state, Jews sell their property in Europe to European nations and their gentile citizens in the most honest, orderly and honorable manner possible.[42] Herzl's recurrent, detailed references to the splendor and magnificence of public rituals in his Jewish state manifest the deep significance this aspect of statehood held for him.[43]

An illuminating illustration of Herzl's coupling of human dignity with Jewish honor may be found in his treatment of the character of David in his novel *Altneuland*.[44] We first encounter David as a beggar boy, starving on the streets of Vienna together with his East European family. His pathetic condition moves the novel's Jewish protagonist (himself on a self re-creative mission), who bestows all his earthly goods on David. The Jewish family makes good use of the money, and twenty years later, when we (and the now changed, manly protagonist) next encounter David, he is a distinguished, honorable leader of the national Jewish state in Palestine. His undignified

---

[40] *Ibid.*
[41] Kornberg, p. 57.
[42] See, for example, Herzl (1960) vol. I, pp. 37-8, 69-70.
[43] See, for example: 'High priests will wear magnificent costume; the cavalry yellow trousers and white coats. Warlords will have silver armor.' Herzl (1939) vol. I, p. 40, my translation from the Hebrew.
[44] Herzl (1960) vol. I, p.85.

personal situation was redeemed through the honorable Jewish national political independence.

In conclusion, let me quote Kornberg, sketching the psychological origins of Herzlian, honor-based Zionism:

> Herzlian Zionism was ... the outcome of wounded pride... Jews were to free themselves of shame and contempt and gain pride, respect and honor. ... Zionism served as a circuitous route to honor and acceptance. ... Herzl was more preoccupied with issues of Jewish pride and gentile recognition than with the refuge for Jews in distress; more with Jewish honor than with Jewish power.[45]

Max Nordau, Herzl's close friend and political ally, internalized the European honor ideology with even less critical awareness.[46] Concerned about East European Jewry's economic plight and undignified living conditions, he adopted the anti-Semitic portrayal of contemporary Jews as deformed, degenerate and unhealthy.[47] This unmanly collective condition was deeply dishonorable in his view. The main difference between Nordau, a militant Zionist, and contemporary anti-Semites was in his claim that the Jews' dishonorable condition was not inherent or natural, but rather a consequence of their political subordination.[48] Hence the belief that an independent Jewish state would transform Jewish men into the honorable, deep-chested, powerfully built and keen-eyed men they were capable of being and had been in ancient times. It is no coincidence that a play he wrote in 1907, entitled 'A Question of Honor,' features the death of a young Jew in a duel with a German officer who had offended him, and, through him, the entire Jewish nation.[49]

It is significant that Ahad Ha-Am (pen name for Asher Ginzberg), who posed the most powerful opposition to Herzl and Nordau, fiercely rejected both the honor discourse and the whole concept of political Zionism.[50] He argued that Herzl's honor code was a far cry from Jewish religion and morality; it was nothing but an apish imitation of foreign culture, he claimed.[51] Unlike Herzl, deeply rooted in German culture, Ahad Ha-Am, himself an East

---

[45] Kornberg, p. 8.
[46] Mosse.
[47] *Ibid.*, p. 566-7.
[48] *Ibid.*, p. 569.
[49] *Ibid.*, p. 573.
[50] Ahad Ha-Am's was 'spiritual Zionism.' He advocated that Zion be constituted as a spiritual Jewish center for Jews everywhere rather than a sovereign national state. For an example of his harsh criticism of Herzlean Zionism see Ahad Ha-Am, 'Altneuland,' in *The Complete Writings of Ahad Ha-Am* [in Hebrew, *Kol Kitvei Ahad Ha-Am*] (Dvir, Tel Aviv 1965), p. 313.
[51] Ahad Ha-Am, 'The National Morality,' in *The Complete Writings of Ahad Ha-Am* pp. 259, 262-3.

European Jew, looked to the British mentality and political system for inspiration. During his 1893 visit to London:

> He saw firsthand the quiet dignity of a culture whose national characteristics were pronounced without being self-conscious and whose everyday life mirrored a healthy and stable political legacy. The essential decency and orderliness of its social life demonstrated a sensibility that he had discovered long before when he had first come to treasure the writings of English social philosophers.[52]

Interestingly, Ahad Ha-Am was the only first-generation Zionist leader who showed deep concern and respect for the dignity of the Palestinian population.[53] Not having substituted Jewish honor for human dignity, he remained sensitive to the dignity of all humans, including (perhaps especially) those who did not belong to the national Jewish collective. He felt that if Zionism 'failed to create a society in which an Arab minority could live with dignity whatever success it achieved would be worse than tainted...'[54] In 1922, referring to what he perceived as the Zionists' brutality to their neighbors, he wrote: '[I]f this is the Messiah, may he come, but may I not live to see him!'[55]

Ze'ev Jabotinsky, charismatic leader of the militant, revisionist section within the Zionist movement, admired Herzl and Nordau and was greatly influenced by them.[56] Perhaps due to criticism such as Ahad Ha-Am's, he seems to have been more aware of the non-Jewish origin of the Zionist honor code. Such imitation of a foreign honor code must have seemed paradoxically dishonorable to him. His solution, typical of many Zionists to this day, was to seek and ground an honor code in ancient, pre-exile Jewish culture.[57] The Hebrew Bible was the natural place to turn to. Jabotinsky's novel *Samson*[58] is a paradigmatic example of the Zionist reading of 19th-century German notions of honor into ancient Hebrew culture. Jabotinsky's Samson is an ancient

---

[52] Steven J. Zipperstein, 'Between Tribalism and Utopia: Ahad Ha'am and the Making of Jewish Cultural Politics,' *Modern Judaism* (1993) vol XIII, p. 238.

[53] Ahad Ha-Am 'Truth from Eretz-Yisrael,' in *The Complete Writings of Ahad Ha-Am*, p. 23.

[54] Zipperstein, p. 243.

[55] Ahad Ha-Am, p. 462; Zipperstein, p. 242.

[56] Ben Bilskey and Raphaella Hur, *Every Man a King: The Social and Political Thought of Ze'ev Jabotinsky* [in Hebrew *Kol Yachid Hu Melech*] (Dvir, Tel Aviv 1988).

[57] Herzl and Nordau both proudly referred to the Jews' honorable, independent existence in ancient times. Heroic stories from biblical times and the period of the second temple (the Makkabim) were sources of inspiration. Jabotinsky went further and situated his novel in antiquity. Interestingly, Ahad Ha-Am cherished the heritage of Yohanan Ben-Zakai, who (dishonorably) hid in a coffin to escape the Romans and preserve Jewish culture.

[58] Ze'ev Jabotinsky, *Samson* (Tarmil, Tel Aviv 1982).

version of Nordau's deep-chested, powerfully built and keen-eyed 'new Jew.' He is a smart brute, a diplomat and a warrior and a man of honor. Torn between loyalty to his small, weak, unattractive tribe and his admiration for the Philistine nation (strikingly similar to modern Germany), Jabotinsky's Samson marries a blond, blue-eyed Philistine woman, but gives his life redeeming his people's honor. Such rereading of ancient Hebrew sources as a means of appropriating the European honor code has been an indispensable strategy of Zionism.

Most important of the 20th century Zionist leaders is David Ben-Gurion, the actual founder of Israel and the man who shaped the state's ideology, priorities and vision for a significant period in the state's formative years. In his disgust with and contempt for Jewish existence in the Diaspora, Ben-Gurion takes after Nordau and shares much with Jabotinsky.[59] He revealed this tendency in its extreme when, showing deep insensitivity to the dignity of holocaust survivors (as well as other Diaspora Jews), he referred to them as 'human dust.'[60] While distancing himself and Israeli Jews from disgraceful Jewish life in the Diaspora, he eagerly promoted Zionist readings of the Hebrew Bible and its heroes, turning bible reading into a bonding ritual between the Jewish nation and its reclaimed culture, history and land.[61] Ben-

---

[59] Even Jewish existence in liberal, egalitarian countries was despised and unacceptable to him. In a speech given in 1957, a year after the Israeli victory over the Egyptian army in the Sinai war, he said: '... Israeli Jews have no inferiority complexes. On the contrary. But there is not a single country in the world—even where Jews truly enjoy full freedom and equality ... where Jews do not suffer from a sense of inferiority' David Ben-Gurion, *Distinctiveness and Destiny: On Israel's Security* [in Hebrew, *Yehud ve-Yeud: Dvarim al Bitchon Yisrael*] (Maarachot, Jerusalem 1977), p. 301, my translation from Hebrew. See also p. 160.

[60] Referring to new immigrants, holocaust survivors as well as Jews from Arab countries, in a speech to the Knesset given on August 1949 he stated: '...those of us who became part of the homeland, the culture, the Hebrew independence before the establishment of the state are liable to disregard the grave fact that they are but a very small portion of the Jewish people, most of which is still, from a Jewish perspective, human dust, without a language, without tradition, without roots, without attachment to public life, without the habits of an independent society' Ben-Gurion (1977), p. 66. My translation from Hebrew. The phrase 'human dust,' often referring specifically to 'Oriental Jews,' reappears in many speeches. For discussion of attitude towards holocaust survivors see Tom Segev, *The Seventh Million: The Israelis and the Holocaust* [in Hebrew, *ha-Million ha-Shvi'i: ha-Yisraelim ve-ha-Shoa*] (Keter, Jerusalem 1991) pp. 101-110.

[61] Despise for Diaspora and love for bible - David Ben-Gurion, *Biblical Reflections*, [in Hebrew, *Eyunim ba-Tanach*] (Am Oved, Tel Aviv 1969), pp. 48, 94, 219; *Vision and Way* [in Hebrew, *Hazon va-Derech*] (Mifleget Poali Eretz Yisrael, Tel Aviv 1951), vol. II, p. 225; Michael Keren, *Ben Gurion and the Intellectuals* [in Hebrew, *Ben Gurion ve-ha-Intellectualim*] (Ben Gurion University Press, Jerusalem 1988), p. 103; Eliezer Don-Yihya, 'Judaism and the Statism in Ben-Gurion's Thought and Politics,' *Zionism – Studies in the History of the Zionist Movement and of the Jewish Community* (1989) vol. XIV, pp. 53-55, 64, 66; Segev, pp. 404, 417; Shapira, pp.

Gurion attempted to purify Jewish honor by erasing the dishonorable existence in exile and rewriting the Jewish history as consisting of the reinterpreted biblical stories and modern day Zionist and Israeli heroism.

Relying on Ben-Gurion's voluminous writings, it is possible to further reconstruct the complex relationship between dignity and honor theorized and reflected in his world-view. Human dignity, he claims, is a Jewish value, established and developed by the ancient biblical prophets. The unique fundamental respect for human dignity has always distinguished Jewish culture from all others; it afforded Judaism its moral superiority and secured its survival through centuries of persecution.[62] The world's respect for the Jewish commitment to human dignity ensured the honor of the Jewish nation in the international community. But through the hardships of the Diaspora, Jews in exile lost their conviction, their own dignity, their moral superiority and therefore their honor as well. Only through an honorable, independent national life could the Jewish people regain its honor in the international community, while reestablishing human dignity as humanity's central moral value.[63] Clearly, within this philosophy, human dignity and Jewish national honor are almost synonymous.

For decades both before and after the foundation of the state of Israel, the general Israeli public was, by and large, committed to this bonding of human dignity with Jewish honor. This entailed an inability to think of human dignity in and of itself. Assaults on human dignity of Jews were experienced and formulated as disgraces to Jewish honor. Violations of human dignity of non-Jews, including Palestinians, could not be reconstructed as offenses to Jewish honor, and were therefore all but invisible.

The end of the Second World War caused the European powers to rethink their moral priorities. Horrified Germany drafted a constitution proclaiming human dignity its ultimate, absolute value. The conquering allies, celebrating the superiority of their liberal philosophy, drafted the Universal Declaration of Human Rights. For the Zionist Jews in Palestine, and later in Israel, the Holocaust was experienced as the ultimate, unbearable humiliation and disgrace. The Holocaust was too overwhelming for Zionist Jews to cope with through the prism of human dignity. It was far more manageable for them to respond to it as a national dishonor. This 'choice' sacrificed the dignity of

---

209, 217, 228; Ze'ev Tzahor, 'Ben-Gurion as Creator of Myth," in *Myth and Memory: The Metamorphoses of Israeli Consciousness*, David Ohana andRobert Weistrich, eds. [in Hebrew, 'Ben-Gurion ke-Meatzev Mitos'] (Ha-Kibbutz Ha-Meuhad and Van Leer, Jerusalem 1997), p. 136.

[62] Ben-Gurion (1977), pp. 345, 373; Ben-Gurion, (1951) vol. I, p. 183.

[63] 'He [the Egyptian leader, Nasser] cannot understand the source of the great honor and fame which Israel and the Israeli army enjoy in the world and in the two great continents—Asia and Africa. Our people is honored for the human dignity we have.' Ben-Gurion (1977), p. 345, in a speech before soldiers, July 1959. My translation from Hebrew. See also Ben-Gurion (1969) p. 225. For the centrality of universal dignity in the honorable national existence see Ben-Gurion (1951), vol. I, p. 113. See also Keren, p. 73.

the survivors but allowed the community to redeem its honor, in its own eyes, through the establishment of the state of Israel and what it perceived as honorable, militant national behavior. Thus *kvod ha-adam*, human dignity, was not, and could not have been, adopted by the emerging Israeli society as a fundamental value. *Kavod*, honor, took its place. It is no coincidence that the Israeli Declaration of Independence, drafted the same year as the Universal Declaration of Human Rights, mentions equality and other human rights, but does not establish human dignity as one of Israel's fundamental values. *Kavod*'s single appearance in this document is in the context of the claim that holocaust survivors' courageous conduct after the war established their right to a life of *kavod*, freedom and honorable work in their homeland; in this context, *kavod* is closer to (national) honor than to anything else.[64]

III. The Supreme Court's Honor Mentality

This section is based on close reading of every published case handed down by the Israeli Supreme Court from its first day until the 1990s. As most of this data is not currently on-line, the five law students who conducted the textual-empirical work carefully read every volume of the Supreme Court's decisions.[65] They were instructed to note every appearance of *kvod ha-adam* (human dignity), *kavod* and derivations from the root *k-v-d*, and analyze whether, in the specific context of each appearance, it connoted dignity, honor, glory, respect or any combination thereof. They were also instructed to search for references to these values, explicit or implied, made without the use of the root *k-v-d*. In long group meetings they presented their findings and we debated the accuracy of the suggested categorizations. All five students, as well as myself, are native speakers of Hebrew.

The Israeli Supreme Court's decisions indicate that regarding honor and dignity, Israel's legal system acted no differently than the society it served. Despite their familiarity with it, Supreme Court Justices refrained from using the phrase *kvod ha-adam*, human dignity. In the three decades following 1948, the phrase *kvod ha-adam*, human dignity, appears in Supreme Court decisions no more than five times; thrice in reference to procedural rights of (Jewish) suspects and prisoners, and twice in reference to spousal rape (within the Palestinian community in Israel).[66] In eight other cases, the root *k-v-d* appears

---

[64] A close reading of earlier versions of the text supports this reading. I am thankful to Yoram Shachar for making this point.

[65] To be more accurate, they read every decision published up to the 1980s. Decisions published from this time on are accessible on-line and were selectively searched with the assistance of computer software.

[66] In Criminal Appeal Jarjura v. State of Israel, 9 *PD* (1) the Justices determined that fingerprinting does not offend human dignity; in 273/65 Artzi v. The State of Israel and The State of Israel v. Artzi, 20 *PD* (1) 225, the majority rule in favor of the appellant, whose human dignity was offended during police investigation; in Tau v. The State of Israel, 20 *PD* (2) 539, the Justices denied the appeal despite the offense

in a manner that clearly connotes dignity.[67] In dozens of decisions the absence of reference to human dignity (whether through *kvod ha-adam*, the root *k-v-d* or in any other way) is striking. So, for example, discussion of human dignity is never mentioned in reference to deportation, house demolition or expropriation of land. Not once did the Supreme Court debate whether any of the actions taken against Israeli Palestinians were in violation of their human dignity.

During that same period the Supreme Court used the root *k-v-d* in reference to honor no less than eighty times. In many of these cases the court referred to the honor of the state and its authorities such as the court system, the legal profession and the police force. The justices stressed the importance of eradicating the unhappy Diaspora heritage of disrespecting the state and its authorities; in the Jewish state, 'new Jews' were to be reeducated to honor their state, and thus themselves. The Justices were equally concerned that Palestinians honor the Jewish state and its authorities. In several cases where human dignity could have been acknowledged and discussed, honor was acknowledged and discussed instead.

Let me mention two outstanding decisions which best illustrate this honor mentality during the years 1948—1980. On June 6th, 1967, the second day of the 1967 war, Mr. Gofada, an orthodox Jewish farmer, moved his tractor to a neighboring Arab village although it had been conscripted for military use. Two enraged citizens attacked him and cut his sidelocks. Two years later one of the perpetrators was elected to the town council, prompting Mr. Gofada to appeal to the Supreme Court in its capacity as High Court of Justice.[68] Gofada demanded that the perpetrator be prevented from taking office on the grounds that he had committed a disgraceful act. The legal question before the Court was whether the physical attack on Gofada and the cutting of his sidelocks were dishonorable acts.

Justice Haim Cohen, who lost his family in the Holocaust, refrained from referring to human dignity and instead, discussed the issue using the logic of honor. Cohen denounced Gofada's behavior as a treacherous, disgraceful act of villainy. Under these circumstances, he determined, the physical assault on Gofada was not dishonorable. In Cohen's view, Gofada's treachery stained the national honor; the assault on him reconstituted the damaged collective honor and was, therefore, an honorable act. But the act of cutting Gofada's sidelocks, declared Cohen, 'bears such painful national associations that the disgrace it attributes to the perpetrator is undeniable and irrevocable under any circumstances.'[69] The Nazi-like cutting of Gofada's sidelocks was not perceived as violating his human dignity. For Justice Cohen, it was an attack

---

to the appellant's human dignity. The rape cases are Fakir et al. v. The State of Israel 18 *PD* (4) 200 and Katib v. The State of Israel 20 *PD* (2) 137.

[67] Clearly, we may have missed or misjudged certain decisions. If ever on-line, the results may be more accurate.

[68] Gofada v. Chair of Migdal Council 23 *PD* (2) 2.

[69] *Ibid.*, 4.

on Jewish national honor. In this vein, Cohen responded by disgracing the offender in turn. He proclaimed his act disgraceful, depriving him of his honor as well as the right to serve as a council member.

In the summer of 1978, five Israeli policemen searching for drug dealers were physically assaulted by the mayor of the Palestinian town Beit Jala and three council members. Convicted of committing violent acts and assaulting police officers, all four were discharged from their public offices by the Israeli military commander of the area. In their plea to the Supreme Court in its capacity as High Court of Justice, the four claimed that their behavior was not disgraceful, and that there were, therefore, no legal grounds for their discharge.[70] Israel's Supreme Court determined that assaulting mere citizens would not have been deemed disgraceful but the public humiliation of official representatives of the state constituted disgrace. In other words, in response to what the Court perceived as an offense to national honor, it responded by dishonoring the Palestinian offenders.

The Supreme Court: From Honor to Dignity (and Glory) Talk

The 1973 war is said to have caused many changes in Israeli society's attitudes, including those towards Holocaust survivors. From the perspective of this discussion, it may be that the deep trauma caused by that war and by what was experienced in Israel as defeat, led, at least in some sections of Israeli society, to disillusionment with Israel's honor values. This may have allowed for more sensitivity to the discourse of human dignity. When, in 1977, Mr. Begin's right-wing Likud party came to power, establishing Jabotinsky's intense honor mentality as the country's official discourse, segments of Israeli society, including the Supreme Court, may have reacted by enhancing the emerging dignity discourse. In any event, it was in 1980 that a newly nominated Holocaust survivor Supreme Court Justice, Aharon Barak, embraced *kvod ha-adam*, human dignity as a fundamental socio-legal value and basic right. In his landmark decision in *Katlan v. The Prison Administration*,[71] Barak denied the state's right to perform an enema on a prisoner without his consent, constituting human dignity as a fundamental right within the Israeli legal system. In a concurring opinion, Justice Cohen defined an enlightened society as one committed to human dignity. Such commitment, he pronounced, echoing the Universal Declaration of Human Rights, was the basis for all human rights and liberties. At the same time, however, Cohen claimed that human dignity, *kvod ha-adam*, originated in traditional Jewish culture. In so doing, he confused the modern, liberal, concept of human dignity with the traditional notion of glory, an attribute of Man manifesting the image of god. The Hebrew phrase *kvod ha-adam*, connoting both liberal dignity and traditional glory, facilitated Cohen's confusion of the two concepts. Over the

---

[70] Dahud et al. v. The State of Israel 32 *PD* (3) 477.
[71] 34 *PD* (3) 294.

last decade, this unconscious confusion has evolved into an explicit ideological conflict.

Basic Law *kvod ha-adam ve-heruto*, legislated in 1992, has been interpreted by some as supporting the elevation of universal human dignity, and by others as reinforcing the traditional 'glory of Man' approach. The ambiguity of the root *k-v-d*, which allows for either interpretation, is echoed in the basic law's solemn opening statement declaring its purpose to protect *kvod ha-adam* in order to secure the values of Israel as a 'Jewish and democratic' state. In Justice Barak's view (now Chief Justice) the law constitutes the secular, 'democratic' human dignity as the legal system's fundamental value, giving rise to all other human rights. In contrast, Justice Menahem Elon (recently retired) following the interpretation first suggested by Justice Cohen, determined that the Basic Law enforced the Jewish value of Man's glory. In a series of opinions, (although not using the English terms 'honor,' 'dignity' and 'glory') Elon explicitly distinguished *kvod ha-adam* from both honor and dignity, identifying it with traditional, conservative glory.[72] In these decisions, *kvod ha-adam*, derived from God's image, does not entail nor secure the right to die at will, nor the right to use Latin letters on a Jew's gravestone.[73] To date, it is Barak's approach which seems to prevail (despite common reference by the Justices to Man's creation in 'god's image'). In the late 1990s, The Supreme Court has heard hundreds of appeals invoking *kvod ha-adam*, human dignity, consistently forming an Israeli human dignity jurisprudence.[74] In this respect, the Supreme Court seems to be implementing the potential shift of emphasis implied in Basic Law *kvod ha-adam ve-heruto* from honor to dignity.

Thus, the legislation of Basic Law *kvod ha-adam ve-heruto* seems to have encouraged the legal system's tendency to withdraw from its honor mentality and to develop a dignity discourse. This dynamic concomitantly mirrors and influences similar tendencies within certain segments of Israeli society at large, currently struggling with its concepts of honor, glory and dignity. At the same time it deepens the gap between the legal system and large segments (perhaps the majority) of Israeli society, still more committed to *kavod*-honor, *kavod*-glory or a combination thereof than to human dignity per se.[75] This gap has manifested itself in harsh, sometimes militant attacks on

---

[72] The most explicit of these is State of Israel v. Gueta, 46 *PD* (5) 704.

[73] Sheffer v. The State of Israel, 48 *PD* (1) 87 and Hevra Kadisha v. Kastenbaum, 46 *PD* (2) 464. It is significant that many, perhaps most of Justice Elon's decisions promote and guard 'human dignity' as well as 'Man's glory.' It is only in extreme cases that dignity and glory seem to pull in different directions, but these cases are most instructive for this study of the concepts.

[74] David Kretzmer, 'Human Dignity in Israeli Jurisprudence,' in this volume.

[75] For a thorough socio-legal analysis of the Supreme Court's relationship with different segments of Israeli society see Menahem Mautner, *The Decline of Formalism and Rise of Values in Israel's Legal System* [in Hebrew, *Yeridat ha-Formalism ve-Aliat ha-Arachim ba-Mishpat ha-Yisraeli*] (Ma'agalei Da'at, Tel Aviv 1993).

the legal system, the Supreme Court in particular, launched by leaders of the Jewish Orthodox community in Israel. During the years 1996-1999, some government members voiced serious criticism of the legal system, sometimes grave enough to be understood as questioning its legitimacy. In this delicate socio-political-legal situation, the question presents itself whether it is the Supreme Court's prerogative, perhaps duty, to lead the way taking the ideological path which may be implied in the 1992 Basic Law, or whether the legal system should merely reflect and conceptualize social changes once they have already taken place? In the social conflict between honor, dignity and glory tendencies, what is the legal system's appropriate role? Can the legal system, and should it, participate in the possible shift from a more honor-based to a more dignity-based culture? If so, at what stage, how and how much? At this stage, I prefer to leave these questions open.

*Hebrew-speaking Israelis can hardly distinguish between honor, dignity, glory and respect, as all four are denoted by the single term *kavod*, the centerpiece of Israel's Bill of Rights. Nevertheless, Israeli society seems to be pulled in different directions by strong cultural tendencies associated with the distinct notions of honor, dignity and glory. I hope this discussion facilitates a useful analysis of future developments within Israel, as well as cross-cultural comparison.

Bibliography

Ahad Ha-am. *The Complete Writings of Ahad Ha-Am*. Tel Aviv: Dvir 1965 (in Hebrew, *Kol Kitvei Ahad Ha-Am*).

Alcalay, Reuven. *The Complete Hebrew-English Dictionary*. Ramat Gan-Jerusalem: Massada 1970.

Almog, Oz. *The Sabra: A Profile*. Tel Aviv: Am Oved 1997 (in Hebrew, *haTzabar: Profil*).

Ben-Gurion, David. *Biblical Reflections*. Tel Aviv: Am Oved 1969 (in Hebrew, *Eyunim ba-Tanach*).

Ben-Gurion, David. *Distinctiveness and Destiny: On Israel's Security*. Jerusalem: Maarachot 1977 (in Hebrew, *Yehud ve-Yeud: Dvarim al Bitchon Yisrael*).

Ben-Gurion, David. *Vision and Way*. Tel Aviv: Mifleget Poalei Eretz Yisrael 1951 (in Hebrew, *Hazon va-Derech*).

Bilskey, Ben and Raphaella Hur. *Every Man a King: The Social and Political Thought of Ze'ev Jabotinsky*. Tel Aviv: Dvir 1988 (in Hebrew, *Kol Yachid Hu Melech*).

Bourdieu, Pierre. 'The Sentiment of Honor in Kabyle Society.' *Honor and Shame: The Values of Mediterranean Society*. Peristiany, J. G., ed. Chicago: Chicago University Press 1966.

Boyarin, Daniel. 'Colonial Drag: Zionism, Gender, and Mimicry.' 11 *Theory and Criticism – An Israeli Forum* 123 (1997) (in Hebrew, 'Neshef haMasechot haKolonialy').

Campbell, J.K. 'Honor and the Devil.' *Honor and Shame: The Values of Mediterranean Society*. Peristiany, J. G., ed. Chicago: Chicago University Press 1966.

Don-Yehiya, Eliezer. 'Judaism and Statism in Ben-Gurion's Thought and Politics.' 14 *Zionism – Studies in the History of the Zionist Movement and of the Jewish Community in Palestine* 51 (1989).

Eylon, Amos. *Herzl*. Tel Aviv: Am Oved 1976 (in Hebrew).

Fletcher, George P. 'Human Dignity as a Constitutional Value.' 22 *University of Western Ontario Law Review* 171 (1984).

Frevert, Ute. *Men of Honor: A Social and Cultural History of the Duel*. Oxford: Polity Press 1995.

Gewirth, Alan. 'Human Dignity as the Basis of Rights,' *The Constitution of Rights*. Meyer, Michael J. and W.A. Paret, eds. New York: Cornell University Press 1992.

Gluzman, Michael. 'Longing for Heterosexuality: Zionism and Sexuality in Herzl's *Altneuland*.' 11 *Theory and Criticism—An Israeli Forum* 145 (1997) (in Hebrew, 'ha-Kmiha le-Hetrosexualiut').

Herzl, Theodor. *Books of the Days*. Tel Aviv: Mizpeh 1939 (in Hebrew, *Sifrey ha-Yamim*).

Herzl, Theodor. *Herzl's Writings in Ten Volumes*. Jerusalem: ha-Sifriya ha-Tzionit 1960 (in Hebrew, *Kitvey Herzl be-Asara Krahim*).

Herzfeld, Michael. 'Honor and Shame: Problems in the Comparative Analysis of Moral Systems.' 15 *Man* 339 (1980).

Jabotinsky, Ze'ev. 'My Life.' *Autobiographical Writings*. Jerusalem: Ari Jabotinsky Publishing 1958 (in Hebrew, 'Sipur Yamay').

Jabotinsky, Ze'ev. *Samson*. Tel Aviv: Tarmil 1982 (in Hebrew).

Kamir, Orit. 'The Declaration of the Israel's Independence Has Two Faces: The Strange Case of the Zionist Declaration and the Democratic Declaration.' 23 *Iyunei Mishpat* 473 (2000) (in Hebrew, 'laMegila Yesh Shtei Panim: Sipuran ha-Muzar Shel ha-Hachraza haZionit ve-haHachraza haDemokratit').

Keren, Michael. *Ben Gurion and the Intellectuals*. Jerusalem: Ben Gurion University Press 1988 (in Hebrew, *Ben Gurion ve-haIntellectualim*).

Koifman, Yehezkel. *Diaspora and Foreign Land: An Historical Sociological Study on the Destiny of the Jewish People from Antiquity to this Day*. Tel Aviv: Dvir 1971 (in Hebrew, *Gola ve-Nechar: Mechkar Histori Sotziologi be-She'elat Goralo Shel Am Yisrael Miymei Kedem ve-'Ad haZman haZe*).

Kornberg, Jacques. *Theodor Herzl: From Assimilation to Zionism*. Bloomington: Indiana University Press 1993.

Kretzmer, David. 'Human Dignity in Israeli Jurisprudence.' In this volume.

Lahav, Pnina. 'Israel's Supreme Court: The Formative Decade (1948-1955).' 14 *Iyunei Mishpat* 492 (1989) (in Hebrew, 'haOz ve-haMisra: Beit haMishpat haElion baAsor haRishon le-Kiyumo").

Levy, Ya'acov. *Oxford English-Hebrew, Hebrew-English Dictionary*. Jerusalem: Kernerman-Lonnie Kahn 1997.

Mautner, Menahem. *The Decline of Formalism and Rise of Values in Israel's Legal System*. Tel Aviv: Ma'agalei Da'at 1993 (in Hebrew, *Yeridat haFormalism ve-Aliat haArachim baMishpat haYisraeli*).

Miller, William Ian. *Humiliation: And Other Essays on Honor, Social Discomfort and Violence*. Ithaca: Cornell University Press 1993.

Mosse, George L. 'Max Nordau, Liberalism and the New Jew.' 27 *Journal of Contemporary History* 565 (1992).

Ofir, Adi. 'The Declaration of Independence: A User's Manual.' *The Declaration of State: 21 Tablets.* Tartakover, D., ed. Tel Aviv: Modan 65 (1988) (in Hebrew, 'Megilat haAzmaut: Hora'ot Shimush').

Peristiany, J. G., ed. *Honor and Shame: The Values of Mediterranean Society.* Chicago: Chicago University Press 1966.

Piers, Gerhart and Milton B. Singer. *Shame and Guilt: A Psychoanalytic and Cultural Study.* New York: Norton 1971.

Pitt-Rivers, Julian. 'Honor and Social Status.' *Honor and Shame: The Values of Mediterranean Society.* Peristiany, J. G., ed. Chicago: Chicago University Press 1966.

Pitt-Rivers, Julian. *The Fate of Shechem or the Politics of Sex: Essays in the Anthropology of the Mediterranean.* Cambridge: Cambridge University Press 1977.

Raz-Krakotzkin, Amnon. 'Exile Within Sovereignty: Towards a Critique of the "Negation Of Exile" in Israeli Culture.' 4 *Theory and Criticism – An Israeli Forum* 23 (1993) (in Hebrew, 'Galut be-Ribonut: Likrat Bikoret Shlilat ha-Galut ba-Tarbut ha-Yisraelit').

Schachter, O. 'Editorial Comment—Human Dignity as a Normative Concept.' 77 *American Journal of International Law* 848 (1983).

Segev, Tom. *The Seventh Million: The Israelis and the Holocaust.* Jerusalem: Keter 1991 (in Hebrew, *ha-Million ha-Shvi'i: ha-Ysraelim ve-ha-Shoa*).

Shachar, Yoram. 'Criminal Procedure.' *Yearbook of Israeli Law 1992-3.* Rozen-Zvi, Ariel, ed. Tel Aviv: Lishkat Orchei ha-Din 1993 (in Hebrew, 'Seder-Din Plili').

Shapira, Anita. *Land and Power.* Tel Aviv: Am Oved 1992 (in Hebrew, *Herev ha-Yona: ha-Zionut ve-ha-Koach* 1881-1948).

Shapira, Anita. 'Ben-Gurion and the Bible: The Making of an Historical Narrative?' 14 Alpaim, 207 (1997).

Sternhall, Ze'ev. *Nation-Building or a New Society? The Zionist Movement (1904 - 1940) and the Origins of Israel.* Tel Aviv: Am Oved 1995 (in Hebrew, *Binyan Uma o Tikkun Hevra?*).

Tzahor, Ze'ev. 'Ben-Gurion as Creator of Myth.' in *Myth and Memory: The Metamorphoses of Israeli Consciousness.* Ohana, David and Robert Weistrich eds., Jerusalem: Ha-Kibbutz Ha-Meuhad and Van Leer 1997 (in Hebrew, 'Ben-Gurion ke-Meatzev Mitos').

Zertal, Idith. 'The Sacrifice and the Sanctified: The Construction of a National Martyrology.' 48 *Zmanim – An Historical Quarterly*, 26 (1994) (in Hebrew, 'Ha-Meonim ve-ha-Kdoshim: Kinumah shel Martyrologia Leumit').

Zipperstein, Steven J. 'Between Tribalism and Utopia: Ahad Ha'am and the Making of Jewish Cultural Politics,' 13 *Modern Judaism* 231 (1993).

HONOR, DIGNITY, AND THE FRAMING OF MULTICULTURALIST VALUES
David N. Weisstub

At the end of this millennium, the globalization and interdependency of social and economic structures have perplexed us with respect to how to protect and build a society based upon a core of democratically-minded values. Dignity, perhaps more than any other concept, has emerged as a convergence point for what is perceived to be a non-ideological humanistic point of departure towards a social liberal ideal. This is so because the assumption seems to be instinctively made that human dignity at once represents the individualistic morality brought on by the Enlightenment, which defers to the notions of autonomy and respect for persons, while attending to a social dimension of humanity where persons are given a special status of protection that goes to the heart of what it means to be a person or indeed to be a human with all that it comports. In that sense, human dignity appears to stand as an absolute value, being the actualization of certain basic political and moral values such as liberty, self-determination, and equality, while being the paramount value, which in its inalienability and inviolability is at the source of an extended value system that has the capacity to project an assembly of constitutional values.

This tall mandate and description are a challenge and a threat. For in order that dignity be defended as the regal value *par excellence*, we must be able to discern in it a clarity in its moral value from which we could produce markers for a morally justifiable political and legal vision, as well as a logical trajectory through which we should be able to organize a hierarchy of decisions.

Historically, human dignity was a value of intrinsic worth, but arguably its affinity to aristocratic attributes was at odds with a more liberal or subjectivist inward-turning definition. Indeed, because of these origins, it may be that our understanding of dignity still carries with it a confusing element insofar as—in our Western cultures—we naturally associate the concept of dignity with the perceived dignified behavior of social style or high position. In that sense, at least until recently, dignity may well have had more to do with mores than with morals.

Why then has dignity become so central to our moral-liberal thinking at the end of this century? It is incontestable that the Western preoccupation with dignity was accelerated, borne out of the degrading experiences of the Holocaust that shocked democratic observers who had come to the naive conclusion that enlightened values were our best protection against evil. In the post-war years and in view of widespread cynicism with regard to transcendental metaphysical assertions about absolute values, democrats, in order to avoid the punishing consequences of radical relativism, turned to human dignity as the over-arching protector-value. It is no accident therefore, that the German constitutional system fashioned human dignity as the basic and absolute value of the entire constitutional structure. The human dignity-value asserts that no secondary characteristic can ever be put in a position to trump its universalism, and implicitly, it requires of its constitutional membership to shadow all other values in this light.[1] No other value in the German constitutional system is stated as such an absolute, and the pragmatic dispositions of judges to balance and proportionalize values are boldly checked by this absolutist pronouncement. The value is stated so strongly that human dignity is not only postulated as a precondition for the realization of other values, but also as an illuminating value that should, by its force, intrude into all relevant value conflicts that engage the question of humanity or personhood.

In this way, human dignity is proclaimed a value that may never leave the person, even in situations of grave depreciation or degradation. This idealized *cri du coeur* implies in some way that no human act has the power or ability to take away the divine spark in persons, and carries with it a kind of theological overtone which perhaps has a secondary gain of alleviating our guilt with respect to the suffering of the victims in question. To state human dignity as an inviolable absolute in some way elevates our discussion to a higher level, away from victims to an abstract realm of descriptive certitude. In this realm, human dignity can never be taken away, but the attempt to do so only acknowledged.

The difficulty with an absolutist vision is that it carries the definitional closed circle of never agreeing to acknowledge the human experience of dignity being taken away or compromised. In this way, human dignity is never permitted to enter the real world. Personhood is relegated to a paradise or purity where human beings cannot be hurt because they have been angelically defined. The worth of such a concept may, under scrutiny, be unfortunately limited or too precious for any long-term meaning in the conflictual constitutional systems that we currently encounter. It is in fact notorious that some of the worst constitutional orders have the finest constitutional values.

---

[1] The *Grundgesetz* of the Federal Republic of German (Basic Law) of May 23, 1949, stipulates in its article 1: (1) 'The dignity of man is inviolable. To respect and protect it shall be the duty of all public authority;' (2) The German people therefore uphold human rights as inviolable and inalienable and as the basis of every community, of peace and justice in the world.

What we have suggested here is that we should be slow to respect ultimate value statements unless they can be tracked within systems in such a way that we can prove to ourselves that we have a model around which to organize our constitutional thinking, where the core concept is the *sine qua non* of human respect and protection of vulnerability. There is no question, given the trauma that the German cultural elite suffered in the disturbing acquiescence of key professions such as Medicine and Law to the Nazi horrors, that human dignity has been symbolized to such an extent in the German context that it has been a blockade against the historical resurgence of Fascist denigration of despised minorities and/or imperfect members of society. [2]

However it must be seen that other social orders which have had very different historical experiences may relate to the concept very differently, and in so doing expose the extent to which what is interesting about human dignity is how it colours differently, depending upon the social needs in question. Its centrality and attractiveness for global ethics may be, thereby, its malleability rather than the tightness of its logic. Dignity, within a colonial or racist society, seen by pacific observers as noble and virtuous in the guise of a Ghandi or a Martin Luther King, may equally be shaped in favor of the leadership behind a violent uprising, where an enslaved or tortured population might only see its dignity through a series of violent acts against the oppressors.[3]

Some of our definitions of dignified behaviour may seem vacillating and self-serving. In societies where persons see human dignity as a Christian-type virtue, where forgiveness and love are confirmed values, passive resistance will be fully celebrated.[4] However, if such virtues could be seen as aping the attributes of a *noblesse* rather than redeeming the degradation of loved ones through seizing of power realized only through violent acts, it is not clear that there is an inner logic in the concept of human dignity, a logic capable of defying the latter as a legitimate definition, either with respect to the core of the value or the course of action to be taken. [5]

---

[2] See M. Kater, *Doctors Under Hitler* (University of North Carolina Press, Chapel Hill 1989); B. Muller-Hill, *Murderous Science: Elimination by Scientific Selection of Jews, Gypsies and Others, Germany 1933-1945* (Oxford University Press, Toronto 1988); and R. Proctor, *Racial Hygiene: Medicine under the Nazis* (Harvard University Press, Cambridge, MA 1988.)

[3] A compelling psychological rationale is expressed in the works of Franz Fanon, esp. *Les damnés de la terre* (Maspero, Paris 1961).

[4] See Michael J. Meyer, "Dignity, Death and Modern Virtue", *in American Philosophical Quarterly*, vol. XXXII, no. 1 (January 1995), p. 51. It is Meyer's view that dignity should be considered as the key modern virtue.

[5] 'Moralists of various sorts use the terms "human dignity" and "human worth" often, but frequently these words have little more than rhetorical effect, even among professional philosophers. The fact is that we have a fairly vague concept of human worth and dignity, though there is a core that is instructive' G. W. Harris, *Dignity and Vulnerability* (University of California Press, Berkeley 1997). See also, P.R.S. Johnson, 'An Analysis of "Dignity,"' in *Theoretical Medicine and Bioethics 19*

Societies which have a liberal flavor or which have arisen from or committed in principle to the rule of law in a set of common laws or constitutional values of a well-tried historical nature, and in which the role of human dignity plays a preponderant part, would presumably have less invested in the process of prestige predication than would fascistic or colonial orders. Rather than fixating upon human dignity as the dogmatic-penumbrating value, a well-integrated liberal environment might concentrate the role and function of human dignity more naturally in specific discussions of loss of autonomy, such as in the case of death and dying, or the treatment of vulnerable populations such as the elderly and the mentally incapacitated. Some legal or political liberal systems, despite their apparent pragmatism, in fact may carry with them a load of concepts and historical precedent which actually do the work of the human dignity concept, diffused throughout an elaborate process of balancing means and relationships, and where the aim of the project is to maximize the protection of human subjects while attending to legitimate collective interests.

In the range of social models that have included traumatized genocidal societies, revolutionary emancipatory communities, and loosely-described liberal-democratic social orders, the purpose and function of human dignity has varied contours. So much so, that the tightness, or need for abstraction giving rise to an absolutist statement of human dignity may be important as a signifier of an historical need rather than as a compelling philosophical statement about the universalism of the claims or projections about human dignity posited as an absolute. To say this in no way throws into question the rhetorical value or even the constitutional attractiveness of sharing human dignity in the global environment as the preferred value standing at the helm of an international democratic order. However, to acknowledge human dignity as the ultimate value may be, as we have suggested, giving it the function of a social ideal rather than that of a value having any serious directive utility. Furthermore, if no theological value is attributed, namely that dignity, as the core of personhood, is not attached to the image of God in Creation, the ontological origin of the concept remains as puzzling as giving any other highly-valued concept such as privacy a specific place in the hierarchy of values. This dilemma becomes apparent when other values have to be interpreted according to exact terms.[6]

(1998), 339-340, in which the author states: 'Although many use the word dignity, one should not assume the word carries a particular intention. Dignity per se has no overarching descriptive meaning, and cannot be used alone as a capable tool for prescriptive uses. Each individual might have his or her own definition or at least sense of the word, but there is no consensus.'

[6] This line of thinking is more fully developed in D.N. Weisstub, 'La lettre des principes et l'esprit des lois; le problème de l'application dans la jurisprudence analytique' in *La vie des normes et l'esprit des lois,* Lukas K. Sosoe, ed. (Harmattan, Paris-Montreal 1998).

I. Analytical Jurisprudence

The treatment of human dignity in constitutional systems can be best critiqued as part of a wider framework of how we attempt to manage constitutional principles.

It is in the nature of all constitutional decision-making structures in Western society to have attempted, since the earliest inception of legal narrative, to locate the values of a given legal order in an ultimate source, whether it was in the pronouncement of the deity or in higher order values as the embodiment of pure or ultimate reason.[7] In attempts to wed revelation to reason, natural law thinkers have, at various points in Western legal philosophy, singled out certain values as containing within them an authoritative governing force. Both theological and secular traditions of natural law or natural rights thinking have made such attempts, although there has been limited acceptance of these values in their applied form among highly evolved constitutional orders. At best, among different legal communities, we can speak about shared values but not about the certitude of unified absolutes or indeed, any absolute at all.

However, if there were any value that could claim this attribution in our *fin de siècle* thinking, it would have to be human dignity. Despite even an avowed international idealization, there is little or no evidence to suggest what applications are any better or clearer than the political will of a liberal democratic order and its expanding antennae, to protect vulnerable members of a population. Human Dignity as an ideal to be attained is put to the test in a multitude of contexts, ranging from the political arena, where the rights and entitlements of minorities are at issue, to a myriad of examples found in the health care system where vulnerable populations, whether they be children, the elderly, or institutionalized patients, wish to see their dignity protected, or for whom, due to their limits or incapacitation, there is the implied or expressed need to intervene on their behalf.[8]

Seen in this way, military or political interventions to protect minorities might not in any meaningful sense depend on the precise vocabulary of human dignity but may simply be representative of our commitment, acknowledged by many diverse systems of beliefs and attitudes, that humiliation of

---

[7] One can argue that there is an evolutionary frame within Western law to which constitutional values have been attached. See J.C. Smith and D. N. Weisstub, 'The Evolution of Western Legal Consciousness' in *International Journal of Law and Psychiatry*, II, 2 (1980), and more generally, *The Western Idea of Law* (Butterworths, Toronto-London 1981).

[8] Value models in relation to the dignitary protection of vulnerable populations in research ethics are explored in D. N. Weisstub, 'The Ethical Parameters of Experimentation' in D.N. Weisstub, ed., *Research on Human Subjects: Ethics, Law and Social Policy* (Elsevier Science, Oxford 1998).

vulnerable persons is unacceptable, either for theological or pragmatic reasons, or both.[9]

II. Dignity, Rules and Values

What is interesting about contemporary analytical-jurisprudential thinking, is that a great deal of attention has been given to situate constitutional decision-making above and beyond what is perceived to be the mechanistic application of rules, even of a moral nature, insofar as rules have been perceived to operate at a lowly level of bureaucratic or regulatory application.[10] Many rules in the legal system, which could even be termed 'respect' rules, are seen as matters which are addressed with limited discretion, and which somehow lead us to believe that too much attachment to rules un-connects us from contemplation of the values upon which presumably rules are made and the process, in more general terms, justified. Political analysis and custom have even come to be appreciated as more interesting avenues of inquiry in what really matters in the construction of morally based laws. This perspective—found in analytical jurisprudence—has been embellished by the critical legal studies movement.

The pursuit of human dignity as the ultimate governing principle of a legal order is based upon the profound disquiet endemic to pragmatic societies who, in their discomfort with positivistic science, have turned toward value analysis. This avenue has been frustrated however by the inability of legal philosophers to analyze fundamental values as absolutes, given the modernistic rejection of ontological certitude, and the cynicism attendant to it, that it is possible to establish a prioritization of values. The relativism that has lain at the heart of North American jurisprudence since the rapid evolution of American Legal Realism since the 1930's has never been resolved, except insofar as American analytical jurisprudence has utilized the American constitutional value system as the receptacle from which to draw important references about core values in a democratic liberal state.[11] Because this attempt to fashion principles has been superimposed by critical theory (whether it be economic, psycho-analytical, empirical/methodological or feminist), analytical jurisprudence, except for constitutional value-analysis, has never been able to achieve, or justify, the core values of our constitutional system.

---

[9] See R. Macklin & S. Sherwin, 'Experimenting on Human Subjects: Philosophical Perspectives' 25 (3) *Case Western Law Review* 434 (1975), pp. 457-458.

[10] See R. Dworkin, *Taking Rights Seriously* (Duckworth, London 1977) and *A Matter of Principle* (Harvard University Press, Cambridge, MA 1985).

[11] In this regard, it is worth noting that the pinnacle value in the Neo-Realist writings of Harold Lasswell and Myers McDougal is human dignity.

III. Constitutionalism

Albeit ambiguous, dignity is a signaling term that goes to the heart of what constitutes the quality of humanness. Human dignity has come to be the value of first and last resort, the place where morally responsible politicians and members of the judiciary have grounded their interventions on behalf of vulnerable populations. In fact, the crux of where we stand on the issue of human dignity as the universal under which we prevent evil to come to the unarmed or disarmed members of our social communities, is put to the test when we are called upon to pass laws and administer justice with the optimum value of maximizing human dignity. In this perspective, human dignity becomes the stated end-goal of all our respective instruments of social justice. However, having pronounced this value as the most significant moral bonding unit of our international justice sensibility, we are still left, upon reflection, with the challenge of working through the ambiguities that lie at the root of the concept.

One of the first difficulties that we encounter is that, in the context of our very modalities of decision-making and even philosophizing, the systematic analysis of the esthetic, moral and legal dimensions of the term is often lost in the conflating of these dimensions that persist not only in the ambiguities but as well in the ambivalence that we have towards the term which are felt in both public consciousness and subjective feelings. For dignity, above all, wherever it is used explicitly in Western culture, is the object of admired behavior. In fact, rather than being a moral reference point which earmarks an intrinsic quality of soul or the object of divine creation applied to all human beings in the widest possible circumference, dignity is something which is recognized as distinctly regal and indeed even attractive to the eye.

The instinctive response, even in our contemporary culture, which has been infused with the language of human dignity in the context of respect for persons and the value of autonomy, is the most natural use of the term which persists in being how persons come across, one to the other, in social exchange. The aristocratic attributes of being 'above the crowd,' being able to control excessive sentiment or emotion, being un-needy materially (or apparently so), looking like the product of good breeding in dress and mannerisms, still persist as being the attributes to which society aspires and complements in the spirit of the term *dignitas hominis*. To say that a head of state looks dignified, or a member of the monarchy carried him or herself with great dignity still strikes a chord in the hearts of most citizens.

The struggle with the term accelerates when we begin to describe persons in involuntary states of committal, the mentally and medically incapacitated, minorities and the under-classes, as dignified. Of course, one's 'liberal' instinct is to avow the human dignity of all these groups as a moral given. However, this flies in the face of popular use, indicating why it is so difficult for us to advance the term unencumbered by its problematic past. Indeed, the confusions may be so endemic, that apart from being an ideal statement of contemporary virtue, it may even be a term of limited use for moral protection, apart from more precise values like equality and autonomy, with which it must be affiliated in order to give it concrete meaning.

Primo Levi, noted for his disciplined psychological perceptions on the experience of inmate survival in Auschwitz, sadly observed that he and the others condemned not only lost their innocence there, but also their dignity. Our quick retort that no dignity was lost and our insistence that the tortured, the gassed and the insane found there carried their dignity in that hell right to their collective numbered but un-named graves would, it is feared, be immoral arrogance on the part of those who were not there to provide comfort either to those who perished or survived. Rather, true humility would be to find out how human dignity, in those circumstances, was regained against overwhelming odds. Perhaps at that point, the term utilized should be humanity, rather than dignity. The most telling examples of human denigration in this century have occurred where admired elites, highly educated and cultured and, in the classical Roman sense, the most dignified members of historical communities in the West, had participated in and led the profound diminution of other human beings, robbing them of their dignity in all senses which are understood to this day in our public consciousness as being relevant to dignified human behavior. At a lower level of evil, but still demonstrable in the impact on human behavior, institutions under the direction of professional elites, schools, prisons, hospitals, and other places of incarceration or closed environments, the techniques of demeaning of others through the taking of dignity is clearly appreciated.

The evidence of interventions that reduce the objects of our torment to behave in a less than dignified manner should prevail upon us that it is as possible to take away human dignity, as it is possible to give it. It is a truism, therefore, that the wealthy and the powerful appear to have more dignity than those who do not share in their appearances. How to associate our moral vision of dignity with its esthetic dimension is, of course, the test of whether or not dignity has evolved as a concept, or is just an idealized term that hides what we do not wish to express in less celebrated language. The social structure of dignity imaging is relevant to both ordinary language usage and perceptions about how we relate to it as an aspirant value. What we think of as dignified has a great deal to do with how we identify with any given social hierarchy. Acting in an undignified manner may be a signal about the rejection of certain establishment or power images.

States of mind, in terms of identification with the over-class or aggressors, majority as opposed to minority membership in any given community, or gender-related emotions, may all come into play in the stylistics of dignity. Many of the exchanges that occur in society about dignity can be referred back to states of mind. We may indeed conclude in certain circumstances, that because X has behaved in an undignified manner, he or she is deserving of less respect or human approbation. But insofar as dignity is frequently the reflection of a placing within the social hierarchy, it rather begs the question to locate individuals in any human dignity trajectory that is socially specified. The difficulty remains that any a-social definition or referent takes the term to a level of abstraction where it is defeated on the grounds of vagueness.

In the legal sphere, dignity has been entered as a term to breathe life into the heart of constitutional liberalism, which has been the mainstay of a post-war moral/legal articulation of values. Constitutional experts, where there are entrenched rights, have become the modern philosophers of values for their societies. This is so because constitutional law is 'high-profile' and is the public forum where the most contentious value issues are given full airing. Here, we may see citizens debating the rights to die and to live, definitions of the family and its attendant obligations of reproduction, and the bases upon which citizens can make demands for state benefits, even in the context of fiscal restraints and limited resources. [12] In constitutional law, basic freedoms for democratic behavior are conceived and elaborated upon in our societies that have dismissed religion as the source for infusing moral content into the law.

Constitutionalism has taken up the space of the clarifier of fundamental values. The dichotomization between entrenched or fundamental rights and more concrete sets of common law rules lies at the heart of, for example, American moral-constitutional authority. It has been an essential characteristic of American legal liberalism in the twentieth century to downplay both the efficaciousness and moral integrity of taking the historical common law direction of covering cases through existing rules within the system. Over time, the common law, however, has always allowed for the creation, in the light of existing jurisprudence, of new precedents by the process of legal analogy, and the dictates of generalizable or broad rules governed by the legislative process that remains paramount. In contrast, the American constitutional ethos has been to expand the discretionary force of judges by the mandates of higher principles, accepting the belief that it is only through such principles that the integrity of the system can be squarely lodged.

One of the testing grounds for the constitutionality of human dignity has been the privacy value in American constitutional law which has operated as a centralizing principle for autonomy and respect for persons, which in their essence represent the core of human dignity expressed as an ultimate value for constitutional order. Privacy, in American constitutional law, has been a fashionable principle since the 1960's and has covered important matters of personal and political liberty. It has also dealt with many contentious issues ranging from birth control and abortion to state rights, sexual preferences and rights within the welfare state. Dealing with privacy as a centralizing right is an interesting inquiry insofar as it, like human dignity, functions in the American constitutional system as a driving force which obfuscates any clear understanding about its legal ontology, given the fact that we are never certain

---

[12] Laurence H. Tribe, *The Clash of Absolutes* (Norton, New York 1991).

of precisely how it operates as a reference point or directs the content of our decision-making.[13]

If privacy is a so-called fundamental value or absolute, how can it then serve as the pre-condition for the fulfillment of certain basic values familiar to our proper moral functioning as a society? What meaning is it to say that privacy is a base value for certain well-established other values that are central to our system? Is privacy in reality a vehicle to understanding the pragmatic process of balancing the power rights of certain groups over and against others? Finally, should privacy be best understood as an interest, a need, or a fundamental value? Is it the case that, as a stated base-value, the same ambiguities apply to human dignity as to privacy?

IV. Dignity as a Governing Principle and Constitutional Adjudication

Among constitutional adjudicators, we may find literalists, fundamentalists, and pragmatists, all of who lay some claim to having the right model of using constitutional values for purposes of deciding major social conflicts. Constitutional literalists, by definition, do not search the origins of the enterprise beyond the moment of constitutional creation. Here, frozen in time, a text is delineated which becomes the basis for interpretation. For the judge, no application is possible without interpretation. The defining of the constitutional circle, however, is the key issue—what may be permitted to enter the dialogue, and wherein lie the limits of reference in working out a value-base for adjudication. The literalists either work according to references of plain and simple meaning or wed themselves to an historical frame where the meaning of the period and the values contained within the mindset of the founders or framers of the constitution dictate the legitimate boundaries for application. By nature, the fundamentalists weave the web more broadly and take themselves to theories about values which connect to notions about reason and justification found either in philosophy, the Judeo-Christian tradition, or other periods of history (in particular, the Enlightenment).

The overwhelming number of constitutionalists in the Anglo-Saxon framework lures us into a process of decision-making where, according to some organizing principles of higher-ranking values (namely those designated in the constitution itself), there is the omnipresent idea that the constitution has within it the capacity to direct or guide us to a correct decision. The premise is that there is an inherent set of truths in the constitutional document that cannot be contested by reason, but nonetheless is subject to the balancing of interests in the real context of social conflict. These values are justifiably moderated in the light of social, political and economic pressures. This form of soft pragmatism pervades most constitutional decision-making at the end of the twentieth century.

---

[13] The tension between common law adjudication and the constitutional re-ordering of values is explored in D.N. Weisstub and C.C. Gotlieb, *The Nature of Privacy*. (Canadian Federal Department of Communications 1973)

Some legal theorists are wont to profess that principles in law are vested with neutrality or carry with them clear and precise dictates which can be weighed and thereafter applied as being not only meaningful, but afford us the criteria for making true or precise conclusions which should not be subjected to extra-legal considerations such as political or economic factors. In this sense, these theorists choose to treat constitutional principles as ends in themselves and will not take into account consequentialist arguments. In this respect, such constitutional pure-theorists share with Kantians the ideal of veering towards a notion of constitutional universalism. In reality, very few theorists or judges share in this description of a puristic state of affairs.

The pressing problem within the current constitutional framework as we know it, is that there is a widespread cynicism in the majority of Western legal systems and institutions of higher learning, about our ability to delineate where the political overlay is justified as a referent to guide judicial decisions.

V. Human Dignity as Relatively Absolute: The German Experience[14]

The moral ammunition necessary to protect human subjects was certainly present in the philosophical and legal realities that preceded the Third Reich.[15] Nevertheless, the enshrining of human dignity as an inviolable provision stands at the helm of the German Basic Law that laid the cornerstone for a new legal order in postwar Germany. In so doing, the burden of proof shifted dramatically against the state in the eyes of the public and moreover, gave the obligation to the judiciary to treat the long-standing notion of respect for persons with the 'respect' that it had deserved. The imposing super-legal principle was meant to serve as a reminder to the political and judicial systems

---

[14] The German Basic Law and the various cases mentioned in this section are cited and presented more fully by Eckert Klein in his chapter in this volume, 'Human Dignity in German Law.' For example, see: *Bayerische Verwaltungsblaetter* 28 (1982), 47, 50 [examples of violations of human dignity as recognized by the Bavarian Constitutional Court]; BverfGE 84, 90, 121 (1991) [a seizure case under Soviet occupation]; BverfGE 80, 267 (1989) [the use of an accused's diary records in his criminal proceedings]; The Mephisto case, BverfGE 30, 173 (1971) [protection of an individual's reputation after death can trump the freedom of art]; and *Verwaltungsgericht Neustadt*, decision of 21.05.1992, NVwZ 12 (1993), 98 [dwarf-throwing].

[15] In the modern legal era, the concept in law of a person was created, upon which Enlightenment natural law theory began to build, exemplified by the writings of Pufendorf. Enlightenment thinking, in legal theory, which built on the Kantian orientation in moral freedom, linked the concept of a legal subject to human universalism. Despite the influence of positivism, the 20th century thinking in Germany allowed for the articulation of fundamental justice and the socialist-minded notion of a humane existence for all to be found in the constitution of the Weimar Republic of 1919. In constitutional terms, the differentiating factor of post-war German constitutionalism was to give dignity the binding force of an absolute. However, as we have observed earlier, the precise implications of this, in substantive terms, remain unclear.

that, for the prime values stated, they could not be permitted nor indeed permit themselves to regress into the ghost of history. This concept of a basic right, human dignity, in effect a right to rights, applied to all citizens, and presumably emanated to the whole body of law. So understood, it was meant to function as a super-juridical stamp. Such a radical legal statement in the German constitutional rhetoric meant that no individual had the right to give up the right, and even though human dignity could be violated, it could not in any sense be taken away.

What does this mean? It would appear to state that human dignity is, *a priori*, never subjected to any unpredictable balancing against other interests, principles, or values, either individual or communitarian. Stated as a lofty principle, the interpretation of human dignity in German law means that persons are not to be treated as mere objects, flowing from the pre-war Kantian understanding; and in concrete terms, individuals cannot be treated contemptuously or in a degraded fashion. This is not meant to be an isolated value, as there is implicitly an obligation on the part of society to integrate individuals into a common goal of mutuality and exchange. Courts have interpreted the principle to apply to any act of discrimination, libel and slander, stigmatization, excessive punishment, etc. In other words, wherever courts could see that the human being was the subject of abuse, the first order of principle, constitutionally, could be properly invoked. It is of course morally unacceptable to question such moral sensibility, as it would be to attack human dignity as a cornerstone of the best intentions of the German constitutional statement.

As an idealized first right, human dignity is as suitable as any other to fuel the judicial system with appropriate respect for its human members. However, the question still remains whether, apart from an idealized statement which really amounts to a proclamation of respect for humanity, there is anything residing in the concept itself that clarifies its relationship to other fundamental values, gives us a logic with respect to the flow of decision-making, and really does direct the opinion of the judges on hard cases where there are conflicting values or interests between or among individuals, groups, and/or the state. Furthermore, the concept itself does not through its own intrinsic logic equip us with how to override established common law that respects special populations. It does not inform us about whether the core and substance of human dignity is best articulated through a consensus morality, if it can be located alternatively among the professional elite of the judiciary, or whether it can only be articulated over a long process through the amalgamation and interaction with other rights, values, principles and rules established nationally and trans-nationally in law and legislation.

What does human dignity add, *tout court,* apart from reasons of political necessity and idealization? Finally, if human dignity must be invoked wherever cases of abuse are extreme, then the lesson of history should be vigorously underlined that when the judiciary need such rhetoric to protect the violation of humanity, they have already become the victim of a larger apparatus.

In the actual application of human dignity law, the German courts have found it easier to deal with its absolute quality in protecting property, for example in seizure cases under Soviet occupation, than with more troubling issues such as abortion, the right to personality, issues relating to privacy, and evidentiary interests of the state in criminal cases. What is submitted here are that the German constitutional decisions are no better equipped for dealing with these matters than any liberal pragmatic court which would not have at its disposal a super-dignitary right as a basic law.

Once the collective interests are exposed, matters of proportionality implicitly present themselves as part of the resolution of conflict. It is not surprising that the German court was equally divided on the matter of whether diary records could be used of an accused murderer in his criminal proceedings. The question of where the state can encroach and where in fact the private sphere remains an absolute is precisely reflective of the confusion about whether the human dignity value applied, reigns absolutely. The absolute application, once the private sphere has been determined, can be said to apply absolutely, but this is a tautology. Put in another way, how absolute is an absolute, when it is balanced even when standing on its own head?

The line of retreat for its articulations in the German courts has been to park the human dignity value in the territory of other related values, such as the invocation of privacy or the right to personality. In so doing, the courts have been led to protect a dead individual against an unflattering portrayal of him as an actor during the Nazi regime, and the freedom of art invoked by the publisher was trumped. In looking at this piece of German constitutional history we cannot appreciate the proper legal meaning of the decision without understanding the sensibility in Germany around the treatment of 'degenerated art' by the Third Reich. It is not clear whether in hard cases, human dignity functions as a hand maiden to back up other rights, having an almost relative strength of an absolute (illogical) or whether it behaves with a clear logical finality once the proportionality test has been administered and the decision of the court has become clear. In the former instance, human dignity serves with primarily a rhetorical function while in the latter it may have the force of an *imprimatur* without properly reasoned justification.

There are some places in German constitutional law where the courts have risen to a proper moral level of responsibility in acting against the denigration of persons who, despite consensual practices, have allowed themselves to be publicly degraded for the amusement of others, such as in peep shows and dwarf-throwing. We are hard-pressed to imagine any civilized court within the Western legal world as we know it which would not be able to roundly condemn ugly practices of publicly condoned humiliation through utilizing the limitations on consensual practice provided by common law jurisprudence, other constitutional values, legislative enactments, or judicial responses to notions of public morality. In any event, the case could be made that there is no harm in bringing human dignity forward as the value to support our condemnation of clear occurrences of human denigration. In circumstances, however, where participants in a denigrating act cannot be demonstrated to be acting under any form of duress, are fully consensual, do not appear to have the handicap of low self-esteem, and can be proven to benefit from secondary gains such as improving their own standard of living or that of those close to them, then the question can be, how absolute should our prohibition be? Once again, the German record of the treatment of the handicapped is a daring lesson for all humanity and cannot be culturally separated from the impetus behind the German courts' post-war decisions.[16]

The balancing between collective and individual interests comes to the fore whenever there is a real threat to the social cohesion or physical well being of the group in question. The limits of state interference against for example the mentally-disordered population in terms of preventive detention, the culling of suspected terrorists from within the population for surveillance or interrogation, the subjugation of proven terrorists to stiff forms of interrogation and even forms of duress or torture, are all examples where the tests of the democratic limits of individualism in the name of human dignity are put under collective modalities of scrutiny. In the best of all ideal universes, it is presumed that humanity, that is the prime value of human dignity, will trump all other rights and prevail absolutely. The truth however is that the absolute of German constitutional law is no more clear than Hegel's absolute in which the dialectical progression has the danger of ending in unpredictable vocabularies of intolerance.[17]

The question of how and when we ground our fundamental values, even if we cannot philosophically protect them, becomes an interesting question for governments who are committed to a democratic political system, but who forthrightly, because of special pressures upon their political will and social reality feel compelled to admit proportionality into rights/decision-making. Naming a value an absolute may symbolically have real utility given a particular social history. However, in liberal democratic societies which do not perceive themselves to have traumatic histories with human rights violations from the inception of their political definition, nor any momentous guilt-producing periods within their histories, (although admittedly, even in liberal democracies, it is difficult to imagine the absence of some measure of trauma,

---

[16] We are not suggesting here that any decisions to the contrary should be easily taken, even in cultures where historical conditions are highly variant from the German experience. Nevertheless, it is arguably the case that there could be situations where we might wish to moderate our thinking.

[17] We must distinguish between ambiguous moral rigidity (absolutist thinking) and prohibition, that is, absolute denial or rejection of certain cases of improper behavior which violate international senses of decency, such as torture. It is enough for domestic jurisdictions to defer to such decisions taken by a large international community. This can be accomplished without declaring a series of rights as being absolute in themselves.

which would include slavery, colonialism, unjust wars, and serious mistreatments of minorities and women) proportionality, rather than relinquishing commitment on human rights protections, may be the modality of decision-making which the political culture feels most comfortable with in meting out its desserts and punishments.

VI. The Israeli Constitutional Debate

An interesting case study is the Israeli political and legal history surrounding the enshrining of human dignity as a base value. The self concept within Israel of the political majority and the judicial elite is that Israel is a democratic and liberal society connected to the history of Jewish values. The Jewish value input is regarded as humanistic and not inconsistent with the Christian conceptualization of human dignity understood as respect for humanity. Nevertheless, there is a tension that has arisen between the humanistic self concept issuing from centuries of Jewish suffering, which culminated in the Holocaust, and the presence of an Arab minority within its geographic map which regards itself as a victim of majoritarian thinking. Other groups within this society, including Christians, regard the theocratic element which governs certain aspects of social life in Israel as ethno-centric and oppressive. The Jewish/Israeli history is very distinct from the German history, and yet demands are being made that Israel should follow the German example of declaring human dignity the absolute basic value of its constitutional reform.

Given the history between German and Jewish realities, the debate currently underway about how Israel should define, in actual decisions, its human dignity provision is worthy of comment.

The Israeli judicial responses to the newly-introduced human dignitary vocabulary of the Basic Laws[18] carries with it ambiguous references for human dignitary content, such as 'the enlightened public in Israel', and references, in other decisions, to encode the "divine image in man," which further reveal different realities within the Israeli judiciary.[19]

Actual phrasing of dignity in the Israeli Law carries within it the component of honor, again a complicated feature which can be connected, psychologically and culturally, to the cumulative experience of Zionist reaction to the Holocaust, ongoing hostilities, and public concern about

---

[18] *Basic Law: Human Dignity and Liberty.* Fundamental principles. (1) 'Fundamental human rights in Israel are founded on recognition of the value of the human being, the sanctity of human life, and the principle that all persons are free; these rights shall be respected in the spirit of the principles set forth in the Declaration on the Establishment of the State of Israel.' *Purpose*: (1a) 'The purpose of this Basic Law is to protect human dignity and liberty, in order to entrench in a basic law the values of the State of Israel as a Jewish and democratic state.' *Respect for life, body and dignity* (2) 'No one's life, body or human dignity shall be violated.'(1992)

[19] See Ploni v. Almoni (1992) 48 *PD* (3), 843; See Vickselbaum v. Minister of Defence (1992) 47 *PD* (2), 827/ See State of Israel v. Goata (1992) 6 *PS* (5), p. 708.

terrorism. Human dignity in current Israeli law, albeit a value of the highest order, is supreme only insofar as it can come out on the right side of other associated rights, such as liberty, property, and privacy. From the point of view of clarity of decision making, one of the frustrating aspects, given the partiality of the Israeli Enactment of Rights which fell short of a general bill, is that judicial incentive has promoted a host of rights which were not intended by the Human Dignity Enactment.This could lead both to confusion and trivialization of an optimal role for a potentially clarified developed concept of human dignity. There is a danger, as Kretzmer[20] rightly points out, that the so-called super-right of human dignity could become washed away in a morass of tangled specificities.

What we have earlier suggested in this analysis, is that it is no better than a form of moral arrogance to assume that the human dignity right absolutely described gives a clear direction for the moral life of any given community, either in content or with respect to aspirant goals.

In a society that operates with a psychology of siege and/or fear relating to the prospect of terrorist acts, there is a *prima facie* tendency to escape into self-serving rationalizations or to shift the burden of evidence to an unjustifiably low standard directed against the suspect target group. In the Israeli example, this puts a strong moral obligation on the judiciary to exercise moderation and to assist the society at large to resist its own hyper-sensitivity or urges for revenge. Such judicial initiatives will undoubtedly contribute to the enhancing of the "human dignity value". What makes Israel instructive as a reference is that it is perceived that sensitivity and victimization can be causally related to the propagation of other injuries.

It is a legitimate question to ask where in the experience of post-50's German jurisprudence, human dignity has been applied as an absolute where it could be of real significance to a political culture either under severe ethnic stress or where the human dignity value is not stated as an absolute. In point of fact, the Law on Human Dignity, in German jurisprudence, has never been in any broad sense, applied absolutely. Despite the rhetoric, the law carries with it the same range of ambiguities that are more overtly expressed by the different components of the dignitary universe as exposed in the Israeli political and value realities. Israel as a society faces daily human confrontation relating to questions about citizensip and rights,as it struggles, with its relationship between Jewish and democratic content. The contradictions and pressures are obvious and disturbing. However it is when the stakes are high that dignity can find merit and ennoble an environment, or become degraded as a concept.

It is the public nature of the debate that is the best protection of the society against evil. When the 'balancing feature' of the debate is subdued because the philosophical world or judicial rhetoric have been made profoundly irrelevant by the political will, then the society is put to high risk with respect to its expressed constitutional value system. To conflate the Israeli

---

[20] D. Kretzmer, *Human Dignity in Israeli Jurisprudence*, in this volume.

difficulties in defining the role and function of human dignity as a core value with the sacrifice of standards that were part of the Fascist reality, however, is provocative and misleading.[21]

VII. The Intra-Psychic Dimensions of Dignity: A Paradigm

Depending upon how we define dignity, certain philosophical assumptions become part of the direction of what is relevant to a full and complete understanding of how dignity operates intra-psychically, and thereafter in its relation to a wider social circumference. If dignity is a God-given characteristic to all human beings who have the appearance of being human, even those who are incapacitated will receive, at least at the abstract level, all the benefits of human dignity owed to the species. Even in acts of charity, those whose appearance is deemed 'borderline' with respect to "human being-ness" become the recipients of an obligation that is squarely placed on the political will. However, once a definitional dignity veers away from mirroring God's image, secular options are considerably less clear in their direction. Enlightenment postulates concentrate on human capacity for reason, particularly the art of moral reasoning, and those who fall short of the mark would appear to have less claims on the system than they would in the more tightened and closed universe of religion. In either case, as our societies are not mainly governed by theological or metaphysical precepts, and Enlightenment theories have been replaced by many critical vantage points such as the politics of victimization and the emancipatory movements of minorities, the feminist critiques of 18th century theories of entitlement, the various perspectives loosely associated with anti-elitism (including Marxism), and the critical viewpoints oriented in psycho-analytical frameworks, post-modern conceptions of dignity cannot escape some process of radical redefinition.

It is insightful to attend particularly to the psychological dimension, as it is through this optic that we might begin to more fully understand and appreciate the underbelly of the dignity concept. Some commentators have rightly expressed the point that humiliation exposes the warping of the human psyche such that a normal person's response when treated in a degrading fashion is, even in circumstances where the perpetrator has disrespected the traumatic impact, a lowering of self-esteem with far-reaching human consequences for the personality and its capacity to assert itself in a comfortable and mature moral fashion. Unfortunately, the damaged personality becomes morally incapacitated; given the nature of a person who is diminished and debased. Undoubtedly instincts such as revenge and desire to reconstitute

---

[21] In this volume, it is the view expressed by Dr. Orit Kamir that the over-identification of the Zionist movement with Aryan imagery has produced an intra-psychic conflict affecting even the Israeli judiciary. The implication of this point of view is that, in such a sick reality, the value of human dignity can only find perverse forms of application.

the psyche through acts of distancing and even denigration of the opposing forces may be necessary for intra-psychic rejuvenation and for the exercise of a healthy political will.[22] In Christian theory, this perspective is rejected, but in actuality, historical patterns of social reconstitution suggest that the matter is considerably more complicated. How to adjust our political thinking to these necessities is no small order because notions of moral and psychological health may quickly come into conflict. In many instances they are clearly distinguishable and challenge our thinking about issues like forgiveness and collective responsibility for the development of a liberal/humanistic set of directions.[23] It is counter-productive to reject psychological components that give rise to individual and social needs, because whether we wish to accept it or not, these variables have the means of conditioning and influencing, even dramatically, the outcome of our private and public interactions.

Once dignity has been denied to persons, the experience of many minorities in particular, they must attend to the psychological depth of the experience. Shylock's words in *The Merchant of Venice* carry with them a biting clarity:

> To baite fish with all, if it will feede nothing else, it will feede my revenge; hee hath disgrac'd me, and hindred me halfe a million, laught at my losses, mockt at my gaines, scorned my Nation, thwarted my bargaines, cooled my friends, heated mine enemies, and whats his reason, I am a Jewe: Hath not a Jewe eyes, hath not a Jewe hands, organs, dementions, sences, affections, passions, fed with the same foode, hurt with the same weapons, subject to the same diseases, healed by the same meanes, warmed and cooled by he same Winter and Sommer as a Christian is: if you pricke us doe we not bleede, if you tickle us doe wee not laugh, if you poyson us doe wee not die, and if you wrong us shall wee not revenge, if we are like you in the rest, we will resemble you in that. If a Jewe wrong a Christian, what is his humillity, revenge? If a Christian wrong a Jewe, what should his sufferance be by Christian example, why revenge? The villanie you teach me I will execute, and it shall goe hard but I will better the instruction.[24]

Shylock's outburst tells us something about the impact of dignity-denial on the intra-psychic struggle for re-affirmation. With other relevant support systems lacking, Shylock's only retort is to hold up the limited power of material gain

---

[22] J. L. Herman, *Trauma and Recovery* (Harper/Collins, New York 1992).

[23] The difference between Jewish and Christian perspectives, victimization, and guilt is discussed in D. Thomasma and D. Weisstub, 'Forgiving and Forgetting: A Post-Holocaust Dialogue on the Possibility of Healing' *Cambridge Quarterly of Healthcare Ethics*, vol. IX (2000).

[24] William Shakespeare, *The Most Excellent Historie of The Merchant of Venice*, ed. Annabel Patterson (Harvester Press, London, etc. 1995) p. 71.

and accompanying revenge. However, it is a self-defeating battle, because as he rightly recognizes, his dignity is denied, *qua* his identity as a Jew. Ultimately, he can never get beyond the condition of the wounded animal which is not allowed, by definition, to enter into the realm of humanity. This infliction is the deepest wound that others can make upon our person, so much so that any process of incarceration and/or accompanying torture is necessarily built upon this premise. The conditioning of any group which includes transgenerational realities to feel itself socially excluded, informs us about how dignity patterns are played out in reality. Without the tracking of experiences of shame and humiliation, the imaging of dignity in a particular culture will at best be partial and distorted, and even in some cases, perverse. What victims believed in any given circumstance as dignified may relate to disturbing factors such as identification with the aggressor, spurious notions of elitist or aristocratic affect which, although perceived as noble or lacking in self-interest, are more revealing about the psychology of victimization than any objective set of values. This can be seen in descriptions of the psychology of Victorian domestics toward children or extended family members, as much as in the psychology of survival in German concentration camps. When people are humiliated, they frequently turn against each other, denying mutual self-respect, and through fear, grudgingly begin to believe in the dominant structure of values in order to be able to survive. Taking away any material viability reveals that there is a slope reaching deeper into degradation than that experienced by Shylock. Relieving persons of any identity, except for being a member of a disgraced group, and making people enfeebled physically, in most cases brings individuals to apathy and then to a living death. Such a slide represents the severe process of the dialectical interplay between the external and the internal, to the point where human dignity ceases to be a meaningful term of reference to the parties involved, and where the psychology of humiliation takes hold. Responsible analysis of those circumstances where dignity loss is the issue requires that we closely study the humiliation pattern that has been put into place.[25]

Psychological understanding is paramount to an analytically complete accounting of dignity as an applied concept. If the purpose of our understanding of dignity is to enhance the human predicament and to maximize the condition for moral judgment and mutuality of social conduct, then failure to deal with the psychological component should be seen as a dignitary violation in itself.

Shylock's perception is psychologically accurate. It addresses the cycle of inward-turning anger that is the subject of humiliation turned into a desire for revenge using whichever resources are still left available to the victim, given the structure of abuse. In the case of the Jew in Western society, as it has

---

[25] See J.C. Smith, *The Neurotic Foundations of Social Order* (New York University Press, New York and London 1990), and S.A. Luel and P. Marcus, eds., *Psychoanalytic Reflections on the Holocaust: Selected Essays* (KTAV Publishing House, New York 1984).

been with other minorities, the phenomenon relates to material superiority becoming part of a cycle of spurious dominance followed by revenge at the hands of the majority population. An interesting twist of fate occurs when the content of theology is reversed, such as in the Western example where Christians avow a passive and non-violent morality, but where there is revenge upon the Jew whose theology is perceived to be vengeful and materialistic. This interplay between abstract morality and applied abuse is, as we have stated, important to note and analyze in undertaking a psychological investigation into any pattern of humiliation. This was well articulated by Hegel's dialectical analysis of the relation between master and slave, but is more importantly revealed in the larger picture of inquisitions, torture and genocide which are now part of the twentieth century record of indignity to mankind.[26]

The telling moral limit of what Shylock has to proffer as a justification for improved treatment falls short of what one might call a dignified statement, because the psychology of his victimization already bears the result of the moral infliction which has produced his studied identity. He appeals to a moral sensibility which relates to the Jewish response to suffering *qua* animal, rather than as a future actor exchanging human benefits and charitable acts. That is, he appeals to the universality of revenge rather than to the dialectic of reciprocity and recognition, namely the dialogue of mutually-respectful parties: he is incapable of reaching the world which is dignified, in the sense that the definition of human-ness allows for real autonomy and respect to take force. Like a caged animal, he is acting for release from pain rather than for the impossible and unreachable standard for the Jew in a Christian universe, to be treated as an equal with interchangeable capacities for moral conduct.[27]

Some philosophical traditions postulate an implicit escape from attempts at psychoanalysing dignitary loss, while producing the model which is psychological in the very limited sense of addressing self-consciousness as a closed circuit. The moral aristocrat projected in the stoical personality is the individual so well integrated, that there is apparently no need for external confirmation. This flies in the face of what we know about the conditioning of all humans, from monarchs to peasants, and has an underlying premise which is often exposed in material aristocracies (that greatly outnumber philosophical ones) where dignity is self-contained at the expense of valuing the other. To be guillotined by persons who are unworthy socially, morally, and intellectually, produces the kind of snobbery that made it possible for many to die a dignified death during the *Règne de la terreur*.

Shylock's identity is a-dialogical, moving naturally from the torment of intra-psychic conflict into an archetypal self-definition of the Jew as

---

[26] Hegel, *Phenomenology of Spirit*, trans. A.V. Miller. (Oxford University Press, Oxford 1991).

[27] Shylock's statement is taken here as a paradigmatic artifact. Shakespeare's interpretive mindset and the role of the Jew in Elizabethan England, however relevant, is not part of this discussion.

determined and understood by external forces. In this sense, it is irrelevant what a Jew might feel at the truly personal level except to suffer the indignity of the archetypal definition unfolded in an overly-determined fashion. The compensation for being despised is to survive through material gains, but this is a self-defeating path because the results are anticipated in advance. There is no freedom, even if intelligence fuels action, where one's *liberté intrinsèque* has been ghettoized. In ethical terms, the universe is an I-We[28] conflation where the victim's identity, response and revenge are all interconnected to a collective over-identification with the experience of shame and humiliation. As history is reality, we must take care in looking at any subjugated or minority community in view of its psychological need for being 'born again' in the experience of freedom and equality. Without such a psychic exemplar out of which to build a political footing, the likelihood of an integrated or balanced society emerging where the diverse and distinct parts are reunited in the general will of citizen equality will have little chance of reaching its objective. The deep problem facing cultures that have an ethnic history of being disgraced is to ensure that the ethical evolution is psychologically credible while denying to the group the right to subjugate or violate others. This objective, however, may regrettably be seen as facile insofar as there are deep ethnic conflicts which historically remain even when this move is made.

VIII. Honor and Dignity

The taking-on of honor as a dimensional pre-condition for achieving distinct cultural recognition may be the ground upon which dignity must be placed. This is not honor in the sense of aristocratic stature, nor is it *les préférences* that Rousseau rebuffed,[29] but rather the honor of being made to feel human after the experience of humiliation. It might be argued that to use honor in this way has a special modern meaning, insofar as according to many commentators, dignity has replaced honor for this purpose. But that would mean not admitting into the discussion the special need to be honored as a baseline which is a perceived need and want of humiliated populations. In this sense, the psychological need for honor has no time; it is neither feudal nor a child of the Enlightenment, nor modern in the sense in which persons locate their own self-worth through principles like equality or a notion of the authentic self.[30] It is more deeply felt as the human need to be valued and precedes modern concepts of dignity, which in any event may have less

---

[28] This *Weltanschauung* is dialectically contrasted with or by the I-Thou, or dialogical dimension.
[29] 'La nature de l'honneur est de demander des Préférences et des distinctions...' Montesquieu, *De l'esprit des lois*, Book 3, Ch. 7. Rousseau's critique is found in the *Discours sur l'origine et l'inégalité parmi les hommes*.
[30] See C. Taylor, *The Malaise of Modernity* (Anansi Press, Concord, Ont. 1991) and *The Sources of the Self: The Making of the Modern Identity* (Harvard University Press, Cambridge, MA 1989).

meaning to the populations it is meant to address than the more timeless concept of honor. It is possible that the oppressed, the handicapped and the vulnerable would rather choose to feel honored and valued as members either equal or specially regarded because of their compensatory needs, than be lifted to the abstract language of human dignity which, as a universal, may have greater difficulty in reaching the depths of their highly personal tribulations. We can imagine religious communities or secular humanist ones where honoring certain members in non-condescending ways, would, from the point of view of respect, be superior as a humane point of reference than dignity, and might be another way of avoiding harm rather than giving benefits. When dignity is taken away from a rights vocabulary and is turned into a language of charity and benevolence, perhaps it should be better understood as approximating the concept of honor, broadly appreciated.

Both dignity and honor in their most positive forms can be connected to a dialogic process of recognizing the 'other'. Yet the difficulty with any community honoring itself is that it appears to create a framework for valuing distinctness over and against the 'other,' realizing the promise of a given culture and attending to its history and mores. This can, in some significant ways, be at odds with liberal proceduralism, the democratic vision associated with recent decades of American post-war constitutional protections.

The question is how to balance diversity and protection. What we are slow to reveal however, is that the recognition of diversity is so deep that it will, regardless of our interest in and our fear of homogeneity or of radical political equality, never stem the tide of human energy that pulls identity back into its familial and communal roots. What we can reasonably ask of communities, given their specifications, is a negotiable which we should not be permitted to answer through abstraction. What would truly be the justified terms of reconciliation or forgiveness with the outer community, that we must be prepared to ask—as the 'outer community'—from traumatized and wounded populations? Unless we assist these populations in their political turmoil by substantial endeavors at our own human cost, we will continue to ask of them results which they have no intention of giving. Our failures in this regard should give us no sense of moral superiority. Whether the stressed environments are Ireland, Israel, Yugoslavia or Rwanda, we have the moral obligation to appreciate the psychological dynamics at play before imposing moral absolutes which have never been achieved, either in our international community to any significant degree, nor in national communities which have espoused major legal-moral concepts of justice and the rule of law, such as Ancient Rome and Germany.

IX. The Socio-Legal Dialectic

Mutuality, regardless of whether there is a power imbalance, replaces the hierarchical thinking familiar to status-oriented societies that are often regarded as pre-modern. What earmarks the modern world in law is the model of autonomous-acting individuals who are able to contract relations amongst themselves. However, so many relations in life, emotional, political and commercial, have to address issues of difference, incapacity, power, wealth, and even emotional maturity, and appropriate ethics of recognition must proceed beyond a contractualist perspective. Recognition brings us to notions relating to the authenticity or difference of the other party, or even further, to the possibility of a covenental relation, where differences of power are recognized, but obligations and duty flow morally from the historic, creational or unique moral commitments that are part of the relationship in question, whether it be between God and persons, or professionals and their patients or clients.[31]

In the political sphere, Charles Taylor is sympathetic to the idea that modern views of dignity have systematically escaped from the trappings of honor-based political thinking which objectified and inferiorized the poor, minorities, and all vulnerable parties in status systems (such as the feudal one), where to know one's place was to recount specific moral and political narratives.[32] Taylor's view of dignity and its relationship to political reality is an attractive accounting of the mutual support that arguably comes in any mature system of relations, where persons can sympathetically accept differences. Alas, in the history of modern hospitals, mental asylums, and other such establishments, the right to difference or weakness has been overpoweringly diminished by the hierarchical nature of closed institutions and professional elites. Taylor is right in seeking the ground of authenticity of self and mutuality as the cornerstones of a productive ethics in politics, as well as, we can assume, for a reflective individual existence.

In my view, a respectful approach to otherness is without question the correct ethic, in the context of both individual relations and political systems. Nonetheless, the distinction drawn between dignity and honor is less helpful than it may appear at the outset. Honor, in its pre-modern incarnation, was undoubtedly shackled by pomp and accompanying derision towards those who, being lower in the pecking order, were left only with the right to applaud and remain solely with their limited self-respecting identity. However, as ancient as the biblical use of the word *kavod,* which was connected to one of the earliest precepts of recognition, namely, the respect of parents ('honor thy father and thy mother'), is the notion of honor as a sustaining force of mutuality. This notion is of greater support to us than *dignitas,* which in its historical role was linked to worthiness or, simply put, attributes deserving of

---

[31] See W.F. May, 'Code and Covenant or Philanthropy and Contract?' in S.J. Reiser, A.J. Dyck & W.J. Curran, eds., *Ethics in Medicine: Historical Perspectives and Contemporary Concerns* (The MIT Press, Cambridge, MA 1977) p. 65. See also L.R. Tancredi & D.N. Weisstub 'Malpractice in American Psychiatry: Toward a Restructuring of Psychiatrist-Patient Relationship,' in *Law and Mental Health: International Perspectives* II, D.N. Weisstub, ed. (Pergamon Press, Oxford 1986) 83 at 90-94.

[32] C. Taylor, 'The Politics of Recognition,' in *Multiculturalism,* Amy Gutmann, ed. (Princeton University Press, Princeton 1994).

our social respect. It thus may be that in its historical roots, the notion of honor has, in relative terms, a stronger moral core in respect of so-called modernist or post-modernist values than dignity. For our comprehension of dignity must attend, on the one hand, to the very strong element of aristocratic virtuousness that it carries. On the other, dignity has achieved a high level of abstraction because of its reductions into universalist-minded texts, making its moral efficacy diffused and oftentimes unclear.

On the sociological plane, the submission was made by Peter Berger in his classic statement in 1970, that honor occupies about the same place in contemporary usage as chastity...: 'At best, honor and chastity are seen as ideological leftovers in the consciousness of obsolete classes, such as military officers or ethnic grandmothers.'[33] Berger was right in saying that it is an improvement to have fled from phobic morality, superstition and an exaggerated sense of insult found for example among the military gentry and the *débutantes* of the old South. The difficulty with Berger's point of view is that with the benefit of hindsight, his exaggerated claims about chastity and grandmothers are now as dated as his carefully-chosen parodies of the *ancien régime*. Sociological observation of the 1970's underlined the emancipation of the moderns from worn-out institutions. Corporativism and 'bigness' were replaced in the progressive rhetorics of sociology by the vocabularies of authenticity, individuality, de-centralization and 'smallness'.[34] From that point of view, the 1990's are certainly in massive regression. The question remains however, whether we can articulate both the notion of community or even corporation which still allows for the discovery of self and a meaningful mutuality among parties. In the intervening decades popular psychology has suggested that we have come a far way in that dignity-equality is a real reference point for the way in which persons relate to each other.

What is the reality? More than in any other period in the twentieth century, well-educated elites are harnessed to the workplace and to dependency on corporations. Constant competition and fear of future unemployment, despite the fact that there is lessened loyalty to the corporate name, has not meant a lessening of corporativist fanaticism ad dependency. Now people simply speak about serial relationships and serial loyalties. Communitarian thinking is strengthened and atomistic behavior abhorred. Patterns of alternative modes of thinking, nutrition, therapy and healing, reveal conformism in the extreme. The space for authenticity may arguably be narrowing rather than expanding in our modern age of media control and extensive state surveillance, and globalization has intensified these realities. Perhaps one of the reasons why there is such a stampede in favor of vocabularies such as those of authenticity, dignity, and privacy, is that there is a crisis about how to preserve the self in the face of momentous pressures.

---

[33] P. Berger, 'On the Obsolescence of the Concept of Honor' in the *Archives européennes de sociologie* II (1970), pp. 339-47.

[34] N. Kittrie, *The Right To Be Different* (John Hopkins University Press, Baltimore 1971).

Therefore, there has been a pronounced retreat, albeit sometimes unreflective and regressive, into the world of chastity and 'forgotten grandmothers'.

It is true, as Peter Berger describes, that Victorian-type claims were dismissed with intentional torts, for a remedy in common law, and replaced by the preserve of violations of human dignity. However, if we look at the evolution of the protection of dignitary interests in this century, intentional infliction of mental suffering has blended in with the vague category of protection of privacy. It is no longer the case that damages are required for a psycho-physical injury. Mere dignitary violation is a sufficient condition for privacy recovery. This circumvention of the carefully-developed rules of common law which required an intention and proof of damages, have a broadened ground of recovery to the extent that we can now find a poorly-categorized grab-bag of injury. When carefully developed categories have been set aside, dignity may, as we have suggested earlier in this discussion, appear as airy as Victorian honor appeared to contemporary observers.

In the universe in which we live and which we must face, it may be that pouring new wine into the old bottle of honor will be the source where dignity will locate meaningful moral vitality. If we can show that honor and dignity have interchangeable vocabularies of respect, concern, and even mutuality, then the choice of words should by this fact recede as a matter of importance and give way to the more pressing question of how to concretely, in different categories of vulnerability, protect honor and dignify those for whom these concepts were created.

X. Multiculturalism: A Case-Study

Because many dignitary claims are made by groups with respect to each other's entitlements and are related to emancipatory vocabularies and express a psychological component with respect to self-fulfillment, it is instructive to look at an example of emancipatory thinking that has occurred within a democratic political framework. Such is the case in Canada, where a wide range of political sentiment has produced a movement toward the geographic and ethnic separation of one part of the population from the larger unit. Because this movement is grounded in a long military and political social history which carries with it linguistic and cultural elements, and given that the leaders of the movement continue to commit themselves to democratic values and to a very strong charter of human rights to protect minorities, Québec remains a fascinating study about balancing emancipation with dignitary protections. Within this political movement, philosophical justifications have been made for the right to difference as a particular aspect of encouraging and actualizing identity and self over and against more plastic varieties of contemporary liberal rhetoric based on extreme forms of individualism.

There are great controversies about how to link a charter of rights with the multiculturalist reality. This is so because certain minorities, depending upon how the geographical lines are drawn within the body politic, have made special claims about exclusivity of language in the workplace, for example, or the prioritization of language entitlements relating to such basic daily realities as education and health. These claims can be directly related to sensibilities about the nature of human dignity. They give rise to discussions about human indignities stemming from linguistic incapacity or the limitation of what are perceived to be fair and just choices made by individuals about how they wish to have themselves or their extended families treated by government systems. Given the recent events in the international community around questions of ethnic strife involving religion, language, and race, it is timely to reflect on our immediate political environment. Such inquiries reveal the extent to which, despite the existence of charters of rights and professed fundamental values such as human dignity, equality, and autonomy of choice, we should acknowledge that legal and political justifications continue to surface that protect group interests over individual assertions of rights which are not necessarily in all cases admitted by their supporters as contradictory of liberal/humanistic values understood in a broad sense.

Emancipatory movements and claims about multicultural entitlements are the political focus of human dignity. What is being told is that, in order to achieve at the psychological plane, a level of acceptable self-respect, certain conditions must be fulfilled in the political sphere. Because of the commitment of the majority of Western legal cultures to charters of fundamental values and rights, the human dignity component, as a post-war liberal creation, is a puzzling presence in the light of continuing ethno-centric assertions.

Part of the psychological meaning of emancipatory political claims is that, in order to properly evolve as a social reality, certain groups need to go through a process of denial towards the other, or at least compromise the others' rights in order to achieve an integrated political whole. This is frequently expressed as a way of redressing historical imbalances. Charters of rights do not exist in historical vacuums: apart from formal egalitarianism, we have become aware in most liberal democracies of the follow-through tensions that arise with respect to social equality. These quarrels raise questions about the relationship between human dignity and the nature of liberal values. They lie squarely at the heart of discussions about how to constitute a civic order which can reflect the need for the socio-cultural expression of divergent groups while at the same time maintaining a baseline standard of respect for diversity. Governments rise and fall depending upon the extent to which they touch the chords relating to the psychology of human dignity as it in turn relates to consciousness in the locale. Unfortunately, wars have ensued, inflamed by these heightened sensibilities. In this way, emancipatory political movements in the name of human dignity have given rise to acts of violence, and minorities have in many cases been attacked in other circumstances where, it is argued, they have not sufficiently respected the human dignity interest of the majority population. Economic, social, and political elites have been slaughtered from Western Europe to Indonesia and Africa, based on claims that the opposing populations were diminished, humiliated, or denigrated by the acts of economic, military or political power of the perceived dominant elites, even where these elites have been numerical minorities. Unfortunately, the rhetoric of human dignity changes hands rapidly in the battlefronts of religious, racial, and ethnic strife.

In the Canadian reality, multiculturalism has been central to reflections on the specific nature of the Canadian 'mosaic', including its Charter of Rights and Freedoms with built-in conditions for adjustment to the Canadian political reality. The role of basic rights in Canada cannot be separated from its indigenous, political and linguistic history, nor from its historical immigration policies. The relationship between multiculturalism in Canada and liberal values reveals the connection between human dignity and how claimants see the 'other' when there is the fear or experience of denigration or humiliation. Human dignity is the other side of the humiliation coin, such as, in the instance of privacy, there is always a linked claim about a right to information.

Furthermore, claims about human dignity inform us about a host of relations with regard to power, dominance and imbalances of entitlement. Even when we use absolutist vocabularies, we are called upon to redress wrongs by re-apportioning the commodities or goods associated with the survival of either individuals or groups, wrongs that are hard-felt when employment, health, and education are at stake. To speak about human dignity in the Canadian political and legal realities without attention to the actual multiculturalist fabric of Canadian society would be to enter a debate which is dissociated from the way dignitary violations are actually experienced.

XI. The Social Psychology of Multiculturalism

Multiculturalism, as a coined phrase, is a relatively recent term, suggesting that special recognition or status should be given to minority cultures coexisting within a larger political framework. This need for recognition stems from a social environment which is either dominated by a particular culture, including non-liberal, or represents a claim made in a liberal culture that equal, or in the alternative, respectful recognition be given in a heterogeneous social structure to diverse collective memberships. In a strictly homogeneous society, where there are small and marginalized minorities, it would be odd to wish to re-order or describe the society as multicultural, the coexistence of the minorities alongside the ruling group would not presumably rise to a proportion of expecting or needing a particular recognition. The rules surrounding the dominance of the majority culture and its recognition and entitlements of the few minority entities would not be a matter of political or social concern unless grave violations of liberties had become an issue. Even then, it would surprise us if the redress of these infractions were part of 'cultural-dignitary' claims on the society to become multicultural.

Multiculturalism is permitted political and social meaning in a society which presumes at once to be liberal and also to be in need, because of actual diversity of its memberships, of acknowledging in politically and socially relevant ways, the viability of a series of groups whose populations and value systems have reached the level of seriousness in claims, one against the other, to have become a real political force. This is why liberal societies which are immigrant-based, such as those of the US and of Canada, are ripe for analyzing in terms of their multiculturalist integrity. Other societies which are also liberal, such as the more homogeneous entities, for example of Scandinavia and Holland, surely boast minorities. Tolerance of them is made against a dominant linguistic and social culture of a long standing history, including that of state religions, monarchies, and specific social institutions which have integrated other groups, but nonetheless allowed for the continuation of cultural and religious identity to be differentiated within the terms of a liberal-minded citizenship. This is not done, however, on the basis of arguments for individualized institutions and special political status for ethnic minorities.

In other Western, less liberal societies, there is certainly no shortage of ethnic minorities to be found, in particular in Central and Eastern Europe, but it would be strange to describe the former Yugoslavia or Poland as multicultural societies. This is so because these societies have within their histories crippling strife among the different populations that have shared citizenship under some loose concept of coexistence, and where the lapses or rejections of entitlements of certain groups towards rights have been endemic. Where religious intolerance has been the critical issue, such as in Ireland, or indeed throughout the long history of the Middle East, we would hesitate to treat such turmoil under the veil of multiculturalism. The existence of different or opposing cultures in the same geographic locale, or within identical political and institutional historical structures, is not a sufficient ground to constitute a multicultural society.

It is important therefore to explore the foundations of the liberal thinking which has given rise in the post-war years to a particular brand of liberal pluralism, upon which certain progressive political instincts have laid before us their claims and ambitions. This undertaking is timely because it is part of this history that the colors of multiculturalism have not remained steadfast nor clear. They have altered according to the redefinition of entitlements that have veered away from an individualistically based multiculturalist concept to one that has latterly shown greater affinities to collectivist claims, sometimes associated with anti-liberalist positions. These transitions in the orientation of multiculturalism must be looked at carefully in order to test the strength of our commitments to specific liberal values, such as autonomy and freedom to choose one's language and religion, as part of a more general social vision based upon the previously-discussed dimensions of mutuality and respect for 'otherness'. The difficulty has become that collectivist arguments made by groups, which perceive themselves as under siege, have in the reconstitution of either geographical political entities, or demands for autonomous regions of decision-making to reflect cultural uniqueness, over time become 'exclusionist,' and therefore problematic to the sustenance of a multiculturalist liberal ethos.

In the North American context, Canadians normally reserve a greater claim on multiculturalism than their American counterparts. The assumption is made that the 'melting pot' liberalism, demonstrated in a powerful way by the constitutional apparatus of the post-war years, reveals an overwhelming melting down of differences among immigrants in the name of a dynamic civic participation in the concept of Americanism. This can be seen as distinctive from what has been articulated in Canadian terms for its culture as a mosaic pattern of cultural survival, which is taken as the ideal, or the mandate of a liberal politics which places greater emphasis on differences over similarities. This has led to a weaker nationalism in Canada and has exacerbated both problems of regionalism and social integration of immigrant groups, against the background of the trespass of groups against each other's ethnic territory and integrity in the constitutional wrangling between Québec and its neighboring provinces, and within its own political boundaries.

The US received and was created upon the arrival of essentially the same ethnic populations that constituted the federation of Canada, but from the actual establishment of even transplanted ghettoized village populations, the American challenge to a new citizenship was to alter or forget old hatreds and differences. This was regarded as feasible on the basis of shared values and entitlements seen as part of the level playing field where all Americans could be protected according to constitutional entitlements, which would always remain paramount in the broader legal and political culture. In Canada by contrast, there was much greater caution in assuming that the eradication of differences was either healthy or necessary to establish a framework for political and legal survival. In fact, the tendency was to foster a *'culture des ancêtres,'* where the celebration of the old world was seen to give flavor to the new. It was conceived that in the preservation of particularity, a stable social order was predictable and highly valued. In defense of this philosophy of particularity, Canadians have often wished to contrast lower levels of crime, greater social commitments to social caring, more affordable access to health care and education, and greater respect for authority in a less litigious society, which despite its regionalism and ethnic conflicts, remains essentially a tolerant liberal body politic.

The Canadian brand of multiculturalism was instantiated in the Trudeau era as a curious blend of mosaicism and cosmopolitanism. Trudeau began a course of action which at once supported the development of cultural minorities within the country, while at the same time ensuring that Québec's claims on Canada were relegated to those of another minority, albeit of a greater political significance. Having so reconstituted the Canadian map, Québecers were then thrown into the frustrated condition of having to reaffirm their own sense of political minority, along with other groups, in the light of the introduction of a Charter of Rights, which made all claims a subject of citizenship rather than collectivity. , Québec was thus reduced to a cultural minority rather than a contester of political wills within the concept of founding nations. Trudeau has never been forgiven this seeming cosmopolitan move because beyond the Canadian fabric, there was an apparent agenda of defending the notion that citizens and indeed Canadians should ultimately keep in mind the ideal of universal citizenship. This, to any group which lives with a strong psychology of ethnicism, could only be regarded as a direct threat to the viability of the group whose siege mentality would require ongoing symbolization of victimization and affronts to political dignity.

It is difficult to ascribe too much to this Trudeau liberalism in the absence of any elaborate proof if intent or assumptions. This is so in the view of Trudeau's utilization of the *War Measures Act*, which was exercised on scant evidence, pronouncements on the Biafran conflict in Nigeria, and his celebration of non-liberal, even totalitarian regimes, such as Cuba and the former Soviet Union. An unsympathetic account of Trudeau's policy on multiculturalism would be to say that he ethnicized Canada as a way of punishing Québec for its own parochialism, and this done with a typical flair which teased his fellow Québecers with the arrogance of an aristocratic, rootless cosmopolitan.

In the Trudeau years, Canada was overlain with celebrations of ethnic revivalism. This was highly welcomed by Canada's ethnic minorities who had, at least in English Canada, suffered the normal North American degradations, in the immediate years following the Second World War, of being displaced persons. Despite the preceding sufferings of the ravages of Western Europe, Canada's ethnic populations were familiarly cast into second-class citizenship, made the subject of restrictions in entries to private clubs and universities, and moreover to prestigious positions in public life or business. It was only with Trudeauism that Canada's lag time, in comparison with US patterns of integration, kicked in with the introduction of minorities into the upper social structures of the country. So much so, that Trudeau still remains the hero of Canada's multiculturalist policies, much revered by the ethnic minorities who see their upgrading as directly flowing from his initiatives.

Whether Trudeau should be regarded as a true liberal, however, for our purposes, is not the issue. The more precise challenge is whether there is, within this genre of thinking, a series of claims that are part of what could be called a liberal point of view from which to give direction to a philosophy of multiculturalism. Such a philosophy could suggest a way of approaching claims made in the name of cultural diversity, or for that matter, even more significantly, legal claims either of entitlements or with respect to the nature of the legal decision-making apparatus itself. If we accept the view that we are to behave as a liberal society, we might wish to know on what basis we can define the limits of collective claims for support and enhancement, as opposed to simply guaranteeing that citizens are to be left alone to develop their own inner cultural integrity. To see the society as being politically and socially responsible for the enhancement of minority cultural identities, in anything other than manners of soft support, would strike most Americans as an anathema to their way of constituting their civil order. In Canada, however, in part because of the Trudeau policies, but moreover due to the patterns of regionalist integration, citizens have been predisposed to accepting certain liberal rationales of how a multiculturalist policy can in fact enhance tolerance among groups.

Such a view contains within it the seeds of certain liberal notions which have been enshrined in the popular psychology of recent progressive cultures in both Western Europe and North America. There is the idea that proximity to differences and an acceptance and dialogue between such groups should naturally lead to exchanges of friendship, trust, and tolerance. The fact that such proximity in other regions of the world has never led to such equanimity, but rather to prolonged suspicion over generations, has not frustrated North American liberals, who continue to believe that openness of communications eventually triumphs over ignorance and suspicion. Regarded in this way, Citizenship in Canada has been seen as the context for realizing shared purposes reflected in public institutions and responsibilities, indeed far a field from the fabric of cultural alienation, despite the proximity factor of diverse cultures in their countries of origin, where ethnic conflict was the mainstay of those environments.

Other assumptions are intrinsic to a commitment to a liberal concept of multiculturalism. Firstly, that for a group to be respectful to other cultures, it must be made socio-economically viable; and secondly, that the conditions must be fulfilled for inner identity, to be enhanced in the group to the point where a shared security would make the group more flexible and tolerant of others. Such views have been supported historically by economists and psychologists to explain why certain countries have acted intolerantly towards others, precipitated either by periods of economic duress or low self-esteem held by certain groups due to both internal and external forces.

There is evidence to support the view that this is reductionist thinking and inadequate insofar as the revamping of the Japanese and German economies, to take two notable instances, cannot be easily correlated with greater tolerance of ethnic minorities.[35] Equally, when groups have achieved greater confidence due to advancement in socio-economic or political terms, there is little proof to suggest that socio-psychological well being necessarily leads to a more liberal perspective with regard to other groups' entitlements. In short, economic and psychological empowerment, which have usually been assumed by liberals to lie at the basis of an effective multiculturalist policy, have shown many counter-examples to frustrate our widely held beliefs.

Nevertheless, we persist in the view that our commitment to the empowerment of minorities, if sustained, should ultimately lead to the tolerance goal of multiculturalist policies. This commitment is connected to the view that a mature pluralism takes place when groups have achieved a level of psycho-political maturation, where anger over past conflicts has been dissipated due to having passed through stages of an evolutionary ethic.

---

[35] Perceptions were held that Québec historically suffered from a two-faced indignity, firstly of course, the defeat of the French at the hands of the English, and secondly, an elaborate system of subjugation to church interests which, some argue, lasted until the 1960's.

Included in this is the demand that collective guilt should lead the majority or dominant groups to repay social and political debts. This subsides when the minority group ultimately feels secure enough in its own accomplishments that such claims appear either dated or irrelevant.

The issue of political maturation remains central to current quarrels about multiculturalist policies in Canada relating to ethnic communities, native peoples, and finally to the heated political debates surrounding Québec's relationships with the rest of Canada. Who can claim what against whom, for whatever past deeds, is now part of the fabric of multiculturalism insofar as many dissimilar groups, for varying motivations and highly diversified socioeconomic and political histories, have begun to make claims about their own specificities and entitlements.

Liberal minded observers are left confused by this host of claims, because many of them stem from groups which have little affinity with liberal values, have origins in communities with long standing histories of intolerant attitudes towards other groups, and have actually practiced, through rituals or laws, policies which directly violate human dignity.

XII. Conclusion

If there is any benefit in standing at the beginning of a new millennium, it is to understand the failure of large systems of abstraction to prevent evil. We have become more aware in this century, of human feelings and the need for communication, crossing the lines of wealth, race, and gender. It is only through such a process of dialogic evolution that we have any chance at all of baring our hearts credibly before and around the conflicts before us. When such dialogic attempts fail, we have the limited tools at our disposal of exercising laws that attempt to protect and actualize the constitutional freedoms that we now regard as the baseline of a civilized order. These rights are mainly procedurally in place. However, the specific demands of cultural groups have changed the rules of the game for placid liberals who believed a few decades ago, that love and burgeoning economies could diffuse conflict. What we have seen is that the urges to be different and culturally distinct have re-surfaced with a vengeance, threatening stability in all contexts. Individual cultures now have the obligation of demarcating where the line cannot be crossed before abuses become intolerable. Denying the right to live and work in a given language may be such a line, but once again, each history is specific, and it is moral arrogance to think that there are absolutes that can instruct us on how our moral geography is to be re-drawn. It is only through quarrelling short of violence that we can continue to aspire towards stability. Democratic controversy coupled with a judiciary devoted to the protection of basic, liberal human values is the only model on which we could be justified in placing our trust. This does not mean that we can logically derive an absolute consensus, even if there is a judgment about commitment to certain values. On what basis could we have expected otherwise?

LIST OF CONTRIBUTORS

Yehoshua Arieli is the James G. McDonald Professor Emeritus of American History and Modern History at the Hebrwe University of Jerusalem.

Hubert Cancik teaches at the Philologische Seminar and the Seminar für Religionswissenschaft of the Eberhard-Karls-Universität Tübingen.

Arthur Chaskalson is the President of the Constitutional Court of South Africa.

Klaus Dicke is Professor of Political Theory and History of Ideas at Friedrich Schiller - University Jena, Germany.

Joern Eckert holds the Chair of German and European History of Law, Civil Law and Trade Law at Christian Albrechts University of Kiel.

Jochen Frowein is Director of the Max Planck Institute for Comparative Public Law and International Law.

Orit Kamir is a lecturer at the Hebrew University Faculty of Law.

Eckart Klein is the Director of the Human Rights Centre at the University of Potsdam and holds the Chair of Constitutional Law, Public International Law and Law of the European Union. He has been a member of the United Nations Human Rights Committee since 1995.

David Kretzmer is the Bruce W. Wayne Professor in International Law at the Hebrew University of Jerusalem and the former Director of the Minerva Center for Human Rights. He is Vice-Chairperson of the United Nations Human Rights Committee.

Yair Lorberbaum lectures on the philosophy of *Halakha*, law and culture at the Bar-Ilan University Faculty of Law. He is also a Fellow at the Shalom Hartman Institute for Advanced Judaic Studies.

Michael J. Meyer is an Associate Professor of Philosophy at Santa Clara University in California.

Dietrich Ritschl teaches at the Ecumenical Instutute of the University of Heidelberg.

Chana Safrai is a Visiting Lecturer in Jewish Thought at the Hebrew University of Jerusalem and a Fellow at the Shalom Hartman Institute for Advanced Judaic Studies.

Christian Starck is a Professor at the Faculty of Law of Georg August University of Göttingen.

Daniel Statman is an Assistant Professor in the Department of Philosophy at Bar-Ilan University.

David Weisstub holds the Philippe Pinel Chair of Legal Psychiatry and Biomedical Ethics at the University of Montreal Faculty of Medicine.

INDEX

Adultery
  punishment for, 69-70
American Jewish Committee
  Declaration of Human Rights, 113
Anthropology
  discipline of, 182
Aristocracy
  ideology, rejection of, 202
Autonomy
  moral, 182

Beheading
  corporeal damage, 61
  defiled blood, purging, 62-76
  disfigurement, prevention of, 77
  implementation of, 62-64
  Mishnah's depiction of, 62
  murder, for, 76
  murder, prohibition of, 64
  origin and rationale as capital punishment, 61
  sacrificing, and, 73
  scriptural basis of, 64
  source of law, 68-73
  sword, with, 62-64, 77
  tannaim, judicial execution of, 59-60
Blaspheming
  punishment for, 70
Blood
  Bible, warning against consumption in, 65, 67
  Deuteronomy, depiction in, 67
  execution by spilling of, 72, 82

expiation, and, 73-76, 82-83
purifying characteristics, 66
soul, identification of, 65-67
soul, of, 73-74

Canada
  Charter, rights and freedoms in, 137
  multiculturalism, 289-294
Capital punishment
  abolishing, 78-80
  beheading. *See* Beheading
  Bible, designation in, 65
  corporeal damage, limiting, 60-61, 77
  divine image, diminishing, 78-83
  internal burning, 60
  monetary indemnification, substitution of, 58
  murder, for, 57
  Roman forms of, 64
  sanctity of human life, and, 83-84
  spilling of blood, by, 72, 82
  strangulation, 60, 70
  teliyah, 61
Christianity
  human dignity, as root of, 180-181, 186
  individualism, seeds for, 183
  modern law, influence on formation of, 180
  spiritual and secular realm, distinction between, 17
Concepts
  classes of, 88
  condition humaine, concerning, 89, 94
  frame, 88, 90
  human dignity as, 89-93
  inductive operation, gained by, 89
  theologians and lawyers, of, 88-91
Conflict
  causes of, 142
Constitutional core
  values at, 232
Constitutional law
  human dignity, role of, 87
Constitutionalism
  adjudication, 272-273
  clarifier or legal values, as, 271
  dignity in, 269-72
  privacy law, 271

Corporal punishment
  judicial, 124
  juvenile offenders, of, 139
Criminal law
  Biblical, 57

Darwinism
  effect of, 210
Declaration of Human Rights
  American Jewish Committee, of, 113
Deduction
  logics of, 89
Democracy
  historical move to, 5
Dignity
  concepts of, 112-113
  Hebrew term for, 56
  human. *See* Human dignity
  natural law concept, 113
Discrimination
  impairment of dignity, and, 140

Emotions
  morality, claims to, 220
  rationality of, 217-221
  reasons for, 218
Enlightenment
  dignity, concept of, 113, 117
  human rights theory, 7
  meaning, 6
  motto of, 6
  natural law doctrine in, 48
  philosophy of man, 7
Equality
  dignity, interdependence with, 140
  moral, 213
Ethics
  assertions, 94
  global, dignity in, 265
  human dignity, role of, 87
  law, and, 92-94
  medical, 92-93
European Convention on Human Rights
  human dignity,
    element in interpretation, as, 24-126

no reference to, 123
Extradition
  torture, to face, 157

Fear
  behaviour tending to cause, 219
  exclusion, of, 221-226
  humiliation, analogy with, 219
  rationality of, 217-218
French Revolution
  credo of, 5
  dignity and rank, separation of, 45
  Germany, influence in, 46
Frightening behaviour
  definition, 218
  fear, tending to cause, 219

German law
  Basic Law, 41
    Article 1, architecture of, 146-149
    Article 1 Para 1, substantial meaning of, 149-157
    different needs, facing, 146
    focal point of order, 152-153, 159
    fundamental statements and conclusions, 146-147
    goal of, 145
    guarantee of inviolability, 146, 148
    human dignity clause, 147, 187
    human dignity, guarantee of, 179
    human rights, inviolability of, 145
    inalienable human rights, 149
    new legal order, as cornerstone for, 273
  capital punishment, abolition, 190
  concept of person and human rights, link between, 51
  Constitution,
    Basis Rights, 135-136
    Bismarck, 146
    Herrenchiemsee draft, 122-123
  dignity, legal roots of, 47-51
  equality, idea of, 47
  human being, image of, 150
  human dignity,
    abortion cases, 151, 154
    application by courts, 275
    beneficiaries of, 187
    clauses on, 41, 187

collective and individual interests, balance between, 276
compulsory military service not violating, 191
contemptuous treatment, intention of, 151
criminal law, issues of, 190
criminal procedure, issues of, 190
data protection provisions, 192
duty to forbid and to sanction, and, 192-193
duty to respect and protect, 189
dwarf-throwing, 158
encroachment on, 148
explicit acknowledgement of, 51-52
force-feeding of prisoners, 191
freedom of art, and, 156
general procedural law, issues of, 191
guarantee of inviolability, 146, 148
guarantee of, 179, 187-188
human life as basis of, 153-154, 190
inviolability, 188
jurisprudence on, 153
life imprisonment, and, 157
meaning, 149
objective scope of protection, 149-152
observation of prisoners, 191
other basic rights, and, 148, 152-157
other values, balanced against, 158-159
personal scope of protection, 152
police action, use of firearms in, 192
proportionality, matters of, 275
relatively absolute, as, 273-277
trivialities, and, 151
violation of, 156
voluntary behaviour, impact of, 157-158
waiver of, 148
Weimar Republic, constitution of, 52
Lander, Constitutions of, 52-53
length of court proceedings in, 125-126
life, right to, 153-154
personality, right to, 155-156
Second World War, after, 52-53
theory of object, 150
Weimar Republic, constitution of, 52
Glory
Christian formulations, 245
duties imposed in name of, 244
godly element, referring to, 244

k-v-d qualities, 243-244
  metaphysical nature of, 244
Guilt culture
  honor culture, and, 231-232
  shame, and, 238

Homosexuality
  illegality, 129
Honor culture
  class distinctions, 240-241
  contemporary usage, 286
  definition, 239, 243
  dignity, and, 241-243
  dignity in, 283-284
  distinct recognition, 283-284
  earning honor in, 242
  emotional economies, 239
  faces of k-v-d, 238
  glory, and, 243-245
  guilt culture, and, 231-232
  honor as disciplining tool, 240
  respect, and, 245
  social status, social rights and self-esteem in, 239
  specifics and linguistic terms, 238
Human dignity
  analytical jurisprudence, 267
  ancient history, meanings in, 43
  anthropological and ethical argument, 26
  basis of, 27
  Biblical and modern era contrasted, 58
  Biblical tradition, 95
  Christian-type virtue, as, 265
  Cicero, core treatise of,
    commentaries and translations, 27
    date, addressee and genre of, 20
    text, 20
    topic and aim, 19
  coining of expression, 19
  concept of, 196-197
  constitutional guarantee, 179-180
  constitutionalism, 269-72
  constitutions and international legal instruments, central to, 41-42
  contents of, 90, 96-97
  core of person's worth, at, 241
  descriptive of normative notion, as, 211

developments after Second World War, effect of, 52
dialogical concept, 98
dignified behaviour, definitions of, 265
dignitas,
  definition of, 22
  majesty, and, 23-24
  quality of, 23
  visible and social quality, 22-23
dignity of the state, as response to, 123
English philosophers, works of, 45
expansion of, 243
first legal provision, 52
first occurrence of expression, 27
first persona,
  Cicero, core treatise of, 19-21
  context and source, 21-22
foundations of, 42
Garve, writings of, 35-36
German law, in. *See* German law
governing principle, as, 272-273
gross impairment of, 142
Hebrew term for, 56
historical background, 43-47
history of formula, 36-37
human nature, in, 24-26
humiliation, connection with, 209-212. *See also* Humiliation
identity, and, 129-131
Imago Dei as basis for, 55
impartation, by, 97-98
inductive operation, concept gained by, 89
inherent,
  man and God, relationship of, 10
  meaning, 9
  ontological status of man, reference to, 9
  principle and theory of, 12
international law, in. *See* International law
intra-psychic dimensions, 279-283
intrinsic worth, 263
inviolable absolute, as, 264
Jewish honor, coupled with, 249
Jewish value, as, 253
judicial meaning, 42
Kant's concept, Stoic impact on, 33-36
legal concept, whether, 87
legal essence of, 42

length of court proceedings, relationship with, 125-126
meaning, 210-211
metaphysical dimension, 184-187
modern idea of, 84-85
modern sense, in, 99
modern view of, 285
moral minimum, as, 195
moral thinking, central to, 264
notions of, 95-97
pedagogy, in context of, 34-35
persons possessing, 46
philosophical roots of, 180-181
physio-concept, 95
political order, as basis of, 180
political philosophy, approach of, 181-182
prisoners, of, 128
protection of interests, 287
Pufendorf, writings of, 30-33, 44
Quattrocentro Italy, treatises in, 28-30, 44
Rabbinical Literature, in. *See* Rabbinical Literature
ratio, 25-26
regal value par excellence, as, 263
relatively absolute, as, 273-277
rules and values, and, 268
sense of, 197
social orders, in, 265
socio-legal dialectic, 284-287
Stoic context, in, 32
theologians and lawyers, concepts of, 88-91
theological perception, 55
torture, and, 126-128
treaty, by means of, 96
Universal Declaration, provisions of. *See* Universal Declaration of Human Rights
virtue of, 195, 197-207. *See also* Virtue
Human rights
  core elements, development of, 46
  English philosophers, works of, 45
  first declarations of, 111
  gross abuses, prevention of, 143
  jurisprudence, development of, 137
Humiliation
  Autarky Problem, 215
  behaviour tending to cause, 220
  concept of, 210
  criminals, of, 222-223

denial of dignity, as, 281
fear of exclusion, and, 221-226
fear, analogy with, 219
Grounds Problem, 215-216
hurt feelings, claims about, 227
injury to self-respect, as, 209-210, 213-217, 226
irrational, 219, 225-226
meaning, 211-214
moral views, not contingent on, 223
multi-layered issue, as, 218
Nazi behaviour as, 217
notion of dignity, connection with, 209-212
paradoxes of, 216
possibility, establishment of, 216
rationality of, 215-216
reasons for, 218-219
violation of human dignity, as, 209
Humility
exemplars of, 199
misplaced, 197-198
vice, as, 200
Hungary
Constitution, 136

Identity
childhood, access to information on, 130-13
human dignity, and, 129-131
sexual, 129-130
Image
interpretations, 56
Imago Dei
ancient perceptions, presentation of, 59
basis for concept of human dignity, as, 55
Bible, descriptions of man in, 57
Genesis, in, 55-56
interpretations, 56
origin of idea, 55
Individuality
idea of, 46
Induction
process of, 89
International Convention on Civil and Political Rights
dignity, foundational role of, 135
International Criminal Court
establishment of, 144

International Labour Organization
  Philadelphia Declaration, 114
International law
  crimes in, 144
  declaratory tradition, 115
  enforcement, 143
  human dignity in,
    early references, 121
    identity, and, 129-131
    new texts, 122-124
    prisoners, of, 128
    slaves, common rule against trade of, 122
    torture, and, 126-128
    Treaty of Amity and Commerce, 121
    young persons, treatment of, 131
  representatives of state, protection of, 144
Ireland
  Constitution, legal provision of dignity and freedom of the individual, 52
Islam
  spiritual and secular realm, no distinction between, 16
Israel
  administrative detention, 171-172
  Basic law: Human Dignity and Liberty,
    versions of, 9
    constitutional debate, 277-279
    fundamental principles, declaration of, 9
    herut and *kvod ha-adam*, translation of, 233, 257
    logic of *kavod*-dignity, shift to, 235-236
    passing of, 233
    purpose of, 9
    text of, 176-178
  Basic Laws, 233
  bill of rights, core values, 232-234
  constitutional debate, 277-279
  constitutional revolution, 165
  Declaration of Establishment, 9
  Declaration of Independence, 161, 234
  emergency regulations, 166, 169
  equality, right to 172-174
  expression, freedom of, 174
  formal constitution, lack of, 233
  fundamental human rights in, 9
  human dignity,
    Basic Law provisions, 165-174, 180
    constraint on other rights, as, 169

detainees or prisoners, in relation to, 163-164
equality and freedom of conscience, protection of, 172-173
examples of, 168
faces of k-v-d, 236-245
general value, as, 167-169
honor, glory and respect, and, 237
inviolability, 169
kavod, translation of, 237
kvod ha-adam, 166-167, 233, 236, 254
notification of arrest to family of arrestee, 164
notion of, 163
other rights and interests, accommodation of, 169-171
period prior to Basic Laws, in, 163-165
refining of concept, 174-175
right, limited protection of, 166
separate right, as, 169-172
super-right, as, 172-174
Supreme Court, honor mentality of, 254-258
value of, 233
human rights,
absolute protection, absence of, 170
Basic Laws, 161
constraints, background to, 162
decisions on, 163
human dignity and liberty, 162
judicial interpretation, 173
legal system, place in, 161-3
occupation, freedom of, 161, 170, 177-178
status prior to Basic Laws, 163
kavod-honor,
kavod-dignity and *kavod*-glory, and, 234-235
logic of *kavod*-dignity, shift to, 235
Supreme Court, mentality of, 254-258
values of, 234
Zionist adoption of, 245-254
marriage and divorce, regulation of, 162
norms of, 9
political system, coalition, 162
primary legislation, judicial review of, 165
religious practices, laws enforcing, 162
rights, catalogue of, 123

Jews
Christians, baptism as, 248
Diaspora, 253

harsh living conditions, subject to, 246
Holocaust, effect of, 253

Language
  entitlements, 287-288
  primary and tertiary, 88
Law
  ethics, and, 92-94
League of Nations
  Covenant of, 2
  United Nations, differences in nature and aims of, 2
Legal capacity
  features for, 48
  modern doctrine, 48-49
Liberalism
  historical move to, 5
  human dignity, approach to, 183-184
Life
  right to, 135, 153-154

Minorities
  denial of dignity to, 280-281
  empowerment of, 293
  language entitlements, 287-288
  multiculturalism, 287-294. *See also* Multiculturalism
  protection of, 267
Multiculturalism
  Canada, in, 289-294
  case study, 287-289
  charter of rights, linking, 287
  emancipatory movements, 288
  language entitlements, 287-288
  political and social meaning, 289
  social psychology of, 289-294
  United States, in, 291

Natural law
  dignity, concept of, 113
  Enlightenment, doctrine in, 48
  equality, idea of, 45
  Hart's criticism of, 186
Nature
  law of, 14
Nobility
  misplaced, 198

Office
  dignity of, 203

Palestine
  incremental settlement, policy of, 249
  national state in, 245
  population, dignity of, 251
Person
  civil laws accepting human beings as, 50
  concept, foundations of, 47-48
  element in legal relations, as, 50
  rights in society, having, 49
  Saxon Code, in, 50
Personality
  right to, 134, 155-156
Political philosophy
  human dignity, approach to, 181-182
Positivism
  human dignity, approach to, 184
Pride
  virtue of, 206
Prisoners
  human dignity of, 128
Privacy
  breach of, 140
  constitutionality, 271
  fundamental value, as, 272

Rabbinical Literature
  base of, 99
  Boshet, 105-108
  bride, dignity of, 102
  creatures or people, dignity of, 101
  Dignity as official attribute of God, 99
  human dignity, expression of,
    commitment, hierarchy of, 105
    golden rule, and, 104
    issues, 100
  Kavod, concepts of, 100
  Kvod Aniyim, 103
  Kvod ha-Adam, 100-101
  Kvod ha-Am, 103
  Kvod ha-Briot, 101, 105
  Kvod ha-Kala, 102

Kvod ha-Nashim, 102
Kvod ha-Shabbat, 103-104
Kvod ha-Tsibur, 101-102
  literary, 104-105
  shame, and, 105-109
  summation, 104
 nature of, 99
 people, dignity of, 103
 poor, dignity of, 103
 public dignity, 101-102
 quest for human dignity, 109
 Rabban Yohanan b. Zakkai, dictums explained in name of, 107-109
 Sabbath and Holy Days, dignity of, 103-104
 Sacrifice regulations, 107-108
 shame in, 105-109
 women, dignity of, 102
Reformation
 crisis of authority, as, 45
Religion
 Marx, analysis of, 184
Res publica
 idea of, 16
Respect
 k-v-d qualities, 245
Rights of man
 political, social and legal order, foundation of, 6
 theory of, 5
Roman Law
 achievements of, 12, 13
 fundamental structure of, 15
 history of the West, influence in, 15-17
 secular law, as rational system of, 12
 Stoic philosophy, influence of, 13-15
 universal validity, claiming, 15
 Western history, role in, 12
Rule of law
 commitment to, 266
Rwanda
 genocide, 144

Secularization
 process of, 182-183
Self-determination, right of
 Milton demanding, 45
 historically, 5

Self-respect
  basal, 224
  damage to, 224
  fragility of, 225
  humiliation as injury to, 209-210, 213-217, 226
  moral concept of, 213-214
  normative understanding of, 215
  objective-normative and subjective-psychological notion of, 210, 220
  self-esteem, and, 221-222
  subjective attitude, as, 213
Servitude
  prohibition, 50-51
Slavery
  prohibition, 50-51
Slaves
  common rule against trade of, 122
Social dignity
  concept of, 196, 203
  hierarchy of, 203-207
Social models
  range of, 266
South Africa
  apartheid, 138
  Bill of Rights, interpretation and application of, 139
  colonialism, 138
  Constitution, 136, 138
  dignity, constitutional value of, 139
  juvenile offenders, corporal punishment of, 139
  reconciliation and reconstruction, 138
  social and economic rights, questions of, 141-142
State
  dignity of, 123
Subsumption
  process of, 89

Tannaim
  judicial execution, 59-61
Teliyah
  practice of, 61
Tort
  remedies for, 287
Torture
  definition of, 127
  extradition to face, 157
  human dignity, and, 126-128

Transsexuals
 identity of, 129-130

Underdevelopment
 causes of, 142
United Nations
 Charter, 3, 41, 111, 113-115
  faith in human rights, reaffirmation of, 133
  new world order, aspirations for, 133-134
  pledge, living up to, 137-138
 establishment of, 133
 League of Nations, differences in nature and aims of, 2
 task of, 2-3
 United States and the West, pre-eminent role of, 5
United States
 Declaration of Independence, 5, 7
 self-incrimination, privilege against, 136
 shaping of UN, role in, 5
Universal Declaration of Human Rights
 adoption of, 3, 111, 134
 concepts and terms, understanding of, 1
 concepts, values and ideas, 5
 dignity of man,
  context of, 1
  inherent, declaration of, 1, 8
 drafting history of, 112-114
 future international order, as cornerstone of, 1
 growing impact of, 4
 human dignity,
  autonomy of persons, 134
  concept of, 111-112, 114-118
  critical functions, 119
  definition, absence of, 115, 118, 120
  founding function of, 114, 118-120
  fundamental value, as, 135
  legitimizing function of, 118-119
  reference to, 114
  religious or philosophical traditions, reference to, 117
  social rights, and, 117-118
  worth, combined with, 116
 humanity, conception of, 4
 incentive for, 112
 just and favorable remuneration, right to, 118
 justification, 8
 life, right to, 135

personality, rights of, 134
philosophical underpinning, 7
political experience, reference to, 116
preamble, 3, 41, 134
regulatory ideal, as, 4
social and economic rights, 134
style of reasoning, 115
versions of, 4

Virtue
dignity, of, 195, 197-202
haughty man, elitism of, 198
modern, dignity as, 202-207
noble man, elitism of, 198
opposing vices, location of, 197
perfectionist thinking, whether requiring, 201
pride, of, 206
trait of excellence, as, 200

Western civilization
common ground, 11
evolution of, 11-12
law and jurisprudence, uniqueness of, 11

Young persons
treatment of, 131
Yugoslavia
ethnic cleansing in, 144

Zionism
Ben-Gurion as leader of, 252-253
honor discourse, as, 245-247, 250
incremental settlement in Palestine, policy of, 249
kavod-honor, adoption of, 245-254
militant, 251
political, 249-250